# ANCIENT JERUSALEM REVEALED

# ANCIENT
## JERUSALEM
### REVEALED

EDITED BY HILLEL GEVA

ISRAEL EXPLORATION SOCIETY
JERUSALEM 1994

BIBLICAL ARCHAEOLOGY SOCIETY
WASHINGTON D.C.

This volume contains articles adapted from

QADMONIOT

Quarterly for the Antiquities of Eretz-Israel and Bible Lands
Published in Hebrew by the Israel Exploraton Society

First Editor: Y. Yadin (1968–1978)

*Editor:* E. Stern; *Editorial Board:* M. Broshi, A. Eitan, Y. Tsafrir,
D. Ussishkin; *Hebrew Style:* R. Eshel; *Layout:* A. Pladot; *Adminstrative
Editor:* J. Aviram

*English version:* Joseph Shadur
*Layout:* Avraham Pladot
*Administrative editor:* Joseph Aviram

ISBN 965–221–021–8

Typeset and printed in Israel by Ben-Zvi Printing Enterprises, Jerusalem
Plates by Old City Press Ltd., Jerusalem.

Cover Photograph: Aerial view of Jerusalem, including the excavations along the southern
side of the Temple Mount
Photo: Duby Tal and Moni Haramati, Albatross Aerial Photography

# Contents

## JERUSALEM—SECOND TEMPLE PERIOD

## JERUSALEM—LATER PERIODS

This publication was made possible by a grant from
The Kaplan-Kushlik Foundation.

*Dedicated to Teddy Kollek,*
*Visionary and Rebuilder of Jerusalem.*

## To Teddy Kollek

In 1976, Teddy Kollek, the Mayor of Jerusalem, visited South Africa and brought me a gift, hot off the press—*Jerusalem Revealed*. This exciting book aroused in me the desire to participate in the archaeological discoveries being made in Jerusalem, and led to discussions with Teddy and others regarding a new, comprehensive dig at the site of the City of David. As a result, the City of David Society was founded with Mayor Kollek as President and myself as Vice-President. The help of friends from South Africa and elsewhere joined the efforts of the Jerusalem Foundation.

The excavations at the City of David, under the direction of Prof. Yigal Shiloh, began in 1978 and continued until 1985, and up to his untimely death in 1987. The scholarly reports of the many important discoveries are published in the *Qedem* series of the Hebrew University Institute of Archaeology. A large part of the present, attractive second volume of *Jerusalem Revealed*, presents this fascinating material to the English-speaking public at large for the first time in concise form.

For the past quarter of a century, Teddy Kollek has been the moving factor behind many of the important archaeological projects in Jerusalem—at the western and southern walls of the Temple Mount, the Jewish Quarter of the Old City, the City of David, the Citadel, and others. Many of the results of this intense work have been imaginatively preserved in the form of restored sites and archaeological parks freely accessible to the public. All the relevant discoveries spanning three thousand years of Jerusalem's history are also represented in *Ancient Jerusalem Revealed*.

It is fitting then that this volume published by the Israel Exploration Society be dedicated to Teddy Kollek. May it inspire many others, as it did myself, to take an active part in the development of Jerusalem as we approach our fourth millennium.

*Mendel Kaplan*

Illuminated western side of Old City wall at night (view from Sultan's Pool)
Photo: David Harris, Jerusalem

# Foreword

The archaeological exploration of Jerusalem began in the middle of the 19th century and continues uninterruptedly to this day. From its inception, it fired the imagination of explorers and scholars from many different backgrounds and nations who came to the city in search of its past. As Archaeological research progressed, the analysis and interpretation of the ancient remains unearthed from early strata of occupation, have required constant revision. This research received new impetus with the reunification of Jerusalem in 1967, after the Six-Day War. A new generation of highly motivated Israeli archaeologists, who had been separated physically from the historic areas of Jerusalem since the city was divided in 1948, was spurred to extensive, systematic excavation of the city's ancient, hidden remains.

Excavations and archaeological research, of an intensity and scope unprecedented during the preceding one-hundred years, have accompanied the last quarter century of dynamic urban development in all parts of Jerusalem. The new excavations spread throughout the extent of the ancient city, and for the first time penetrated into the densely populated Old City—*terra incognita* from the point of view of archaeological research until then.

From the early 1990s, comprehensive surveys and numerous excavations have also been conducted in former agricultural areas that surrounded ancient Jerusalem and are today within the municipal boundaries of the city. Previously unknown evidence testifying to the close interrelation of the city proper with its rural periphery, which in antiquity served as its economic hinterland, is beginning to accumulate. This aspect of Jerusalem's past will be subjected to comprehensive review in a future publication.

The antiquities of Jerusalem have proven to be an inexhaustible source of study. Already at the outset, the new archaeological excavations in the city uncovered a variety of finds of unique value. These discoveries shed light on the material culture of the Land of Israel in past ages, and particularly on the development and the spectrum of daily life in ancient Jerusalem. The time has now come to crystallize conclusions and delineate more precisely the topographic structure of ancient Jerusalem throughout six thousand years of eventful history.

The previous volume of *Jerusalem Revealed*, which appeared in 1976, summarized the results of archaeological research in Jerusalem up to the time of publication. It presented preliminary reports and assessments of the new discoveries being made at the time. In the following years, the increasing excavation activity in Jerusalem exposed ever more remains and finds of the city's past. The full extent of these discoveries and interpretations of their significance could not be included in the first volume.

*Ancient Jerusalem Revealed* fills this void and presents the archaeological discoveries made in the soil of Jerusalem from the mid–1970s, through the 1980s and into the 1990s. It continues and complements the first volume of *Jerusalem Revealed*. Together, both volumes broadly summarize the results and achievements of the recent archaeological activities in Jerusalem. These two books testify to the tremendous efforts invested during the last two-and-a-half decades by Israeli scholars and archaeological institutions, representing a wide range of academic approaches, in the comprehensive study of Jerusalem's ancient remains. They cover all of its historical periods—under Jewish, Christian and Muslim rule; times of achievement and prosperity, and eras of decline and neglect.

This new research in Jerusalem is characterized by ceaseless improvement in excavation methods through the application of modern scientific innovations, and, above all, by a free academic spirit and a deep sense of the trust borne by the scholars engaged in the exploration of Jerusalem's past.

The antiquities of Jerusalem exposed by the new excavations are being preserved in many sites throughout the city, presenting the visitor with a tangible perception of all its historic periods. The labor of excavation and careful restoration of the ancient remains is the appropriate reply to those institutions and circles who, for reasons far removed from scholarly or scientific considerations, attempt to denigrate and restrict Israeli archaeological research in Jerusalem.

The articles presented in *Ancient Jerusalem Revealed* appeared originally in Hebrew, in the quarterly archaeological journal *Qadmoniot*. They have now been expanded and revised by their authors. The first article in this volume offers a summarizing overview of archaeological research in Jerusalem in the past twenty-five years, and an evaluation of the results and achievements. Most of the articles deal with the results of the main excavations during that period in Jerusalem. Other studies focus on the analysis and interpretation of particularly significant categories of finds. The book ends with a list of the excavations published in both volumes of *Jerusalem Revealed*, accompanied by a map of Jerusalem locating their sites.

Several persons have contributed to the publication of this volume: J. Aviram, the Director of the Israel Exploration Society, initiated this series which, besides *Jerusalem Revealed*, includes also *Ancient Synagogues Revealed* and *Ancient Churches Revealed*. His guidance and assistance were forthcoming at all stages of the preparation of this book. Thanks are also due to D. Louvish who translated some of the articles into English; to A. Paris who translated and edited some of the material; and particularly to J. Shadur who translated, edited, and saw this book through the press.

Hillel Geva,
Jerusalem 1994

# List of Plates

# Abbreviations

All biblical quotes are from the Revised Standard Version.

| | |
|---|---|
| Jer. Tal. | = Jerusalem Talmud (Danby ed.). |
| Bab. Tal. | = Babylonian Talmud (Danby ed.). |
| *Ant.* | = Josephus: Antiquities of the Jews (Thackeray ed.) |
| *War* | = Josephus: The Jewish War (Thackeray ed.) |

| | |
|---|---|
| *AASOR* | Annual of the American Schools of Oriental Research |
| *BA* | Biblical Archaeologist |
| *BAR* | Biblical Archaeology Review |
| *BASOR* | Bulletin of the American Schools of Oriental Research |
| *BR* | Bible Review |
| *HUCA* | Hebrew Union College Annual |
| *IEJ* | Israel Exploration Journal |
| *INJ* | Israel Numismatic Journal |
| *JA* | Jewish Art |
| *JJA* | Journal of Jewish Art |
| *JJS* | Journal of Jewish Studies |
| *LA* | Liber Annuus (Studii Biblici Franciscani) |
| *PEFA* | Palestine Exploration Fund Annual |
| *PEFQS* | Palestine Exploration Fund Quarterly Statement |
| *PEQ* | Palestine Exploration Quarterly |
| *POC* | Proche Orient Chrétien |
| *QDAP* | Quarterly of the Department of Antiquities of Palestine |
| *RB* | Revue Biblique |
| *TA* | Tel Aviv |
| *ZDPV* | Zeitschrift des Deutschen Palästina-vereins |

# Twenty Five Years of Excavations in Jerusalem, 1967–1992: Achievements and Evaluation

## Hillel Geva

For nearly a century-and-a-half ancient Jerusalem has been the focus of untiring archaeological exploration and historical study. Dozens of larger and smaller excavations in the city and its environs, carried out by several generations of archaeologists from many countries, have brought to light a rich variety of remains spanning six thousand years of the city's history. The evidence we have today for the topography of ancient Jerusalem includes defensive fortifications, public and religious buildings, private dwellings and residential quarters, ingenious water supply systems, and crowded cemeteries spread over the valleys and slopes of the surrounding hills.

Systematic study of the remains of Jerusalem's past began in the mid–19th century. E. Robinson and T. Tobler were typical of the perceptive scholarly pioneers of this research. They were followed by many other outstanding explorers—F. de Saulcy, Ch. Wilson, C.R. Conder, Ch.W. Warren, Ch. Clermont-Ganneau, C. Schick, to name but a few. These founding fathers of the archaeological exploration of Jerusalem documented and investigated the still visible ancient remains of the city, and sometimes also engaged in limited digs—often under trying physical conditions and personal danger. We marvel today at their detailed reports, exact drawings, and photographs.

The first large-scale archaeological excavation in Jerusalem was carried out at the end of the 19th century by F.J. Bliss and A.C. Dickie along the southern slope of Mount Zion and at the southern issue of the Tyropoeon Valley. Among their important discoveries were large sections of the ancient fortifications on Mount Zion—recognized today as the First Wall of

the Second Temple period—and the Byzantine city wall. Early in the 20th century, R. Weill, R.A.S. Macalister and J.G. Duncan, and J.W. Crowfoot and G.M. Fitzgerald excavated and studied the ancient remains of the City of David. It was the first time that new stratigraphic methods of excavation were employed in Jerusalem. Most of their finds—mainly the city walls—were thought to be of

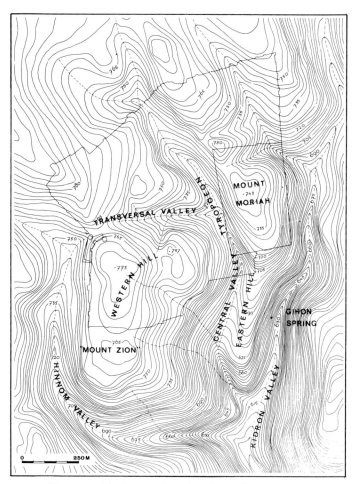

Topographical map of ancient Jerusalem

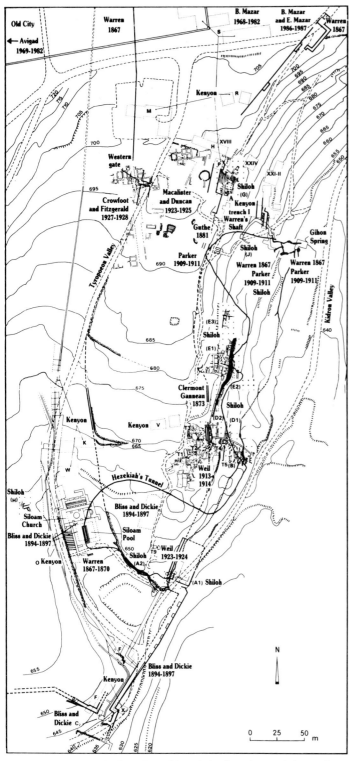

Map of City of David and the locations of the main
areas of the archaeological excavations

at the earliest. At about the same time, remains of the Third Wall of ancient Jerusalem were uncovered north of the Old City by E.L. Sukenik and L.A. Mayer, thus establishing the northern boundaries of Jerusalem at the end of the Second Temple period. No significant excavations could be conducted at this stage of the research within the densely built-up Old City itself. One exception was the excavations conducted by C.N. Johns in the courtyard of the Tower of David Citadel south of the Jaffa Gate, where an impressive section of the northwestern corner of the First Wall and its towers of the Second Temple period were uncovered.

While revealing extensive and tangible remains of the city's distant past, this initial excavation and research activity in Jerusalem also aroused serious disagreement about the dating of various finds, interpretations of their significance, and their contribution to the understanding of the topography of the ancient city.

Between the years 1961 and 1967, large-scale excavations by K.M. Kenyon marked the beginning of modern, scientific archaeological research in Jerusalem. Kenyon's excavations were carried out in small areas at scattered locations, mainly in the City of David, but also within and north of the Old City, and on Mount Zion. Her chief objective was to uncover new archaeological evidence which might provide answers to complex unresolved problems concerning the topography of ancient Jerusalem. Kenyon was the first to discover remains of the early-2nd millennium B.C.E. city wall of Jerusalem at the lower part of the eastern slope of the City of David. Thus, the entrance to Warren's Shaft, the city's ancient water supply system, was shown to have been within the walled city.

The reunification of Jerusalem in 1967 sparked a dramatic surge of archaeological activity in the ancient city. Widespread investigation of the ancient remains was initiated on a scale which overshadowed all such previous work. Excavations were conducted throughout the entire extent of ancient Jerusalem, including places within the

biblical Jerusalem, and particularly its ancient city wall. Subsequent excavations at the site, however, showed that several of these remains should be dated to the Second Temple period

Aerial view of the Temple Mount and the remains uncovered in the Ophel area south of it; looking west

Old City walls where the spade of the archaeologist had never broken ground. Building and structural remains, and the artifacts that have come to light in the course of the last twenty-five years of intensive archaeological research in Jerusalem, now make it possible to re-evaluate and summarize some of the key questions concerning the topography and architectural features of the city during various periods of its history. As a result, much of our understanding of the city's past has been revolutionized. The results of the major archaeological excavations of the last twenty-five years are presented and examined in the two volumes of *Jerusalem Revealed*. The first volume, which appeared in 1976, is now complemented and brought up to date in *Ancient Jerusalem Revealed*.

One cannot summarize the decades of archaeological research in Jerusalem without mentioning the enormous and often insoluble difficulties—some of them specific to Jerusalem—that have always been inherent in archaeological excavation there. Most of the urban area of ancient Jerusalem today lies within the walls of the densely-built Old City and the adjacent neighborhoods. This sever-

ely limits the possibilities for excavating large areas, which is the only way to obtain a comprehensive overview of the city's topography. Religious sensitivity and political factors also hinder archaeological research in key parts of the city. Jerusalem has been inhabited continuously and intensively for thousands of years. On the slopes upon which the city was built, and in the surrounding valleys, archaeological deposits consisting of layers of occupation and accumulated debris were later covered by large, deep dumps. Buildings constructed upon steep hillsides collapsed and suffered erosion, leaving only foundations in some places. With each subsequent rebuilding, foundations had to be sunk more deeply through the previous occupational levels to achieve the necessary stability. Earlier structures were dismantled and their building stones reutilized. Sometimes, as a result of official building activities in the city, such as the construction of the Temple Mount in the days of Herod, all previously existing structures along its outer sides were razed to make room for the new foundations. In view of the difficulties and limitations on the investigation of Jerusalem's past, the overwhelming

3

The City of David (below) and the Old City and Temple Mount (above). An aerial view looking north

achievements of archaeological activity, and particularly the excavations of the last twenty-five years, are the more remarkable.

## The Bronze Age

The excavations by Y. Shiloh in Area E on the eastern slope of the City of David in 1978–1985 revealed significant remains of the earliest settlement of the city, indicating a limited occupational presence in the Chalcolithic period—as early as the 4th millennium B.C.E. During the 3rd millennium B.C.E., in the Early Bronze Age, the first structures were erected on the bedrock of the steep eastern slope of the hill above the Gihon Spring. In the course of these excavations, a long segment of the city wall of the beginning of the 2nd millennium B.C.E. was uncovered. This was part of a southern extension of fortifica-

tions first found by Kenyon in the 1960s. A succession of remains of Middle and Late Bronze Age settlements discovered in Kenyon's, and mainly in Shiloh's, excavations presents firm evidence for occupational continuity in the City of David in its early days.

## The First Temple Period

So far no evidence has been encountered at the City of David for its conquest by members of the tribe of Judah or, at a later date, by King David, as described in the biblical narrative. These recorded events of the earliest history of Jerusalem still remain without satisfactory explanation from an archaeological point of view and perhaps manifest the need for reevaluating the correlation of the historical and archaeological data.

Shiloh's work in Area G provided new evidence that the stepped stone structure at the top of the northeastern slope of the City of David, previously excavated by Macalister and Duncan, and later by Kenyon, dates to the 10th century B.C.E. Shiloh assigned these remains to King David's Fortress of Zion mentioned in the Bible. Recent analysis of finds from this area for final publication has led J.M. Cahill and D. Tarler, members of the Shiloh expedition, to propose the possibility that the stepped stone structure was constructed in the days of the Canaanites-Jebusites (13th–11th century B.C.E.) before David's conquest of the city.

Warren's Shaft, the ancient water supply system of the City of David, was uncovered and cleared in the framework of Shiloh's excavations. However, there still is no conclusive dating for its construction. Shiloh himself favored a date at the beginning of the Israelite city's existence (10th–9th century B.C.E.). Geological examinations of the rock walls of Warren's Shaft by D. Gill indicate that it consists largely of natural caves created by karstic action which were enlarged and interconnected in several places to facilitate access to the source of water. This may well constitute a breakthrough in determining an earlier date for Warren's Shaft—with implications regarding the biblical narrative. Cahill and Tarler reexamined a view commonly held during the early years of research in Jerusalem which ascribed Warren's Shaft originally to the Canaanite-Jebusite period and identified it with the *zinnor*, mentioned in the Bible in connection with David's conquest.

In the eastern part of the Ophel, south of the Temple Mount, B. Mazar and E. Mazar uncovered a complex of monumental buildings attesting to royal construction activities during the 9th–8th centuries B.C.E. This complex consists of several contiguous construction units which together formed a massive fortification system—the eastern defense wall of the city—during the First Temple period. Among these buildings are a tower and remains of an adjacent structure which the excavators identified as a four-chambered gatehouse—the biblical Water Gate.

Discoveries by N. Avigad in the Jewish Quarter have finally resolved the long-standing debate concerning the date of Jerusalem's westward expansion over the Western Hill of the ancient city. The many structures and artifacts (Pl. IIa) he found on bedrock throughout the Western Hill, particularly the remains of the Broad Wall, indicate that settlement on the hill began as early as the 8th century B.C.E. At the end of that century, King Hezekiah fortified the Western Hill by encompassing it with a strong wall. Additional sections of fortifications excavated by Avigad north of the Broad Wall probably indicate a second phase of fortification-building activity toward the end of the First Temple period—to strengthen the northern side of the

The Broad Wall built at the end of the First Temple period uncovered in the Jewish Quarter; looking northeast (and see Pl. Ia)

Corner of an Israelite tower (right) and a Hasmonean tower abutting it (left) as uncovered in the Jewish Quarter (and see Pl. Ib)

segments dating to the end of the First Temple period on this side of the city. To my mind, it conclusively confirms the view held by most scholars that the late First Temple period city wall encompassed the entire Western Hill up to the present Jaffa Gate, and continued southward above the Hinnom Valley around Mount Zion, and down toward the southern tip of the City of David. A minority opinion visualizes a smaller city on the Western Hill.

Shiloh's excavations brought up evidence for the existence of a sparse extramural residential neighborhood in the 8th century B.C.E., located outside the eastern wall of the City of David and contemporary with the early stage of the settlement of the Western Hill. An unfortified squatters' neighborhood north of the Western Hill (in the present-day Christian and Muslim Quarters) began to develop during this period. A contemporary workshop building, discovered by M. Broshi outside the western wall of the city, should also be seen in the context of such extramural construction. It would seem that the impetus

city which lacks deep natural barriers. These remains of fortifications exposed on the Western Hill confirm Josephus's account that the First Wall of Jerusalem dates originally to the time of David and Solomon (the First Temple period). It is also clear now that portions of the early city wall of the end of the First Temple period were later incorporated into the reconstruction of the First Wall erected around the Western Hill by the Hasmoneans in the late 2nd century B.C.E. As a result of numerous excavations and studies conducted along the western sections of the First Wall above the Hinnom Valley, there is growing evidence pointing to the existence of fortified

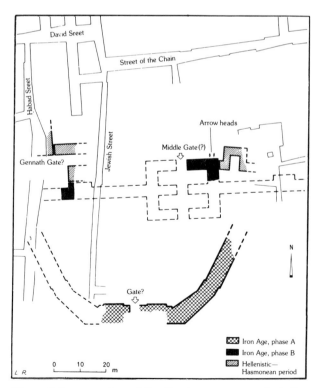

Plan of the complex of fortifications uncovered at the northern side of the Jewish Quarter

for construction of residential areas outside the walls of Jerusalem at the late First Temple period ceased with the Assyrian siege by Sennacherib in 701 B.C.E. and the resulting deterioration of security. Unfortified quarters were probably abandoned at that time, their residents preferring to live within the walled city.

The First Temple period cemeteries around Jerusalem have also been thoroughly investigated in the past twenty-five years. This research has contributed significantly to our growing knowledge of the city, its inhabitants and its boundaries during this period. Over a hundred First Temple period tombs are known to us from surveys and excavations around the city, although, regrettably, only a few were found with their contents intact.

In 1968–1970 D. Ussishkin surveyed and documented tens of burial caves in Silwan Village on the eastern slope of the Kidron Valley opposite the City of David. We now have a comprehensive picture of this sumptuous cemetery, which served Jerusalem's upper classes during the First Temple period (9th–7th centuries B.C.E.).

Several groups of burial caves dated to the end of the First Temple period (8th–6th centuries B.C.E.) were excavated on the slopes of the Hinnom Valley by M. Broshi, A. Kloner and D. Davis, by G. Barkay, and by R. Reich. Their location provides further evidence for the city's westward expansion at the end of the First Temple period. Among the many artifacts discovered by Barkay in the Ketef Hinnom cemetery are two small, rolled silver plaques bearing the biblical priestly benediction from Numbers 6:24–26.

A few rock-cut tombs of the end of the First Temple period, some of them known from previous research north of the Old City, were reinvestigated and published by G. Barkay, A. Kloner and A. Mazar. Two such tombs in the grounds of the St. Étienne Monastery are the largest and most luxurious of that period known to date in Jerusalem—or elsewhere in the Land of Israel. Their unexpected location is indicative of the northward expansion of Jerusalem's unfortified residential areas at the end of the First Temple period. Although it is difficult to establish whether they can be identified as the royal tombs mentioned by Josephus to have been situated in this vicinity, they probably give an idea of the monumental sepulchers in which the kings of Judah and high-ranking officials were buried.

Avigad's excavations on the Western Hill, B. Mazar and E. Mazar's excavations at the Ophel, and Shiloh's work in the City of David provide archaeological evidence that sheds light on the biblical account of the destruction and burning of the city by the Babylonians in 587/6 B.C.E. The most important testimony for this event comes from Area G in the City of David, where fragmentary remains of several burnt buildings containing assemblages of vessels characteristic of the period were discovered. In one of the rooms which once contained an archive of documents were more than fifty clay bullae that had been fired in the conflagration. This important epigraphic find provided a long list of Hebrew names, two of which have been identified with biblical personages active in Jerusalem on the eve of its destruction by the Babylonians: Gemariah son of Shaphan and Azariah son of Hilqiah.

Unique artifacts relating to the Temple and to the political administration in Jerusalem at the time of the First Temple have been published recently. The most important is a small ivory pomegranate bearing the Hebrew inscription: "sacred donation for the priests of (in) the house of Yahweh." It apparently belonged to a group of objects utilized in the Jewish Temple in Jerusalem, of which no architectural remains are yet known. Also of great interest are two identical bullae depicting two figures, a king and a high personage facing each other. Beneath them is the Hebrew inscription: "governor of the city." These impressions were most probably made by the seal of an official who may have served as the governor of Jerusalem under one of the last kings of the Judean monarchy.

## The Second Temple Period

Finds from recent excavations of the City of

David have provided new information on the extent and urban features of Jerusalem during the Persian and early Hellenistic periods, before the renewed expansion of the city toward the Western Hill. For the first time, an occupational level of the Persian period was uncovered—by Shiloh at the City of David—in a clear stratigraphic context. Kenyon's and Shiloh's excavations also provide important evidence that the remains of fortifications on the crest of the eastern slope of the City of David were originally constructed during the Second Temple period, and possibly even as early as the time of Nehemiah (mid–5th century B.C.E.)—but not in the Bronze Age (the Canaanite period) or the Iron Age as had been thought previously. This shows that at the beginning of the Second Temple period the earlier line of fortification of the City of David, at the lower part of the eastern slope above the Gihon Spring, was abandoned in favor of one better placed, along the crest of the hill. Evidence of continued—if limited and sporadic—Jewish burial during the Babylonian and Persian periods (6th–4th centuries B.C.E.) was derived from several late First Temple period tombs in the Hinnom Valley.

The early Hellenistic (pre-Hasmonean) period in Jerusalem is so far best represented by the many hundreds of Greek—mainly Rhodian—seal impressions on the handles of amphoras found in excavations in the northern part of the City of David. The extensive work at the Western Hill, however, produced no evidence for the existence of permanent settlement there during the Persian and early Hellenistic periods. In all, the information gleaned from the new excavations clearly indicates that settlement in Jerusalem after the destruction of the First Temple and until the Hasmonean period (6th–2nd centuries B.C.E.) was once again confined only to the traditional boundaries of the City of David, the Ophel, and the Temple Mount.

The exact location of the Seleucid Akra

◁ Aerial view of the southern part of the Temple Mount (below) and the southern part of Old City—the Western Hill (above)

Remains of Hasmonean construction uncovered in the Jewish Quarter

fortress, known from historical sources to have been erected in Jerusalem during the 2nd century B.C.E., is still enigmatic after a hundred-and-fifty years of archaeological research in the city. The absence of any supportive finds on the Western Hill no longer justifies looking for it at the western side of the city, as had been suggested by some scholars. Several locations proposed more recently for the Akra focus upon controversial archaeological remains in the southeastern part of the Herodian Temple Mount precinct, or on the Ophel. So far, such proposals remain inconclusive. The information we do

9

First wall

Aerial view of the Tower of David Citadel (looking east). In the center of the courtyard, the northwest section of the First wall of the Second Temple period can be seen

have may lead us to reconsider one of the older hypotheses: that the Seleucid Akra was one in a series of citadels erected from the time of the Ptolemies (and perhaps even earlier, during the First Temple period or the return from Babylonian exile) until the construction of the Antonia fortress by Herod on the dominating hill next to the northwestern corner of the Temple Mount.

All the excavations on the Western Hill attest to a resumption of permanent settlement there during the 2nd century B.C.E. This process apparently reflected a change in the status of Jerusalem during the middle of that century, when it became the capital of the emerging Hasmonean kingdom. Toward the end of the Hasmonean period, in the mid–1st century B.C.E. and particularly from the time of Herod, large, elaborate, lavish dwellings were built in the wealthy suburb on the Western Hill known as the Upper City. At the beginning of Hasmonean rule (the second half

of the 2nd century B.C.E.) the First Wall was rebuilt around the Western Hill along the line of the circumvallation at the end of the First Temple period. The excavations along the line of the First Wall in the north, west, and south exposed long sections of the wall and several of its towers. This provided us with the key for understanding the various stages and features of its construction in the Hasmonean and Herodian periods. Evidence was found for the incorporation into the Hasmonean First Wall of older sections of fortifications of the late First Temple period.

In the Tower of David Citadel, R. Sivan and G. Solar brought to light impressive testimony of the siege of Jerusalem by the Seleucid King Antiochus VII Sidetes in 134–132 B.C.E., which left hundreds of ballista stones and arrowheads at the foot of the wall.

Only traces of the foundations attributed to Herod the Great's palace that stood at the northwestern corner of the Upper City were

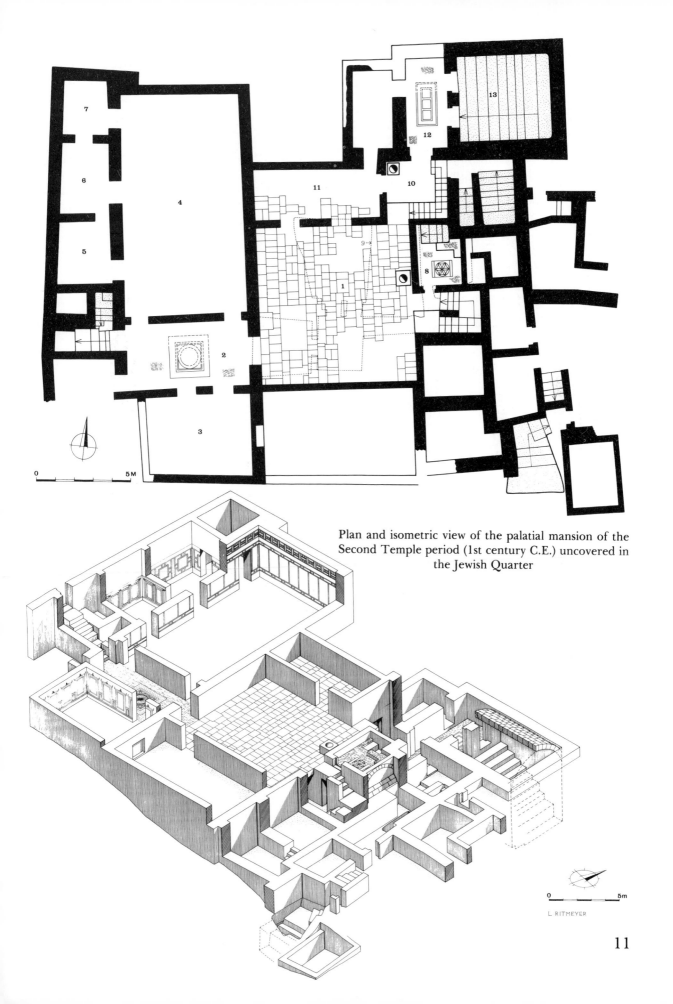

Plan and isometric view of the palatial mansion of the
Second Temple period (1st century C.E.) uncovered in
the Jewish Quarter

L. RITMEYER

11

Artist's reconstruction of the reception hall (No. 4) in the palatial mansion of the Second Temple period uncovered in the Jewish Quarter

uncovered in excavations by K.M. Kenyon and A.D. Tushingham, by R. Amiran and A. Eitan, and by M. Broshi and D. Bahat in the area of the present-day Tower of David Citadel and the Armenian Garden south of it. This extensive royal palace is generally believed to have occupied most of the area of the present Armenian Quarter up to the Old City wall in the south.

Avigad's excavations in the Jewish Quarter revealed remains of large, sumptuous private dwellings in Jerusalem's Upper City from the days of Herod the Great (the second half of the 1st century B.C.E.) until the destruction of the city in 70 C.E. (Pl. IV; VIIb). Of these, the most impressive is a palatial Herodian mansion that included several dozen rooms arranged around a central courtyard. The dwellings built in the Upper City at that time had some particularly splendidly decorated rooms with colored mosaic pavements, and fine-quality plastered, frescoed and stuccoed walls (Pl. VIa,b,c,d,e). In the houses, Jewish ritual baths (*miqva'ot*) were found cut into the bedrock. These installations raise a number of unanswered questions that still require further research to explain their fairly ubiqui-

Stuccoed wall in the reception hall (No. 4) of the palatial mansion

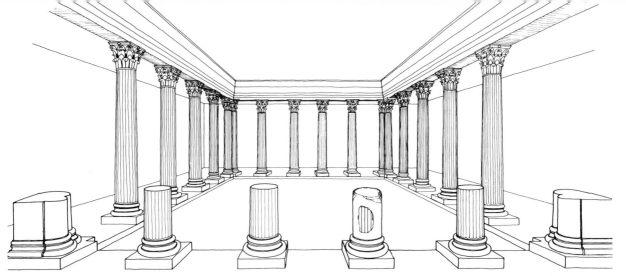

Conjectured reconstruction of the peristyle uncovered in one of the opulent dwellings of the Second Temple period (1st century C.E.) in the Jewish Quarter

Mosaic floor of the Second Temple period from the Jewish Quarter (drawing)

Sundials of the Second Temple period from the Jewish Quarter

tous occurrence, how they functioned, and other questions.

Through the excavations in the Upper City we have become acquainted with household articles made of stone, an industry that flourished in Jerusalem at the end of the Second Temple period. Particularly attractive among these products are stone tables of different forms and decorative features, and both hand-made and lathe-turned vessels of many sizes and shapes. These, together with a wide variety of elegant ceramic and glass vessels, many of them imported, and many other artifacts

13

found in the buildings, attest to the wealth of the inhabitants of the Upper City at the end of the Second Temple period. One of the most outstanding finds in the Jewish Quarter excavations is a graffito of the Menorah (the seven-branched candelabrum) on two plaster fragments. This has come to be considered the most detailed, authentic early depiction of the Menorah that stood in the Temple in Jerusalem during the Second Temple period.

B. Mazar's excavations at the Ophel exposed the massive foundations of the southern wall and the southern corners of the Herodian Temple Mount platform. These discoveries followed up and complemented the thorough investigation along the outer walls of the Temple Mount started by Warren a century earlier. Abutting the walls of the Temple Mount, remains of impressive Herodian public works now uncovered to their full extent

The Temple Mount and the monumental stairway at the Ophel along its southern wall; looking north

include wide, paved streets, flights of stairs, and plazas used by those who came to the Temple. Robinson's Arch was found to be part of a series of vaults that supported a staircase giving access from the level of the main street in the Tyropoeon Valley to a gate once located high at the southwestern corner of the Temple Mount.

The Western Wall of the Temple Mount was exposed along its entire length, north of the present prayer plaza, by means of a tunnel excavated with considerable difficulty beneath the buildings of the Old City under the supervision of M. Ben-Dov and later by D. Bahat. The dating of Wilson's Arch remains uncertain. Some scholars consider it to be the original arch—part of the bridge built during the Second Temple period over the Tyropoeon Valley; others prefer an Early Arab period dating and consider that it was built over the remains of the original arch. The recent discovery of a Roman-Byzantine street pavement above the complex of vaults extending westward from Wilson's Arch might testify to the earlier dating, but the issue can be decided only by additional excavations. In the Wall north of Wilson's Arch, a gigantic stone weighing over 300 tons(!) was discovered. Further north, the facade of Warren's Gate, as it was rebuilt in the Early Arab period, was entirely exposed. At the northern end of the Western Wall, the builders of the Herodian Temple Mount had to cut into the living rock

Herodian construction of large ashlars at the southern wall of the Temple Mount

of the hill in order to continue building the Wall in a straight line. The pavement of the street hugging the Wall here remained unfinished for some reason. Still further north, a rock-cut aqueduct, apparently of the Hasmonean period, that had been reported by Warren, was rediscovered and investigated anew. It seems to support the increasingly prevalent view that Herod's Antonia fortress was confined only to the rock outcrop between the Temple Mount and the Convent of the Sisters of Zion to the north.

The location and date of the Second Wall still remain unresolved problems in the topography of Second Temple period Jerusalem.

Hebrew inscription from the southwestern corner of Temple Mount "to the house of the trumpeting to pr[oclaim]"

The discovery of what was once a stone quarry at the site of the Holy Sepulcher and the adjoining Muristan in the present Christian Quarter led Kenyon to propose that the Second Wall ran somewhat to the east of this area. Avigad's discovery at the northwestern side of the present Jewish Quarter of the remains of a fortification system in the line of the First Wall, which he identified as the Ginat Gate complex, is perhaps indirect evidence that the Second Wall indeed passed north of there, along a course largely corresponding to that proposed by Kenyon.

The long-standing controversy among scholars concerning the precise line of the Third Wall of Jerusalem, constructed at the northern side of the city during the reign of Agrippa I in the 1st century C.E., now seems to be near resolution. Results of new excavations conducted by K.M. Kenyon and E.W. Hamrick, and later by S. Ben-Arieh and E. Netzer, along the remains of the Third Wall previously excavated by E.L. Sukenik and L.A. Mayer north of the Old City, confirm that this wall of Jerusalem was constructed during the 1st century C.E. Moreover, several recent soundings at the foundations of the present (Ottoman) north wall of the Old City failed to uncover remains of a Second Temple period city wall along the same line, and M. Magen's important excavation of the Roman city gate beneath the present Damascus Gate demonstrated that the gate complex was entirely built during the period of Roman Aelia Capitolina in the 2nd century C.E. All of this negates J.B. Hennessy and K.M. Kenyon's view that at least the foundations belong to a gate in the Third Wall of the Second Temple period. The accumulating evidence thus conclusively confirms Sukenik and Mayer's identification of the fortification remains north of the Damascus Gate as the Third Wall, and clearly shows that the Third Wall did not follow the course of the present north wall of the Old City.

Surprisingly, a number of excavations along the conjectured eastern and western line of the Third Wall have not yielded any results. A possible explanation for this may be inferred from the excavations along the northern line of the Third Wall which seems to have been extensively robbed of its stones, mainly for the building of Aelia Capitolina, leaving only fragments of its foundations. It may be, therefore, that those eastern and western sections of the Third Wall that were closest to Aelia Capitolina were dismantled to the last stone without leaving a trace. A hypothetical reconstruction of the line of the eastern and western portions of the Third Wall would perhaps have it running slightly inside the present wall of the Old City.

A. Mazar's new archaeological survey and study, in the late 1960s, of the remains of ancient aqueducts that supplied water to Jerusalem brought to light new information on their exact course and the engineering details of their construction. Segments of the Lower Aqueduct were recently uncovered south and west of the city limits. Particularly impressive is the long tunnel piercing the Armon Hanaziv ridge (the Hill of Evil Counsel). The generally accepted view that the Lower Aqueduct, which carried water to the Temple Mount, was constructed during the Second Temple period (perhaps as early as the Hasmonean period) can now be proven archaeologically. The Upper Aqueduct may also have been constructed as early as in the Second Temple period, probably during the reign of Herod the Great, to provide water to his palace and to the Upper City on the Western Hill.

The extensive cemeteries which surrounded Jerusalem during the Second Temple period have been the subject of intensive excavations and research in the years after 1967. Tens of new tombs excavated primarily north of the city in the area of Mount Scopus and the new Giv'at Hamivtar and French Hill neighborhoods, have raised the known number of Second Temple period burial caves in Jerusalem cemeteries to over 830. Notable among recently discovered tombs is the burial cave of the Nazirite family excavated by N. Avigad, and a burial cave uncovered by V. Tzaferis in which an inscription was found mentioning one "Mattathiah son of Juda(h)," identified by some scholars with Mattathias Antigonus, the

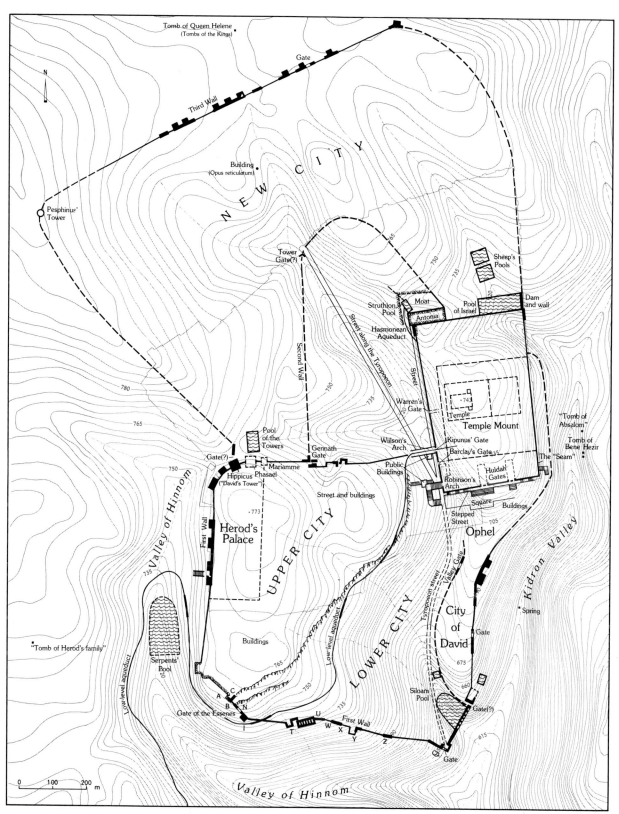

Map of Jerusalem at the end of the Second Temple period. (*The New Encyclopedia of Archaeological Excavations in the Holy Land*, p. 718)

Paved Herodian street at the foot of the Western Wall of the Temple Mount, north of Robinson's Arch; heaps of fallen stones from the wall cover the street

containing unusual artifacts are also described in the present volume.

For the first time we have vivid, concrete evidence for the violent conquest of Jerusalem by Roman Legions in 70 C.E. and the intensive destruction of its buildings. Deep accumulations of stones from the walls and buildings of the Temple Mount were encountered in B. Mazar's excavations next to the southern and western walls. These substantial remains, which included ornamented architectural fragments, covered destroyed buildings and streets alongside the Temple Mount. Next to the southwestern corner of the Temple Mount, a fragmentary Hebrew inscription incised in stone was found, reading: "to the house of the trumpeting to pr[oclaim]." This stone was originally embedded in the masonry high at the top of the corner here. Avigad's excavations in the Jewish Quarter uncovered evidence of the total destruction of the luxurious structures of the Upper City. The destruction wrought by the Roman conquest is particularly evident in the Burnt House found buried under a thick layer of charred remains and collapse (Pl. Va,b,c). A stone weight inscribed "(belonging) to bar (son of) Kathros" —the name of a well-known priestly family of Jerusalem during the Second Temple period —was found in this building.

## The Roman Period
### (2nd–3rd Centuries C.E.)

Recent excavations have shed new light on the construction activities of the Roman Tenth Legion which after 70 C.E. built its camp on the Western Hill of Jerusalem over the ruins of the Upper City of the Second Temple period. The most important testimony for the character of the construction there are thousands of fragments of ceramic rooftiles, bricks, and pipe sections, hundreds of which, impressed with the Legion's stamp:

L(egio) · X · F(retensis),

were found on the Western Hill, particularly in Avigad's excavations in the Jewish Quarter. Of the camp headquarters, apparently concentrated in the northwestern corner of the hill, only poor foundations were found in the

last king of the Hasmonean dynasty. Another tomb, excavated by Tzaferis, contained an ossuary bearing the inscription: "Simon the Temple builder" and the bones of a man executed by crucifixion. South of the city, Z. Greenhut recently excavated a tomb containing an ossuary inscribed "Joseph son of Caiapha,"—perhaps related to the family of the Jerusalem high priest Caiaphas mentioned in the New Testament in connection with the crucifixion of Jesus. A number of other important tombs with sumptuous decorations or

18

Rooftiles with stamp impressions of the Roman Tenth Fretensis Legion; note the Legion's emblems—galley and boar—on No. 1

excavations at the Tower of David Citadel. The finds from the Western Hill seem to contradict the accepted conception of a standard, fortified Roman army camp occupying the southern part of the Old City in the 2nd–3rd centuries C.E.—or even only its western portion in the area of the present Armenian Quarter. More probably, a small unit of the Tenth Legion occupied several scattered buildings on the Western Hill, of which fragmentary remains came to light mainly in the vicinity of the Tower of David Citadel.

The northern gate of Aelia Capitolina with its tripartite arched entrance flanked by two towers, located under the present Damascus Gate, was entirely exposed by M. Magen. The gateway is built mainly of large ashlars taken from destroyed Second Temple period buildings. Magen's work confirmed that this monumental gateway, modelled on Roman triumphal arches and preserved to an impressive height, was originally constructed at the time of the foundation of the Roman colony Aelia Capitolina by Hadrian at the beginning of the 2nd century C.E.

The exposure of the Roman Damascus Gate again raises the fundamental question regarding the topography of Roman Aelia Capitolina: was the city protected by walls? Excavations and soundings conducted throughout the years along the foundations of the present Old City wall—presumably the line of the city

wall of Aelia Capitolina—revealed no signs of Roman fortifications. There is, however, growing evidence that the northern wall of the Old City was first built along its present course at the very beginning of the Byzantine period, and that the line of the present southern Old City wall, crossing Mount Zion, is not earlier than the 10th–11th century C.E. Thus, the excavation results seem to indicate that Aelia Capitolina was an unfortified city, with the possible exception of the three massive Herodian towers and the western section of the First Wall which, as Josephus tells us, were left in place to protect the camp of the Tenth Legion stationed in the city after 70 C.E.

Information concerning various public and religious buildings in the northern, civilian, portion of Roman Aelia Capitolina is still very fragmentary. We are mainly familiar with Roman street pavements and plazas. Inside the Damascus Gate, M. Magen uncovered part of a massive Roman pavement which is firmly identified with the open plaza depicted on the Madaba mosaic map. The pavement in the basement of the Convent of the Sisters of Zion, northwest of the Temple Mount, venerated as the Lithostrotos in Christian tradition (the courtyard of the Antonia fortress) can now be dated more confidently to the Roman period. Apparently, it was part of the eastern forum of Roman Aelia Capitolina where a tripartite triumphal arch stood—of which the central, highest archway is the Ecce Homo arch in the Via Dolorosa.

Structural remains attributed to the Roman period were discovered from the 1960s on in a survey and in excavations of limited extent conducted by V. Corbo and others during the restoration of the Church of the Holy Sepulcher. These may be contemporary and connected with the architectural elements that have been known for many years in the basement of the Russian Alexandrovsky Hospice, east of the Church of the Holy Sepulcher. The most impressive of these Roman remains are the walls attributed to the raised platform (temenos) constructed here by Hadrian in the 2nd century C.E. next to the forum. Other walls may have been part of the

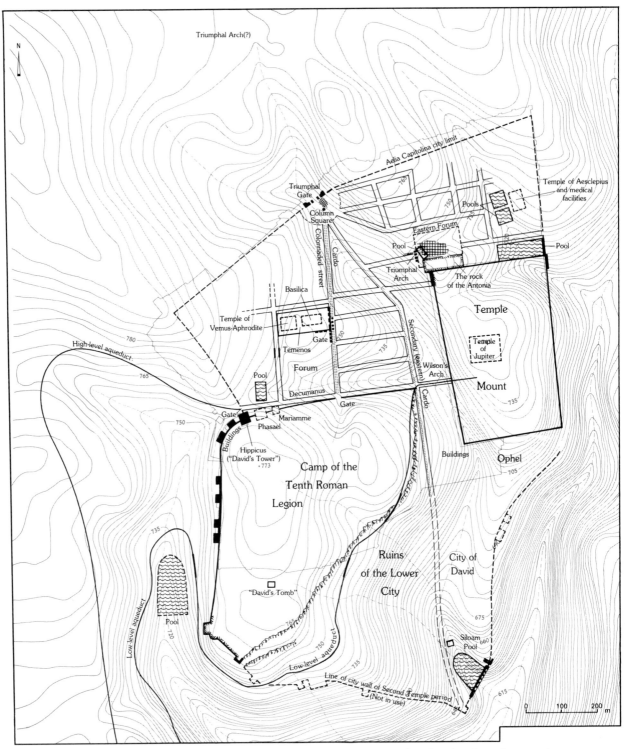

Map of Jerusalem during the Roman period. (*The New Encyclopedia of Archaeological Excavations in the Holy Land*, p. 758)

foundations of the Roman temple, and possibly also of a basilica that stood here. The attribution of some of these walls to the Roman period is still not conclusively proven

in the final published reports of the archaeological excavations at this site.

The remains of several buildings of the Roman period uncovered by B. Mazar's excavations south of the Temple Mount and next to its southwestern corner are of great interest due to their location and functions in connection with the activities of the Roman Tenth Legion.

## The Byzantine Period

Various aspects of the topography of Jerusalem in the Byzantine period—its fortifications, streets, residential quarters and churches—particularly in the southern part of the city, have been reexamined and reconstructed on the basis of the many new archaeological discoveries relating to this period.

Several architecturally uniform sections of the Byzantine city wall and its towers are known today from both past and recent excavations. These seem to indicate that the Byzantine city wall stretched along the line of the Damascus Gate in the north, the Jaffa Gate in the west, around Mount Zion in the south, and along the eastern side of the City of David and the Ophel in the east. It was probably erected originally as one concentrated construction project at the beginning of the 4th century C.E. and several of its sections were reconstructed during the late Byzantine and the Early Arab periods.

Important, unique discoveries by Avigad in the Jewish Quarter give a new perspective on the development and urban character of the Byzantine Zion Quarter. Remains of the southern portion of the main north-south street of Jerusalem—the Cardo with its two colonnades as depicted in the Madaba mosaic map—were uncovered, thus extending the northern part of the Cardo which dates to the period of the foundation of Roman Aelia Capitolina in the 2nd century C.E. The archaeological evidence shows this southern portion of the Cardo (Pl. VIIId) to have been constructed in the mid–6th century C.E., during the reign of Justinian, to connect in a straight line the Church of the Holy Sepulcher with the new Nea Church.

At the southern end of the Cardo, in the southern part of today's Jewish Quarter, several sections of foundation walls of the Nea Church complex, also built by Justinian in the

Inscription of Justinian in the vaulted cistern of the Byzantine Nea Church uncovered in the Jewish Quarter

mid–6th century C.E., were uncovered and identified by Avigad, thus enabling us to appreciate its huge dimensions and massive construction. The estimated length of the church proper is 115 m.(!) The southern part of the church complex was supported by the vaults of an immense underground cistern (Pl. VIIIc). An inscription in plaster on one of its walls commemorates the emperor Justinian and this monumental project. These discoveries now permit conclusive identification of the exact location of the Nea Church, solving a problem long debated among scholars.

The Kenyon-Tushingham excavations in the Armenian Garden, Broshi's excavations on Mount Zion, and Y. Margovsky and Ben-Dov's excavations on the eastern slope of Mount Zion all revealed many additional remains of streets and private, public and religious buildings that densely covered the Zion Quarter during the Byzantine period.

B. Mazar's excavations at the Ophel uncovered remains of a residential quarter established there already at the beginning of the Byzantine period. The structures are more-or-less uniform in plan. They include many rooms arranged around central courtyards, many of them paved with mosaics. Their well-preserved remains give us a clear picture of the domestic architecture in Jerusalem at that time. Later in the Byzantine period, this neighborhood became more crowded with additional construction. In one of the structures near the southwestern corner of the

21

Reconstruction of the southern section of the Cardo in the Jewish Quarter

The eastern wall of the Nea Church uncovered in the Jewish Quarter with the southern lateral apse

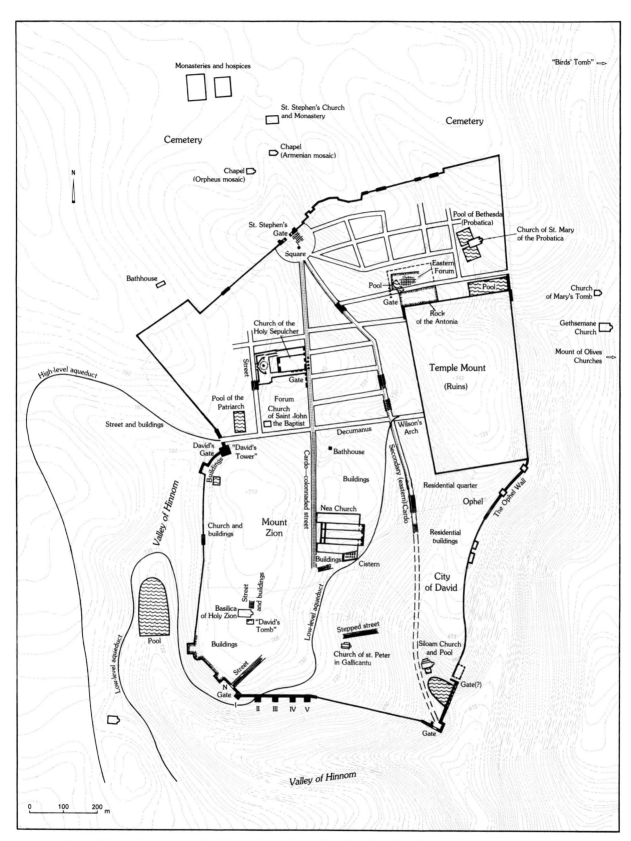

Map of Jerusalem during the Byzantine period. (*The New Encyclopedia of Archaeological Excavations in the Holy Land*, p. 769)

Temple Mount unexpected evidence attests a brief period of Jewish settlement there at the end of the Byzantine period, perhaps following the Persian conquest of the city in 614 C.E. The finds demonstrate that some of the Byzantine buildings continued to be used alongside the palaces constructed south and west of the Temple Mount at the beginning of the Early Arab period.

Southwest of the Dung Gate, Ben-Dov uncovered the remains of the secondary (eastern) Cardo which probably only had one row of columns and shops on its western side. The street seems to have been constructed at the beginning of the Byzantine period, perhaps along the line of an earlier Roman street. The significant change in the course of this eastern main street of Jerusalem from the time of the Second Temple to the Roman-Byzantine period is of interest: During the Second Temple period the street followed the Tyropoeon Valley, along the Western Wall of the Temple Mount, whereas during the Roman-Byzantine period, it followed a higher, western course, constructed along an artificial rock scarp which is still visible at the eastern edge of the Jewish Quarter, opposite the Western Wall prayer plaza.

Several segments of pavements discovered in recent years below the present main streets of the Old City consist of massive Roman-type slabs, mostly in secondary use. These indicate that the main thoroughfares of Jerusalem underwent extensive renovation at the beginning of the Byzantine period (4th–5th century C.E.), entailing large-scale secondary use of Roman paving stones.

The archaeological survey and limited excavations conducted by Corbo and others since the 1960s in the Church of the Holy Sepulcher have uncovered building remains dating to the original Constantinian church complex at the beginning of the 4th century C.E. The most important among these remains is the apse of the basilica oriented to the west, toward the traditional sepulcher of Jesus. Differences of opinion between V. Corbo and Ch. Coüasnon concerning the architectural details of the various structures built here during this period focus primarily on the reconstruction of the rotunda around the Tomb. According to Corbo, the rotunda with its three apses was completed already under Constantine, thus leaving the Tomb within a roofed space. Coüasnon, on the other hand, argues that during the Constantinian building phase the Tomb was left enclosed in a niche at the western side of an open courtyard which underwent changes and was roofed only toward the end of the 4th century C.E.

The picture which has emerged from exca-

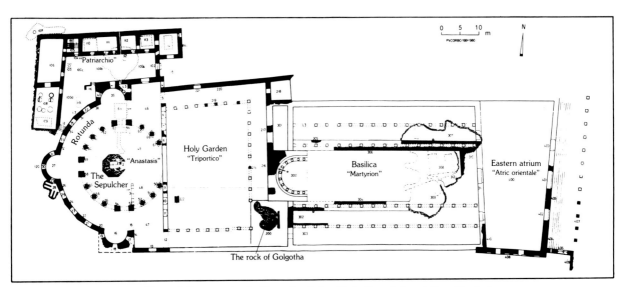

Plan of Constantine's Church of the Holy Sepulcher (after Corbo)

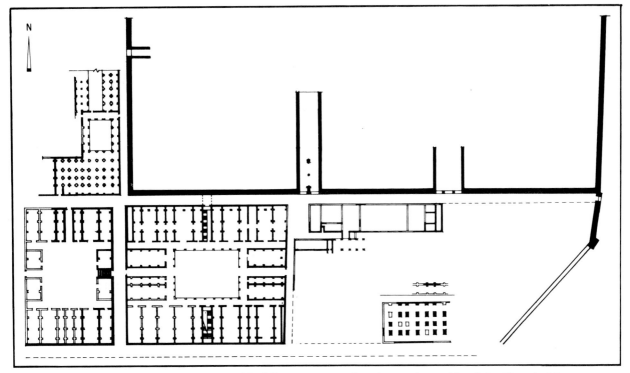

Plan of the Early Arab period royal buildings uncovered at the southern side of the Temple Mount

vations north and west of the Old City, regarding the extensive Byzantine construction beyond the city walls, is both important and innovative. North of the Old City several Byzantine-period structures serving religious functions were previously known. The most famous of these are the Armenian and the Orpheus floor mosaics. Near these Ben-Arieh and Netzer uncovered the remains of a large building which they identified as a Byzantine monastery. Additional monastic buildings were discovered nearby by Tzaferis and others. These include a large number of rooms, burial chapels with a mosaic pavement, and many tombs. Remains of another monastery which belonged to the Armenian community in Byzantine Jerusalem were uncovered by D. Amit and S. Wolff. The excavated finds illustrate the development, during the latter part of the Byzantine period (5th, and mainly 6th centuries C.E.), of an unwalled urban quarter of Christian religious character, north of the city wall. At the same time, remains of commercial complexes with workshops were excavated by A.M. Maeir and R. Reich just beyond the present-day Jaffa

Gate—outside the western Byzantine city gate.

## The Early Arab Period

Finds of the period following the Muslim conquest attest to the efforts of the new rulers in changing the city's Byzantine-Christian character. The most important discoveries dating to the Early Arab period are the remains of two large palaces and several other royal buildings uncovered in the course of B. Mazar's excavations at the Ophel and near the southwestern corner of the Temple Mount. These impressive palaces—part of a royal administrative center—were constructed next to the walls of the Temple Mount during the rule of the Umayyad caliphs toward the end of the 7th and beginning of the 8th century C.E. They are contemporaneous with the foundations of the earliest mosques on the Temple Mount and incorporate also restorations of parts of the destroyed walls and gates of the Temple Mount. The palaces follow a nearly identical plan with a central courtyard surrounded by porticos and rooms. Building materials taken from collapsed and destroyed

25

walls of the Second Temple period Temple Mount, as well as columns and various architectural components from destroyed Byzantine churches, were utilized in their construction. The palaces were in use for only a short time. They were severely damaged by the earthquake that shook Jerusalem in the 747 (or 749) C.E. and were subsequently abandoned. Various structures were erected upon their ruins during the Fatimid period.

In the context of royal building activity in Jerusalem at the beginning of the Early Arab period, a new fortress was erected in the area of the present Tower of David Citadel south of the Jaffa Gate. Johns's excavations there in the past, and Geva's more recent excavations at this site, exposed a round corner tower and sections of adjoining, massive defensive walls. These were included within the southeastern corner of the small citadel constructed during the late 7th–8th centuries C.E. to safeguard

and overlook Jerusalem. Apparently at the same time, several sections along the line of the Byzantine city wall, which continued to protect the city during the Early Arab period, were restored.

The picture emerging from excavations within the limits of the city and its outlying quarters reflects a general continuity of its Byzantine-Christian character at the beginning of the Early Arab period. The decline of Jerusalem as a Christian city began with the inception of Abbasid rule in the mid–8th century C.E. and continued through the 9th century. During this period the city gradually became Muslim, both architecturally and demographically.

Avigad's excavations along the southern wall of the Old City uncovered a section of fortifications—the earliest city wall found along this line—with a gateway protected by a pair of inner towers dated to the end of the

Construction remains including a columned room of the Crusader period uncovered in the southern part of the Jewish Quarter; looking north

Ayyubid tower (or gate) beneath the inner side of the southern wall of the Old City uncovered in the Jewish Quarter

Early Arab period (10th–11th century C.E.). This indicates that the southern city wall was not shortened before this period to the line of the present-day southern wall of the Old City, leaving Mount Zion, the City of David and the southern issue of the Tyropoeon Valley outside of the walled area of the city.

## The Medieval Period

New information is now available about the fortifications of Jerusalem in the Medieval period. In digs conducted by Ben-Dov, Avigad and Broshi along the southern and western lines of the present Old City wall and at its foundations, from the Tower of David Citadel in the west and as far as the Dung Gate in the south, uncovered long sections of an earlier city wall with towers and gates. The foundations of the new wall were laid during the Ayyubid period (or perhaps previously, under the Crusaders) over the line of the even earlier wall of the 10th–11th centuries C.E. Inscriptions uncovered on Mount Zion by Broshi also clearly indicate fortification-building activity there at the beginning of the 13th century C.E. But as we know from literary sources, this construction was purposely dismantled shortly afterwards by the Muslim rulers. At the northwestern corner of the Old City wall, D. Bahat and M. Ben-Ari uncovered remains of the facade of the Medieval Qal'at Jalud (Goliath's Tower) and the moat which protected it from the outside. During the Crusader period the Damascus Gate was refurbished by the addition of an outer fortified gateway, the remains of which were excavated by Kenyon and Hennessy.

The digs conducted in the Tower of David Citadel have exposed only fragmentary remains of the foundations of the Medieval fortress. It seems that the present Ottoman Citadel, which dates originally to the Mamluk period, had the same proportions and plan as the one constructed there by the Crusaders.

Within the Old City, several underground Mamluk building complexes, west of Wilson's

Arch, were cleared and reexamined. These consist of a series of vaulted subterranean rooms along a central vaulted passageway which served also as substructures of the houses above. In the Jewish Quarter, A. Ovadiah cleared the ruins of a Crusader monastery comprising a church and other buildings on two levels. Along the course of the Byzantine Cardo Avigad uncovered a two-storied vaulted Crusader bazaar with buildings added at some indeterminate time. A public building, probably of monastic character, its central room having a roof supported by four heavy, round stone pillars, was also found by Avigad in the southern part of the Jewish Quarter. In the Armenian Garden, Bahat and Broshi uncovered a few remains of the royal Crusader palace. South of it, Kenyon and Tushingham excavated a public building which may have served as a caravanserai during the Ayyubid period. In the Muslim Quarter west of the Temple Mount, Bahat investigated and identified an intact Crusader church used today as a workshop. The first comprehensive survey of Muslim buildings, primarily of the Mamluk period, was conducted on the Temple Mount and in the Muslim Quarter west of it by M.H. Burgoyne and D. Richards.

## The Periphery of Jerusalem

In addition to archaeological activity within the ancient urban area of Jerusalem, comprehensive archaeological surveys and excavations of the rural agricultural settlements on the outskirts of the city have also been carried out. Remains studied include small villages, farmsteads and monasteries, as well as various agricultural installations. All these attest to a developed agriculture and intensive land use over thousands of years in the narrow valleys and on the terraced hillsides. This densely occupied rural hinterland was a major economic factor in the growth and prosperity of the city throughout its long history.

Research has shown that the population density in Jerusalem's rural periphery peaked at the end of the First Temple period (8th–7th centuries B.C.E.), during the Hasmonean and Herodian periods (2nd century B.C.E.–1st century C.E.) and in the late Byzantine and early Arab periods (6th–8th centuries C.E.). There is a close correlation between periods of maximum expansion of the city limits and the development and population density of its rural hinterland.

For the first time, the archaeological investigation of Jerusalem is accompanied by wide-ranging restoration and preservation projects comprising excavated remains of all periods. It is now possible to visit many sites that illustrate and bring to life much of ancient Jerusalem, and to follow and understand the urban and architectural history of the city—from its beginnings thousands of years ago, through the Ottoman period.

## General Bibliography

Avigad, N., *Discovering Jerusalem* (Nashville, 1983).
Bahat, D., *The Illustrated Atlas of Jerusalem* (Jerusalem, 1990).
Ben-Dov, M., *In the Shadow of the Temple. The Discovery of Ancient Jerusalem* (Jerusalem, 1982).
Kenyon, K.M., *Digging Up Jerusalem* (London, 1974).
Shiloh, Y., *Excavations at the City of David I* (Jerusalem, 1984).
Stern, E. (ed.), *The New Encyclopedia of Archaeological Excavations in the Holy Land* (Jerusalem, 1993), pp. 698–804.
Yadin, Y. (ed.), *Jerusalem Revealed. Archaeology in the Holy City 1968–1974* (Jerusalem, 1976).

**Note:** Detailed bibliographical listings are given with the articles in both volumes of *Jerusalem Revealed* and in the *The New Encyclopedia of Archaeological Excavations in the Holy Land*.

# JERUSALEM — FIRST TEMPLE PERIOD

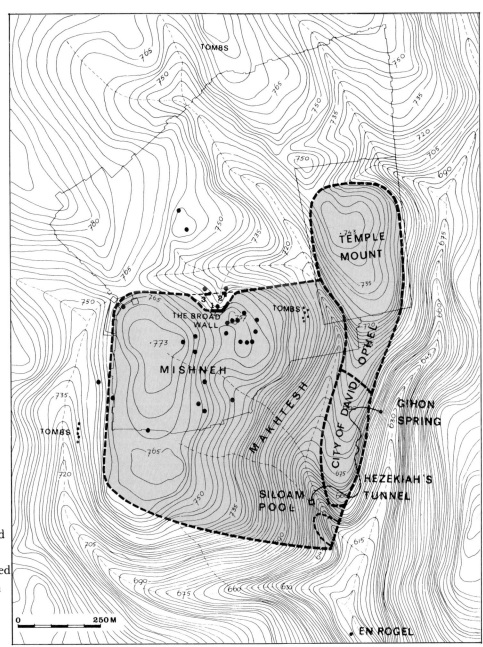

Map of Jerusalem at the end of the First Temple period. The dots represent excavated Israelite sites at the western side of ancient Jerusalem (N. Avigad, *Discovering Jerusalem*, Fig. 36)

Aerial view of the City of David with the location of the excavation areas and the Old City

# Excavations Directed by Yigal Shiloh at the City of David, 1978–1985

## Jane M. Cahill and David Tarler

The earliest settlement of Jerusalem is situated on a long, narrow, triangle-shaped hill stretching south of the Temple Mount— commonly known by its biblical designation, the City of David. To the east, this hill is bounded by the steep Kidron Valley; to the west and south it is delimited by the Tyropoeon (Central) Valley joining the Kidron. The only perennial source of water in the immediate vicinity is the Gihon Spring, located in a cave at the foot of the eastern slope. The area of the City of David covers about 49 dunams (12 acres). From earliest times the inhabited area expanded down the eastern slope toward the Gihon Spring.

## The New Excavations

Since the mid–19th century, numerous archaeologists of various nationalities have worked within the City of David. The most recent excavations were those begun in 1978 under the direction of Professor Y. Shiloh of the Hebrew University as part of a municipal development project sponsored by the City of David Society.[1] Twenty-one strata ranging in

date from the Chalcolithic Age (4th millennium B.C.E.) to the late Medieval period (14th–15th centuries C.E.) have been revealed.

Twelve excavation areas, encompassing approximately 4 dunams located primarily along the eastern slope of the City of David, were investigated during eight consecutive seasons in 1978–1985. The location of these areas reflected a problem-oriented strategy aimed at elucidating the component parts of the Canaanite and Israelite cities of the Bronze and Iron Ages. Excavation in Areas A1, A2, B, and J, located in the southern half of the site, was directed primarily toward gaining a better understanding of the subterranean water supply systems and the tunnels linking the Gihon Spring to the Siloam (Shiloah) Pool. The investigation of Areas D1–2, K, and H, located along the southern edge of the eastern slope, the summit, and the western slopes of the Tyropoeon Valley, focused on exposing structures and fortifications of the Hellenistic, Roman, and Byzantine periods. Work in Areas D1–2 and E1–3, close to the center of the eastern slope, concentrated on revealing architectural remains of the Early and Middle Bronze Ages, as well as a large Iron Age domestic quarter. Excavation in Area G, located just below the hillcrest toward the northern end of the site, centered on exposing remains of a massive substructural support system of the Late Bronze or Early Iron Age, and two terraces of Late Iron Age structures destroyed by the Babylonians in 587/6 B.C.E.

## Neolithic-Chalcolithic Ages

Artifacts from the City of David that may be dated to the Neolithic Age include a single

[1] The excavations in the City of David were directed by the late Yigal Shiloh, until his untimely death in 1987. The City of David Society comprises the Hebrew University Institute of Archaeology, the Israel Exploration Society, the Jerusalem Foundation, and a group of sponsors from South Africa headed by Mendel Kaplan. The mayor of Jerusalem, Teddy Kollek, serves as its president. Generous financial assistance for conducting the excavations was received from the Ambassador International Cultural Foundation, the Rothschild Foundation, and the Jerusalem Municipality. Excavation work was carried out by an international body of volunteers supervised by a senior staff of archaeologists and technicians associated with the Hebrew University Institute of Archaeology. (Some of the conclusions in this article differ from those of Y. Shiloh as presented in various publications.)

General view of City of David: eastern slope with excavation Areas D, E, J, G; looking north

these structures were discovered beneath the fortification wall and associated structures of Middle Bronze Age II excavated at the eastern edge of Area E1. The exposure of large numbers of similarly planned broadroom structures at the Negev site of Arad has earned them their name, Arad-type house.

## Middle Bronze Age II
Historically, Middle Bronze Age II is contemporaneous with the Egyptian Middle Kingdom Execration Texts which name Jerusalem. Archaeologically, it is represented by several phases in the City of David. The earliest of these contains a massive fortification wall built of cyclopean limestone boulders found skirting a steep scarp in the bedrock located midway between the hillcrest and the Gihon Spring. During its initial phase, this fortification wall was approximately 3 m. wide. In subsequent phases, buttressing was added to its inner face, and floors bearing chronologically indicative pottery were laid up to it. K.M. Kenyon, who cleared 12.5 m. of this wall in an area farther to the north, noted the presence of two angular turns which she initially interpreted as the corner of a gate tower. Ultimately, she concluded that they belonged to one of a succession of offsets and insets. Shiloh uncovered an additional 30 m. of the wall in Areas E1 and E3, revealing a second offset, or jog, similar to the one exposed by Kenyon. Concurring on the date of the wall's construction, Kenyon and Shiloh both ascribed its appearance to the 18th century B.C.E. In addition to the fortification wall, Shiloh uncovered fragmentary structural remains in Areas E1 and E3, including one floor which yielded an assortment of carved bone inlays and pieces of gold leaf.

## Late Bronze Age
Architectural remains of the Late Bronze Age are known primarily from the upper part of the eastern slope. The earliest of these are portions of two poorly preserved rooms belonging to a structure built upon the bedrock in Area G and tentatively dated to the early part of the Late Bronze Age.

sherd bearing an incised band of herringbone decoration and a flint arrowhead. Sherds ascribed to the Chalcolithic Age have been found in a layer of soil excavated in Area B at the foot of the City of David's eastern slope. In addition, Chalcolithic pottery was also found in natural depressions in the bedrock, together with sherds from the Early Bronze Age.

## Early Bronze Age
The earliest architectural remains uncovered in the City of David consist of rectangular broadroom structures with benches lining their interior walls. Founded on the bedrock,

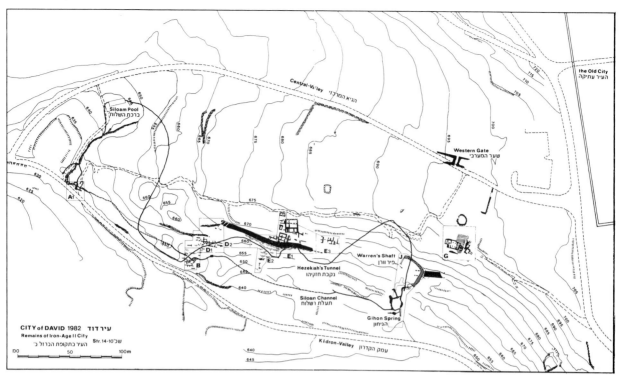

General map of the City of David and excavation areas

City of David: the early city wall in Area E

Evidence of Jerusalem's status as an Egyptian satellite during the 14th century B.C.E. is provided by six letters from the king of the city, 'Abdi-Hepah, discovered in the archive at Tell el-Amarna in Egypt. Although archaeological remains ascribable to this period have been retrieved from tomb deposits on the Mount of Olives nearby, none have been found at the City of David.

## Late Bronze Age II/Iron Age I

The transitional period between the Late Bronze Age II and Iron Age I is represented by a massive stepped stone structure with undefined boundaries built along the upper

City of David: fragment of cultic stand, 10th century B.C.E.

reaches of the eastern slope during the 13th/12th century B.C.E. Shiloh's excavations in Area G have shown that this structure consists of a substructure and a superstructure. The substructure comprises a series of interlocking terraces formed by north-south running spine walls and closely-spaced, east-west rib walls, which together created rows of rectangular compartments filled with loosely packed boulders topped by layers of compacted soil. Sections of two, and possibly three, substructural terraces descending from the eastern edge of the hillcrest toward the Kidron Valley for a distance of about 20 m. have been investigated. The substructural terraces were capped by a stone-built superstructure, also of two parts: a rubble core and a stepped mantle. The rubble core consisted of loose boulders keying the mantle to the substructure. The mantle was constructed of partially dressed, dentiform limestone blocks laid like rooftiles in a series of overlapping courses, rising from east to west in a stepped fashion toward the hillcrest. Shiloh interpreted these substructural and superstructural components as independent architectural features dating, respectively, to the Late Bronze Age II (ca. 13th century B.C.E.) and to the early Iron Age II (ca. 10th century B.C.E.). He regarded the substructural compartments as a means for expanding the level area of the hillcrest, atop which he located the Canaanite Citadel of Zion. Shiloh interpreted the stepped stone mantle as a buttress added to the substructural fills sometime during the 10th century B.C.E. Although he dated the substructural compartments from the pottery found within them, he determined the date of the superstructural mantle on the basis of the pottery extracted from the covering layers of soil. Pottery dating to the 13th/12th century B.C.E. recovered from a probe cut through the mantle's lower courses during the 1983 season of excavation was identical to that revealed within the substructural fills during the earlier seasons. The structure's stepped stone mantle appears, therefore, to have been contemporary with the substructural compartments. In light of the ceramic evidence, both features

City of David: general view of Area G, looking west

should be considered as components of a single architectural unit constructed during the transitional period between the end of the Late Bronze Age II and the beginning of Iron Age I. Pottery and fragmentary structural remains from this period were also revealed in Areas B, E1, and D1.

## Iron Age II

Historically, Iron Age II is the period of Jerusalem's preeminence as the capital of the United Monarchy, and later, the Kingdom of Judah. Archaeologically, it is the most physically defined period in the City of David: it was the last period during which the lower part of the eastern slope lay within the city walls and was clearly delimited by the Babylonian destruction in 587/6 B.C.E.

TENTH CENTURY B.C.E. David captured the Jebusite stronghold of Zion and made it his capital early in the 10th century B.C.E. Remains of this period have been recovered from Areas B, D1, E1, and G. Slightly north of Area G, Kenyon exposed structural remains which she interpreted as part of a casemate fortification wall similar to those attributed to Solomon at Gezer, Hazor, and Megiddo. The location of Kenyon's purported casemate wall, slightly north of Area G, led Shiloh to view the stepped stone structure to its south as the southeastern corner of a 10th century B.C.E royal compound. But as concluded above, the stepped stone structure and its terraced foundations appear to form a single architectural unit originally constructed during the 13th/12th centuries B.C.E. In Area G, therefore,

35

the 10th century B.C.E is represented solely by the fragmentary remains of structures and soil fills found covering the lower courses of the stepped stone structure. Evidence of the 10th century B.C.E. in Area E1 includes clay installations, two ceramic chalices, and the lower half of a fenestrated cultic stand.

NINTH-EIGHTH CENTURIES B.C.E. Remains ascribable to the 9th century B.C.E. consist solely of poorly preserved structures and soil fills found in Areas E1 and G. During the 8th century B.C.E., the Iron Age city of Jerusalem expanded greatly. Perhaps due to the arrival of Israelite refugees fleeing the Assyrian conquest of the northern kingdom of Israel in 721 B.C.E., and Judahites displaced by upheavals along the Judah-Philistia border, the city's growth appears to have peaked during the reign of Hezekiah, when it already included the Western Hill within its walled limits.

Sections of a massive fortification wall ascribed to the 8th century B.C.E. have been found towering above a vertical escarpment located near the middle of the eastern slope. This wall, which was traced for approximately 120 m. across Areas D1, D2, E1, E2, and E3, followed virtually the same course as its Middle Bronze Age II predecessor, and in places even incorporated remnants of the older wall. It was constructed in a jagged, sawtooth line and was preserved up to 5 m. in width and 3 m. in height. Remains of a 2–3-m.-wide cobbled pavement revetted by a retaining wall were found abutting it on the outside. Presumably this extramural street paralleled the entire length of the city wall, segments of which were traced by Shiloh through Areas D2, E1, and E2, and by Kenyon further to the north.

City of David, Area G: (1) L.997 = plaster floor of Burnt Room destroyed in 587/6 B.C.E.; (2) north wall of the House of Aḥi'el; (3) stepped stone structure; (4) rubble core of stepped stone structure

Within Areas E1 and E3, the fortification wall supported a system of structurally integrated buildings that were linked by a stepped alleyway having a drainage channel emptying into the Kidron Valley via a small rectangular opening built into the wall. Integrated with the fortification wall to the west was the Lower Terrace House. This structure, excavated in Area E1, consisted of three parallel rooms at three different levels following the rise in the bedrock. Like the fortification wall, it served throughout the final three phases of Iron Age II, each phase being represented by a floor bearing a chronologically indicative assemblage of ceramic vessels.

A number of structures dating to the 8th century B.C.E. were also revealed on the lower slopes of the bedrock, outside the fortification wall in Areas B, D1, D2, and E2. The 8th century B.C.E. pottery found both inside and outside these buildings suggests that their abandonment coincided with the Assyrian siege of 701 B.C.E.

**SEVENTH-SIXTH CENTURIES B.C.E.** Most intramural areas excavated within the City of David have produced evidence of occupation at the end of the Iron Age II. Four prominent structures, however, are particularly significant for elucidating both the city's material culture and the intensity of the 587/6 B.C.E. Babylonian destruction. These are the Ashlar House, excavated in Area E1, and the House of Aḥi'el, the Burnt Room, and the Bullae House, uncovered in Area G.

The Ashlar House was a large (13 x 13 m.) structure, spreading across two terraces located in the upper reaches of Area E1. Its 80 cm.-thick walls, preserved in places to a height of 3 m., were built of roughly dressed, rectangular blocks of limestone and well dressed ashlars positioned mainly in corners subjected to the greatest static pressure. Although its entire floor plan was not revealed, Shiloh believed that the Ashlar House followed the so-called four-room or four-pillared house plan characteristic of Israelite architecture. Its large size, its elevated topographic position, and the quality of its construction led

City of David, Area G: toilet chamber appended to House of Aḥi'el

him to identify it as a public structure. The ceramic and stratigraphic evidence indicated that the Ashlar House was constructed during the early part of the 7th century B.C.E. and destroyed at the end of the Iron Age in 587/6 B.C.E.

The House of Aḥi'el was an 8 x 8 m., four-room or -pillared house, situated along the higher of two structural terraces in Area G. Its name comes from the discovery there of a storage jar fragment bearing a Hebrew inscription containing the personal name Aḥi'el. The walls of this building were constructed of both roughly dressed fieldstones and ashlars, including one with an inscription in paleo-Hebrew script. Two stone monoliths and two built piers supported the ceiling above the ground floor and separated the central courtyard from two side chambers.

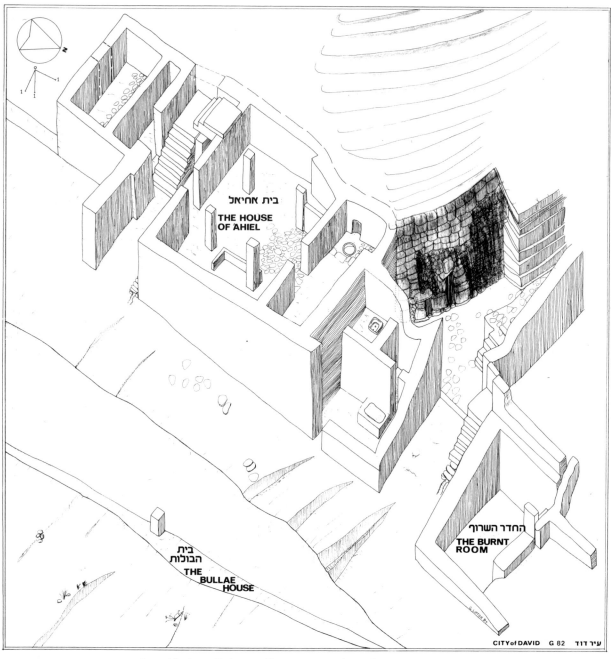

בית אחיאל
THE HOUSE OF AHIEL

החדר השרוף
THE BURNT ROOM

בית הבולות
THE BULLAE HOUSE

CITY of DAVID   G 82   עיר דוד

City of David, Area G: isometric reconstruction of Late Iron Age buildings

Attached to the northern wall of the House of Aḥi'el was a three-room addition housing a storeroom with over fifty restorable ceramic vessels, mostly storage jars. The floor of a small chamber adjoining the storeroom consisted of a thick layer of lime plaster. Embedded in one side of this plastered floor was a limestone toilet seat with a plaster-lined cesspit beneath it. An identical toilet seat was discovered by J.G. Duncan in 1925 during previous excavations in this area, and another one was found *in situ* in an Iron Age II structure excavated in Area E3.

An alleyway separated the House of Aḥi'el from a building containing the Burnt Room, named after the thick layer of charred debris found on its floor. A staircase built of finely cut ashlars abutted the southern wall of the structure and led to its upper or second story. The rectangular Burnt Room is located immediately north of the wall bounding the external staircase and constituted the southern,

38

City of David: floor of Burnt Room after removal of stone collapse

ground-floor room of a partially excavated structure. Evidence for the second story was provided by both the position of the landing above the external staircase and the corresponding ledge in its western wall, 2.5 m. above the floor, along which were found the carbonized remains of wooden ceiling beams. Among the charred debris extracted from this room were pieces of burnt wood, including fragments that had been carved with motifs identical to those known from ornamental ivories. Although most of this wood was from local trees, some of the finely carved pieces were identified as boxwood (*Buxus*), a species native to Cyprus, northern Syria, and southern Turkey.

East of the House of Aḥi'el, on the next lower terrace, is the Bullae House, named after a cache of over fifty clay sealings, or bullae, found in its northwest corner (see in this volume, pp. 55–61 and pp. 62–63). As only a narrow strip (7–8 x 1 m.) located at the structure's western edge was excavated, little can be said about its plan. Its western wall, however, served both as the exterior wall of the building and as the revetment for a street

or walkway leading to the upper terrace structures. As in the Burnt Room, a thick layer of charred debris covered the structure's hard plaster floor.

The massive destruction of Jerusalem by the Babylonians is apparent not only in the thick layers of charred remains unearthed in

City of David: collapse in Burnt Room

39

City of David, Area G: ceramic vessels from final phase of Iron Age II

structures such as the Burnt Room and the Bullae House, but also in the deep stone rubble from collapsed buildings found covering the eastern slope. The biblical descriptions of the city's destruction (2 Kings 25:8–10; Jeremiah 39:8; 2 Chronicles 36:18–19) complement the archaeological evidence, and the 587/6 B.C.E. date is documented in other historical sources. The pottery recovered from the destruction level unearthed along much of the eastern slope of the City of David is identical to that typifying the final phase of Iron Age II at other Judean sites.

**Persian Period**

Following the Persian conquest of Babylonia in the late 6th century B.C.E., the Judean exiles received permission to return to Jerusalem and rebuild their Temple (Ezra 1:1–4; 6:2–5). Although reconstruction initially focused on the Temple itself (Ezra 3:8–10), the City of David and its fortifications were eventually rebuilt as well.

Probably because of the massive accumulation of collapsed masonry covering the eastern slope of the City of David, new structures were not built there. Immediately below the hillcrest, however, the Ashlar House in Area E1 was partially reused. Sloping layers of limestone chips revetted by flimsy walls have been found along the eastern slope in Areas D1, D2, and E1. These stone chips may be interpreted as refuse originating from a stone quarry located atop the hillcrest.

The line of the fortification wall built under Nehemiah's direction has not yet been traced with certainty, for no correlation exists between the landmarks listed in his description of it (Nehemiah 3:1–32) and the archaeological remains. Nevertheless, the biblical narrative clearly states that large portions of the old wall were repaired rather than built anew. The repaired portions are commonly identified with the western line of the pre–8th century B.C.E. fortifications. Nehemiah described the ruins along the eastern slope as impassable (Nehemiah 2:12–14), and accordingly the earlier wall line located at midslope is thought to have been abandoned in favor of a new one skirting the eastern edge of the hillcrest. A short segment of fortification wall excavated there by Macalister and Duncan was reinvestigated by Kenyon, who identified it as Nehemiah's wall. Renewed examination of this wall under Shiloh's direction showed it to have been built of roughly dressed limestone blocks laid in successively receding courses atop a steep escarpment. Although this segment is clearly the earliest component of the fortification line in this area of the hillcrest, Kenyon's discovery of Late Bronze Age deposits on the bedrock close to its inner face suggests that it may actually have originated much before the Persian period.

Sandwiched stratigraphically between the stone collapse resulting from the Iron Age II (587/6 B.C.E.) destruction and strata dating to the early Hellenistic period, the Persian period layers in the City of David yielded a varied assemblage of pottery including storage jar handles bearing several types of seal impressions. The well-stratified deposits of the Persian period discovered in the City of David stand in sharp contrast to the lack of comparable remains from other excavated areas of Jerusalem. This suggests that the City of David was the city's main center of occupation during this period.

## Hellenistic Period

Historically, this period has two major subdivisions: the early Hellenistic period, which began with the conquest of Alexander the Great in 332 B.C.E. and ended with the Maccabean revolt in the year 167 B.C.E.; and the late Hellenistic, or Hasmonean period, which followed this revolt and ended with Jerusalem falling to the Roman army led by Pompey in

City of David, Area G: close-up of one of the layers of the Hellenistic glacis; additional layers can be seen in the section behind

63 B.C.E. Archaeological remains of the early Hellenistic period revealed in Shiloh's excavations include part of a structure, uncovered just below the hillcrest in Area E1, that had been destroyed by fire. Additional evidence of the period comes from a large corpus of imported Greek amphora handles bearing seal impressions ranging in date from the late 4th to the early 1st centuries B.C.E. but clustering between 260–150 B.C.E. Although most of these stamped handles derive from post-Hellenistic archaeological contexts within the City of David, the large number found there, in contrast to the few recovered from other excavated areas of Jerusalem, suggests that the City of David remained the center of occupation throughout the early Hellenistic period.

Following the establishment of the Hasmonean dynasty in the mid–2nd century B.C.E., Jerusalem experienced a period of expansion during which the populated area spread from its ancient nucleus in the City of David to the Western Hill. Subsequently, the City of David became the Lower City, while the Western Hill became the Upper City. The defensive system described by Josephus as the First Wall (*War* V, 142–145) was erected during this period. Although the northern and western lines of this defensive wall largely followed the course of its Iron Age II predecessor, and in places even incorporated it, its eastern line presumably followed the course established during the Persian period, skirting the crest atop the eastern slope of the City of David. A sloping glacis, the remains of which were uncovered in Area G, may also have been constructed during the 2nd century B.C.E. Although direct contact between the glacis and the First Wall had been severed by earlier excavators, Shiloh projected its continuation to the base of the fortification wall skirting the upper edge of the eastern slope of the City of David. Farther south, in Areas D1, D2, E1, and E3, the eastern slope was found to be covered by a series of stepped terraces, formed of single-faced, dry-built stone walls securing layers of soil fill. These terraces were apparently linked by stone-built stairways.

## Roman Period

The Roman period, too, may be divided historically into two unequal phases: the early Roman period, beginning with Pompey's campaign of 63 B.C.E. and ending with the Roman destruction of Jerusalem in 70 C.E.; and the late Roman period, beginning with the end of the First Jewish Revolt and ending with the start of the Byzantine period during the reign of Constantine the Great at the beginning of the 4th century C.E.

Archaeological evidence for the early Roman period in the City of David, or Lower City, largely parallels that described in relation to the Hasmonean period. The line of the city wall along the crest above the eastern slope remained unchanged. Alternating uniform layers of compacted soil and pebbles were added to the glacis in Area G. Similarly, the soil-filled terraces farther to the south, along the eastern slope, were maintained and supplemented throughout the period. Three small sections of burnt buildings and an alleyway containing the scattered remains of human skeletons, that were uncovered along the eastern slope of the Western Hill in Area H, bore witness to the violent destruction of Jerusalem by the Romans in 70 C.E.

Sometime after the Roman destruction, tons of debris originating on the hillcrest were dumped down the eastern slope of the City of David, destroying and completely covering the soil-filled terraces. In places, these dumps reached more than 10 m. in depth. The deposition of debris along the eastern slope in this period inhibited construction there and determined its modern-day appearance from that time on.

## Byzantine Period

During the Byzantine period, which began during the reign of Constantine and ended with the fall of Jerusalem to the Muslims in 638 C.E., the City of David was presumably included within a fortification wall. However, no such wall constructed during this period has been clearly identified in the area of the City of David. Remains of soil-filled terraces, as well as the facade of a structure carved out

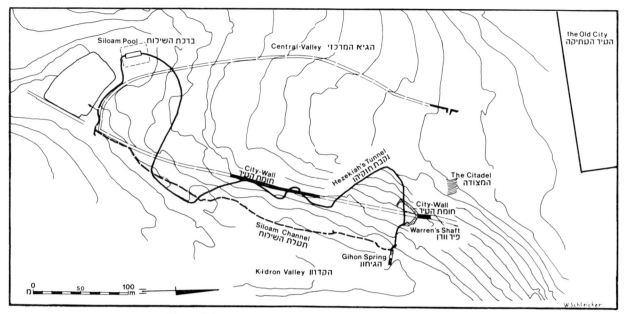

Plan of the Iron Age water systems of the City of David

of the bedrock and fronted by a large court-yard, were found in Area K excavated at the southern end of the hillcrest. In addition, remains of buildings possibly related to the church built above the Pool of Siloam during the 5th century C.E. were unearthed in Area H.

## Early Arab and Medieval Periods
Few remains belonging to these periods were revealed during Shiloh's excavations. Building activity relating to the Early Arab period came to light primarily in Area A1, where walls and a stone pavement were found in association with the water installations located at the foot of the City of David's southeastern slope. Other remains include a tower and a group of plastered installations found on the hillcrest in Area G.

## Subterranean Water Supply Systems in the City of David[2]
GIHON SPRING. Ancient Jerusalem's only perennial source of water is in a cave located in the Kidron Valley, beyond the bounds of the fortified city. The Gihon does not maintain a

[2] This section on Jerusalem's water supply systems is a short supplement to the articles published by R. Amiran and Y. Shiloh on the subject. It is based on evidence gathered from the geological survey conducted by D. Gill as part of the City of David Archaeological Project directed by Y. Shiloh.

constant flow, but is a syphon-type karst spring, fed by groundwater that gushes intermittently through cracks in the cave floor. The frequency of the outflow varies with the season of the year and the annual precipitation. Water from the Gihon could be drawn from either the spring cave or a small pool cut in the bedrock close to it. Three subterranean water supply systems were devised to capture, store, distribute, and protect its waters. These three systems are known as Warren's Shaft, the Siloam channel, and Hezekiah's Tunnel. Although their absolute dates are difficult to determine, their relative chronology is fairly well established.

WARREN'S SHAFT. Warren's Shaft is Jerusalem's earliest strategic water supply system. Named after its discoverer Ch. Warren, this system was initially cleared by M. Parker between 1909 and 1911. Under Shiloh's direction, it was again cleared, surveyed geologically, and opened to the public as part of an archaeological garden (see in this volume, pp. 46–54). The underground system enabled the residents of Jerusalem to draw water from the Gihon without having to leave the fortified confines of the city. It comprises an entrance area, a cavernous tunnel, a vertical shaft, and a feeder tunnel linking the Gihon to the bottom of the shaft. Natural encrustations found

43

City of David: the interior of the Siloam Channel

cal logic and analogy to other subterranean water systems. On this basis, Shiloh compared Warren's Shaft to the underground water systems found at Meggido and Hazor, which have been dated stratigraphically to the 9th century B.C.E. The discovery that Warren's Shaft incorporates a number of natural geological features, all of which existed long before David's conquest of Jerusalem, suggests that the question of its relationship to the biblical *zinnor* should be reassessed. Moreover, as similar subterranean water systems were operative in Mycenaean Greece as early as the 13th century B.C.E., the possibility that the technology for constructing such systems was introduced into the Land of Israel during the Late Bronze or Early Iron Ages cannot be summarily rejected.

SILOAM CHANNEL. The Siloam channel is thought to be either contemporary with or slightly later in date than Warren's Shaft. Three sections of this water system located in the lower parts of Areas A1, B, and J, totalling some 120 m. in length (out of an overall length of ca. 400 m.), were investigated under Shiloh's direction. Unlike the other two water systems connected to the Gihon Spring, which were entirely subterranean, the Siloam channel was a composite system, consisting partly of a narrow, rock-hewn tunnel, and partly of a rock-hewn and stone-capped channel. Several window-like apertures pierced its eastern side and an additional number of openings penetrated its roof. This channel appears to have served three functions: it conveyed water from the Gihon along the eastern slope of the City of David to a reservoir situated at the southern end of the Tyropoeon Valley; it released water through the window-like openings in its eastern wall into agricultural plots located in the Kidron Valley; and it collected runoff from the slope above through the openings in its roof. As it lay outside the city's fortification wall, it was not a strategic system. Indeed, the construction of Hezekiah's Tunnel prior to the Assyrian siege of 701 B.C.E., superseded and partially canceled the function of the Siloam channel, both by blocking it

in the geological survey to be adhering to the walls of both the vertical shaft and the cavernous tunnel have led to the conclusion that the system was engineered by integrating natural and man-made features.

Although Warren's Shaft is chronologically the earliest of Jerusalem's three strategic subterranean water supply systems, its absolute date is still debated. Following its discovery, it was commonly identified with the *zinnor* mentioned in the Hebrew text of 2 Samuel 5:6–10 in connection with David's successful conquest of Jerusalem. This identification, which predicates a pre-Davidic date for the water system, was subsequently rejected on various grounds by most scholars. As no stratigraphic or other archaeological evidence useful for dating its construction has been found, any date proffered for it must rely on both histori-

and by changing the direction in which water flowed through its southern end. The Siloam channel must therefore predate Hezekiah's Tunnel, and may be identified with "the waters of Shiloah (Siloam) that flow gently" (Isaiah 8:6).

**HEZEKIAH'S TUNNEL.** Hezekiah's Tunnel was Jerusalem's third and chronologically latest subterranean means of water supply. It conveyed water from the Gihon Spring to a reservoir located in the southern reaches of the Tyropoeon Valley known as the Pool of Siloam. Its ascription to the time of Hezekiah is based primarily on the biblical description of Hezekiah's efforts to prepare Jerusalem for the Assyrian siege by bringing the waters of the Gihon into the fortified area of the city (2 Kings 20:20; Isaiah 22:11; 2 Chronicles 32:2–4, 30).

During the Hellenistic and Roman periods, the Gihon Spring was replaced as Jerusalem's primary source of water by aqueducts built to bring water to the city from springs located in the Judean Hills. Hezekiah's Tunnel and the Pool of Siloam, however, continued to function throughout these periods. Shiloh believed that Warren's Shaft may also have remained accessible through a vault constructed over its upper entrance.

## Bibliography

Amiran, R., "The Water Supply of Israelite Jerusalem," in: Yadin, Y. (ed.), *Jerusalem Revealed: Archaeology in the Holy City, 1968–1974,* (Jerusalem, 1976), pp. 75–78.

Ariel, D.T., *Excavations at the City of David 1978–1985 Directed by Yigal Shiloh* II. Qedem 30 (Jerusalem, 1990).

Cahill, J., Rheinhard, K., Tarler, D. and Warnock, P., "It had to Happen—Archaeologists Examine Remains of Ancient Bathroom," *BAR* 17/3 (1991): 64–69.

Chapman, R., "A Stone Toilet Seat Found in Jerusalem in 1925," *PEQ* 124 (1992): 4–8.

De Groot, A. and Ariel, D.T. (eds.), *Excavations at the City of David 1978–1985 Directed by Yigal Shiloh* III. Qedem 33 (Jerusalem, 1992).

Geva, H., "The Western Boundary of Jerusalem at the End of the Monarchy," *IEJ* 29 (1979): 84–91.

Gill, D., "Subterranean Waterworks of Biblical Jerusalem: Adaptation of a Karst System," *Science* 254 (1991): 1467–1471.

Gill, D. and Shiloh, Y., "Subterranean Water Supply Systems of the City of David: Utilization of a Natural Karstic System," *Annual Meeting 1982: Eilat and Eastern Sinai* Israel Geological Society (Eilat, 1982), pp. 32–34.

Hamblin, D. J., "Bearing Witness to the City of David's Life and Death," *Smithsonian* 13/4 (1982): 72–80.

Kenyon, K. M., *Jerusalem: Excavating 3000 Years of History* (London, 1967).

———, *Digging Up Jerusalem* (London, 1974).

Macalister, R.A.S. and Duncan, J.G., *Excavations on the Hill of Ophel, Jerusalem 1923–1925.* PEFA 4 (London, 1926).

Shiloh, Y., "Tables of Major Archaeological Activities in Jerusalem since 1863," in: Yadin, Y. (ed.), *Jerusalem Revealed: Archaeology in the Holy City 1968–1974* (Jerusalem, 1976).

———, "Jerusalem's Water Supply During Siege—The Rediscovery of Warren's Shaft," *BAR* 7/4 (1981): 24–39.

———, *Excavations in the City of David I, 1978–1982: Interim Report of the First Five Seasons.* Qedem 19 (Jerusalem,1984).

Shiloh, Y. and Tarler, D., "Bullae from the City of David: A Hoard of Seal Impressions from the Israelite Period," *BA* 49/4 (1986): 196–209.

# The Rediscovery of the Ancient Water System Known as "Warren's Shaft"

## Yigal Shiloh

A key problem in the planning of large cities in Judah and Israel during the Iron Age was how to ensure a regular supply of water in peacetime and in time of war. The security of a city was gauged by the strength of its fortifications, but its ability to withstand a siege, particularly in the hot, dry climate of the Land of Israel, depended on other factors of which one of the most important was a regular supply of water.

Archaeologists have uncovered several underground water systems in ancient Israelite cities—at Megiddo, Hazor, Gezer and Gibeon. These systems tell us something about the engineering techniques employed in assuring a water supply in those times. When planning the archaeological excavations in the City of David it was agreed that the ancient city's waterworks would be one of the prime targets for investigation.

The City of David had one major source of water—the Gihon Spring. It was next to this source, on the southeastern hill of Jerusalem, that the earliest settlements in this area were established during the Chalcolithic period and Early Bronze Age I. By the Iron Age there were three water systems connected with the Gihon Spring: the water system known as Warren's Shaft, the Siloam channel, and Hezekiah's Tunnel. These systems fulfilled different functions and therefore operated in different ways. The expedition directed by the present writer studied the components of each of these systems. In addition to excavating the area around the Siloam Pool (Area A) and reexposing the Siloam channel for a stretch of some 120 m. (Areas J, B and part of Area A), we conducted an investigation of Warren's Shaft at the northern end of the eastern slope (Area J)—the main topic of this article.

This system, which connects with Hezekiah's Tunnel, is named after the Englishman Ch. Warren who discovered it in 1867 while exploring Hezekiah's Tunnel. Warren worked under extremely difficult conditions which demanded considerable courage and physical strength. His thrilling account of the discovery of the shaft, the attempts to scale it, and the description of the upper tunnel were constantly in our minds during our reexamination of the system. A further stage in the investigation of the shaft was undertaken by the M. Parker expedition, active at the City of David from 1909 to 1911. Thanks to the account by L.-H. Vincent, we have some reliable information concerning the expedition's activities and discoveries. As it turns out, Parker and his team made more accurate and detailed measurements and drew better plans than Warren's. K. Kenyon's excavations in the City of David (1961–1967) solved one problem that had previously puzzled scholars: the connection of the City of David's fortifications with the water system. Kenyon uncovered a system of city walls from the Bronze and Iron Ages at the foot of the slope, and was able to verify that the entrance to the water system was inside the city, within the line of fortifications.

## The Excavations

When we began to investigate Warren's Shaft, we had several questions in mind. How did it operate? What were its main components? When was it made? Was it really a Jebusite (Canaanite) invention, and does it, therefore, antedate the Israelite city? What was the con-

46

nection between Warren's Shaft, the Siloam channel, Hezekiah's Tunnel, and the Gihon Spring? How long was it in use? How did it relate to the fortifications higher up on the eastern slope? Did it relate to the historical events described in the Bible, such as the conquest of Jerusalem by David and his men? Some of these questions had already been dealt with in the past, and we were able to provide some new answers to others. But in the course of our work new problems emerged that still await solution.

Warren's Shaft consists of several parts. Those known today, beginning from the top of the mound and following the system down to the Gihon Spring are: the upper access tunnel (1); the vaulted chamber (2); the stepped tunnel (3); the horizontal tunnel (4); the vertical shaft (5); the tunnel linking the base of the shaft to the spring (6); the Gihon Spring (7); the side cave (8); and the so-called "trial" shaft (9). Clearly, there are several missing links between the vaulted chamber and the city's fortifications and residential areas. One of these, the upper access tunnel (1), which was exceptionally important for our understanding of the system, was uncovered by our expedition.

When we began our research in 1978, we discovered that the area at the top opening of the water system was completely buried under tremendous piles of debris from Kenyon's Trench A just to the north. We were therefore forced to give up any idea of a systematic excavation starting at the surface, and reverted instead to Warren's underground methods. During the 1978 season we reached the base of the vertical shaft (5) and tried to climb it to the horizontal tunnel (4). The width of the oval-sectioned vertical shaft is about 2 m. and its height some 15 m. Despite repeated attempts, we were unable to scale the shaft; it was obvious that we would have to enlist the help of skilled climbers. Our experience convinced us that the ancient city could not have been penetrated through the shaft by climbing. (Warren had scaled it by means of wooden scaffolding.)

In the summer of 1979, after completing all

Aerial photograph of the eastern slope of the City of David, looking south: 1. entrance to Gihon Spring; 2. upper entrance to tunnel leading to vaulted chamber at top of Warren's Shaft; 3. Kenyon's Trench I—location of city walls during the Bronze and Iron Ages; 4. Area E—retaining walls and structures of the Israelite town above the city's line of fortifications; 5. line of fortifications of the Canaanite and Israelite cities (Bronze and Iron Ages)

necessary technical arrangements, we again planned to climb this shaft from the tunnel linking its base to the Gihon Spring (6), accompanied this time by three alpinists, Z. Bernstein, I. Kantarovich and K. Evans. For two hours they slowly inched their way up the vertical shaft, using special equipment. When the first climber reached the top and threw down ropes so that we, the archaeologists, could follow, it really looked like a relatively simple climb. We soon learned that it was not quite as easy as it looked.

The view from the top was breathtaking: the horizontal tunnel (4), partly cleared by

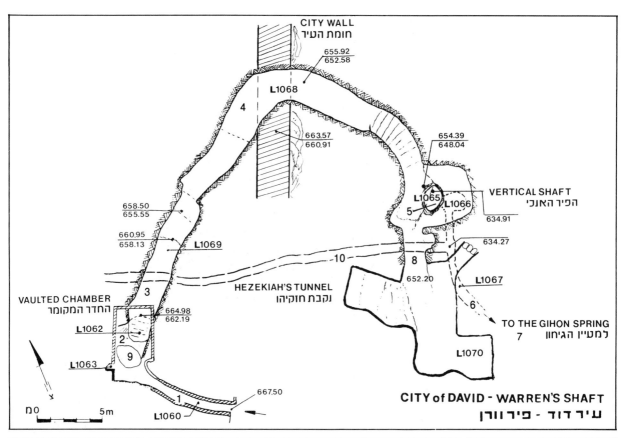

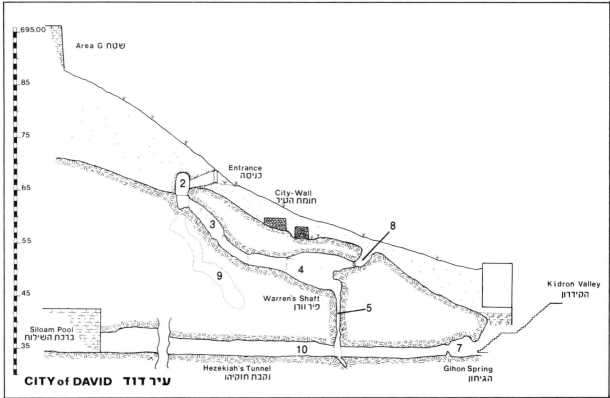

City of David: plan and section of tunnels in Warren's Shaft: 1. access tunnel; 2. vaulted chamber; 3. stepped tunnel; 4. horizontal tunnel; 5. vertical shaft; 6. tunnel linking up to spring; 7. Gihon Spring; 8. side cave; 9. trial shaft; 10. Hezekiah's Tunnel

City of David: view from bottom of vertical shaft to top while being scaled by mountaineers

City of David: top of vertical shaft; excavator is climbing rope-ladder from the Gihon Spring to beginning of horizontal tunnel

Parker, is most impressive. It extends for approximately 29 m., and is 2.5–3 m. wide and 1.5–5.5 m. high. We advanced along the tunnel, following its twists and turns, first northward and then toward the southwest, finally reaching the point where it meets the stepped tunnel (3). Here we encountered debris and discovered that the stepped tunnel was completely blocked along its entire length, obstructing our advance upward. Returning to the shaft to descend and find our way out to the Gihon Spring, we were troubled by the idea that our plans to open and

explore Warren's Shaft might be thwarted because of the huge accumulation of debris which blocked the stepped tunnel and under which the top of the water system lay buried. It was evident that we would have to solve some formidable engineering problems and find a way to penetrate the upper part of the system, since it would be impossible to remove debris through the Gihon Spring. We therefore attempted to reach the top of the system by way of a tunnel with a gable roof constructed of stone slabs (1), the opening of which had been discovered a few years earlier.

City of David: the blocked meeting point in Warren's Shaft of the stepped tunnel and the horizontal tunnel

City of David: vaulted chamber during clearing

After crawling approximately 3 m. on hands and knees in this tunnel, we found that it, too, was impassable.

During the 1980 season, two South African mining engineers, J. Quail and H. Espach, experts at clearing debris from abandoned mines, arrived in Jerusalem. Archaeologist D. Glick, who directed the excavations in this area, and a few enthusiastic volunteers would disappear into the mouth of the upper access tunnel (1) each morning. Only the baskets of earth moving outside betrayed the fact that people were at work somewhere in the bowels of the earth. The first section was easily cleared. The tunnel proved to be ancient and led straight to the vaulted chamber (2). The last section, between the upper access tunnel and the vaulted chamber, was excavated with the mining engineers' guidance, using props and beams to shore it up. Here and there we found traces of Parker's excavations. Upon reaching the chamber, we had to dig down 6 m. from the top of the vault. After three weeks, the vaulted chamber had been cleared down to bedrock and we could distinguish two clearly defined stages in its construction. In the first stage, the stepped tunnel (3) ended in a rock-cut chamber, from which it was probably possible to continue the ascent toward the southwest. In the second stage, the vaulted chamber (2) and the upper access tunnel (1) were built—and the tunnel, perhaps slightly later than the vaulted chamber.

At the bottom of the vaulted chamber, in the northern wall, we found the upper entrance to the stepped tunnel. At this point, we began to dig from both sides. One team scaled the shaft with a rope-ladder and cleared the debris from the lower end of the stepped tunnel into the horizontal tunnel; the second team made its way in from the vaulted chamber, working at the upper end of the stepped tunnel. As the teams approached one another, they could hear each other's voices, recalling the similar experience of Hezekiah's workers as recorded in the Siloam inscription: "There was heard a man's voice calling to his fellow." Contact was made during the last week of the season, and a passage was thus opened from the vaulted chamber to the other parts of the system. The team members felt highly gratified as they slid down the debris. Finally, access to the water system from above, as in ancient times, had been achieved.

In subsequent years the remaining debris was cleared and restoration and conservation of the entire water supply system were completed. Today, all parts of the system are accessible to the public. The continuation of the system toward the top of the slope and the manner in which it fit within the Iron Age fortifications still remain a puzzle. Both Warren and Parker recorded a side entrance leading to the lower end of the horizontal tunnel, but since the entire area is now built up, it is impossible to examine this part of the system.

## How the Water System Functioned

We now understand the functioning of this water supply system. The main entrance to it was clearly on the eastern slope, inside the walls. The stepped tunnel recalls similar structures in other Israelite water systems, such as

City of David: the upper access tunnel with gabled ceiling after being cleared

those at Hazor, Gezer, Gibeon and Ibleam. Since the system was entered from the slope rather than the top of the hill, it was unnecessary to cut a large entrance shaft, as had been done at Hazor, Megiddo or Gibeon ("the pool"), and perhaps also at Beersheba and Lachish. The horizontal tunnel leads to a point from which water can be drawn, as in the horizontal tunnel at Megiddo or the stepped tunnels at Gezer, Hazor and Gibeon.

The ingenious feature of this system, unparalleled in any other known water system, is the function of the vertical shaft. A disadvantage of Iron Age water systems was that the connection between the interior of the city and the spring outside constituted a weak point in a city's defenses: The enemy could penetrate a city through its water-supply tunnel. One solution to this problem may be seen in the water-supply systems of Hazor and Gezer and the "pool" at Gibeon, where the tunnels led to an aquifer (water-bearing stratum) within the mound of the city, obviating the need to go outside the walls for water. This was an ideal solution, but not feasible in Jerusalem because of the nature of the Gihon Spring. For this reason, planners utilized a unique technical obstacle: a vertical shaft, which virtually cut off access to the city through its water supply.

One as yet unclear point is the link between the base of the shaft and the Gihon Spring, particularly as the spring also feeds Hezekiah's Tunnel and the Siloam channel. These systems have been examined by D. Gill of the Israel Geological Survey. The results of his investigations may give us a better answer to the question of why the shaft was located in this particular position, and if it made use of a natural fissure in the rock as suggested by our research. We must also determine the significance of the "trial" shaft (9), the top of which has been exposed at the base of the vaulted chamber, and ascertain the relationship between this system and the other water systems in the City of David. There is, however, no doubt that water flowed into Warren's Shaft through the lower feeder tunnel, and that the residents of the city, standing at the top of the shaft, drew it up in buckets.

In the course of our study we discovered various new details about the water system. The builders of the vaulted chamber and entrance tunnel presumably wished to protect the entrance to the subterranean system from loose debris on the eastern slope. Architectural considerations assign the vaulted chamber and the gable-roofed entrance tunnel to the Second Temple period, perhaps the reign of Herod. If this is correct, Warren's Shaft must still have been in use during the Second Temple period. This conclusion, in turn, reinforces our conjecture that the

City of David: horizontal tunnel; view from upper section to top of vertical shaft

system must have connected in some fashion with the top of the eastern slope, where the southern part of the Hasmonean First Wall was located.

These conclusions raise certain questions about the dating of the other Jerusalem water systems and their interrelation. Here are some of the issues that merit reconsideration in light of our new findings: It was previously believed that Warren's Shaft was the earliest of the three water systems. Some scholars assigned it to Jerusalem's Jebusite-Canaanite period, while the Siloam channel was generally thought to date from the 10th–9th centuries B.C.E. Hezekiah's Tunnel, for which we have accurate chronological data based both on the biblical account and on archaeological and epigraphic finds, is universally believed to have been hewn toward the end of the 8th century B.C.E. The common view is that Warren's Shaft, and perhaps the Siloam channel, fell into disuse when Hezekiah's Tunnel was cut. However, there is really no reason to assume that the creation of the tunnel made the other systems superfluous; after all, each of them had its own function, contributing in a specific way to an efficient supply of water for Jerusalem.

Warren's Shaft was the system regularly used by the people of Jerusalem, allowing them easy access to the city's main water source in times of peace and war alike; similar systems may be found in other important cities. The Siloam channel directed water along the base of the eastern slope of the City of David, part of the way as a rock-cut tunnel, and part of the way as an exposed channel outside the wall, watering nearby agricultural plots in the Kidron Valley through special outlets in its eastern side. Other openings, at the top of the channel, were designed to collect runoff from the eastern slope outside the city walls, divert it into the channel and then into reservoirs in the Tyropoeon Valley, at the southern end of the City of David. Hezekiah's Tunnel was the most sophisticated element in the Iron Age waterworks of Jerusalem. The waters of the Gihon, a typical karst spring, gush intermittently for roughly forty

City of David: Warren's Shaft after clearing

minutes every six to eight hours. This may, in fact, be the origin of its name, which derives from a Hebrew verb meaning "to erupt," or "burst forth." This made it impossible to draw water from the Gihon as one would from a conventional spring such as the one at Megiddo or from an aquifer such as the one at Hazor. Hezekiah's Tunnel was designed to solve this problem: it received the water gushing from the spring and diverted it to the only place—in view of the location and nature of the city fortifications in Hezekiah's time—where large reservoirs could be built. Collection of the water in these pools made it possible to regulate the water supply independently of the intermittent flow of the spring.

Conceivably, in Hezekiah's time all three water systems of the City of David were in operation simultaneously, each fulfilling a specific function. If the wall separating the branch of the tunnel leading from Hezekiah's Tunnel to the bottom of Warren's Shaft were removed, water would continue to flow in

Hezekiah's Tunnel but some of it would collect at the bottom of the vertical shaft. The residents of the City of David could stand on a platform—perhaps of wooden planks—at the top of the shaft and draw water by means of a bucket at the end of a rope, as from a well. At the same time, the water in Hezekiah's Tunnel would continue to flow into the reservoirs at its southern end. The Siloam channel would continue to operate independently. Nevertheless, it is clear from our findings in the southern part of the City of David that certain changes were made in the Siloam channel over the years, perhaps related to the operation of Hezekiah's Tunnel and the Siloam Pool.

## The Date of the Water System

Vincent devoted much attention to the biblical account as related in the Hebrew text of 2 Samuel 5:6–10 and 1 Chronicles 11:4–9, of how David and the commander of his forces, Joab, penetrated Jerusalem through the *zinnor*. Vincent suggested that *zinnor* meant "water course" and that it was Warren's Shaft. Other scholars, such as W.F. Albright, B. Mazar, Y. Aharoni and Y. Yadin rejected this interpretation out of hand, each for his own reasons—whether on the basis of his reading of the biblical text or of archaeological and architectural data.

To accept Vincent's interpretation, we would have to regard Warren's Shaft as a Jebusite, i.e., Canaanite, structure. Subterranean water systems were a major factor in the planning of fortified towns in Judah and Israel during the Iron Age. None of the water systems that can be confidently dated by precise stratigraphic considerations—such as those at Gibeon, Megiddo, Hazor and Tell es-Saʿidiya, and perhaps also Lachish and Beer-sheba—are earlier than the 10th century B.C.E. It is a reasonable assumption that the water supply of the royal capital, which was based on a karst spring, took advantage, at least from the time of Hezekiah, of three water systems operating in parallel. For the moment, we have no data permitting a more accurate dating of Warren's Shaft. There is good ground for the suggestion that it was part of the original planning of the Israelite city of the 10th or 9th centuries B.C.E.* The Siloam channel was probably in use simultaneously, and Hezekiah's Tunnel was added toward the end of the 8th century B.C.E.

With the destruction of Jerusalem at the end of the Iron Age, part of the water system was destroyed too. Possibly the Siloam channel was then blocked up and fell into disuse, but the Gihon Spring, Hezekiah's Tunnel and the Siloam Pool have continued in use up to the present day. It is also possible that Warren's Shaft was still used in the Second Temple period. With the growth of Jerusalem under the Hasmoneans and Herod, however, town planners needed larger and more reliable sources of water, originating at a higher altitude. These they found to the south of Jerusalem.

* Regarding an earlier dating of Warren's Shaft, see in this volume, pp. 43–44 (ed. note).

# A Group of Hebrew Bullae from Yigal Shiloh's Excavations in the City of David

## Yair Shoham

The excavations in the City of David under the direction of the late Y. Shiloh were conducted in the years 1978–1985 (see in this volume, pp. 31–45). In the course of these excavations remains dating back to the beginnings of settlement in Jerusalem were uncovered. Among these are also some epigraphic discoveries of the Iron Age II period, the most important of which is a group of Hebrew bullae.[1]

### The Discovery

The bullae were discovered in 1982, during the fifth season of excavations at the City of David. They were found in Area G at the top of the northeastern slope of the City of David ridge, in a complex of structures related to Stratum 10 of the second half of the 7th–beginning 6th century B.C.E. The complex of buildings apparently dates to the reign of King Josiah and was destroyed together with the city and the Temple in 587/6 B.C.E. The bullae were found in one of the buildings which was later given the name House of Bullae. The buildings extend over two terraces, one about 5 m. higher than the other, with a massive supporting wall (W. 753) between them. On the upper terrace, west of this wall, the remains of several dwelling houses were uncovered, among them the

House of Aḥiel and the Burnt Room. In all these buildings finds of the late First Temple period came to light.

The House of Bullae (Locus 967) is built on the lower of the two terraces. The supporting wall that separates the terraces serves also as the western wall of the House of Bullae. Because of the narrow dimensions of the excavation area here, the other walls of this house were not found and only a narrow strip, about 7 × 1 m., was uncovered. Two levels of floors

City of David: the House of Bullae during excavation

[1] The bullae from the City of David were first published by Y. Shiloh. More recently the bullae were again examined by J. Naveh and the present writer in preparation for final publication. The drawings of the bullae are by A. Yardeni who also assisted in reading them. Area G, where the bullae were discovered, was excavated under the supervision of D. Tarler and J. Cahill. Their publication of the stratigraphy and the finds in this area is in preparation.

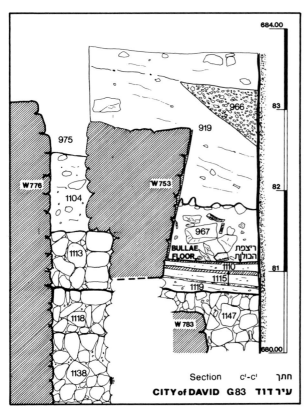

City of David, Area G: section in the House of Bullae

City of David, House of Bullae (on left) on the Lower Terrace of Area G; looking south

made of beaten earth were revealed. The earlier level (Locus 1110) most probably belongs to the second half of the 7th century B.C.E. The floor of the house had been res-

City of David: assemblage of finds from the House of Bullae

tored and covered with a new layer of plaster (Locus 967) still before the destruction of the city in 587/6 B.C.E. This floor was covered with remains of the destruction about 70 cm. thick—containing the bullae and various pottery vessels, arrowheads and other metal objects. Among the twenty-five vessels found there are wheel-burnished bowls, kraters, storage jars and decanters. The assemblage of finds is typical of the late Iron Age in Judah. The bullae were therefore found in a context clearly dated to the end of the 7th-early 6th century B.C.E.

In the House of Bullae were also four square, worked, limestone stands, about 20 cm. high, with a shallow, round depression at the top of each. Their form seems to indicate that they served as cult stands. Next to the stands were found two kraters with high bases and a drainage hole at the bottom of the body. The entire body of the kraters above the base is finished with a fine wheel-burnish. Such vessels are rare in the City of David, and in

Jerusalem generally. That these unusual pottery items were found together with the bullae attests to the special character of the House of Bullae, which apparently served some public function and was used to store written documents.

Most of the bullae were found concentrated in the northwestern corner of the House of Bullae within an area of less that one square meter. On completion of the work there, 53 bullae and fragments of bullae had been discovered. Already at the outset of the examination two of the fragments proved to be very small and much damaged, with not even one letter being legible. These fragments were later used for Neutron Activation Analysis in the laboratory of the Hebrew University Institute of Archaeology in Jerusalem. Several other fragments could be restored to make up two entire bullae (Nos. 24 and 38). The total number of bullae therefore comes to 49: four of them uninscribed seal impressions, and 45 inscribed bullae.

## The Bullae

The word "bulla" derives from Latin and denotes the seal of an important personage. Documents in the ancient Near East were either written on parchment or papyrus, and were rolled, tied with string, and sealed with bullae to assure that only those authorized would read them. Such seals were made by forming a lump of soft clay into a small, fingernail-sized flat disk; the clay was affixed to the string binding the document and would then be stamped with the appropriate seal. In time the clay would dry and harden. In order to open the document, the bulla(e) sealing it had to be separated from the string, or broken. The separated bulla was proof that the scroll had been opened. This practice comes to life in Jeremiah 32:9–14:

> And I bought the field at Anathoth from Hanamel my cousin, and weighed out the money to him...I signed the deed, sealed it, got witnesses...Then I took the sealed deed of purchase...and the open copy...and I gave the deed of purchase to Baruch...in the presence of Hanamel...in the presence of the witnesses who signed the deed...and in the presence of all the Jews who were sitting in the court of the guard. I charged Baruch in their presence...Take these deeds, both this sealed deed of purchase and this open deed, and put them in an earthenware vessel, that they may last for a long time.

The bullae from the City of David, average 14 mm. in length, 12 mm. in width and 2–6 mm. in thickness; the actual oval impressions are about 11 mm. long by 9 mm. wide. The largest bulla in the group (No. 12) measures $19 \times 16$ mm., and the smallest (No. 17) $11 \times 10$ mm. The reverse sides of most of the bullae show impressions of the string used to tie the rolled papyrus, as well as traces of the fibers of the papyrus to which the clay lump was affixed.

Most of the seal impressions are readily legible. The conflagration that destroyed the City of David burnt the scrolls but hardened the clay, and so helped preserve the seal impressions on the bullae. Missing or corrupt letters can usually be reconstructed with fair certainty. Only two of the seal impressions (Nos. 22 and 43) are so illegible that not even one name can be made out. In four of the bullae (Nos. 6, 11, 38, 40) only one out of the two names can be read. All the other bullae are fully legible.

The list of the bullae—after addition of the missing letters—is as follows:[2]

1. לבלגי בן דליהו (Belonging) to Bilgai son of Delayahu
2. לגמריהו בן שפן (Belonging) to Gemaryahu son of Shaphan
3. לחנמלך—ישמעאל (Belonging) to Ḥnmlk son of Yishma''el
4. לטבשלם בן זכר (Belonging) to Ṭbšlm son of Zkr
5. לטבשלם בן בנזכר (Belonging) to Ṭbšlm son of Bnzkr

[2] The numbering of the bullae in this article is not always identical with the identifying numbers given the bullae as they were being found, and which were employed in the interim publications by Y. Shiloh.

6. לטבשלם] בן זכר הרפא‎ (Belonging) [to *Ṭbšlm*] son of *Zkr* the Healer

7. לאלשמע בן סמכיהו‎ (Belonging) to ʾElishamaʿ son of Semakhyahu

8. למכיהו בן חצי‎ (Belonging) to Mikhayahu son of *Ḥṣy*

9. לאפרח—אחיהו‎ (Belonging) to ʾEphraḥ (son of) ʾAḥiyahu

10. לאפרח—אחיהו‎ (Belonging) to ʾEphraḥ (son of) ʾAḥiyahu

11. להושעיהו—...יהו‎ (Belonging) to Hosha‛yahu (son of) [...]yahu

12. לידעיהו בן משלם‎ (Belonging) to Yedaʿyahu son of Meshullam

13. לגדיהו בן עזר‎ (Belonging) to Gadiyahu son of ʿEzer

14. לשמעיהו—מחסיהו‎ (Belonging) to Shemaʿyahu (son of) Maḥseyahu

15. לשמעיהו בן יאזניהו‎ (Belonging) to Shemaʿyahu son of Yaʾazanyahu

16. לנתניהו בן רחם‎ (Belonging) to Netanyahu son of *Rḥm*

17. לרפאיהו בן אפרח‎ (Belonging) to Rephaʾyahu son of ʾEphraḥ

18. לאלשמע בן יהואב‎ (Belonging) to ʾElishamaʿ son of Yehoʾab

19. לגמריהו בן מגן‎ (Belonging) to Gemaryahu son of Magen

20. לאלנתן בן בלגי‎ (Belonging) to ʾElnatan son of Bilgai

21. לאלנתן בן בלגי‎ (Belonging) to ʾElnatan son of Bilgai

22. ל ..... .....‎ (Belonging) to [          ]

23. לשמעיהו בן פלטיהו‎ (Belonging) to Shemaʿyahu son of Pelaṭyahu

24. לעמדיהו—אשיהו‎ (Belonging) to ʿImmadiyahu (son of) ʾAshyahu

25. לדליהו בן הושעיהו‎ (Belonging) to Delayahu son of Hoshaʿyahu

26. לעזיהו אלשמע‎ (Belonging) to ʿUziyahu (son) of ʾElishamaʿ

27. לעזריהו בן חלקיהו‎ (Belonging) to ʿAzaryahu son of Ḥilqiyahu

28. לאחימה—חניה‎ (Belonging) to ʾḥymh (son of) Ḥananyah

29. לאליקם בן אוהל‎ (Belonging) to ʾElyaqim son of ʾOhel

30. לאליקם בן אוהל‎ (Belonging) to ʾElyaqim son of ʾOhel

31. לבניהו בן הושעיהו‎ (Belonging) to Benayahu son of Hoshaʿyahu

32. לעזרקם—מכיהו‎ (Belonging) to ʿAzriqam (son of) Mikhayahu

33. לברכיהו בן מלכי‎ (Belonging) to Berekhyahu son of Malki

34. לחנניהו בן אחא‎ (Belonging) to Ḥananyahu son of ʾAḥaʾ

35. לסילא בן אלשמע‎ (Belonging) to Sillaʾ son of ʾElishamaʿ

36. לנריהו—דמליהו‎ (Belonging) to Neriyahu (son of) Demalyahu

37. לאחיאב בן יהואב‎ (Belonging) to ʾAḥiʾab son of Yehoʾab

38. לי.... בן עזריהו‎ (Belonging) to Y[        ] son of ʿAzaryahu

39. לשפטיהו בן צפן‎ (Belonging) to Shephaṭyahu son of *Ṣpn*

40. לברכיהו בן ע...‎ (Belonging) to Berekhyahu son of ʿ[          ]

41. ליאזניהו בן מעשיהו‎ (Belonging) to Yaʾazanyahu son of Maʿaśeyahu

42. לעזריהו בן אחא‎ (Belonging) to ʿAzaryahu son of ʾAḥaʾ

43. ליה... בן ב...‎ (Belonging) to Yh[        ] son of B[        ]

44. לשפטיהו בן דמליהו‎ (Belonging) to Shephaṭyahu son of Demalyahu

45. לנחם בן שאלה‎ (Belonging) to Naḥum son of *Šʾlh*

Fifty-three different personal names appear on the bullae:

| | |
|---|---|
| ʾAḥaʾ—34, 42 | ʾElnatan—20, 21 |
| ʾAḥiʾab—37 | ʾElyaqim—29, 30 |
| ʾAḥiyahu—9, 10 | ʾEphraḥ—9, 10, 17 |
| ʾAshyahu—24 | |
| ʿAzaryahu—27, 38, 42 | ʿEzer—13 |
| ʿAzriqam—32 | Gadiyahu—13 |
| Bilgai—1, 20, 21 | Gemaryahu—2, 19 |
| *Bnzkr*—5, 4?, 6? | Ḥananyah[u]—28, 34 |
| Benayahu—31 | Ḥilqiyahu—27 |
| Berekhyahu—33, 40 | *Ḥnmlk*—3 |
| Delayahu—1, 25 | |
| Demalyahu—36, 44 | Hoshaʿyahu—11, 25, 31 |
| ʾElishamaʿ—7, 18, 26, 35 | *Ḥṣy*—8 |

58

'hymh—28
'Immadiyahu—24
Magen—19
Ma'aseyahu—41
Mahseyahu—14
Malki—33
Meshullam—12

Mikhayahu—8, 32
Nahum—45
Neriyahu—36
Netanyahu—16
'Ohel—29, 30

Pelatyahu—23
Repha'yahu—17
*Rhm*—16

Semakhyahu—7

Shaphan—2
She'ila—45
Shema'yahu—14,
  15, 23
Shephatyahu—39,
  44
Silla'—35
*Spn*—39

*Tbšlm*—4, 5, [6?]
'Uziyahu—26
Ya'azanyahu—15,
  41

Yeda'yahu—12
Yeho'ab—37
Yishma''el—3
*Zkr*—4, 6

Inscribed bullae from the City of David

Most of the names appearing on the bullae from the City of David are known from the Bible. Those that are not are nevertheless not foreign to Hebrew onomastics, being known from inscriptions and other seal impressions. One man—'Elnatan son of Bilgai—had apparently two different seals (Bullae 20, 21). *Tbšlm* son of *Zkr* may have owned three seals— if indeed the assumption is correct that Bullae 4, 5 and 6 relate to the same person. In Bulla 6, the profession of the owner of the seal is mentioned—"the healer." Altogether, there are twenty-six theophoric names ending in "yahu."

Two of the personages mentioned in the bullae have names familiar from the Bible. One of these is Gemaryahu son of Shaphan of Bulla 2 (Pl. IIc), a high official and scribe at the court of King Jehoiakim of Judah eighteen years before the destruction of Jerusalem in 587/6 B.C.E., and a contemporary of the prophet Jeremiah: "In the fifth year of Jehoiakim the son of Josiah, king of Judah...all the people in Jerusalem and all the people who came from the cities of Judah to Jerusalem proclaimed a fast before the Lord. Then, in the hearing of all the people, Baruch read the words of Jeremiah...in the house of the Lord, in the chamber of Gemariah the son of Shaphan the secretary, which was in the upper court, at the entry of the New Gate of the Lord's house..." etc. (Jeremiah 36:9–12; and see also 25–26). The script in Bulla 2 is easily legible. The seal, of a quality befitting a man who holds high office, was clearly the work of a skilled artisan. The second biblical personage is mentioned in Bulla 27—'Azaryahu son of Ḥilqiyahu—perhaps a member of the family of high priests who officiated in Jerusa-

Bullae from the City of David; Bullae 21 with reverse side; note the uninscribed bulla (below) with depiction of a bird and reverse side

lem at the end of the First Temple period. Both names appear as father and son in two priestly genealogical lists in 1 Chronicles 5:29–41 and 9:10–11 (see in this volume, pp. 62–63).

The script in the bullae is not of an even quality. In some of the bullae it is indeed fine and clear (e.g., Bullae 2, 7, 17, 20, 21); in others the script is slovenly, while most are somewhere between these extremes of proficiency. There does not seem to be any chronological connotation to the quality of the script and the forms of the letters. Apparently all the bullae were produced within a short time at the end of the First Temple period (second half of the 7th century to the beginning of the 6th century B.C.E.).

The names appearing in the bullae are usually rendered according to the common forms in Hebrew inscriptions of the late First Temple period, i.e., 'defective' grammatical orthography (without vowels—matres lectiones—in the middle of the word), and 'plene' orthography (with added vowels) at the end. Defective orthography in the middle of the names appears in many names: 'Elishama', 'Eliyaqim, Meshullam, Naḥum, 'Uziyahu, 'Azriqam, etc. Only a few names are written in Hebrew plene orthography, such as 'Ohel. At the end of the names the form is always plene.

Decorative motifs are not common in bullae from the City of David. The few that do appear seem to serve one of two purposes: to separate the lines of script, or to fill empty space (Bullae 6, 12, 20, 36, 39, etc.). The decorative motifs are exclusively geometrical or floral; not one of the inscribed bullae has human or animal figures. This is characteristic of Judean seals of the late First Temple period. Nevertheless, together with the bullae described here, another four uninscribed bullae feature animal figures.

## Summary

The significance of this group of Hebrew bullae uncovered in the City of David lies in their being the first assemblage of easily legible Hebrew seal impressions to be found in a controlled excavation, in a clear stratigraphic context and accompanied by architectural, ceramic and historical evidence. The paucity of documented finds of this type from the Iron Age underlines the importance of this discovery of the last days of the Judean monarchy. As Shiloh has pointed out, the full name list from this group of bullae gives ground for the assumption that it was not a family archive, since in that case more of the names would be repeated. The multiplicity of unrelated names probably attests to the public nature of the archive. The mention of the scribe Gemariahu son of Shaphan and of the priest Azariahu son of Hilkiahu strengthens this supposition.

## Bibliography

Avigad, N., *Bullae and Seals from Post-Exilic Judean Archive*. Qedem 4 (Jerusalem, 1976).
———— , *Hebrew Bullae from the Time of Jeremiah* (Jerusalem, 1986).
Hestrin, R. and Dayagi-Mendels, M. *Inscribed Seals, First Temple Period. Hebrew, Ammonite, Moabite, Phoenician and Aramaic from the Collections of the Israel Museum and the Israel Department of Antiquities and Museums* (Jerusalem, 1979).
Naveh, J. *Early History of the Alphabet* (Jerusalem, 1982).
———— , "Nameless People," *IEJ* 40 (1990): 108–123.
Schneider, T., "Azariahu Son of Hilkiahu (High Priest?) on a City of David Bulla," *IEJ* 38 (1988): 139–141.
Shiloh, Y., *Excavations at the City of David 1978–1982*. Qedem 19 (Jerusalem, 1984).
———— , "A Group of Hebrew Bullae from the City of David," *IEJ* 36 (1986): 16–38.
———— , "A Hoard of Israelite Seal-Impressions on Bullae from the City of David," *Qadmoniot* 73–74 (1986): 2–11 (Hebrew).
Shiloh, Y. and Tarler, D., "Bullae from the City of David. A Hoard of Seal Impressions from the Israelite Period," *BA* 49/4 (1986): 196–209.

# A Biblical Name on a City of David Bulla: Azariah son of Hilkiah (High Priest?)

## Tsvi Schneider

Matching names from ancient epigraphic material with biblical counterparts is always risky. Only five of the hundreds of names discovered on bullae, seals, and ostraca have with fair certainty been identified with biblical figures. N. Avigad made four such identifications and Y. Shiloh found a fifth. I propose a sixth name.

According to Avigad, minimum conditions must be met when attempting such a match. First, the names of the father and the son must be identical in both cases; and second, chronological correspondence between the two cases is essential. This means that the epigraphic finds must have been discovered in an archaeological context that can be dated to the period in which the biblical namesakes lived. Avigad added that "if a title of some sort accompanies the names, so much the better."[1]

Until the discovery of the group of bullae by Shiloh in the City of David excavations in Jerusalem (see in this volume, pp. 53–61), the provenance, and therefore the date, of most other seals and bullae was unknown or unreliable. As Shiloh wrote about his find: "...this is the first time that so large a group of easily legible Hebrew sealings has come to light in a controlled excavation, in a clear stratigraphic context and accompanied by architectural, ceramic and historical evidence."[2]

This unique collection was found in Stratum 10 which was destroyed by the Babylonians in 587/6 B.C.E. In his discussion of the onomastics, Shiloh concluded that "...though this is a rich group of names of persons in Jerusalem, all except one are 'nonentities,' historically speaking."[3]

The exception is Gemariah son of Shaphan, who is mentioned several times in Chapter 36 of Jeremiah. The biblical text, unlike the bulla, provides additional information by calling him "Gemariah son of Shaphan, the scribe" (Jeremiah 36:10). The title "scribe" apparently refers to his father Shaphan, who was, in fact, scribe to King Josiah (2 Kings 22). The location of Gemariah's office, "in the upper court, at the entry of the New Gate of the Lord's house" (Jeremiah 36:10) testifies to the importance of his position in the administration of the later Judean kings.

The name of a second biblical figure appears in the bullae collection from the City of David. Bulla 27 bears the name לעזריהו בן חלקיהו "(belonging) to 'Azaryahu son of Hilqiyahu." Both these names appear, as father and son, in two priestly genealogical lists (1 Chronicles 5:39–41 and 9:10–11) and in the

Bulla 27 from the City of David

[1] N. Avigad, "On the Identification of Persons Mentioned in Hebrew Epigraphic Sources," *Eretz Israel* 19 (Jerusalem, 1987), p. 235 (Hebrew).

[2] Y. Shiloh, "A Group of Hebrew Bullae from the City of David," *IEJ* 36 (1986): 16–18.

[3] Ibid., p. 33.

record of Ezra's ancestors (Ezra 7:1). Consequently, it seems that the 'Azariahu and Hilqiahu of Bulla 27 must be two of the high priests who officiated in Jerusalem during the last decades of the First Temple period.

Whereas Azariah is not specifically referred to in any biblical episode, his father Hilkiah was a major figure. His discovery of a scroll in the Temple during renovations there in 622 B.C.E. precipitated King Josiah's reforms, one of the major religious turning points in the First Temple period. The high priest Hilkiah said to Shaphan the scribe, "I have found the book of the law in the house of the Lord" (2 Kings 22:8; a similar verse is found in 2 Chronicles 34:15). Shaphan then brought the book to Josiah, who set the reforms in motion.

The collaboration of Hilkiah the high priest with Shaphan the scribe gives added support to the chronological correspondence of the two bullae with the biblical evidence. Moreover, it stands to reason that their sons, namely Azariah and Gemariah respectively, continued to serve the state in the years preceding the destruction of Jerusalem, when these bullae were impressed.

Though no title accompanies the name, the evidence supporting the identification of 'Azariahu and the Hilqiahu on Bulla 27 with the biblical high priests is nevertheless compelling. Just as in the case of the Gemariah son of Shaphan bulla, the names, relationships, chronology and locations all conform. It seems an almost impossible coincidence that this bulla may have belonged to another seal-owner named Azariah son of Hilkiah who lived in Jerusalem just prior to the Babylonian destruction of the city.

## Bibliography

Avigad, N., "Baruch the Scribe and Yerahme'el the King's Son," *IEJ* 28 (1978): 52–56.

Schneider, T., "Six Biblical Signatures: Seals and Seal Impressions of Six Biblical Personages Recovered," *BAR* 17/4 (1991): 26–33.

Shiloh, Y. "A Group of Hebrew Bullae from the City of David," *Eretz Israel* 18 (Jerusalem, 1985), pp. 73–87 (Hebrew).

# The Royal Quarter of Biblical Jerusalem: The Ophel

## Eilat Mazar

The Jebusite settlement selected by King David for his capital stood on a small hill surrounded by deep valleys, with the perennial Gihon spring gushing from the eastern slope below. In a daring action—the details of the biblical passages are unclear (2 Samuel 5:6–9; 1 Chronicles 11:4–6)—he captured the town, known since then as the City of David. The hill on which the city was built is not completely isolated: in the north a narrow ridge, called the Ophel, gradually widens and connects it with Mount Moriah—the Temple Mount. Topographically, ancient Jerusalem comprised three areas: the hill of the City of David, the Ophel and the Temple Mount. Their development is of primary importance in understanding how Jerusalem's plan changed through time.

The term *ophel* is known from the Bible. Its origin is the Hebrew root *'pl* which means "to climb," "to rise up," or "to swell." It was the exalted place to which one ascended. Quite naturally, it was also the location of the inner fortress, the royal throne, and the kingdom's administrative center. The term should be understood simply as the acropolis—that part of the city that is higher than the rest and is enclosed with a wall.

The earliest recorded reference to an *ophel* appears on the victory stele erected by Mesha, King of Moab, in the mid–9th century B.C.E. Among the construction projects of which Mesha boasts in the lengthy inscription on the stele is the building of a "wall of the *ophel*" (lines 21–22) at Dibon, his capital.

From the Bible we know of another *ophel* at Samaria, the capital of the northern kingdom —Israel—dating to the second half of the 9th century B.C.E. (2 Kings 5:24). The prophet Elisha resided in this prestigious section of Samaria which was apparently located between the palace fortress at the top of the tell and the "lower wall" around it.

Finally, there is the Ophel of Jerusalem, the capital of the united monarchy of Israel, and later, the capital of the kingdom of Judah. The Ophel is first mentioned in the Bible during the time of King Jotham of Judah in the middle of the 8th century B.C.E. Jotham, we are told, "did much building on the wall of Ophel" (2 Chronicles 27:3). The Ophel wall was thus already in existence by that time. Like the *ophel* at Samaria and at Dibon, it probably dates to the 9th century B.C.E. All three "ophels" known to us refer to a definite town section characteristic of capital cities.

The first step in expanding the Jebusite town northward was taken by King David himself. Immediately after he conquered the city, which occupied a mere 50 dunams and had already existed for some two thousand years, he dwelt inside the Jebusite fortress known as the Stronghold of Zion (*mezudat ziyyon*; 2 Samuel 5:7). Soon afterward, however, King David built a new palace for himself with the help of his ally, King Hiram of Tyre, who sent his Phoenician craftsmen to Jerusalem (2 Samuel 5:11; 1 Chronicles 14:1). It is now generally agreed that the Stronghold of Zion was built at the top of Area G of the City of David excavations (see in this volume, pp. 31–45). David's new palace probably stood in the southern part of the Ophel, near the northern edge of the Jebusite city, and remained unfortified until King Solomon appointed Jeroboam son of Nebat, a future king of Israel, to head the building enterprise, one purpose of which was to protect that area:

"Solomon built the Millo, and closed up the breach of the city of David his father" (1 Kings 11:27). The Hebrew word for "breach" can also be translated as "an extension." Therefore, the text can be understood to say that King Solomon enclosed this addition to the city with a wall that apparently connected with the earlier, Jebusite wall. King Solomon also extended the city farther north by building a separate new acropolis on the highest area, Mount Moriah. In this way, he gave Jerusalem its definitive form, clearly dividing it into a lower city, populous and fortified, and, at a distance of more than 250 m., an acropolis that included his own royal palace and the magnificent Temple for the God of Israel.

The absence of pre-9th-century-B.C.E. building remains on the northern Ophel may probably be ascribed to the concentrated development of the Davidic city in the south, and of the Solomonic acropolis on the Temple Mount during that period.

The development of the new acropolis and its southward expansion toward the northern part of the Ophel is described in biblical passages concerning the construction enterprises of the kings of Judah in the 8th and 7th centuries B.C.E. It is further clarified by the findings of excavations in the area of the Ophel, described below.

### Excavations by B. Mazar: 1968–1977

Ten years of excavations in the northern part of the Ophel led to the view that, as a result of intensive quarrying and construction over a period of 1,500 years, nothing remained from the First Temple period but a few fragmentary walls and sporadic finds of little informative value. Then, in May 1976, a portion of a public building (Building C) was exposed on the far southeastern edge of the excavation. It was preserved to a considerable height and contained numerous vessels datable to the Babylonian destruction of Jerusalem in 587/6 B.C.E. Although only part of its plan could be discerned, much was learned about the nature and construction of this building. As the bedrock here slopes sharply to the southeast, it

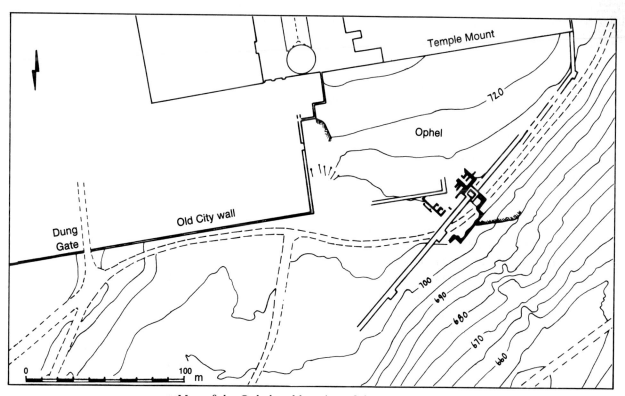

Map of the Ophel and location of the excavation area

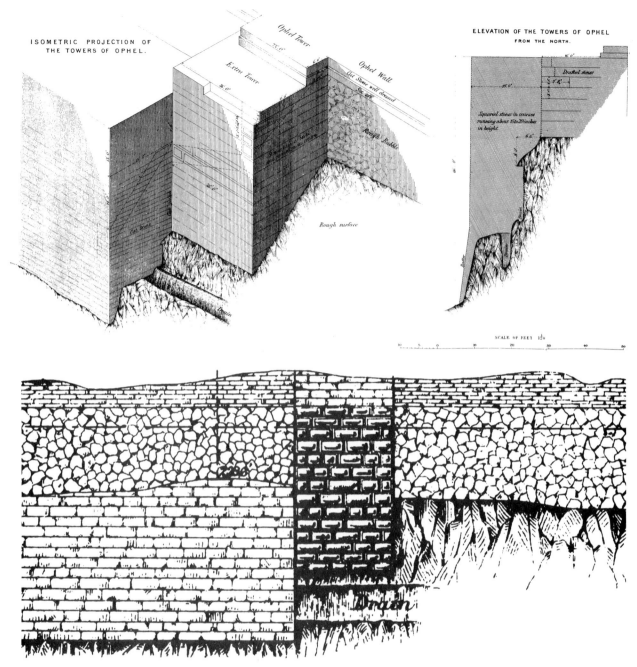

Plan and Sections of Warren's excavations at the Ophel

was necessary to solve the problem of leveling the area in order to provide a stable base for the building. The successful adaptation of the structure to the difficult topography reflects a high level of technical skill on the part of its builders. In order to create a level surface on the slope, a base consisting of layers of large stones was first built up. Foundations were constructed upon this to provide support for floors and walls. In accordance with the topographic conditions, the superstructure was built either upon the stone base, on the foundations, or on exposed bedrock. To the northwest, the bedrock was hewn in places and integrated into the actual structure that was built of rough stones. Doorposts and corners were constructed of ashlars laid in header and stretcher fashion.

B. Mazar excavated two identical, nearly square rooms (2.8 × 2.4 m.) of the structure (Building C), preserved to a maximum height of 3.3 m. In the southern room, dozens of

66

vessels were discovered, including over forty storage jars, all of the same type, together with small finds including a small pendant with an image of Sekhmet the Egyptian goddess of war, and a jar handle bearing a Hebrew seal impression inscribed with the name of a woman: lḥnh bt 'zryh "Hannah daughter of Azariah." In the second room of the building (to the west), which was partly destroyed by early Roman construction, a "rosette" storage jar was found—a type characteristic of the end of the Iron Age. Northwest of this western room, part of an additional room was found. Upside-down on the burnt floor lay six large bowls, one inside the other, apparently fallen from a wooden shelf when it burned.

The public character of Building C, its sophisticated construction technique, and its dating to the period of Judean monarchy led B. Mazar to tentatively identify it as the "house of Millo, on the way that goes down to Silla" (2 Kings 12:20), where King Joash of Judah (836–799 B.C.E.) was assassinated as the result of a conspiracy by his courtiers.

## The Warren and Kenyon Excavations

A review of the earlier archaeological investigations in this area is essential for a complete understanding of the results of the renewed excavations.

In 1867, Ch. Warren undertook a comprehensive topographic exploration of the Temple Mount and the Ophel on behalf of the Palestine Exploration Fund. He dug shafts straight down to bedrock and then followed lines of ancient construction and fortification by tunneling. One of these shafts was in the area to which we returned in 1986. Warren published the results of his research in the Jerusalem volume of the *Survey of Western Palestine*, in which he stated that in this area he found two immense, very well preserved towers built of ashlars and constructed on bedrock. The towers belonged to a fortification system that Warren assigned to the First Temple period. The larger tower (Building B), about 24 m. long and 19 m. wide, is

preserved to a height of 20 m. The other tower (Building A), located northeast of the first, is about 16 m. long, 8 m. wide and 9 m. high. The ashlars in the large tower measure 60–90 by 30–60 cm. In the other tower the ashlars are much larger—up to 2.4 m. long by 90 cm. wide.

In 1967, K.M. Kenyon, on behalf of the British School of Archaeology, returned to the site. She opened an excavation square (SII) at the entrance to the shaft that Warren had dug a hundred years earlier. Here, she uncovered an additional section of the smaller tower. The massive ashlar masonry, unlike anything found elsewhere in Jerusalem, reminded Kenyon of stonework she herself had excavated a half-century earlier at Samaria, which was dated to the 9th century B.C.E. In

Ophel: massive ashlar masonry uncovered by Kenyon in Area SII (Building A)

the publication of the results of her excavation, Kenyon dated the wall, and hence the entire tower, to the 8th century B.C.E. at the latest, adding: "It seems highly probable that these stones were derived from a near-by Solomonic structure."[1]

[1] K.M. Kenyon, "Excavations in Jerusalem," *PEQ* 100 (1967):104.

Ophel: aerial view of the excavations at the end of the 1986 season; looking northeast

## Renewed Excavations: 1986–1987[2]

### The Royal Building

From the outset of our excavations in the area, northwest of the small tower (Building A), the plan of a royal building (Building D) began to emerge. Since only the bottom story, which probably served as storage space, was preserved, it is impossible to know its exact purpose. It had been destroyed in an intense conflagration, signs of which were abundant.

The eastern corner of the building was preserved to a height of more than 4 m. The width of the external walls on the northeast and southeast was 2–2.5 m. The eastern room, measuring 5.75 × 2.5 m., was exposed in its entirety. In this room two superimposed floors were found. On the upper floor, of beaten earth above a reddish earth fill, seven

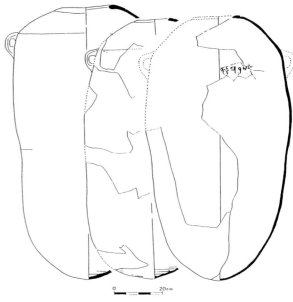

Ophel: pithoi from royal Building D, one of them bearing incised inscription: "belonging to the official in charge of the o..." on its shoulder

[2] The Ophel excavations were conducted under the auspices of the Institute of Archaeology of the Hebrew University of Jerusalem, with the assistance of the Department of Antiquities of the Israel Ministry of Education and Culture, the East Jerusalem Development Company and Dr. R. Hecht. Seven weeks of excavation were conducted in 1986 and four additional weeks were conducted in 1987. B. Mazar and E. Mazar headed the expedition. Members of the team included: Y. Nadelman (principal assistant and area supervisor); A.M. Maeir, T. Shabi, Y. Yisrael, S. Yisraeli, S. Wimmer and Z. Shamir (area supervisors); P. Davies (assistant supervisor); M. Hayush and D. Shmuel (registration); L. Ritmeyer, W. Schleicher, D. Chen, D. Milson and G. Lipton (surveyors); G. Lipton prepared the final plans; I. Sztulman and G. Laron (photographers); Y. Kalman and M. Zahavi (field administration); R. Rivak (restoration); M. Goetz (laboratory); S. Eisenstein (drafting). Special thanks are due to archaeologist E. Lass for his assistance in the project's initial stage. Also, thanks to the workers and volunteers who participated in the excavations.

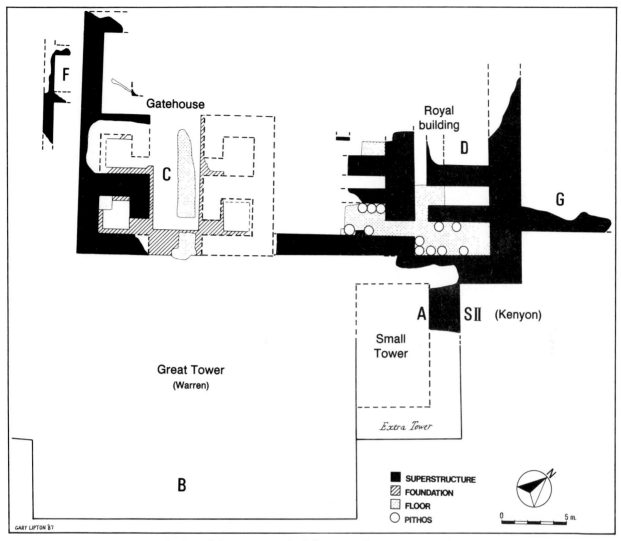

GARY LIPTON '87

General plan of the Iron Age building complex in the Ophel excavations

large pithoi of a type not previously encountered in Jerusalem were arranged along the walls. The average dimensions of each pithos are 1.1 m. high and 80 cm. in diameter. These storage jars probably held oil or wine. The pithoi were found *in situ* but broken, having been crushed by a large fall of stones. Between the stones were remains of carbonized wooden beams, some of which have been identified as cedar from Lebanon. The fill underlying this floor contained an abundance of pottery sherds, apparently vessel fragments that had been collected from other locations and mixed with the earthen fill in order to stabilize it. These sherds provide a basis for dating the upper floor to the 8th century B.C.E. at the earliest—possibly part of King

Manasseh's construction works described in 2 Chronicles 33:14.

The lower floor was very different from the upper one. It was made of lime, below which was a light-brown earthen fill containing very few pottery sherds, many of them dating to the Middle Bronze Age. More significant for dating purposes was an intact black juglet characteristic of the 10th and 9th centuries B.C.E. This juglet was found hidden between the stones of one of the foundation walls of the room, as if it had been placed there intentionally by the builders. On the basis of the pottery, including this juglet, the laying of the lower floor and hence the original construction of the entire building can be dated to the 9th century B.C.E. The lower floor showed no

69

signs of fire or destruction of any kind. The upper floor was probably laid as part of the renovation of the original structure.

The same two superimposed floors were also found in other parts of the building. In the room to the southwest, similar huge pithoi were found arranged along the walls. They were crushed, burnt and broken beyond repair as a result of the intense heat of the conflagration that destroyed the room.

On the shoulder of one pithos there is a clearly incised, though fragmentary, inscription in Hebrew lettering characteristic of the 7th century B.C.E., reading: *lśrh'w...* "belonging to the official in charge of the o..." The reference to a *śr*, a high official functionary, is beyond doubt. The missing portion of the inscription leaves us guessing if this was the official in charge of the bakeries (*'wpym*), of the treasury (*'wẓr*), or possibly, of the stables (*'wrwwt*). In any case, this inscription provides additional evidence for the royal character of the building.

### The Gatehouse

Southwest of Building D, exposure of Building C continued. This structure is noteworthy for its symmetrical plan and the uniform width (1.6 m.) of the walls of its super-structure.

A new plan encompassing the entire complex consisting of buildings A, B, C and D emerged. Building C was a four-chambered gatehouse; Building B was a projecting tower or bastion in front of the inner gatehouse; Building A was an additional tower; and Building D, a royal building of undefined function. Together, they made up a fortification line composed of distinct structural units forming a serrated line, following the gradually rising topography northwards and encompassing the Ophel.

The four gatehouse chambers of Building C are laid out with two chambers on each side of a central passage. The southwestern wall of the gatehouse continues to the northwest, apparently enclosing a part of what appears to have been a plaza inside the city. The northeastern portion of this gatehouse was to a large extent destroyed by later construction. Nevertheless, enough of the foundation walls are preserved to permit a reconstruction of the symmetrical plan of the gatehouse. Since nothing remains of the gate's doorposts, it is difficult from the plan alone to determine where the entrance was located. The 1987 excavation season clarified this matter with the discovery of a fine lime floor, more than 1 m. above bedrock. The floor was preserved over most of the length of the passageway between the chambers, extending to connect Building C with the large projecting bastion (Building B) to the southeast. Someone approaching the Ophel would first pass through

Ophel: general view of the southwestern chamber of the gatehouse (Building C) looking southeast

Ophel: the foundation walls and foundation of the southwestern chamber of the gatehouse.

Ophel: storage jars from the southwestern chamber of the gatehouse (Building C)

an outer gatehouse (as yet undiscovered) at the southwest side of Warren's large tower, then make a 90-degree turn left to enter the Ophel's inner gatehouse.

Gate complexes of Biblical cities vary in detail. These differences sometimes seem to outweigh the similarities they share. Each gate complex is adapted to local needs and topographic conditions. Because of this, it was especially thrilling when D. Milson, our surveyor, discovered that the dimensions of the four-chambered inner gate we had excavated are almost identical with those of the palace gate (No. 1567) of Stratum VA-IVB at Megiddo.

The inner gate of the Ophel must have been built along the same plan as the palace gate at Megiddo, probably relying, in both cases, upon the services of Phoenician royal architects, thus reflecting Phoenicia's close cultural relations with both cities.

The Ophel gate was a city gate in every

Ophel: pottery vessels from the southwestern chamber of the gatehouse (Building C)

71

|                              | Megiddo gate | Ophel gate |
| ---------------------------- | ------------ | ---------- |
| Overall length               | 10.2 m.      | 10.4 m.    |
| Overall width                | 14.6         | 14.8       |
| Width of passageway          | 4.2          | 4.0        |
| Length of each chamber       | 2.8          | 2.8        |
| Width of each chamber        | 2.2          | 2.4        |
| Width of superstructure walls| 1.6          | 1.5        |

respect; one of several gates in the fortified city walls. At the same time, it served as a palace gate, leading to the royal quarter of the city—the acropolis of Jerusalem. On the basis of historical sources, and from the chronology indicated by pottery from the fill of the floor of the gatehouse and from the fill of the lower floor of the adjacent royal building, it may be assumed that the palace complex on the Ophel was built in the 9th century B.C.E.

The numerous storage jars B. Mazar found in the southern chamber of Building C do not conflict with our identification of the structure as a gatehouse. As we know from the Bible, the city's gate complex served, in addition to its defensive functions, as a center of civic and commercial activities, the site of municipal markets and a meeting place.

In the mid–5th century B.C.E., Nehemiah returned to Jerusalem from exile with the objective of rebuilding the city destroyed by the Babylonians. He counted ten gates, in order of their location along the city wall. Warren identified the large tower he discovered as "the tower that projects" mentioned in Nehemiah 3:25. We believe that Warren was right. Accordingly, we identify the gatehouse with the Water Gate, and the entire complex as part of the "upper house of the king" referred to in Nehemiah 3:25–27.[3]

[3] A model of one chamber of the gatehouse (Building C) is exhibited in the Bible Lands Museum, Jerusalem, with its pottery finds and most of the pithoi from Building D.

## Bibliography

Aharoni, Y., *Beer Sheba I. Excavations at Tel Beer-Sheba, 1969–1971 Seasons* (Tel Aviv, 1973).

Avigad, N., "A Note on an Impression from a Woman's Seal," *IEJ* 37 (1987): 18–19.

Herzog, Z., *The City-gate in Eretz-Israel and its Neighboring Countries* (Tel Aviv, 1976) (Hebrew).

Kenyon, K.M., "Excavations in Jerusalem," *PEQ* 95 (1962): 7–21.

———, *Jerusalem: Excavating 3000 Years of History* (London, 1967).

———, "Excavations in Jerusalem, 1967," *PEQ* 100 (1967): 97–109.

———, *Royal Cities of the Old Testament* (New York, 1971).

Lamon, R. S. and Shipton, G. M., *Megiddo I, Seasons of 1925–1934, Strata I–V* (Chicago, 1939).

Mazar, B., *Excavations and Discoveries* (Jerusalem, 1986) (Hebrew).

Mazar, E., "Royal Gateway to Ancient Jerusalem Uncovered," *BAR* 15 (1989): 38–51.

Mazar, E. and Mazar, B., *Excavations in the South of the Temple Mount; The Ophel of Biblical Jerusalem. Qedem* 29 (Jerusalem, 1989).

Shiloh, Y., "The Material Culture of Judah and Jerusalem in Iron Age II: Origins and Influences," in: Lipinski, E. (ed.), *The Land of Israel: Cross-Roads of Civilizations. Proceedings of the Conference Held in Brussels, December 3–5, 1984*, (Louvain, 1985), pp. 113–146.

Warren, C. and Conder, C.R., *The Survey of Western Palestine, Jerusalem* (London, 1884).

# A Fragmentary First Temple Period Hebrew Inscription from the Ophel

## Meir Ben-Dov

In the Ophel area south of the Temple Mount, a fragment of a stone slab bearing a paleo-Hebrew inscription was found in 1982 while excavating private dwellings dating to the end of the Byzantine period (6th–7th centuries C.E.).* The buildings cleared in this area were quite large and surprisingly well preserved, some of them remaining to a height of two stories. This is rare in the archaeology of Jerusalem, and especially in the excavations around the Temple Mount, for continued building activities in the city, particularly in the region of the Ophel, caused severe destruction. Stones were robbed for reuse in new construction and to be burned for lime. The private dwellings of the Byzantine period here are well preserved because they were almost unaffected by Umayyad construction of the 7th–8th centuries C.E. The room in which the fragment of the inscribed stone slab was revealed is located some 20 m. south of the Single Gate in the eastern side of the southern wall of the Temple Mount. The fragment had been reused as a building stone in one of the walls.

Beneath these Byzantine structures were found the remains of buildings and quarries of the Second Temple period, including walls, *miqva'ot* (ritual baths) and cisterns. First Temple period pottery was found here and there on the bedrock. The best-preserved buildings, which date to the 9th–6th centuries B.C.E., are located only a few dozen meters south of the place where the inscribed stone fragment was found at the southeastern side of the Ophel (see in this volume, pp. 00–00).

The slab bearing the inscription is of soft Jerusalem limestone, in which the stonemason cut handsome letters with a chisel. The fragment is 27 cm. high, 24 cm. wide and 10 cm. thick. Examination of the inscription shows it to be merely a small section from the middle of a larger one, for originally there were additional lines both above and below the surviving portion of the text. It is most probable that the text continued to the left, and possibly letters and words are missing also to the right, before the remaining lines.

The fragment comprises four lines, each containing at least one complete word. In keeping with the practice in First Temple period inscriptions, the words were written without spaces between them, but with dots as word-dividers. The inscription is in the paleo-Hebrew script of the First Temple period and can be dated on paleographic grounds to the 8th–7th centuries B.C.E.

| | |
|---|---|
| ]מתחת · לז[ | ]*mtht · lz*[ |
| ]ר[.]כ · המי[. | ]*r*[.]*k · hmy*[. |
| ]בירכתי[. | ]*byrkty*[. |
| ]נסחהכס[ | ]*nsḥhks*[ |

**FIRST LINE.** The letters and the dot between the words are perfectly clear: the first word is

* During the years 1977–1984 a comprehensive conservation project was undertaken on the Ophel, planned and directed by the author. In the framework of this work a residential neighborhood of the Byzantine period was exposed, whose outskirts had been excavated in previous years by B. Mazar. The Byzantine remains conceal remains of the First and Second Temple periods beneath them. After the discovery and first reading of the inscription, I delivered it to Professor J. Naveh for publication: J. Naveh, "A Fragment of an Ancient Hebrew Inscription from the Ophel," *IEJ* 32 (1982): 195–198. The photographs are by the author; the drawing is by M. Ritmeyer.

Photograph and facsimile of the First Temple period inscription found on the Ophel

complete, but of the second only two letters remain. The *lamed* at the beginning of the second word is a preposition of the first. Thus, the second word may be completed to ז[רם] *z[rm]* "stream" as in the Hebrew text of Isaiah 28:2. This completion seems reasonable considering that the inscription obviously has something to do with water (see below).

**SECOND LINE.** The first letter *resh* can be read quite clearly. After it comes a damaged, illegible letter, and then an unmistakable *kaf*, which is the last letter of the word as it is followed by a dot. At the beginning of the second word we can read three letters: *he, mem* and *yod*. These are followed by the upper end of a broken letter which cannot be confidently identified, but from the form of the other letters in the inscription it seems plausible that the letter was a *mem*. Thus the word would be completed to המי[ם] *hmy[m]* "the water." As to the preceding word, which consists of three letters, the missing middle letter may be completed to *bet*, i.e., ר[ב]כ *r[b]k*, from the same root as the word מרבכת *mrbkt* in Leviticus 6:14 and elsewhere in the Bible, where it means "mixed." This would go well with the word

"water," the whole phrase thus meaning "mixing of the water." According to J. Naveh, there was no letter between the two letters of the first word—only a flaw in the stone; the engraver having skipped it, proceeded directly to the next letter. Naveh reads the two letters as adjoining in one word and adduces similar cases of a stonecutter passing over a flaw in the stone in the middle of a word in two Phoenician inscriptions in basalt of the 9th–8th centuries B.C.E. In the present case, however, the inscription was cut in limestone and there are no precedents for faulty writing because of a flaw in limestone, which is soft enough to be easily smoothed. More probably, therefore, the "flaw" is a missing letter which was damaged, either when the original building of the First Temple period was destroyed, or when the stone was set in the Byzantine wall.

**THIRD LINE.** All except the last letters in this line are clearly legible. They combine to form one word בירכתי *byrkty*, meaning "at the far end," "at the back," etc. The last letter is badly preserved, but may be a *waw*, in which case we have the word בירכתי[ו] *byrkty[w]*, i.e., "at the end of..." The word [ם]ירכתי *yrkty[m]* "the remote parts of..." is also quite common in biblical Hebrew.

FOURTH LINE. Six letters can be read with fair certainty without dividing dots. At first sight it might seem to be six-letter word. However, the fourth letter *he* in this seemingly unintelligible line, indicates that it is a combination of two words. We have no explanation for the absence of the dot; however, similar phenomena may be pointed out in other ancient inscriptions of this period, as on the Mesha Stone. In our inscription there was no need for a dot, because the *he* in the middle of the line sufficed to tell the reader that the text comprised two words. The letter *he* probably belongs to the second word and is simply the definite article. The fourth line would therefore read נסח הכס *nsḥ hks*, or, in modern orthography, נסוח הכס *nswḥ hks*. The biblical meaning of the root נסח *nsḥ* is "tear down," as in "The Lord tears down the house of the proud" (Proverbs 15:25), or "root out" as "...the treacherous will be rooted out of it" (Proverbs 2:22). The beginning of the second word in this line is thus כס *ks* that may be completed as [כסות] *ks[wt]* "a covering." But there are other possible ways to complete this word, such as [כסא] *ks['e]* "seat." Perhaps the text concerns the removal of some kind of object in a religious ceremony (see below).

The form of the second and sixth letters *samekh* in this line are not quite identical. Possibly the intrusion of the fifth letter *kaf* under the lines of the second *samekh* made it impossible for the stonecutter to fashion the latter in the same way as the first *samekh*. Whatever the case may be, it is interesting that two different script forms of *samekh* appear in the same formal inscription in cursive script. It follows, therefore, that the engraver did not devote special care to the precise form of the letters. This implies that chronological conclusions sometimes drawn from such differences are not necessarily on safe ground.

The location of the inscription—admittedly, on a stone in secondary use—at the upper, northern part of the Ophel may indicate that it had not been moved very far from its original position. The fine stonecutting and the import of the words may imply that the inscription had some ritual significance. Perhaps it was part of a plaque with written instructions for the priests in matters of the sacred ritual in the region of the Temple Mount, sometime toward the end of the First Temple period. At any rate, the inscription was originally located in the royal palace or within the Temple precincts of Jerusalem. This fragment, which has survived in the ruins of a building of the Byzantine period, as well as the sparse remains of a few First Temple period inscriptions found in Jerusalem, indicate that it was not uncommon for stelae, inscriptions and plaques bearing texts in praise of rulers, or instructions to various functionaries, to be installed in the capital of the kings of Judah.

## Bibliography

Naveh, J., *Early History of the Alphabet* (Jerusalem and Leiden, 1982).

# Mount Zion: Discovery of Iron Age Fortifications Below the Gate of the Essenes

Doron Chen, Shlomo Margalit, Bargil Pixner

Between 1977 and 1988 new excavations were carried out intermittently at the southern edge of the Protestant cemetery on Mount Zion, where a gateway in the line of an ancient city wall was uncovered in the past. The objective of the digs was to verify earlier excavations conducted at the top of the southern slope of Mount Zion, to extend these, and to establish an accurate chronology of the city walls and successive gates discovered there.*

## The Early Excavations

In 1894–1897, F.J. Bliss and A.C. Dickie discovered part of an early defensive fortification line of Jerusalem at the site. Owing to restrictions imposed by the Turkish authorities, Bliss and Dickie's excavation work was conducted in an unusual manner: they followed ancient structural remains by means of subterranean shafts dug as they progressed underground. In these dangerous excavations, and with only rudimentary lighting facilities, they discovered and traced several sections along the ancient outer defenses of Jerusalem. Their detailed descriptions and precise drawings showed that at the southern part of Mount Zion were two fortification lines following identical courses, including sections of walls, towers, and a gateway. The fortification lines are built one next to, or one

over the other, or sometimes in combination with each other, representing two separate construction periods.

The lower—earlier—wall built of ashlars having marginal dressing and prominent bosses was ascribed by Bliss to the time of the First Temple, and some of the wall's later modifications to the Second Temple period. The upper wall—the latest, chronologically— which follows the same line as its predecessor, is built of smooth-faced ashlars, some of which have marginal dressing and very slightly protruding, smooth bosses. This line of wall was dated by Bliss and Dickie to the Byzantine period, and identified by them with the wall described in the literary sources as the one built by the empress Eudoxia in the mid–5th century C.E. to bring Mount Zion within the city limits of Jerusalem. Bliss and Dickie's dating, which bore no relation to the numismatic and pottery finds, may today only be considered as tentative.

At the southwestern corner of Mount Zion, Bliss and Dickie uncovered Tower ABC in the earliest line of the two walls. At the tower's southern side they revealed a deep rock-cutting that continued northeastward for a considerable distance. This they identified as a defensive moat at the upper, eastern side of the Western Hill of Jerusalem. From Tower ABC, the wall stretched about 45 m. southeast to the corner Tower I in which two stages of construction were apparent. In the center of this stretch of wall, in the Protestant cemetery area, they uncovered a gate which they identified with the Gate of the Essenes mentioned by Josephus. Bliss and Dickie detected in the construction of this gate four main stages of use in the Byzantine period. The construction

---

* The excavations were carried out under the auspices of the Dormition Abbey on Mount Zion. The first seasons were directed by B. Pixner and S. Margalit, while the 1988 excavations were directed by D. Chen with the assistance of D. Milson. The Iron Age pottery was examined by E. Mazar. The Roman and Byzantine pottery was examined by S. Loffreda, B. Mazar and R. Rosenthal-Heginbottom. The Coins were examined by R. Barkay.

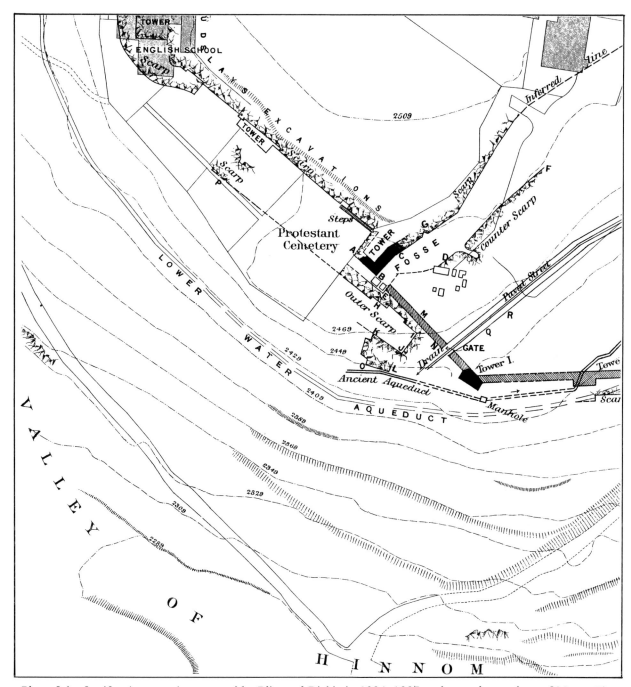

Plan of the fortification remains exposed by Bliss and Dickie in 1894–1897 at the southwest slope of Mount Zion

phases of the gateway are reflected in the level of the entrance having been raised successively by new sills superimposed one over the other. At the end of the last stage of the gate's use the gate opening was blocked by stone construction.

## The Recent Excavations

Rediscovering the structures described in Bliss and Dickie's reports, we continued exca-

vating in order to reach bedrock. At a level below that of the Gate of the Essenes we found Iron Age pottery and an earlier wall. We then extended our dig inside and outside the cemetery to include Bliss's Tower I. In the course of the limited sounding to verify the breadth, orientation, and chronology of this earlier wall, we came upon the remains of an adjacent structure. Both these early structures were found to date to the Iron Age.

Mount Zion: general view of the excavations; looking north

## The Post-Iron Age Finds

The first structures uncovered in our excavations were some poorly preserved walls and an irrigation channel of the Umayyad period, built onto the inner face of the uppermost (Byzantine) city wall. Nearby, the bedding of a mosaic floor, loose tesserae, and several Umayyad coins dated to 700–750 C.E. were found.

Below the Umayyad level we rediscovered remains of the upper—the latest—Byzantine gate and the road leading to and through it. An important key for dating ancient buildings is the identification of the units of measure, in whole numbers, employed by the planners and builders. In the present case, this criterion was applied in checking the chronology of the successive gateways. The width of the Byzantine city wall here is 2.79 m. (or 9 Byzantine feet of 30.89 cm.). The width of the gate at its inner side is 3.09 m. (10 Byzantine feet), and 2.47 m. (8 Byzantine feet) at its outer side. Pottery found at this level comprises types

typical of the 4–6th centuries C.E. At the same level were found two coins of Elagabalus (218–222 C.E.) and a coin of Galerius Maximianus (308–313 C.E.). Bliss's attribution of this Byzantine gate to the empress Eudoxia could thus be confirmed.

Below the Byzantine gate, Bliss and Dickie discovered two layers of limestone slabs used as thresholds. However, they were unable to determine whether this structure was the remains of a single earlier gate or of two successive gates. We believe that these two slabs were actually parts of a stepped sill. At the southern end of the lower inner slab is a hinge socket. In addition, both slabs had been bonded together by cement plaster, traces of which remained on the outside face of the sill.

This gate led into the walled-off compound of the early Christian community reestablished on Mount Zion after 70 C.E. The Bordeaux Pilgrim, who visited Jerusalem in 333 C.E. vividly described this area:

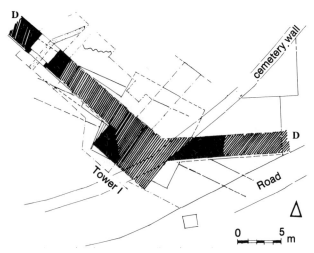

Mount Zion: the Herodian Gate of the Essenes inserted into the breach in an already existing city wall (D–D) of the Hasmonean period

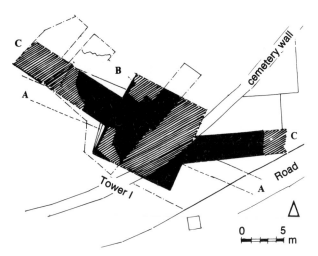

Mount Zion: massive Wall C–C and the early corner Tower I of the Hasmonean period

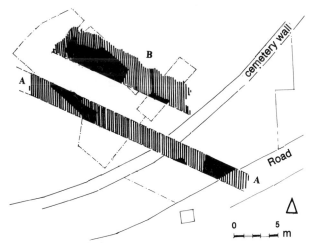

Mount Zion: Wall A-A and adjacent Structure B of the late Iron Age

Now these going out of Jerusalem to go up to Mount Sion have to their right side and down in the valley near the city wall the pool, which is called Silua;...from there one ascends to Sion and there appears the place where the house of Caiphas the High priest stood, and the column is still there where Jesus has been scourged. Inside, though within the wall of Sion, appears the site where David had his palace. And of the seven synagogues which had been there just a single one remains, while all the others have been plowed and tilled, just as the prophet Isaiah had said (Is. 1,8). When from there you go out of the wall of Sion those proceeding to the Neapolitan Gate have to their right side, towards the valley, the walls of the house of Pontius Pilate and to their left the hill of Golgotha...

We found that the lowest-level gate was exactly as described by Bliss. The outer width of this gate is 2.66 m. (9 Roman feet of 29.57 cm., or 6 Roman cubits, a cubit being a foot and a half). Underneath the paving we found the sewage channel (y–y) which Bliss followed eastward into the city. We were able to trace intermittent remains of the sewage channel and the street above it ascending northeast for nearly 50 m. Pottery from beneath the original paving slabs of the road leading to this gate is dated to the 1st century C.E., and no later than 70 C.E. We noticed that the southern jambstone of the gate had been built into a breach made in an already existing Hasmonean city wall (D–D). Apparently, the upper courses of the corner Tower I belong to this wall. In addition, ceramic evidence below and next to the jambstones appears to be Hellenistic and early Herodian. Thus, ceramic evidence and the fact that the gate is now conclusively dated to the Second Temple period give much weight to Bliss's initial identification of this gate as the Gate of the Essenes. Clearly, this section of the wall and gate are what Josephus refers to in *War* V, 143, where he traces the course of the First Wall of Jerusalem: "Beginning at the same point (from tower Hippicus) in the other direction, westwards, it descended past the place called Bethso to the gate of the Essenes, then turned southwards above the fountain Siloam..."

79

Mount Zion, outer side of the three superimposed gate sills: 1. the Gate of the Essenes of the Second Temple period; 2. the Roman gate; 3. the Byzantine gate; 4. northern gate-jamb of the Byzantine gate; 5. modern retaining wall

Following the line of the Second Temple period and Byzantine city walls to the southeast of the Gate of the Essenes, we came upon another, even earlier city wall—below the level of the lowest course of the later city wall (D–D). Much destroyed, this ca. 3.43–3.55 m.-wide wall (C–C) seems to be connected to the lower courses of the corner Tower I. In Wall C–C, northwest of corner Tower I, we were able to discern three courses of large ashlars with traces of gray plaster in the joints. East of the tower, below Wall D–D, another section of Wall C–C was rediscovered. Several architectural fragments of distinctly classical carving, in secondary use, were found in the core

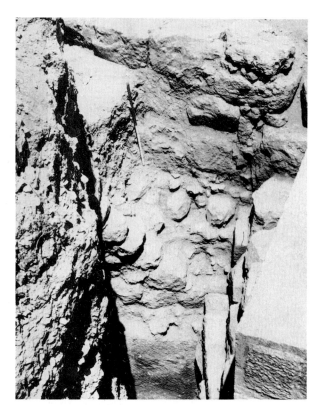

Mount Zion: center—outer face of the Iron Age Wall A–A above rock scarp; right—corner of Tower I

of the wall. We attribute this wall and the lower part of Tower I to the early stage of the First Wall built by the Hasmoneans.

## The Iron Age Finds

In the course of the excavations in 1988, remains of an Iron Age wall and an adjacent structure were uncovered. North of the northwestern corner of Tower I and below Wall C–C, we found remains of the earliest wall (A–A), which is 2.4 m. broad and stands to a height of nearly 2 m. This wall was built on a 1.45 m.-high, finely-hewn rock scarp. At the bottom of the scarp there is a small groove in the rock which indicates that there once was a stone quarry at the site. The outer face of Wall A–A is built of medium-sized fieldstones, slightly worked into near-rectangular shapes. We were able to discern the inner face of this wall ca. 1.5 m. further to the north, where traces of up to three courses remain. In our sounding south of corner Tower I, beyond the wall of the cemetery and next to the nearby modern road, we discovered another section of this same wall. The total length from the extremities of both uncovered sections of Wall A–A is nearly 20 m. The wall is aligned northwest-southeast in a straight line. Pottery sherds extracted from within the core of this wall at both sections, north and south of Tower I, belong to vessels typical of the 8th–7th and beginning of the 6th centuries B.C.E. The massive construction and its dominant position atop the steep slopes of Mount Zion prove that Wall A–A is a part of the late Iron Age fortifications.

Within the cemetery compound, adjacent to Wall A–A and north of Tower I, just above bedrock we found three courses of large stones which are the remains of another structure (B); it parallels Wall A–A, ca. 3 m. to the east. Pottery from within the core of Structure B also belong to vessels typical of 8th–7th and the beginning of the 6th centuries B.C.E. Since much of that structure is still unexcavated it is not yet clear whether we came across another city wall, a building, or a platform of the late First Temple period. Traces of a plaster floor between Wall A–A and Structure B were also identified. Since city Wall C–C still covers much of the space between Structure B and Wall A–A, we were not able to verify the chronology of that floor.

The late Iron Age fortifications uncovered on Mount Zion are conclusive evidence that the walled city of Jerusalem before the Babylonian exile extended to the western slopes of the Western Hill. However, since the pottery recovered from the core of Wall A–A and adjacent Structure B generally dates to the 8th–7th and beginning of the 6th centuries

Mount Zion: center—the inner face of the Iron Age Wall A–A; above—the city wall of the Second Temple period

B.C.E., little chronological distinction can be made. The strategic situation of the late Iron Age fortification line below the Gate of the Essenes shows that the preexilic wall determined the course of the First Wall of the Second Temple period.

## Bibliography

Bliss, F.J. and Dickie, A.C., *Excavations in Jerusalem, 1894–1897* (London, 1898).

Pixner, B. OSB, Chen, D. and Margalit, S., "Mount Zion: The 'Gate of the Essenes' Re-excavated," *ZDPV* 105 (1989): 85–95.

Pixner, B. OSB, "The History of the 'Essene Gate' Area," *ZDPV* 105 (1989): 96–104.

Riesner, R., "Josephus' 'Gate of the Essenes' in Modern Discussion," *ZDPV* 105 (1989): 105–109.

# Iron Age Remains in the Chapel of St. Vartan in the Church of the Holy Sepulcher

## Magen Broshi

Besides being the holiest site in Christendom, the Holy Sepulcher is also one of the most interesting archaeological complexes in the world. This is not surprising for it incorporates a number of structures, the earliest dating back as far as the 4th century C.E., which still fulfill their original functions.

Although archaeological excavations have been conducted in Jerusalem for over a century, only recently has it been possible to excavate in the Church of the Holy Sepulcher. In 1960, the three Christian denominations holding rights of possession—the Roman Catholics, Greek Orthodox, and Armenians —came to an agreement concerning the restoration and renovation of the entire complex. Within that framework, limited excavations have also been conducted, making a substantial contribution to our knowledge of the different components of the site.

Toward the end of 1975, I was invited by the Armenian Patriarchate to supervise an excavation at the Chapel of St. Vartan and the Armenian Martyrs. This chapel is located at the eastern edge of Holy Sepulcher, east of the Chapel of St. Helena, or, as it is called by the Armenians, the Chapel of St. Krikor (Gregory) which dates to Crusader times. It is bounded on the west by the latter chapel, on the north and east by walls of Constantine's time, and on the south by bedrock. Important remains were found in the space that was cleared: from Iron Age IIC (7th century B.C.E.), parts of the Hadrianic forum, parts of Constantine's basilica, and Crusader structures.*

## The Excavations

The maximum dimensions of the cleared space are 10.3 × 9.8 m. This space is the result of quarrying: the quarry workers removed the *meleke* limestone, in some parts leaving the overlying *mizzi ḥilu* to form a ceiling roughly 13 m. above the bottom of the quarry. The quarry bottom was later covered with a floor made of beaten earth mixed with ashes. This has survived only to a maximum length of about 6.5 m. after walls of later periods—three of the time of Hadrian and one dating to the reign of Constantine—were built on this floor, and so, its limits could not be ascertained. Nor could we determine whether it

Church of the Holy Sepulcher: plan of the excavated area and its surroundings: 1. Chapel of St. Helena (Chapel of St. Krikor); 2. Chapel of the Finding of the Cross; 3. Chapel of St. Vartan: excavation area; 4. the northern space; 5–6. ancient cisterns

* Later remains, of the Roman-Byzantine period at this site are described in M. Broshi, "Excavations in the Holy Sepulchre in the Chapel of St. Vartan and The Armenian Martyrs," in Y. Tzafrir (ed.) *Ancient Churches Revealed* (Jerusalem, 1993), pp. 118–122.

Church of the Holy Sepulcher: Chapel of St. Vartan,
Iron Age quarry; looking east

Church of the Holy Sepulcher: Chapel of St. Vartan,
section of the Iron Age floor surrounded by walls of the
Roman and Byzantine periods

was the floor of a roofed building or an open occupational level. The floor was laid on a fill of earth and stones to a depth ranging from a few centimeters to 1.3 m. All sherds found in the fill, including an ostracon on which a few letters were inscribed, date to the end of the Iron Age (8th–7th centuries B.C.E.). Almost every spot in the Holy Sepulcher where the

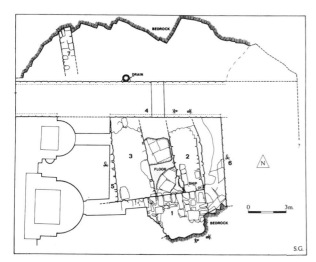

Church of the Holy Sepulcher: plan of the excavated
area in the Chapel of St. Vartan

excavators reached bedrock showed signs of quarrying and contained Iron Age potsherds. This site is the only one featuring a floor as well, indicating that the area was inhabited at the time by squatters.

The quarry is of particular interest. It undoubtedly dates to the Iron Age—almost the only quarry in Jerusalem that can be confidently ascribed to that period. The whole surrounding area stands on a deep quarry, which was a source of *meleke* stone, while the overlying *mizzi ḥilu* rock was left in place. The excavations by U. Lux, in the Church of the Redeemer some 85 m. south of our site, also included Iron Age IIC finds, but this material was not stratified. K.M. Kenyon, on the other hand, digging in Area C in the courtyard of the Lutheran school in the Muristan, about 165 m. south of our site, unearthed similar material *in situ*, and what may have been an occupational floor. Here too, there was a quarry predating the occupational level, but the physical difficulties involved in the dig—the excavator reached a depth of about 15 m.—precluded the exposure of more than a small segment.

## Conclusions

Recent excavations in Jerusalem have revealed a sudden and substantial increase in the area of the city toward the end of the Iron Age. During the 8th century B.C.E. the city was encompassed by a new wall, enclosing an area more than twice as large as in the 10th–8th centuries B.C.E. A considerable part of this increase may have been due to an influx of refugees from Samaria after the Assyrian conquest of that city in 720 B.C.E.; additional migrants came from the western settlements of the Shefelah (Judean foothills) that were seized by the Assyrians after Sennacherib's campaign in 701 B.C.E. and given over to the Philistine coastal cities. Credit for the discovery of the most important evidence of this population increase and the consequent expansion of Jerusalem goes to N. Avigad, namely, his uncovering of the Broad Wall in the Jewish Quarter in 1970, and of the nearby tower in 1975.

However, it turns out that the walled area was not the only territory added to Jerusalem at the end of the First Temple period. Recent excavations have disclosed the existence of extramural quarters west and north of the expanded city. Evidence for this has come to light along the western side of the Western Hill in the Citadel (C.N. Johns; R. Amiran and A. Eitan), the Armenian Garden (K.M. Kenyon and A.D. Tushingham; D. Bahat and M. Broshi), and on Mount Zion (M. Broshi)— an area which I believe was left outside the city wall (the Broad Wall). Additional proof for the expansion of the city to the north turned up in the Muristan (K.M. Kenyon; U. Lux), and now also in the Holy Sepulcher. Indirect evidence to the same effect is provided by the tremendous quantities of sherds of that period discovered at a considerable distance from the wall, from the western slopes of Mount Zion to the excavations of the Third Wall.

The limits of the city's expansion are marked by the cemeteries. The burial ground discovered by B. Mazar near the southwestern corner of the Temple Mount on the western slopes of the Tyropoeon Valley indicates the maximum extent of the city up to the 8th century B.C.E., while the long belt of tombs extending from the slopes of Mount Zion to north of the Damascus Gate demarcates the western border of the new city in the 7th century B.C.E. This belt includes the tombs discovered by A. Kloner and myself on the slopes of Mount Zion descending to the Hinnom Valley, the tombs in the Mamilla cemetery published by R. Amiran and more recently excavated by G. Barkay and R. Reich (see in this volume, pp. 85–118), and at least a dozen tombs uncovered by G. Barkay, A. Mazar, and A. Kloner in Suleiman Street, the Garden Tomb, and St. Étienne's in the north of the city.

It is quite possible that a few tombs discovered in the area of the Holy Sepulcher can also be added to this list. Over a century ago C. Schick reported the discovery of several tombs in a gigantic cistern beneath the Coptic monastery. Although his report is not sufficiently detailed, it seems to indicate that these tombs lacked the most typical features of Second Temple period burials, such as loculi, but rather had benches. Such tombs are typical of the Iron Age, allowing us to conjecture that the limits of the necropolis of Jerusalem toward the end of the monarchy were somewhere in the vicinity of the Coptic monastery. Thus, our excavations brought to light additional evidence of the city's expansion—a conclusion of considerable historical significance.

## Bibliography

Broshi, M. & Barkay, G., "Excavations inn the Chapel of St. Vartan in the Holy Sepulchre" *IEJ* 35 (1985): 108–128.

Corbo, V.C., *Il Santo Sepolcro de Gerusalemme* 1–3 (Jerusalem, 1981–1982).

Coüasnon, C., *The Church of the Holy Sepulchre in Jerusalem* (London, 1974).

# Excavations at Ketef Hinnom in Jerusalem

## Gabriel Barkay

In the 130-odd years of archaeological activity in Jerusalem few excavations have yielded a great quantity of finds, for each period tended to destroy and loot the treasures of the preceding one. It is therefore the more remarkable that a relatively small dig in the western part of Jerusalem, conducted during five seasons between 1975 and 1989, revealed a wealth of important finds that shed light on the city's history over thousands of years, from the days of the First Temple to the Ottoman period. The discoveries include a large, early Christian church, rock-hewn burial caves and other tombs, quarries, ancient Hebrew inscriptions, and an abundance of small finds—jewelry, weapons, pottery and other objects.

### The Site and the Excavations

The site is located next to the Scottish St. Andrew's Church which was built in 1927 on a prominent hill giving fine views over the walls of the Old City, the Hinnom Valley and Mount Zion. The slopes of Siloam Village and Judean Desert landscapes can be seen between the hills to the southeast. The hill on which the Scottish church stands rises above the deep bed of the Hinnom Valley to the east, and over the upper reaches of the Rephaim Valley on the west. Near the hill, to the west, is the Jerusalem railway station, the terminal for trains coming up the Sorek and Rephaim valleys.

This rocky knoll towering opposite ancient Jerusalem was known by the Arabic name of Ras ed-Dabbus (pinhead, or head of the thighbone). For want of a historic Hebrew name, we named the place after the adjacent valley and its topographic situation Ketef Hinnom

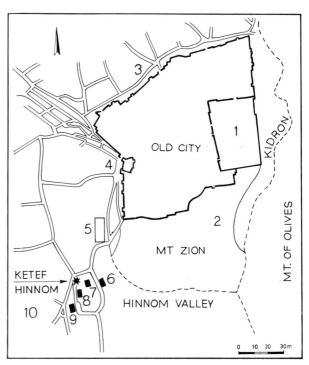

The location of the Ketef Hinnom site: 1. Temple Mount; 2. City of David; 3. Damascus Gate; 4. Citadel; 5. Sultan's Pool; 6. Mount Zion Hotel (formerly St. John's Ophthalmic Hospital); 7. St. Andrew's Scottish Church; 8. Khan Theater; 9. Jerusalem Railway Station; 10. Liberty Bell Park

—the Shoulder of Hinnom. The hill rises to 755 m. above sea level, about 80 m. above the bed of the Hinnom Valley. To the north the ridge dips into a saddle, and beyond it, on the rising ground, stand the Montefiore windmill and the King David Hotel. Ketef Hinnom is situated on the central watershed line of the Judean Mountains ridge, the route of the ancient north-south road between Beersheba, Hebron and Shechem. This is the lowest point of the watershed within the present municipal boundaries of Jerusalem, and at its closest to

Ketef Hinnom: General view of Ketef Hinnom; looking south-west, at the left—St. Andrew's Scottish Church; to the right, among the trees—the tower of Qasr el-Ghazzal (with a flag above it); to the right of the tower—excavations in the area of the Byzantine-period church

historic Jerusalem. In effect, the hill dominates a bottleneck in the road between the beds of the Rephaim and Hinnom valleys, forcing travellers along the north-south thoroughfare to follow one of the natural terraces. At the above-mentioned saddle, north of Ketef Hinnom, a secondary road branches off toward ancient Jerusalem from the main road coming up from the south. Those coming from Beersheba, Hebron or Bethlehem to Jerusalem could not leave this road before reaching Ketef Hinnom because the steep, scarp-like, rocky banks of the lower Hinnom Valley barred the way. Ketef Hinnom was thus the most convenient place for diverging from the main road in order to go to the City of David and the Old City.

The situation of Ketef Hinnom opposite the walls of the Old City not only lent the place a fine prospect but also great strategic importance. Whoever controlled this height dominated the southern approaches to Jerusalem and much of the city's western parts. The walls of the Old City can be easily seen from the hill which was well beyond the effective range of ancient projectiles.

Ketef Hinnom is located on the boundary of the tribal territories of Judah and Benjamin:

> ...then the boundary goes up by the valley of the son of Hinnom at the southern shoulder of the Jebusite (that is, Jerusalem); and the boundary goes up to the top of the mountain that lies over against the valley of Hinnom, on the west, at the northern end of the valley of Rephaim;... (Joshua 15:8; and see also 18:16).

Thus Ketef Hinnom is situated on the main road between Bethlehem, the town of David's birth, and his capital the City of David. The Book of Judges tells us of a man of the Tribe of Levi who made his way north from Bethlehem, with his concubine and servant, to his home in a remote part of the Hills of Ephraim. At sunset they found themselves at a crossroads, probably near Ketef Hinnom, where a

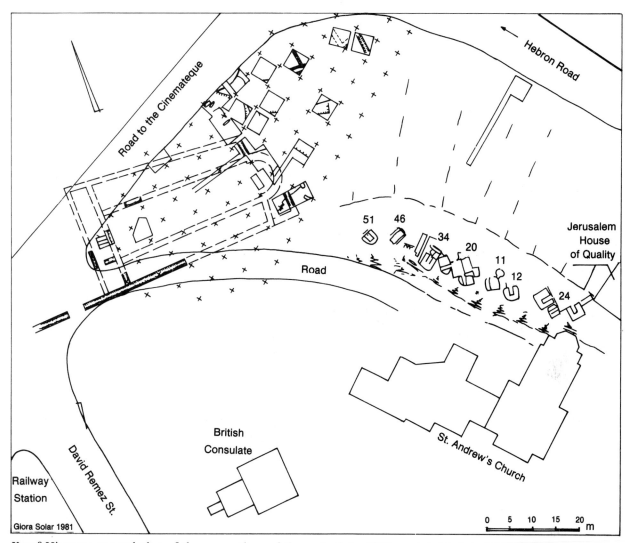

Ketef Hinnom: general plan of the excavations of the end of the 1980 season showing the area of the Byzantine-period church, the scarp with First Temple period burial caves, the series of trial excavations at various points on the hill, the buildings of Qasr el-Ghazzal (the British consulate), and St. Andrew's Church

track led east toward Jerusalem. The man and his servant deliberated whether to go into the city, which at that time was under Jebusite rule:

> But the man would not spend the night; he rose up and departed, and arrived opposite Jebus (that is, Jerusalem). He had with him a couple of saddled asses, and his concubine was with him. When they were near Jebus, the day was far spent, and the servant said to his master, "Come now, let us turn aside to this city of the Jebusites, and spend the night in it." And the master said to him, "We will not turn aside into the city of foreigners, who do not belong to the people of Israel; but we will pass on to Gibeah." (Judges 19:10–12)

The man decided not to enter Jerusalem but

to proceed to Gibeah (Tell el-Fûl) north of Jerusalem.

In the days of the Second Temple, Pompey selected the area of Ketef Hinnom for his encampment opposite the walls of Jerusalem, and from there attacked the city in 63 B.C.E. (*War* V, 506). In 70 C.E., during the First Jewish Revolt, Roman soldiers again appeared at Ketef Hinnom. The siege wall (*circumvallatio*) with which Titus surrounded Jerusalem to seal off the approaches to the city passed near this hill (*War* V, 506). Nearby, or perhaps on the hill proper, one of Titus's auxiliary camps was set up at the time of the siege of Jerusalem.

Almost no ancient remains were known on Ketef Hinnom before we excavated there.

The German scholar K. Galling had noted some destroyed burial caves there, and in a few limited salvage digs conducted during the British Mandate in the vicinity some ruins were uncovered. In 1940, when the roadway leading to the Scottish church was constructed, a salvage dig was carried out by S.A.S. Husseini. At the time, the finds were mainly of the Byzantine period but these excavations were not published. Surface surveys conducted by the present author in the early 1970s recorded many potsherds of the late Iron Age and of the Persian, Hellenistic, early and late Roman, Byzantine, Arab, and Ottoman periods. Visible above ground were also vestiges of structures and of burial caves. The strategic position of the site opposite the Old City walls raised the possibility that interesting remains of these periods might exist there. This, and the promising results of the surface surveys, led us to conduct excavations at this site.[1]

## Remains of the Ottoman Period

Before the Scottish church was built on the site in 1927, Ketef Hinnom was a bare, rocky knoll on property of the Greek Orthodox Patriarchate. The slopes and crest were

planted with olive and mulberry trees. Two major buildings stood on the hill: a fortified watchtower called Qasr el-Ghazzal (Gazelle Fortress) on C.W.M. Van de Velde's map of 1852, which today houses the British consulate, and a complex of warehouses, storage rooms and workshops of a silk factory built by the Greeks—today the Khan Theater. Qasr el-Ghazzal was built at some stage of Ottoman rule to control the southern approach to Jerusalem. Our excavations brought up many finds of that period: sections of a paved road, remains of agricultural terraces, small objects such as clay smoking-pipes typical of contemporary sites, an inscribed bronze seal, and a small metal medallion depicting the baptism of Jesus—probably lost by one of the Greek Orthodox orchard workers in the 19th century. When clearing one of the Iron Age

Ketef Hinnom: six rifles of the Ottoman period found on a late First Temple period rock-cut burial bench in burial Cave 20

[1] The excavations were conducted in 1975, 1979, 1980, 1988 and 1989 under the direction of the present writer on behalf of the Institute of Archaeology of Tel Aviv University and the Israel Exploration Society. The expedition was assisted, among others, by the Israel Antiquities Authority, the Yad Ha-Nadiv Foundation and the B'nai B'rith Organization. In charge of excavation areas and assistants were: D. Hamilton-Murray (1975); N. Mintz-Toyster, L. Sandler, G. Franz (1979–1989); B. Frankel and O. Zimhoni (1979); O. Dan, K. Walker, M. Huwari, L. Hurowitz, B.J. Wilson, G. Franz and O. Zimhoni (1980); G. Suleimani (1988–1989); S. Ortiz (1988–1989); M. Peterson-Suleimani (1989); Y. Rapuano (1989); M. Lev-Teller, Y. Ben-Naeh (1989). The work was carried out by groups of volunteers from Israel and abroad, students of the American Institute of Holy Land Studies and hired workers. Equipment was lent by the Lachish Expedition, courtesy of Prof. D. Ussishkin. Surveying was by R. Reich (1975); J. Dekel (1979); D. Smiley and G. Solar (1980); L. Ritmeyer (1988); W. Schleicher (1988–1989). Photographers were A. Hager, Z. Sagiv and A. Hai (1979); G. Franz and J. Weinberg (1980-1989). The finds were analyzed and restored in the laboratories of the Tel Aviv University Institute of Archaeology.

burial caves we saw that it had been blown up with explosives. The Turkish coins found there indicated that this had happened at the turn of the 19th century. Most likely, until its destruction, the ancient burial cave served the Turkish forces occupying the fortress as an arms and ammunition store. In the cave we found the remains of dozens of rifles, among them a double-barreled Winchester. Some of the rifles were found laid out on the rock-cut burial benches which had been occupied originally by deceased Jerusalemites at the end of the First Temple period. Together with the remains of numerous Turkish weapons were also pieces of small coffee cups, clay pipes, military uniform buttons and insignia, a bone die, horseshoes, decorative beads for horse and mule trappings, and a gold-nib pen.

## Remains of the Byzantine Period

Excavations at the northern part of Ketef Hinnom brought to light a large stone door-sill, a chamber with fine vaulting built of ashlars, as well as parts of walls and a mosaic pavement. All these belonged to a very large Byzantine church dating to the 5th–early 7th centuries C.E.: the length of the building—the nave and the narthex—is approximately 45 m. and it is 25 m. wide. The church was badly damaged during the Ottoman period when the building stones were removed for secondary use, perhaps for the construction of Qasr el-Ghazzal. Only the foundations of the church building were preserved under the floor level. Although our excavations revealed only parts of the church, we were able to reconstruct the plan of the building. We uncovered part of the narthex and a well-preserved vaulted crypt. Beneath the floor of the narthex we found three plastered burial places with fresco decorations on the walls depicting colorful, jewel-encrusted metal crosses. We also found sections of walls and parts of the stylobates and apse. The remains of the church decorations include multicolored and gilt glass tesserae of wall mosaics, and a section of a mosaic floor depicting a partridge pecking at grape clusters surrounded by vines and grape leaves, and the

Ketef Hinnom: fragment of mosaic floor uncovered in the southeastern part of the Byzantine church

hind part of a ram. There were also dozens of sawn-out, flat pieces of marble and other stone in various colors and forms: oblong bands, triangles, discs, shapes suggesting flower petals, squares, and pieces with serrated edges. All these apparently had been part of a splendid *opus sectile* floor.

In the excavations conducted in 1984 under the roadway leading to the Jerusalem Cinemathèque and Mount Zion, a large water cistern was uncovered which apparently belonged to the church complex. In the past, various remains had been found nearby that most probably also were part of the same group of buildings. During the British Mandate, building remains and a water cistern which may have been part of a monastery

Ketef Hinnom: colored stone tiling sawn into various shapes of *opus sectile* floor from the Byzantine church

were found west of Ketef Hinnom where today there is a gas station. We found Byzantine-period remains also in other parts of Ketef Hinnom. These include auxiliary buildings to the east of the church, plastered channels, a round stone-lined silo, and a quarry. Among objects of the period are oil-lamps decorated with crosses in relief, the cruciform handle of a clay oil-lamp, red bowls impressed with a cross in the center, a clay seal for stamping the Eucharist bread, a small bronze bell and a handsome earring of the same material. On the earring, in which a blue stone is mounted, is a dove surrounded by a wreath. We also found many coins, and among them a tiny bronze coin minted by King Ezana (330–358 C.E.) of the kingdom of Axum in Ethiopia. It is the first coin struck in that distant Christian country to have been found in a controlled excavation in Israel.[2] Presumably the coin was brought to Jerusalem by Christian pilgrims sometime in or after the 4th century C.E.

Byzantine literary sources mention many churches in Jerusalem and the question is whether the remains of our church can be identified with one of these. Apparently it is the Church of St. George Extramuros (outside the walls) or the Church of St. George outside the Tower of David listed among the churches of Jerusalem in which Christian clergy were slaughtered by the Sassanian Persians who conquered the city in 614 C.E. Before the discovery of the church at Ketef Hinnom, the Church of St. George had been ascribed to a location in the region of Binyanei Ha-'Uma, near the Hilton Hotel in the New City.[3] Now with the discovery of this large, previously unknown, church on Ketef Hinnom, we have a more suitable site for the Church of St. George Outside the Walls. Foremost among

the reasons for this identification is the mention of the name Georgius in one of the Byzantine-period inscriptions carved on the facades of burial caves in the rocky escarpments of the Hinnom Valley nearby. The Byzantine-period church on Ketef Hinnom was one of a series of churches built along the road between Jerusalem and Bethlehem. Other churches on this route are known also in the Abu Tor neighborhood and at Ramat Raḥel. The discovery of the Ketef Hinnom church is an important addition for the reconstruction of the historical topography of the environs of Jerusalem in the Byzantine period.

## Finds of the Late Roman Period

When digging under the remains of the Byzantine church, we found lentil-shaped conglomerations of black and dark-red burnt ash in the balks of our excavation grid. Later, we also uncovered several intact cooking pots that had been placed in the earth as though on purpose. These cooking pots contained remains of burnt, broken or calcinated bones, ash, and here and there also bits of small iron nails. In some cases, the bone material had compounded with the ash into a hard, white, calcified conglomerate. One of the cooking pots was surrounded by a circle of small stones and was covered by a deep bowl. These were undoubtedly remains of cremated bodies: the lenticular chunks of burnt ash came from the

[2] See: R. Barkay, "An Axumite Coin from Jerusalem," *INJ* 5 (1981): 57–59.

[3] This identification was based on an inscription found at the site mentioning Georgius. And see: M. Avi-Yonah, "The Asylum in Givat Ram," in: M. Avi-Yonah (ed.), *Encyclopaedia of Archaeological Excavations in the Holy Land* Vol. II (Jerusalem, 1976), pp. 615–616.

Ketef Hinnom: Roman-period cooking pot *in situ* containing remains of cremated human bones

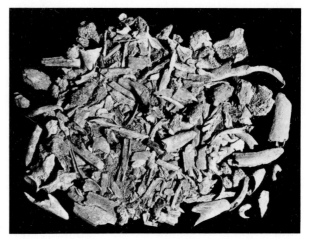

Ketef Hinnom: Roman-period cooking pot and its contents—remains of cremated human bones

funerary pyres in which the bodies were cremated, and the cooking pots were used as urns to store the ashes and bone fragments. Cooking pots of the Roman period containing cremated remains and bones were also discovered elsewhere in Jerusalem and its vicinity: near the Damascus Gate, and in different places along the northern wall of the Old City, as well as near Binyanei Ha-'Uma and at Ramat Raḥel. In these places were also found inscriptions and roof tiles stamped with logograms of the Roman Tenth "Fretensis" Legion. To the best of our knowledge, besides the soldiers of the Tenth Legion, no other population in the history of Jerusalem practiced cremation of their dead. Cremation burials of Roman soldiers were also discovered at the foot of Masada and in the Roman cemetery at Mampsis (Mamshit) in the Negev. Following our dig, cremation burials were also identified at Legio, the camp of the Sixth Legion near ancient Megiddo. The Tenth Legion was stationed in Jerusalem for a very long time, from the destruction of Jerusalem in 70 C.E. and until the reign of Diocletian at the end of the 3rd century C.E. The camp of the Tenth Legion was located in the western part of Jerusalem, near the Tower of David Citadel, just across the valley from Ketef Hinnom. In the Roman burial plot we uncovered about a dozen places of cremation pyres or cooking pots placed in the soil. It is the first burial ground discovered in Jerusalem that can be associated with the Tenth Legion encamped in the city.

In the northern part of the hill of Ketef Hinnom we uncovered three deep rock-cut shaft tombs. At the bottom of each deep, rectangular trench were final resting places for the dead. Around the upper edges, a recess was cut into the rock into which flat stone slabs were fitted to close the tomb. These slabs remained in place in one of the tombs. Inside we found a few funerary offerings—a small loop-shaped golden earring and round bracelets of dark glass dated to the late Roman period, apparently the 3d century C.E., and about a hundred tiny hobnails of Roman military boots.

Cave 34, one of the burial caves of the late First Temple period remained in use also during the late Roman period. We found there evidence of continuous use from the First Temple period through the Persian and Hellenistic periods, and into the early and late Roman periods. It was the first time that a burial cave in such long usage was discovered in Jerusalem. Those who used this cave in later periods did not remove the earlier remains but buried their dead on top of the existing accumulations. In this cave we found pottery, coins and various pieces of jewelry such as two handsome gold earrings, one of them with semiprecious stones mounted in it. Next to one of the skulls was a coin of the emperor Maximianus (286–305 C.E.) which apparently attests to the pagan custom of placing a coin in the mouth of the deceased.

It seems that in the late Roman period Ketef Hinnom served as burial ground for the residents of Mount Zion and the western parts of Jerusalem. In those days Mount Zion was outside the walls of Aelia Capitolina. According to literary evidence (the church-father Epiphanius and the anonymous Bordeaux Pilgrim) Jews and members of the first Judeo-Christian community lived on Mount Zion. Thus it seems possible that alongside the burial ground of the Tenth Legion, Ketef Hinnom also served as cemetery for the Jewish inhabitants on the opposite bank of the Hinnom Valley. Although we lack concrete evidence for identifying the people buried there, the differing funerary practices and the continuity of burial in caves that had undoubtedly been used for burial of Jews in the past, may point to these caves having served part of the Jewish population of Jerusalem at the later date as well.

## The Second Temple Period

In the northern part of Ketef Hinnom, at a lower level than the cremation tombs of the late Roman period, we discovered a group of tombs dating to the time between the end of the Second Temple period and the beginning of the 2nd century C.E. In some places we found cists dug into the ground, lined with rough stones and covered with stone slabs. Some of the graves we cleared did not contain any skeletal remains, possibly indicating that the bones were eventually gathered by family members of the deceased and deposited in ossuaries to be placed in family tombs elsewhere. In some of the tombs, and near them, we found several coins of the Roman procurators of the late Second Temple period—Coponius, Valerius Gratus and Pontius Pilate.

On levels similar to the latter, lower than the late Roman-period tombs, we found several assemblages of elegant, long-necked glass bottles, many of them intact. These candlestick-shaped bottles date to the mid–1st century C.E., but they were made and used also in the 2nd century—that is, after the destruction of Jerusalem by Titus.

Hundreds of rock-cut burial caves of the late Second Temple period have been found around Jerusalem. The custom of burying the

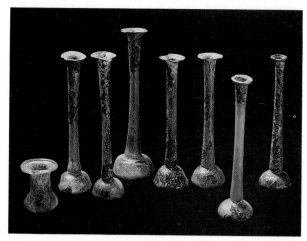

Ketef Hinnom: candlestick-shaped glass bottles of the 2nd century C.E. found next to burial caves at the northern part of excavation area

dead in rock-cut caves with burial niches (*kokhim*) and in stone ossuaries for secondary burial is well-known,[4] but this was the first instance of uncovering a cemetery with graves dug into the ground.

Some of the First Temple period burial caves continued in use in the days of the Second Temple. In Caves 34 and 51 there was clear evidence of use also during the time of the Hasmonean and Herodian dynasties. The evidence consisted chiefly of coins: Seleucid, Hasmonean, of King Herod Agrippa's reign, a Nabatean coin and coins of the First Jewish Revolt against Rome. In addition, we found many pottery vessels of the Second Temple period. In Chamber 25 (of Cave 24), which contained mainly remains of the late First Temple period and the Babylonian and the Persian periods, a small assemblage of vessels of the Second Temple period was found. This included small folded oil-lamps, spindle-shaped pottery bottles (*unguentaria*) of the 1st century B.C.E.

In Cave 34, which was hewn and first used in the days of the First Temple, and later until the late Roman period, were also many finds of the Hellenistic and early Roman periods. In addition to the coins, the finds of that period also included a headless lead figurine, about

[4] See: L.Y. Rahmani, "Ancient Jerusalem's Funerary Customs and Tombs," Part Three *BA* 45 (1982): 43–53; and idem., Part Four: 109–119.

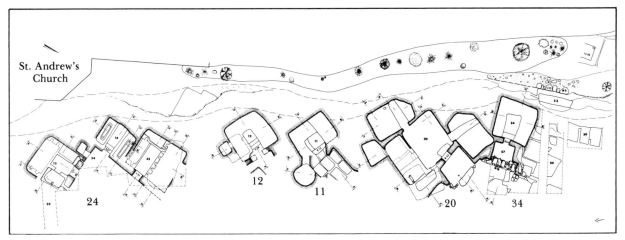

Ketef Hinnom: plan of the scarp with the series of late First Temple burial caves (1980 Season)

10 cm. high, of a nude male with his hands tied behind his back.

The Second Temple period finds are particularly rich and include an abundance of jewelry items—many of silver, beads of various shapes and colors, a seal of blue glass with a stylized figure of a horned animal, stone vessels and a large number of pottery items. Among the latter is an unused cooking pot with a small hole bored into its side. Such pierced pots were found also in the excavations south of the Temple Mount and in the Upper City excavations in the Jewish Quarter of Jerusalem. It has been suggested that these pots were made for the cooking of sacrificial meat by the priests, and once they had been used for that purpose were made unserviceable by having holes bored into them (cf. Leviticus 11:33).

At the eastern side of Ketef Hinnom we uncovered many parts of a large stone quarry of the Second Temple period. In several places the level of the quarry bed was about 4 m. below the surface. Dating was made possible by Second Temple period potsherds found on the lowest level, and by several tombs of the late Second Temple period at levels higher than the quarry bed.

## Burial Caves of the Late First Temple Period

The zenith of the Ketef Hinnom excavations was the discovery of seven burial caves dating to the end of the Judean monarchy (Iron Age II–III) that were cut into the rocky scarp on top of which the Scottish church is built. The apse of the church was positioned directly over Cave 24. All the caves were damaged in one way or another by later quarrying activity. The ceilings of most of them are missing, but in each cave there remains a small section of the ceiling that enabled us to ascertain the original height of the burial chambers. Parts of the facades and the ceilings of the caves had been quarried for building stone for the nearby Byzantine-period church, and other parts were apparently destroyed in the Ottoman period when a road to Bethlehem was built along the terrace in which the caves had been cut.

All the burial caves conform to the usual style of such tombs in the days of the last kings of Judah in Jerusalem and throughout the kingdom. Many parallels to the architectural details of these tombs have been found at other Judean sites, such as Lachish and its vicinity, Beth-Shemesh, Mizpah (Tell en-Nasbe), Khirbet e-Kôm in the Shefelah, and in Motza and Sova west of Jerusalem—as well as in ancient burial grounds of Jerusalem proper (see in this volume, pp. 107–127). The caves were made for the wealthy families of Jerusalem; several generations were buried there. The caves reflect the funerary practices typical of the First Temple period, which are also mentioned in biblical sources. All the caves

Ketef Hinnom: looking southwest to scarp with the burial caves of the time of the kings of Judah; above—St. Andrew's Church; below—Cave 20

the caves. This bench surface has a pillow along its entire length with six headrests recessed into it. This type of arrangement was only found at Ketef Hinnom; nothing like it is known in funerary architecture elsewhere in the country. However, rock-cut headrests exist in other burial caves of the First Temple period—Şova, Gibeon, Khirbet el-Kôm, Silwan, in burial caves of this period in the vicinity of the Damascus Gate and in several caves along the Hinnom Valley. To date we

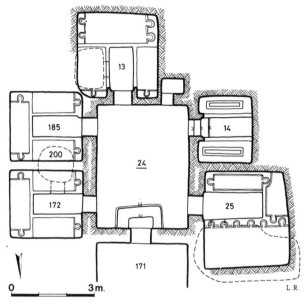

Ketef Hinnom: reconstructed plan of Burial Cave 24; note Chamber 25 and the outline plan of the repository beneath the bench with headrests

were hewn in the rockface during the same period, but each differs from the other in several details. They constitute a diversified sampling of funerary architecture of the late First Temple period. Except for Caves 20 and 24, all have one square chamber about 3 m. on each side. From the opening a step descends to the central space. The three sides facing the entrance are lined with rock-cut benches or shelves on which the corpses were laid. Raised headrests are cut at one end of the benches in Chambers 13 and 25 of Cave 24. On one of the benches in Chamber 13 there is room for four bodies: at each end of the bench, raised pillows are carved in the rock with two headrests and openings for the neck. The bodies were laid head-to-toe, in pairs. In Chamber 25 where similar headrests were found, the surface of one of the benches is wider than usual to permit laying the bodies at right angles to the central passage between the benches, and not parallel to it as on the benches in most of

Ketef Hinnom: view of Chamber 25 of Cave 24; note the wide bench with the row of six headrests; beneath this bench was the repository with all its original contents

94

know of over eighty carved headrests in burial caves of the time of the kingdom of Judah in Jerusalem; but the Ketef Hinnom arrangement is unique.

In six of the burial chambers, a hollow space is hewn out of the rock beneath one of the side benches. They appear in different shapes: two have the form of vertical boxes, one space is L-shaped, another oval, and two are rounded. These served as repositories for secondary burial, i.e., for the collected skeletal remains and funerary offerings removed from the benches. Some time after burial, the bones, pottery vessels and other funerary offerings left with the dead were added to the remains of previous generations of deceased family members in these repositories to make room for new bodies on the benches. Several biblical texts refer to this practice: "And all that generation also were gathered to their fathers;..." (Judges 2:10); and "...I will gather you to your fathers, and you shall be gathered to your grave in peace,..." (2 Kings 22:20). The sizes of the openings of the repositories are fairly similar, but the dimensions of the repository spaces vary from cave to cave. In four of the repositories a small step-like recess is carved in the rock below the opening to facilitate going down and coming out.

Cave 20 (the one used as a Turkish weapons and ammunition store) has a forecourt, an entrance hall and three burial chambers. One of these chambers is hewn out of the rock at a lower level than the others and its opening is carved beneath a wide bench in the entrance hall. Such a split-level cave is unique in First Temple period tomb architecture. At the joint of the walls and the ceiling of the entrance hall, an angular cornice was carved of which only a small part remains. Apparently this cornice imitates a decorative architectural detail in contemporary homes. Such cornices are known from tombs of the Judean aristocracy in Silwan Village, as in the Tomb of the Royal Steward and from the sumptuous burial caves in the grounds of the St. Étienne Monastery. This architectural element exists also in burial caves in Phrygia and Lydia in Asia Minor and in the royal cave tombs of the

Ketef Hinnom: in Cave 20 a small part of the ceiling of the entrance hall with the angular cornice is preserved

kingdom of Urartu (Ararat) at Van in eastern Turkey.

All the caves we uncovered at Ketef Hinnom are hewn in hard limestone. In some of them the stonecutting is of superior workmanship, with the rockface smoothed after the cutting. The burial cave planners took into account natural fissures and veins of harder rock that resulted from geological faults. In planning most of the caves the standard of measure was the royal (or long) Egyptian cubit (52.5 cm.). But the reed measure of 6 cubits (3.15 m.) mentioned in Ezekiel 41:8 ("...measured a full reed of six long cubits") was also used. In Cave 20 the planners used the short Egyptian cubit (45 cm.) as a standard. The simultaneous application of two different standards of measure is also known from the Bible: "...cubits of the old standard..." differing from the earlier cubit (2 Chronicles 3:3). Evidence for the use of two different standards of measure at the time of the monarchy was found also in the burial caves at St. Étienne's and in Iron Age buildings at Megiddo and Lachish.

## The Repository of Chamber 25 in Cave 24

As mentioned above, the burial caves dating to the First Temple period had been destroyed and plundered. The original contents were removed in antiquity mainly from those caves that continued in use in later periods. Nevertheless, in some of them we found remains of funerary offerings that had

Ketef Hinnom: isometric representation of Cave 24, looking south; at the right side can be seen the repository in Chamber 25 where the two silver scrolls were discovered

Ketef Hinnom: the repository of Chamber 25 at the time of excavation; the darker, lower part of the wall marks the level of the acummulation

escaped the notice of tomb robbers or of those who used the caves subsequently. In most cases, no First Temple period burials were found *in situ*, and only rarely did we come upon original objects—which appeared jumbled together with finds of later periods. In Chamber 25 of Cave 24, the one that has the bench with the row of six headrests, we were lucky to discover a repository with its original contents. The burial chamber proper was totally empty, but the repository hewn beneath the right-hand bench was spared the fate of most other repositories and burial chambers: the layer of rock from its ceiling had collapsed and hidden the contents of the repository from view. The repository was oval-shaped; 3.7 m. long, about 2 m. wide and 2.25 m. high. In all the history of archaeological research in Jerusalem, this is one of the very few First Temple repositories to be found with all its contents.[5] It contained over one thousand objects. According to P. Smith who studied the anthropological finds, there were remains of at least 95 individuals.

[5] A burial cave that had not been looted was discovered at the foot of Mount Zion, but it had no repository, and the bones and burial offering of the previous generation were placed on the floor between the benches.

**Metal, Bone, Ivory, Glass, and Stone Objects**
Besides the rich pottery finds, we found in the repository about forty iron arrowheads, and two bronze ones of the so-called Scytho-Iranian type introduced to this region by the Babylonian army that destroyed Jerusalem in 587/6 B.C.E. Some of the arrowhead tips were bent; apparently they were put into the repository after having been used in battle. Could it be that among those buried in the cave were persons killed fighting the Babylonians in the war that brought on the destruction of the First Temple?

Among the other metal objects in the repository were needles, kohl-sticks, and a fibula—all of bronze. There was also an iron knife and a chisel.

In the repository we also found many objects of bone and ivory. There were very many rectangular inlay pieces, some with incised concentric circles. Traces of red paint could be discerned on several of these. Most probably, these pieces were used to decorate wooden boxes which did not survive. Among the bone items is a group of elongated cylindrical handles with grooves incised around them. One side of the cylinder is slightly flattened and pierced by two rivet holes. These grooved handles were attached to bronze cooking pots or cauldrons for easier handling when hot. Possibly, the bronze vessels in the caves were removed for remelting and only the bone handles remained. Until now such handles were not found anywhere else in Israel, but a large assemblage of similar handles is known from excavations of the temple of Hera on the island of Samos, where some of the handles were still attached by means of rivets to the pots and cauldrons. Originally, metal rings were inserted through the cores of the handles for lifting the vessels.

Among the more important items in the repository is a small white-cream colored glass amphoriskos with light blue and yellow decoration. The amphoriskos was molded on a sand core the remains of which can still be seen inside. Fragments of another core-molded glass vessel of dark color were also collected there. Core-molded glass vessels were found in other locations on Ketef Hinnom in our excavations. In Cave 34 two small delicate, particularly beautiful, amphoriskoi stand out by their bright colors—dark blue, light blue and yellow (Pl. IId). Our excavations uncovered three such glass vessels that could be restored, plus fragments of another eight. Glass vessels molded on sand cores dating to the 7th–5th centuries B.C.E. are rare in archaeological excavations in Israel. Similar glass vessels were found in Gibeah (Tell el-Fûl) north of Jerusalem, in En-Gedi, 'Atlit, and Beth-Shean. Another glass object from Cave 34 is a pendant in the form of a grotesque head of a bearded male. It is also colored dark-

Ketef Hinnom: group of ivory and bone objects from the repository of Chamber 25; the small pieces of bone and ivory probably served as decorative inlay of wooden boxes; the two cylindrical items held metal ring handles that were riveted to the sides of metal cooking pots and cauldrons

Ketef Hinnom: two glass amphoriskoi from Cave 34 molded on sand cores; these handsome little vessels date to the 7th–5th centuries B.C.E.

blue, light-blue and yellow. Similar objects were discovered at various sites along the Mediterranean coast, including in Israel, but it is the first time that such items were found

97

Ketef Hinnom: glass pendant in the form of a grotesque head of a bearded male from Cave 34; the glass is light blue; the decoration is dark blue and yellow

in Jerusalem excavations.[6] These glass vessels were expensive luxury items for they were laboriously crafted before the invention of glass-blowing techniques made glass a common, widely distributed material (cf. Job 28:17).

Ketef Hinnom: oil-lamps, small decanters, perfume juglets, and various bottles *in situ* at the time of clearing the repository of Chamber 25

In the repository of Chamber 25 we also found a small alabaster cosmetic bowl and fragments of other alabaster vessels. Among the other stone objects were four pierced, dome-shaped spindle whorls made of different kinds of stone.

## The Pottery from the Repository

A total of 263 complete pottery vessels, and sherds of many more, were found in the repository of Chamber 25. We distinguished three groups of pottery. The first comprises pottery of the end of the Iron Age—the 7th and early 6th centuries B.C.E. These items are similar to the pottery found in Level II at Lachish and in sites that were devastated at the time of the conquest of Judah and Jerusalem by the Babylonians in 587/6 B.C.E. The second group is a continuation of the first and dates to the Babylonian and early Persian periods—6th and early 5th centuries B.C.E. The third group, of only eight items, is of the end of the 1st century B.C.E.

The pottery found in the repository is typical of burial caves, with no storage or cooking vessels. Most of the items are decanters and juglets, perfume bottles and oil-lamps. The number of pottery items predating the Babylonian conquest roughly equals that of the Babylonian and early Persian periods. There is a whole group of pottery typical of the Babylonian period (6th century B.C.E.) of which very few examples are known from excavations throughout Judah. In a few places, such as in Tomb 14 in Beth-Shemesh in the Judean foothills, and in Bethany east of Jerusalem, similar assemblages were encountered. The pottery most similar to ours is that found in a group of graves discovered at the beginning of the 20th century at Gibeah (Tell el-Fûl) north of Jerusalem, where archaeologists were later able to identify a Babylonian-period stratum with an assemblage of pottery.[7] The vessels of the Babylonian period found in the repository include also many carrot-shaped bottles, pottery bottles model-

[6] See: E. Stern, *Material Culture of the Land of the Bible in the Persian Period, 538–332 B.C.* (Warminster, 1973), pp. 151–153.

[7] See: P. Lapp (ed.), "The Third Campaign at Tell el-Fûl—The Excavations of 1964," *AASOR* XLV (1981): 81–101.

ed on alabastra with two tiny nipples on the upper body, flasks, pyxis-like vessels of black clay, oil-lamps with a flat base and decanters with lower parts that widen to a sack-like shape. Together with these vessels we discovered pottery typical of the late Judean monarchy such as wheel-burnished bowls, classic Judean decanters with horizontal burnishing, late Cypro-Phoenician bottles, a cup and saucer, as well as high, thick-stemmed oil-lamps. The main importance of the ceramic find from the repository is in the types dating to the period following the destruction of the Judean monarchy by the Babylonians but antedating the Persian period, that is, pottery of the time-span between Levels II and I at Lachish. Many of the pottery vessels of the Babylonian period reflect Assyrian influences of the 7th century B.C.E. and have some affinity to Ammonite pottery of the late Iron Age.

Among the most notable finds in the repository are fragments of the body and lid of a bathtub-shaped clay coffin having one rounded end and the other straight. To date, only a few such coffins have been found in Israel, mainly in the north: at Megiddo, Dothan, Tirza (the northern Tell el-Farʿah), in the region of Beth-Shean, and Shechem, and they are also known from Tell Mazar in the Jordan Valley and from Amman. Since parallels to these coffins have been found outside Israel—in Mesopotamia and northern Syria—it may reasonably be assumed that they reflect Assyrian burial practices. In the 19th century, Ch. Clermont-Ganneau reported finding a coffin of this type in Manaḥat (Malḥa) southwest of Jerusalem; and after the Six-Day War a similar coffin, apparently from the Shefelah (Judean foothills), was acquired in the antiquities market by the Hebrew Union College. Perhaps, during the Babylonian period, some of the inhabitants of Judah and Jerusalem adopted the Assyrian practice of burial in bathtub-shaped clay coffins.

**Jewelry from the Repository**
The jewelry found in the repository of Chamber 25 in Tomb 24 constitutes a rich

Ketef Hinnom: group of decanters from the repository of Chamber 25; some of the types are well-known from finds of the late monarchy in Judah (7th and early 6th centuries B.C.E.); other decanters, of more degenerate form, represent the Babylonian period that followed the conquest of Judah and Jerusalem (6th century B.C.E.)

treasure without precedent in Jerusalem digs. The Bible tells of the jewelry worn by the "daughters of Jerusalem" and of their resplendent dress:

> In that day the Lord will take away the finery of the anklets, the headbands, and the crescents; the pendants, the bracelets, and the scarfs; the headdresses, the armlets, the sashes, the perfume boxes, and the amulets; the signet rings, and nose rings;...(Isaiah 3:18–21)

Until the excavations at Ketef Hinnom, no representative collection of personal adornment worn by the women of Jerusalem during the monarchy had ever been found. The many pieces of jewelry found in the repository attest to the wealth of the family whose members were buried in this chamber, and to the prosperity of Jerusalem at the end of the First Temple period. In all, six gold and ninety-five silver jewelry items were found in the repository. In addition, there are many beads of various materials in a multitude of shapes and sizes. Part of the items are made of semiprecious or rare stones—agate, carnelian, rock crystal, and partly of more common materials such as glass, faience, seashell, etc. Among the abundance of beads, the most beautiful are colorful eye-beads in which were inserted a kind of faience or paste eyes. One of the most attractive pieces, showing Egyptian

Ketef Hinnom: faience amulet in the form of the Eye of Horus with a silver pupil, from the repository in Chamber 25

cultural influence, is a small faience amulet in the form of the eye of Horus, with the pupil made of silver.

The gold jewelry (Pl. IIe) included boat-shaped earrings, often called crescentic earrings. The body of these earrings consists of a small piece of folded gold sheet formed into a cushion filled with light-colored clay or paste and having a soldered-on spur in the form of an elongated loop. In the repository of Chamber 13 in this tomb, which had been partially robbed in antiquity, the looters overlooked a pair of small gold earrings of rare beauty. The earrings are formed to represent delicate, highly stylized lions' heads executed in filigree technique, that is, by soldering exceedingly thin, twisted gold wires together to form the designs. This pair of earrings was apparently influenced by the goldsmiths' art of the Achaemenid Persian kingdom and they probably date to 5th century B.C.E. The silver objects include, among other things, fifteen earrings, four finger-rings, about fifty beads, a pendant, a silver-framed scarab, and two flower-like ornaments. The most interesting of the silver jewelry items are the earrings, of

Ketef Hinnom: silver earrings and finger-rings from the repository in Chamber 25; the decoration on the earrings is in the granulation technique

unusual beauty, in a variety of designs and shapes. Many of them are given various forms by means of the granulation technique—soldering tiny silver balls together on the body of the earring—such as pyramids made of clusters of minuscule silver grains. Outstanding among the silver jewelry pieces is a signet ring depicting a lion-bodied, raptor-headed, winged griffin with a raised, curving tail.

In some of the earrings, the spur or hook is attached to the body of the earring by means of thin silver wire wound around it, a technique found in Phoenician and Syrian silver and gold jewelry. The rich find of jewelry from the repository is reminiscent of other jewelry items found in Iran and Assyria in the

Ketef Hinnom: silver signet ring showing a galloping griffin having a lion's body and crested bird's head, from the repository in Chamber 25; the ring is of the late First Temple period or of the Babylonian period (7th–6th centuries B.C.E.)

East, in Etruria, Sardinia, and Spain in the West, in the royal tombs of Urartu in the North, and in Syria, Jordan and Israel in the South. From the point of view of its character and various typological and technological details, this collection is particularly close to a hoard of jewelry from northern Transjordan kept today in the Ashmolean Museum at Oxford. The latter assemblage was apparently buried at the beginning of the 5th century B.C.E., but many of the items are probably of earlier date. The forms of several of the earrings from the repository are reminiscent of the earrings adorning the ears of Assyrian nobles in bas-reliefs of Sennacherib, the king of Assyria. It is not impossible, therefore, that such ornaments were also worn by men and not only by the "daughters of Jerusalem."

## A Hebrew Seal and an Archaic Coin

Among the finds in the repository of Chamber 25 of Tomb 24 is also a small, brown-colored limestone seal with the name "Paltah" engraved on it in ancient Hebrew script. Paltah is probably an abbreviated form of the theophoric name Pelatiah or Pelatyahu. In the City of David excavations the same name was found incised on a building stone from a

Ketef Hinnom: Hebrew seal of the end of the First Temple period with the word *paltah*; above—the seal; below—the impression

level destroyed by the Babylonians.[8] The inscription is engraved in the upper part of the seal face, while at the bottom is a palm branch. Between the inscription and the branch is a stylized lotus bud pattern that is common in Hebrew seals of the late monarchy.

The discovery of such seals in Jerusalem is of great significance for they are evidence of the administration and officialdom. Since Ch. Warren's excavations in 1867, thirteen seals (not counting seal impressions) have been found in Jerusalem dating to the First Temple period. Of these, about half come from the western edge of the Western Hill and from the burial caves in the Hinnom Valley. Because of their small size, seals are rarely found in archaeological excavations and mainly show up in the antiquities market.

Who was this Paltah whose name appears on the seal? Can it be that since his father's name (the patronymic) is not mentioned on the seal he was known to all?[9] Can he be the person mentioned in the Bible—Pelatiah the son of Benaiah—one of the "princes of the people" at the very end of the First Temple period (Ezekiel 11:1, 13)? We do not have enough information to answer any of these questions.

Another important find in the repository of Chamber 25 is a small, badly worn silver coin. This tiny coin, 11 mm. in diameter, must have been in circulation for a long time before ending up in the repository. On the obverse is a representation of a crab, and on the reverse is an incuse square, as in many of the Archaic Greek coins. The coin apparently originated in Kos, one of the smaller Aegean islands off

[8] See: Y. Shiloh, "Excavations in the City of David, I, 1978–1982," *Qedem* 19 (1984): 18.

[9] The names Eliphelet, Pelet, Palti, Pelatyahu, and Pelatiah were very common at the end of the monarchy and in the early Persian period. However, they were also known in both earlier and later times. In the Second Temple period cemetery at Jericho an inscribed bowl was found that mentions "Ishma'el bar (son of) Shim'on bar (son of) Palta [from] Jerusalem." And see: R. Hachlili, "A Jerusalem Family in Jericho," *BASOR* 230 (1978): 45–49.

the coast of Asia Minor. It was probably minted in the 6th century B.C.E., that is, at an early stage of the history of coinage, for the first coins were minted in Lydia sometime in the late 7th century B.C.E. Archaic Greek coins are very rare in excavations in Israel, and this coin may well be the oldest one discovered in this country. It undoubtedly attests to trade relations between Jerusalem and the Greek islands.

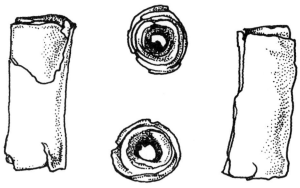

Ketef Hinnom: sheet-silver scroll found in the repository in Chamber 25; the rolled-up plaque was drawn from four sides before being unrolled

## Silver Plaques Inscribed with the Priestly Benediction

The fondest dream of every archaeologist working in Israel, and especially in Jerusalem, is to discover written material. One of the many surprises in the repository of Chamber 25 was a find of two small rolled up silver scrolls. As soon as we came upon them we suspected that they might contain inscriptions and gave them over to the Israel Museum laboratories for unrolling. After much hesitation and technical difficulties, the experts in the laboratory, J. Shenhav and D. Bigelajzen, succeeded in developing a special method for unrolling the brittle scrolls. The larger plaque measures 97 × 27 mm. and the smaller one 39 × 11 mm. An analysis of the metal revealed that the larger plaque was 99 percent pure silver (cf. Psalms 12:7; 1 Chronicles 29:4). The obverse sides of both plaques are covered with ancient Hebrew script, scratched in delicate, extremely shallow lines with a sharp instrument (a "pen of iron"? cf. Isaiah 8:1; Jeremiah 17:1). The scrolls seem to have been worn for a long time and as a result were in poor condition, especially at the two ends. It was extremely difficult to decipher the inscriptions on both of the small plaques.

On the longer Plaque I are remains of 18 lines of writing, out of the original 19. Originally there were 6–8 letters to each line, and altogether traces of 85 letters could be made out, of which 67 were clearly identified. The first word we deciphered was *yhwh*—the Tetragrammaton (the name of the Lord) sometimes rendered in English as Jehovah or Yahweh. This is the first time that the Tetragrammaton was found in Jerusalem, though

the word *yhwh* was discovered in other excavated sites.

In the smaller Plaque II there were 18 lines, of which the remains of 14 lines were preserved with, apparently, 5–7 letters to a line. Altogether 53 letters could be identified. In the second line the letters *nyhw* can be distinguished. These constitute the suffix of theophoric proper names common in Judah in the late First Temple period, such as Ḥananyahu, Netanyahu, Zephanyahu, or Benayahu. From the way the letters are formed, the two inscriptions can be dated to the late 7th century B.C.E.

Ketef Hinnom: Silver Plaque I between two glass plates after being unrolled

102

Inscribed, rolled up metal plaques with amuletic texts have been found in various excavations in the country, but all of these were of the late Roman and Byzantine periods. Small inscribed metal scrolls were also found in synagogues of the Byzantine period, such at Ma'on near Nirim, Ḥurvat Kanaf on the Golan Heights, and at Meroth in Galilee. But this is the first time that this kind of object could be dated to the end of the First Temple period. The contents, the character of the objects and their forms, as well as the parallels with finds of later periods, attest to their function as amulets.

To our surprise both silver plaques were inscribed with benediction formulas almost identical with the biblical Priestly Blessing (Numbers 6:24–26). On the larger Plaque I are the words:

| | |
|---|---|
| יְבָ֫רֶ | Bless |
| כְּ יהוה [וְ] | you YHWH [and |
| יִ]שְׁמְרֶ֫ךָ | |
| [יָ] | k]eep you (may) |
| אֵר יהוה | YHWH shine |
| [פָּ]נָ֫יו | |
| אֵלֶ֫י | [His f]ac[e upon |
| ךָ וִיחֻנֶּ֫ךָ] | you and be gracious to you]" |

The smaller Plaque II has a blessing formula of 10 words, while the biblical Priestly Benediction consists of 15 words. The text reads:

| | |
|---|---|
| יְבָרֶךְ | Bless you |
| יהוה וְ | YHWH and |
| [יִ]שְׁמְרֶךָ | keep you |
| יָאֵר \ \ יה | (may) shine \ \ YH |
| פָּנָיו \ \ | |
| [וֹ]ה | WH \ \ His face |
| [אֵל]יךָ וִ[י] | upon y[ou] and g |
| שֵׁם לְךָ שָׁ | ive you p |
| לֹ[ם] | ea[ce] |

These verses written in the 7th century B.C.E. are the oldest biblical verses known to date. They predate the canonization of the Bible and the sanctification of the crystallized Masoretic Hebrew text. They also predate the oldest biblical texts of the Dead Sea Scrolls by over three centuries. This discovery broadens the scope of the Priestly Benediction: in the

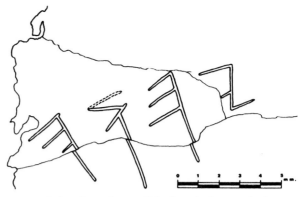

Enlarged drawing of part of the inscription on the larger silver plaque with the letters of the Tetragrammaton YHWH in ancient Hebrew script; the word is less than one centimeter long

Bible it is meant to be uttered orally, while here it is written; in the Bible it is intended for the whole congregation, while here it is in individual use. The Priestly Benediction found on our two little silver plaques has many implications for the study of the culture of the ancient Israelites and for the study of the biblical text. It is surprising to find here tombs of people who worshiped the God of Israel *yhwh*, while from the Bible we know that in this vicinity, in the Hinnom Valley, was the center of foreign cults in Jerusalem (cf. Jeremiah 19:2–6, 32–35).

Wearing inscribed objects was a common practice in ancient Israel, as stated in the Pentateuch: "And it shall be to you as a sign on your hand and as a memorial between your eyes..." (Exodus 13:9, and 16; compare also with Deuteronomy 6:8 and 11:18). Biblical wisdom literature mentions written aphorisms worn around the neck, tied to the fingers, or written on a plaque worn over the heart: "Bind them upon your heart always; tie them about your neck..." (Proverbs 6:21; and compare also with Proverbs 1:9; 3:3, 23; 7:3). The wearing of charms as jewelry is mentioned in Isaiah 3:20 among the ornaments worn by the women of Jerusalem: "the headdresses, the armlets...and the amulets." I have no doubt that the wearing of inscribed amulets was the origin of the *tefillin*—phylacteries. Before the form and contents of the phylacteries crystallized to their present traditional form, the "sign" and the "memory" that were worn on the hand and the forehead were objects like the small silver scrolls we found in

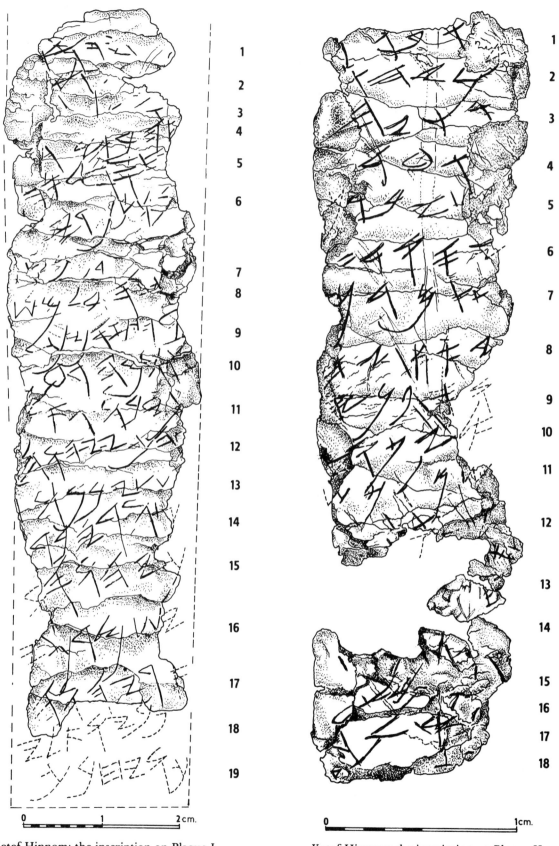

Ketef Hinnom: the inscription on Plaque I

Ketef Hinnom: the inscription on Plaque II

0       1       2 cm.

0                1cm.

104

our excavations. The name *tefillin* for inscribed objects worn on the body is only used in Aramaic translations of passages in the Pentateuch that mention the precept enjoining the wearing of the commands of the Lord. It is appropriate to mention here the interesting appearance of the words *tefilla zi ksaf* "phylactery of silver" in one of the Jewish Aramaic papyri from Edfu in Upper Egypt. The words appear in a document written around 300 B.C.E.[10] Perhaps the object the writer of this papyrus had in mind was of the kind we found at Ketef Hinnom.[11]

## Summary

The finds at Ketef Hinnom are among the richest ever uncovered in a Jerusalem excavation. The burial caves in the scarp of Ketef Hinnom were hewn during the 7th century B.C.E., in the days of the last kings of Judah. The caves are part of the great necropolis that encompassed Jerusalem on all sides. The western part of this necropolis extends along the entire length of the Hinnom Valley, from the upper reaches of the valley in the Mamilla neighborhood where tombs of the Israelite period were discovered about fifty years ago,[12] and more recently in the vicinity of the Jaffa Gate and the Sultan's Pool in the central section of the valley (see in this volume, pp. 107–118),[13] and to its lower reaches where it meets the Kidron Valley. In the survey conducted by R.A.S. Macalister at the beginning of the 20th century, burial caves of the end of the Judean monarchy were discovered in the scarp of the lower Hinnom Valley. These

caves were not dated correctly at the time since nothing remained of their original funerary furnishings and their layout, and Macalister had no information on firmly-dated caves for comparison. The western necropolis of Jerusalem now joins up with the burial ground of the monarchy's aristocracy in Silwan Village,[14] and with the northern necropolis north of the Damascus Gate (see in this volume, pp. 119–127).[15] The discovery of the western necropolis is a most important contribution to our picture of the city's limits at the end of the First Temple period. The hewing of rock-cut burial caves in Ketef Hinnom was a result of the expansion of the city to the far end of the Western Hill—today, the Jewish and Armenian quarters of the Old City and Mount Zion—from the 8th century B.C.E. on. Mapping the burial grounds provides us with a kind of external frame for determining the extent of the "great city" (Jeremiah 22:8) at the end of the First Temple period.

Burial in the cave tombs on Ketef Hinnom did not stop with the Babylonian conquest of Judah and Jerusalem in 587/6 B.C.E. Until now we had no concrete evidence regarding the continuity of the Jewish presence in Jerusalem under Babylonian rule. All the scholars dealing with the study of Jerusalem's history and archaeology concluded that the destruction of the city was absolute, and that it ceased to exist. But it does not make sense, to say the least, that burials continued where there was no community. The tombs of that period are family burials, and it stands to reason that the family members whose forefathers prepared the caves at the end of the First Temple period were the ones who continued to bury their dead there also after the destruction of the Temple. The prophet Jeremiah, who witnessed the cataclysmic events in Jerusalem, tells of a group of people from Shechem,

---

[10] See: A. Cowley, *Aramaic Papyri of the Fifth Century B.C.* (Oxford, 1923), pp. 191–199; No. 81, 1. 30.

[11] For further details on the Priestly Benediction inscriptions see: G. Barkay, "The Priestly Benediction on Silver Plaques from Ketef Hinnom in Jerusalem," *TA* 19 (1992): 139–192.

[12] See: R. Amiran, "Two Tombs in Jerusalem of the Period of the Kings of Judah," *Judah and Jerusalem* (Jerusalem, 1967), pp. 65–72 (Hebrew).

[13] See above, Note 5; and also: M. Broshi, G. Barkay and Sh. Gibson, "Two Burial Caves of the First Temple Period Near the Western City Wall of Jerusalem and their Purification in the Second Temple Period," *Cathedra* 28 (1983): 17–32 (Hebrew).

[14] D. Ussishkin, "The Necropolis from the Time of the Kingdom of Judah at Silwan, Jerusalem," *BA* 33 (1970): 34–46; *idem: The Village of Silwan, the Necropolis from the Period of the Judean Kingdom* (Jerusalem, 1993).

[15] See: G. Barkay and A. Kloner, "Jerusalem Tombs From the Days of the First Temple," *BAR* 12 (1986): 22–39.

Shiloh and Samaria who passed through Mizpah on their way when bringing offerings and incense to the Temple—after its destruction (Jeremiah 41:5). We may therefore assume that it was not only a small remnant of the population that remained in Jerusalem, but that certain ritual activities were still carried on in the ruined Temple. This attracted to Jerusalem also people from distant regions, and even from places outside the boundaries of Judah. During the Babylonian period there existed around Jerusalem an agricultural hinterland of vinedressers and plowmen (Jeremiah 39:10) who were not exiled and who continued to live in hamlets and unfortified villages in the region of Bethlehem south of Jerusalem and in the Land of Benjamin to the north.

The evidence from the burial caves of Ketef Hinnom points to continuous settlement in Jerusalem throughout the 6th century B.C.E. and until the return to Zion and the days of Persian overlordship. The accumulation of pottery and other objects of the Babylonian and the early Persian periods that we uncovered in our excavations are the only finds of those periods found in Jerusalem. Thus, they constitute an important contribution to our knowledge of the city's history.

The gamut of activities represented by the remains found at Ketef Hinnom is typical of sites at the fringes of a city. They include remains of agricultural cultivation and horticulture, roads and fortresses, traces of military units that camped there, quarries of different periods, a large early Christian church, interments and rock-hewn burial caves. In addition to the great variety of finds dating from the days of the First Temple to those of Ottoman rule, our excavations brought to light also individual items from periods that were not represented in the rich accumulation we have described above.

The wealth of finds at Ketef Hinnom that provided so many answers to questions regarding the historical topography of Jerusalem, adds to the mosaic of discoveries in recent years in the area near the Temple Mount, the City of David, the Jewish Quarter, the Citadel, and around the walls of the Old City.

Considering the important discoveries, Ketef Hinnom deserves to be preserved in a suitable manner and to be integrated in the attractive parks embracing the Old City of Jerusalem. It is a fine site for a superb archaeological park that will provide illuminating insights into the history of Jerusalem.

# A Burial Cave of the Late First Temple Period on the Slope of Mount Zion

## Amos Kloner and David Davis

When, in 1975, a retaining wall was dismantled on the western slope of Mount Zion below the southwest corner of the Old City walls, a First Temple burial ground was revealed.[1] Other First Temple period burials around ancient Jerusalem include the tombs in Mamilla Road whose pottery finds were published by R. Amiran, and the tombs uncovered by G. Barkay on the opposite slope of the Hinnom Valley (see in this volume, pp. 85–106). The Mount Zion burial caves are an important link in the late First Temple period necropolis that surrounded Jerusalem on all sides.

The burial caves are situated along a north-south line, in close proximity to each other. The southern caves show signs of later use, whereas the northern one, which is described below, was still sealed with the original blocking stone. These finds are particularly important because they were found undisturbed.

### The Cave Plan

The burial cave consists of two chambers hewn in the Turonian limestone. The

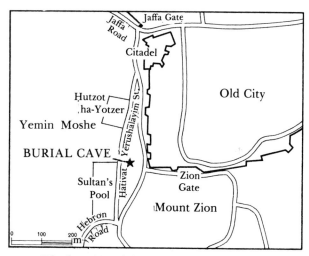

The location of the Mount Zion burial cave

entrance is on the west side through a 1.5 m.-wide recessed forecourt. A single step leads to the southernmost of the two burial chambers in the cave, which measures 3.1 × 2.5 m.; the 1.7 m.-high ceiling enabled the burial workers to stand upright. Along the southern and eastern walls, shelves are hewn into the rock at a height of approximately 90 cm. above floor level. A doorway, from floor to ceiling, connects the two chambers. The northern, inner chamber measures 2.4 × 2.3 m. Shelves are hewn along the three walls of this chamber, with a small niche above the eastern shelf. The cave walls are carelessly aligned and do not meet at right angles.

### The Method of Interment and the Remains

Five of the last interments were found *in situ* on the shelves of the first burial chamber. Two bodies were laid parallel to each other on the southern shelf, the head of one of them

[1] The cave was discovered on 23 January 1975, by Y. Gat and E. Lass. The excavation, which lasted one week, was conducted on behalf of the Department of Antiquities and Museums (today, the Israel Antiquities Authority), with the assistance of the Temple Mount Archaeological Excavations Expedition headed by B. Mazar. The excavation was directed by the authors, with the help of students and volunteers. The photographs of the cave were taken by A. Glick. The objects were photographed by T. Sagiv and Z. Radovan. Surveying was by D. Bahar. A section of the Lower Aqueduct which conveyed water from Solomon's Pools to ancient Jerusalem was also found nearby. As a result of these finds, the original plan to widen Ḥativat Yerushalayim Road to a four-lane roadway was revised. The remains will be incorporated into the National Park area surrounding the walls of the Old City.

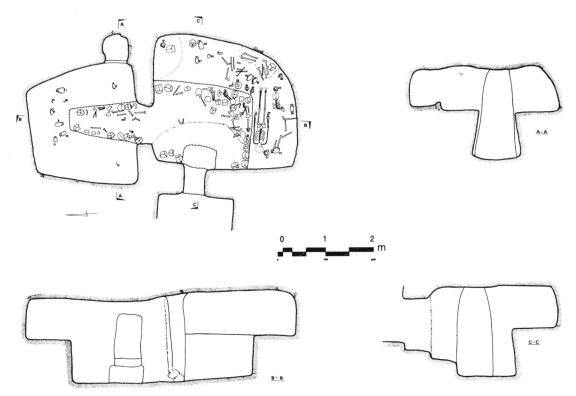

Plan and sections of the burial cave on the slope of Mount Zion

Mount Zion burial cave: general view from main burial chamber looking north, toward the inner burial chamber

facing east and that of the other, west. A lamp was placed at the head and a decanter at the feet of each of these two skeletons. Remains of three skeletons were found on the eastern shelf—two on the southern side and one on

the eastern side, with a lamp placed alongside each skull. Several other pottery vessels were found on the shelves of this chamber, primarily juglets and decanters.

In addition to these five skeletons, the cave contained many others that already in ancient times had been removed from their original resting places and carefully arranged on the floor. The skulls were concentrated at the base of the shelf, while the other skeletal parts were placed on the floor nearby. The bones covered the entire floor surface, except for the step at the entrance. Pottery, jewelry and other personal effects originally buried along with the deceased were placed nearby. Unlike the adjacent burial caves in the cemetery to the south, there are no repositories for the collection of bones in this cave. Juglets, decanter sherds, several small bones and a scaraboid seal made of bone (No. 12 on the plan) were the principal remains found on the shelves of the inner chamber. The seal, 14 mm. in diameter and 7 mm. thick, is pierced lengthwise and a fish with fins and tail is engraved on it. Above and below the fish are

Mount Zion burial cave: view toward the southwest corner of the main burial chamber

Mount Zion burial cave: selection of pottery of the 7th century B.C.E.

engraved the names of the owner and her father:

לחמיאהל בת מנחם (*lḥmy'hl bt mnḥm*)
"(belonging) to Ḥami'ahel, daughter of Menaḥem."

Mount Zion burial cave: seal of Ḥami'ahel daughter of Menaḥem and its imprint

Components of the name Ḥami'ahel appear in the Bible in names like Hamutal, Aholiab, Aholibah, and in the epigraphy of the First Temple period—Ḥami'eden, Aholiba'al and Aholimelekh. Menaḥem is a common biblical name.

The seal, like the pottery, was dated to the late 8th or 7th century B.C.E. The seal is of importance because it was found in a well defined archaeological context. Most known First Temple period seals were not found *in situ* but somehow reached the antiquities market or were found out of context.

Of note are two iron objects, apparently arrowheads (Nos. 81, 82), and an additional arrowhead was discovered while the earth fill on the cave floor was being sifted. These objects probably caused the death of interred individuals and remained on the shelf after their flesh had decomposed and the bones were removed. The pile of bones on the floor of the northern chamber contained a mortar of excellent workmanship in the shape of a small bowl made of polished quartz. This, like the seal, is a woman's article, which perhaps also belonged to Ḥami'ahel the daughter of Menaḥem.

In the niche in the eastern wall of the northern chamber were a few bones of an incomplete skeleton. The shelves, apparently prepared to receive more bodies, remained empty when the cave was no longer used.

## The Population Buried in the Caves[2]

According to the number of bones, the cave must have contained the remains of at least 43 people—26 adults and 17 juveniles and children. Two-thirds of the adults were males. The maximum age was 60 for males and 50 for females. The males were 1.57–1.67 m. tall, the females 1.44–1.52 m. The age distribution was as follows: 0–6 years old—30 percent; 6–16—18 percent; 16–30—10 percent; 30–40—22 percent; 40–50—14 percent; over 50—6 percent. It appears that this age distribution differs from that of other assemblages of skeletons of the same period in which the proportion of adults of over 40 is greater and that of children under 6 is smaller.

Anthropological analysis seems to indicate that at least some of the interred individuals were members of the same family. This supports the prevalent opinion that the First Temple period burial caves served as family sepulchers. There were signs of breaks in some long-bones and blows to some skulls which did not result in death. An examination of dental remains revealed that those interred in the cave, unlike most of the population of the Roman world, did not suffer from dental caries. Sixty percent of the children's skulls showed physiological changes in the eye sockets, an indication of some disease manifested as anemia. The occurrence of this pathological finding is higher (over 90 percent) in the skeletons of the Roman period discovered in caves in the Judean Desert.

Our burial cave was in use in the late 8th and 7th centuries B.C.E.—the time of Jerusalem's maximal expansion during the First Temple period. The discovery of a cemetery in this area is further evidence of the westward expansion of the city and is corroborated by the results of excavations in the Jewish Quarter of the Old City and on Mount Zion.

[2] The anthropological examination was carried out by B. Arensburg and Y. Rak of the Tel Aviv University Medical School. We thank them for permission to publish their preliminary conclusions here. For the final report, see B. Arensburg and Y. Rak, "Jewish Skeletal Remains from the Period of the Kings of Judaea," *PEQ* 117 (1985): 30–34.

# The Ancient Burial Ground in the Mamilla Neighborhood, Jerusalem

## Ronny Reich

One of the largest building projects in Jerusalem is currently being carried out in the Mamilla neighborhood, west of the Old City wall and the Jaffa Gate. The extensive area under development occupies the upper part of Wadi er-Rababi, which is identified with the biblical Hinnom Valley (Joshua 15:8, 18:16).

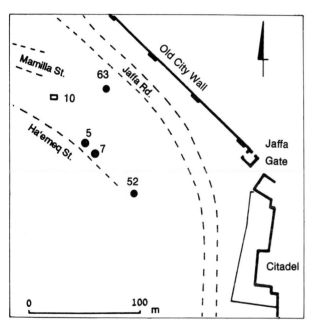

Map of the excavation area at the Mamilla burial ground showing locations of Iron Age Tombs 5, 7 and 52, Hellenistic Tomb 63, and Byzantine Burial Chapel 10

Because of its proximity to one of the most important hubs of historic Jerusalem, archaeological finds were anticipated and inspectors of the Israel Antiquities Authority closely supervised the site at all stages of the earthmoving and foundation work. And indeed, when ancient rock-cuttings came to light, construction on the parking lot planned for the

site was halted to permit excavation, in 1989–1992, of the antiquities there.[1]

### Tombs of the Iron Age

Many Iron Age tombs in various stages of preservation were uncovered, most of them damaged by quarrying in the Roman and Byzantine periods. Among the ten-odd best preserved tombs that were richest in contents, Tombs 5 and 7 were undisturbed. These are described below as representative examples of Iron Age burials in the area.

Both tombs are cut entirely in bedrock and share almost identical plans and architectural features. Tomb 7 has a small rock-cut forecourt, and both tombs have a 70 × 70 cm. typical square opening, sealed by a matching stone, that leads into a rectangular burial chamber with rock-cut shelves. In Tomb 7, which measures 2.9 × 2.65 m., are two wide shelves, one on each side of the central pit-like space. Tomb 5, measuring about 6 × 3.5 m., has three shelves, with the shelf opposite the entrance higher than the other two. In both tombs a roughly circular repository pit was cut into the rock behind the northeastern shelf, that is, on the right-hand side of the burial chamber. The repository of Tomb 5, below the rear shelf of the chamber, reached the considerable depth of 2.55 m.

Of the many tombs dating to the Iron Age that are known in Jerusalem, until now only

[1] The excavation was carried out by the Israel Antiquities Authority under the direction of the author, assisted by E. Shukron and Y. Billig. The dig was financed by the Karta Company. The excavations next to the Jaffa Gate proper may continue in the following years. (For other excavations in this area, see in this volume, pp. 299–305).

111

General view of the Mamilla excavation area, looking northeast

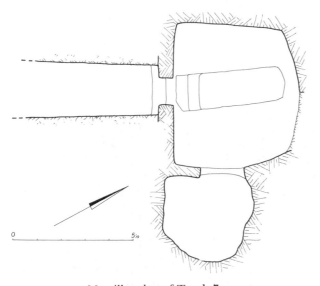

Mamilla: plan of Tomb 7

Mamilla: interior view of Tomb 7

six have been discovered with all their contents. Two of these were found in 1927 and 1935 in the Mamilla area and published in 1956 by R. Amiran.[2] Two tombs were excavated in 1937, north of and near the Damascus Gate, and published in 1976 by A. Mazar (see in this volume, pp. 123–125). In 1975, A. Kloner and D. Davis excavated a tomb close to the Jaffa Gate (see in this volume, pp. 107–110), and G. Barkay excavated another tombs at Ketef Hinnom in 1979–1980 (see in this

[2] R. Amiran, "The Necropolis of Jerusalem in the Time of the Monarchy," in: *Judah and Jerusalem* (Jerusalem, 1957), pp 65–72 (Hebrew).

Mamilla: general view of Iron Age Tomb 5, after removal of the collapsed ceiling material; note deep repository at left, and entrance opposite

volume, pp. 85–106). Of the two latter tombs only preliminary reports were published so far. Four of these six tombs are located in the western necropolis of Jerusalem on the slopes of the Hinnom Valley. Our excavations added at least ten more tombs that could be dated by their contents originally to the late Iron Age, tough some caves were in use also in the Babylonian and Persian periods.

The type of rock in which Tombs 5 and 7 are cut, as well as the level of workmanship, are of inferior quality compared with other contemporary tombs in Jerusalem. This, and the paucity of jewelry and the scarcity of objects other than pottery vessels found in the tombs, suggests that this part of the late Iron Age (8th–6th centuries B.C.E.) cemetery west of Jerusalem was used by the lower classes of society in that period.

The study of the contents of these tombs permits their precise dating. For example, two

Mamilla: Tomb 7 with sealing stone *in situ*

113

Mamilla: general view of Iron Age Tomb 52, after removal of the collapsed ceiling material

Mamilla, Tomb 5: black juglet

types of pottery vessels found in large numbers in the assemblages, and their distribution among and within each of the tombs, serve as good indicators. The black juglet is one of the most common pottery types in late Iron Age tombs, as has been attested in several Judean sites such as Lachish, Beth-Shemesh and Tel Ḥalif. It is, on the other hand, relatively scarce in the late Iron Age strata deposits at the same sites. The black juglet is the only type of vessel made in this technique, implying that it is a typical component of the sepulchral repertoire of late Iron Age tombs.

The distribution of the black juglet in the Mamilla tombs is noteworthy: 49 black juglets were recorded in Tomb 5 (29 percent of 169 pottery vessels); only 3 in Tomb 7 (4.5 percent of 67 items). No black juglets were found in the tomb excavated by Barkay at Ketef Hinnom in which a total of 263 pottery objects was found.

The distribution of the black juglets (37 out the 49 found in Tomb 5) in the deep repository of this tomb is also significant. Their higher density at the bottom of the repository and their diminishing presence higher up in the deposit clearly indicate that the use of the black juglet gradually declined during the 8th century B.C.E. In the second half of the 7th and in the early part of the 6th centuries B.C.E. this type of vessel no longer appears.

Another type of pottery vessel frequently found in these tombs is a brown clay juglet with a globular body, wide neck and outflaring rim. Such globular juglets were distri-

Mamilla: assemblage of Late Iron Age pottery vassels from Tombs 5 and 7

buted equally between both tombs: 16 items in Tomb 5 and 15 in Tomb 7. The distribution of these juglets in the deep repository of Tomb 5 did not show any distinct change in frequency within the upper part of the half-meter-high deposit, indicating that this type

Mamilla, Tomb 5: globular juglet

of vessel was in regular use throughout the 8th and 7th centuries B.C.E. However, it is totally absent in the assemblage of the Ketef Hinnom tomb, meaning probably that this type of juglet was no longer in use at the very end of the 7th or the very beginning of the 6th century B.C.E.

These and other indications point to Tomb 5 having been used in the 8th century B.C.E. and abandoned during the early part of the 7th century B.C.E. Tomb 7, on the other hand, began to be used contemporaneously with the final occupancy of Tomb 5, and was mainly in use during the 7th and the early 6th centuries B.C.E., until the destruction of Jerusalem in 587/6 B.C.E. The tomb excavated by Barkay at Ketef Hinnom came into use toward the very end of the 7th century B.C.E. and perhaps only at the beginning of the 6th century B.C.E.; the repertoire of its pottery vessels differs radically from that of Tomb 5, and significantly from Tomb 7.

115

## Burials and Tombs of the Second Temple Period

The discoveries in the Mamilla burial ground include interesting types of burials and tombs of the Second Temple period. Some of the Iron Age tombs show evidence of continued use throughout the Babylonian, Persian, and up to the late Hellenistic periods. Thus, unlike Tomb 7, Tomb 5 was reused in the Babylonian-early Persian period (the latter part of the 6th century B.C.E.). Several dozen pottery vessels and a few bronze objects—mirror, fibula, carrot-shaped bottle, etc.—occupy the upper part of the repository. In this respect Tomb 5 resembles the contemporary tomb from Ketef Hinnom. But unlike the latter, which had an uninterrupted sequence of use from the very late Iron Age through the Babylonian-early Persian periods, here the renewed use in the latter periods occurred after an interruption of about a century (most of the 7th and early 6th centuries B.C.E.).

Tomb 5 was ultimately used in the Hasmonean period, in the second half of the 2nd and probably the early part of the 1st century B.C.E. This is attested by the pottery and several coins which date no later than Alexander Jannaeus (103–76 B.C.E.). At that later period, the tomb was used in the same manner as in the late First Temple period and the Babylonian and Persian periods: burial on the shelves and the subsequent removal of the

bones and funerary objects into the repository. At that time the repository pit was already full. The last persons to use the tomb

Mamilla: Shaft Tomb 63 of the Hellenistic period

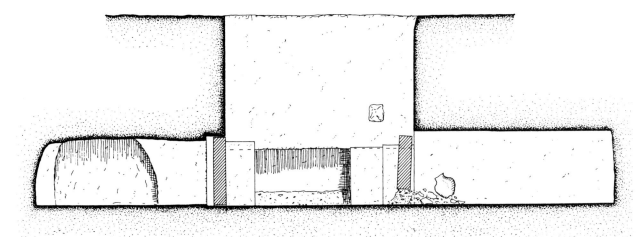

Mamilla: section of Shaft Tomb 63 of the Hellenistic period

left it in a tidy manner by moving all bones and objects into the pit. Almost no bones and only a few small objects (coins, rings, arrowheads, etc.) were found on the benches. The family probably purchased a new burial place elsewhere.

In addition, several types of tombs were discovered that are not characteristic of burials in Jerusalem of the Second Temple period. These include individual inhumations in small rock-cut troughs covered by stone slabs, of which about fifteen were excavated. In some of them Hasmonean coins and candlestick-shaped glass bottles of the 1st century C.E. were found. Another type consisted of vertical shaft tombs with one, two, or four long burial niches at the bottom. An iron strigil was found in one such tomb. These tombs which are dated by the pottery and coins to the 2nd century B.C.E. may well represent the common form of burial in Jerusalem before the introduction of the later *kokhim* (loculi) tomb; possibly, the *kokhim* type developed from these. Only a single burial cave with *kokhim* (without ossuaries) was found at the site. This type of tomb, which is the prevalent type in Jerusalem of the 1st century B.C.E. and the 1st century C.E.—especially on the ridge east and northeast of the city—is uncommon at the western side of the city, including the area of Mamilla.

## Byzantine Burial Chapel

An elongated burial cave (Tomb 10) serving as a crypt, and a small rectangular chapel measuring 5.45 × 2.9–3.45 m. in front of it, to the south, were found on the upper rock terrace near the remains of other rock-hewn tombs uncovered in the area. The crypt and chapel are dated to the Byzantine period. The eastern and northern walls of the chapel are preserved to their entire height while most of the southern and western walls including the entrance, which were built on the lower slope, have fallen off. A small apse is recessed into the eastern wall. Plaster-covered benches to accommodate about thirty people were added at a later stage along the inside walls—except

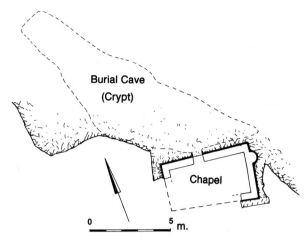

Mamilla: plan of the Byzantine chapel and burial cave (crypt)

the northern wall where the entrance to the crypt is located.

The walls of the chapel are covered with several layers of white plaster most of which show traces of paintings. The painted decoration on the outer layer of plaster is divided into panels by means of vertical and horizontal lines and the panels are painted with wavy lines to simulate colored marble.

The apse in the eastern wall is divided horizontally by means of a marble plate which served as an altar. In the upper part of the apse remain considerable parts of a fresco portraying an angel facing to the right and extending his hand forward. Although details of the angel's face are missing, the head with a round halo, a wing behind his back, and the yellow robe with black folds can still be clearly seen. The central part of the painting is missing but we may assume that it represented the figure of Mary. At the right side are parts (legs, knees?) of another figure. Presumably, the scene is an Annunciation. Next to the apse is a painted representation of a jewel-encrusted bronze cross.

The chapel is paved with rather coarse white mosaic tesserae. Opposite the apse are three crosses in the mosaic floor, and opposite the opening leading to the crypt are the fragmentary remains of a Greek inscription of four lines within a *tabula ansata*. By comparison with similar inscriptions known in Jerusalem and the vicinity, the text may be recon-

Mamilla: the north wall of the Bynzantine chapel with the opening leading to the crypt

structed to read: "For the redemption and salvation of those, God knows their names."

When removing one of the benches, several dozen clay oil-lamps of the simple type common in the Byzantine period were found. Some of the lamps had no traces of soot and it seems that they had never been used.

The burial cave (crypt) is divided in two by a built wall now in partly ruined state. Nevertheless, three small openings can be distinguished in it. The front of the cave—a sort of forecourt—is covered by accumulations of dark-colored soil. The space beyond the wall, about two-thirds of the entire cave, was full of human bones. Several oil-lamps of the type found in the chapel, and coins, the latest of which date to the time of the Byzantine emperor Phocas (602–610 C.E.), were also found in the same space.

It seems that the crypt and the chapel were in use some time during the very late Byzantine period. The burials in the crypt and the formula of the inscription suggest that this was a common burial place of persons whose identity and names were unknown. Perhaps this burial complex may be identified with one of the mass burials, possibly the one referred to as Mamilla in Christian documents relating to the massacres of Christians in Jerusalem during the Persian invasion in 614 C.E.

# The Northern Necropolis of Jerusalem during the First Temple Period

## Gabriel Barkay, Amos Kloner, Amihai Mazar

Archaeological remains of First Temple period Jerusalem are still quite scanty. This magnifies the importance of any new discovery contributing to our knowledge of the capital of Judah during the monarchy. Prior to the discoveries reported here, we knew of three groups of burial caves from First Temple period Jerusalem: 1) Two tombs that were discovered in Mamilla Street, west of the Jaffa Gate. Some of the pottery from these tombs has been published by R. Amiran.[1] 2) The magnificent necropolis in the village of Silwan, recently reexamined by D. Ussishkin, contains fifty burial caves of various types, including sumptuous single burials, as well as

Map of the northern necropolis of Jerusalem; numbers 1–7 indicate the locations of the tombs

rock-cut tombs bearing inscriptions, with above-ground architecture. This necropolis served the aristocracy of Judah. 3) Another group of caves that was dated to the Iron Age was excavated by B. Mazar on the eastern slopes of the Western Hill, west of the Temple Mount. A fourth group, consisting of several rock-cut tombs north of the Old City wall, may now be added to these three.

## Burial Caves in the Grounds of the St. Étienne Monastery

North of the Damascus Gate, in the grounds of the Dominican Monastery of St. Étienne which houses the École Biblique et Archéologique Française, are two large burial cave complexes. They were discovered in the 1880s around the time the monastery was built, and were subsequently excavated. These caves, which were at first attributed to the Second Temple period or even later, lack the most typical features—loculi (kokhim) and arcosolia—of Second Temple or Roman period burials in the Jerusalem area. On the other hand, they have certain typical architectural characteristics of burial caves elsewhere in Judah which have been dated to the end of the late Iron Age. A comprehensive survey was undertaken in the 1970s in order to complete our knowledge of these burial caves.[2]

---

[1] Additional burial caves belonging to the western cemetery of Jerusalem from the end of the First Temple period have been excavated more recently (see in this volume, pp. 85–118).

[2] The caves were surveyed with the kind permission of the late Père P. Benoit, director of the École Biblique. The survey was carried out by G. Barkay and A. Kloner on behalf of the Tel Aviv University Institute of Archaeology and the Department of Antiquities and Museums. The plans are the work of R. Reich and J. Dekel. The photographs are by A. Hai. For further details see: G. Barkay and A. Kloner, "Jerusalem Tombs from the Days of the First Temple," *BAR* 12/2 (1986): 22–39

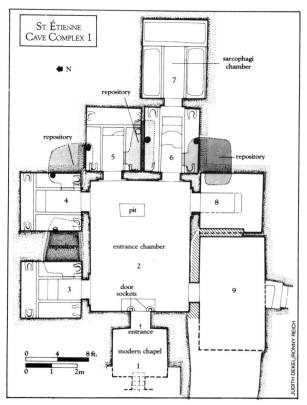

Plan of Cave Complex 1 of the Judean monarchy, near the Church of St. Étienne

## Cave Complex 1

This cave now forms part of a new burial chapel of the Dominican fathers—the last resting place of some of the most important explorers of Palestine, such as F.M. Abel, M.R. Savignac, L.H. Vincent, R.G. de Vaux and P. Benoit. The chapel altar stands in a small courtyard (1) adjoining the cave, and behind the modern altar is the entrance to the large central hall of the cave, one step down. The step is of a typical Assyrian form known from many Assyrian palaces. The hall, 5.25 × 4.2 m., has walls with shallow rectangular panels recessed in the rock-face. Along the joint of the walls and the ceiling is a rock-cut, decorative molded ovolo cornice. In the floor at the northeastern side of the central hall is a rock-cut pit, approximately 1 m. long. When the cave was first excavated in 1885, a decorated metal (bronze?) chest containing bones of animals and birds was found in the pit. The chest disappeared shortly after its discovery. Leading off the central hall are six burial

Central entrance hall of Cave Complex 1 at St. Étienne's: note recessed panels and cornices along joint of walls and ceiling (and see Pl. Ic)

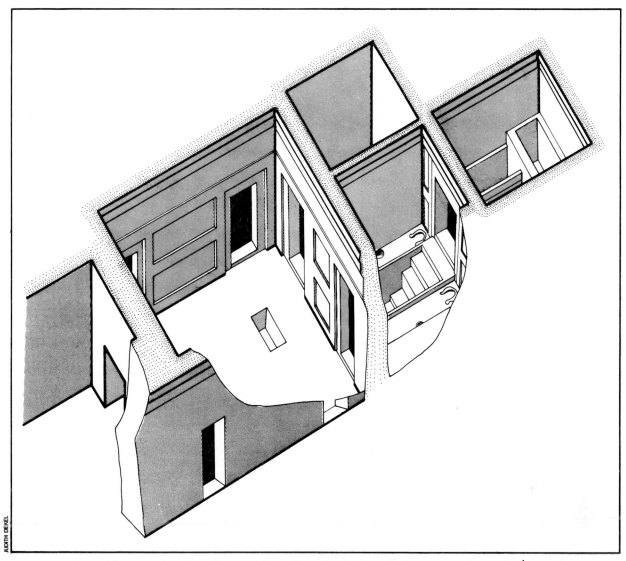

Isometric reconstruction of part of Cave Complex 1 of the Judean monarchy, at St. Étienne's

chambers: two each in the north, east and south. The entrances to these chambers are about 1.8 m. high, with shallow, rock-cut frames around their doorjambs and lintels. The ceiling is 2.3 m. above the floor. Three of the burial chambers (3–5) are identical in design: raised burial benches with low parapets are hewn in the three walls around a central passage; the doorway is in the fourth wall. One or two rock-cut steps lead to the benches opposite the entrances in these chambers. The two benches flanking the central passage have raised, rock-carved, horseshoe-shaped headrests, each with a depression to hold the head of the deceased. These headrests are at the ends of the benches nearest the entrance. The somewhat longer bench opposite the entrance has two headrests, one at either end.

Square openings cut in the wall beneath the right-hand bench of each burial chamber lead to irregularly shaped hollow cavities extending under the left-hand bench of the next chamber. They served as repositories for the bones and funerary offerings cleared from the benches to make room for further burials. Some of them still contained large quantities of bones and sometimes also an earth fill that was apparently not removed when the cave was first excavated. Some of the benches have a circular hole, about 20 cm. in diameter, opening into the repository below.

The southern opening in the eastern wall of the central entrance hall leads to a burial

Burial Chamber 6 in Cave Complex 1 at St. Étienne's: note headrest for deceased on the bench at left, and cornice at joint of walls and ceiling

St. Étienne's, Cave Complex 1: typical burial chamber, including bench with parapet, headrest, and opening to repository beneath the bench

chamber (6) of somewhat different plan from that of the others, containing only two benches, each with two headrests, one at each end. These benches are somewhat longer than those in the other chambers. A stepped cornice, similar to that in the central entrance hall, is hewn in the rock at the joint of the walls and the ceiling. Between the two benches are three rock-cut steps, ascending eastward to the entrance of yet another burial chamber (7). Rock-hewn sarcophagi line three walls of this inner chamber with recesses for the lids carved in their upper edges. In this chamber too, a cornice is hewn in the rock at the joint of the walls and the ceiling. It seems as though these rock-hewn sarcophagi were reserved for particularly important persons such as the father of the family owning the cave and his wives. There are no repositories for collected bones in this chamber.

The southern part of this cave complex was badly damaged during the Byzantine period when it was reused for burial.

## Cave Complex 2

This cave is north of Cave Complex 1, near the Church of St. Étienne. The original opening of the cave was in the south, but it is now blocked by recent masonry work. Access is by way of a modern staircase leading to a spacious central entrance hall measuring 7.19 × 4.5 m. Within the original entrance to the cave is a broad, rock-cut step, and the entrances to three burial chambers are hewn in the eastern wall of the central entrance hall. The southern chamber is larger than the others and also has an angular decorative cornice cut in the rock at the joint of the walls and the ceiling. This room contains no burial installations or benches. Openings in the western wall of the central entrance hall lead into three burial chambers. The openings in the northern wall afford access to only two chambers. The walls of the central entrance hall are smoothed and finely dressed, with much attention given to obtaining straight lines and right angles. Some of the burial chambers show clear signs of damage due to secondary use, probably during the Byzantine period when the Church of St. Stephen was built in the close vicinity of the cave. Today, the central entrance hall and some of the burial chambers are covered over by modern concrete vaulting.

The burial chambers in this burial cave, with the exception of the southeastern one, all have the same plan: each has three benches with low parapets and two steps leading up to the bench opposite the door. The chambers also contain repositories reached through openings usually cut in the wall beneath the right-hand bench. In this cave, too, there are rock-cut headrests for the deceased; here, however, they are shaped differently: the two

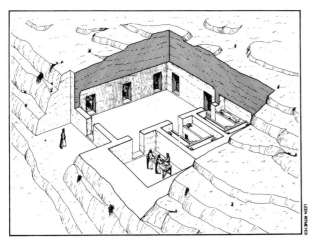

Isometric reconstruction of Cave Complex 2 of the
Judean monarchy, near the Church of St. Étienne

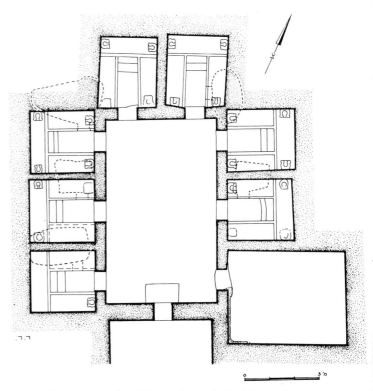

Plan of Cave Complex 2 from the period of the Judean
monarchy, near the Church of St. Étienne

St. Étienne's, Cave Complex 2: headrest in shape of
hairstyle of goddess Hathor

ends of the headrest flanking the neck opening flare outward in a kind of curl, recalling
the hairstyle or the wig of the Egyptian goddess Hathor.

The two burial caves in the grounds of St.
Étienne's are the largest ones known from the
period of the kingdom of Judah; each occupies an area of some 100 sq. m.

## Other Burial Caves North of the
## Old City Wall

An examination of files in the archives of the
British Mandatory Department of Antiquities
revealed a series of photographs of two burial
caves discovered in 1937 in the course of work
for a sewage network north of the Damascus
Gate, along the line of present-day Sultan
Suleiman Street. The plans and descriptions
of the caves were found subsequently, thus
enabling a complete study of these most interesting tombs which escaped the attention of
scholars dealing with Jerusalem of the First
Temple period.[3]

Cave 1 comprises a central chamber, surrounded by four burial chambers. The dimensions of the central chamber (C) are about 2.9
× 2.6 m. and its height approximately 1.5 m.
Cut into the floor in the southwest corner of
the central chamber is an oval repository pit
(H) measuring 70 × 50 cm. and about 80 cm.

[3]  The salvage excavation was conducted under the auspices
of the Department of Antiquities of the British Mandatory
Government. The file was located by A. Mazar, who also
published the tombs with the kind permission of the Department of Antiquities and Museums. For further details see: A.
Mazar, "Iron Age Burial Caves North of the Damascus Gate,
Jerusalem," *IEJ* 26 (1976): 1–8.

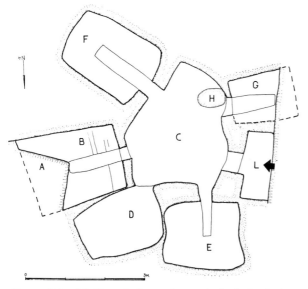

Plan of Burial Cave 1 from the period of the Judean monarchy discovered near Sultan Suleiman Street

Pottery from the period of the Judean monarchy *in situ* in Burial Cave 1 near Sultan Suleiman Street

deep. The entrance (L) to the cave complex was probably on the western side of the central chamber. Along the walls of the central chamber are openings to four burial chambers (B, E, F, G). Some have thresholds raised above the floor of the central chamber. Apparently each of the burial chambers had three benches around a sunken central passage. In the northeastern corner is a chamber (D) which served as a repository. It contained most of the finds found in this burial cave, including six oil-lamps, a decanter, a dipper juglet, two juglets and a trefoil-rimmed jug.

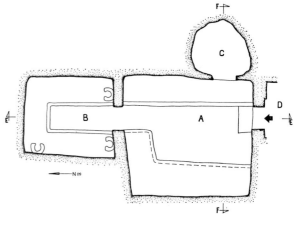

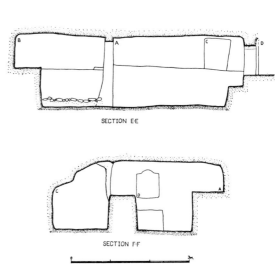

SECTION E-E

SECTION F-F

Plan and sections of Burial Cave 2 from the period of the Judean monarchy, discovered near Sultan Suleiman Street

Burial Cave 1 near Sultan Suleiman Street: interior, looking northwest

These vessels are all typical of ceramic assemblages unearthed at other sites in Judea dated to the 8th–7th centuries B.C.E.

Cave 2 comprises two chambers, the inner (B) accessible only through the first one (A). The entrance is on the south, through a small, ca. 60 × 55 cm., square opening, with a wide step leading down from the entrance into the first chamber which is of asymmetrical plan. To the right of the entrance, at the southeastern corner of the first chamber, is a repository pit (C). Along the eastern, western and northern walls of this chamber are benches with narrow, low parapets. The bench along the northern wall, up to the entrance to the inner chamber, is very short. The arrangement in this chamber is symmetrical, with benches along three sides. At either side of the entrance, on each of the southern ends of the benches, is a headrest, and there is also a rock-carved headrest at the western end of the northern bench. The headrests project about 10 cm. from the bench surfaces and are horseshoe-shaped. The stonecutting in the cave is of very good workmanship, with care taken to obtain straight lines and right angles. According to the excavators, the finds in Cave 2 were few; they included fragments of ceramic vessels and an alabaster bottle.

## Other Caves in the Vicinity

A few meters from the first cave in the grounds of St. Étienne's described above is the famous burial cave known as the Garden Tomb. This site was proposed by General Ch. Gordon in 1882 as the true sepulcher of Jesus.[4] The cave was hewn in the same rock formation and the same escarpment as the burial caves in the grounds of the Dominican monastery. It consists of two rock-hewn chambers; the entrance to the front chamber is from the south, and another opening, breached in its eastern wall, leads to the inner chamber. This cave underwent many transformations over the ages. It was reused during

[4] The cave was reexamined by G. Barkay. See: G. Barkay, "The Garden Tomb, Was Jesus Buried Here?" *BAR* 12/2 (1986): 40–57.

View of the interior of Room B in Burial Cave 2 near Sultan Suleiman Street; note benches with headrests

Benches in Room A in Burial Cave 2 discovered near Sultan Suleiman Street, looking north

Headrest in the north bench of Room B, near Sultan Suleiman Street

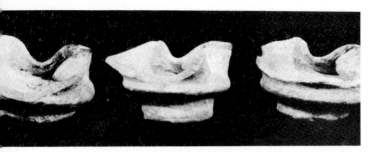

Oil-lamps from the period of the Judean monarchy, from the Garden Tomb

the Byzantine period and again in the Middle Ages for burial and various other purposes. It is therefore difficult to determine the original form of the burial installations. Most probably there was a single burial bench opposite the entrance to the front chamber, while the inner chamber contained three benches. Later, burial troughs were cut in the benches of the inner chamber and crosses with Christian monograms were painted in red on the walls.

The present owners of the site, The Garden Tomb Association, possess a collection of pottery originating most probably from excavations conducted in the area in front of the cave since 1873. It includes Medieval items, a few sherds of the Roman and Byzantine periods, three complete oil-lamps with thick bases, and a rim fragment from a large, deep, wheel-burnished bowl of the 7th century B.C.E. There is evidence that the assemblage included other items from the Iron Age—which were apparently thrown out when the cave was reused during the Byzantine period.

West of the Nablus Road, in the courtyard of a Franciscan White Sisters convent, is another burial cave, discovered and published by C.R. Conder in 1881.[5] In front of the cave is a small courtyard from which an entrance leads westward into the burial cave. The central entrance hall, 2.74 × 1.83 m., gives access to three burial chambers, located in the south, west, and north respectively. Benches

[5] C.R. Conder, "Jerusalem (Lieutenant Conder's Reports)," *PEFQS* 13 (1881): 201–205. The cave was reexamined by G. Barkay and A. Kloner.

about 65 cm. high are hewn in the walls of the three burial chambers. Each of two square openings in the corners of the central entrance hall opposite the entrance leads to a repository. The two windows cut in the facade of the cave, on either side of the entrance, attest to its secondary use.

The French scholar Ch. Clermont-Ganneau referred to a burial cave excavated in 1869 north of the Old City of Jerusalem. He mentioned a bench with a low parapet and a rock-cut headrest. Unfortunately, he published no plan or drawing of the cave and its exact location and form cannot now be determined.

Not far from Conder's cave, both west and east of the Nablus Road, are distinct remains of caves, some of which have been made into cisterns while others were destroyed in varying degrees by quarrying. For example, the openings of two caves, filled with debris, are discernible near the new bus station west of Nablus Road. Other caves, destroyed by quarrying, can be seen in the rocky scarp above the bus station.

The area north of the Old City served as a necropolis of which eight burial caves are known today, together with the remains of about seven other such caves that have suffered more extensive damage.

## Date of the Burial Caves

Burial caves with benches cut along three walls of each chamber are known from various sites in the kingdom of Judah: Beth-Shemesh, Mizpah, Lachish, Moẓa, etc. Benches with square openings beneath them leading to repositories for bones are also known from Iron Age sites such as Khirbet el-Kôm and Tel 'Eton in the southern Shefelah (Judean foothills). In both tombs ancient Hebrew inscriptions have been revealed. Burial caves of the last days of the Judean monarchy, discovered at Khirbet el-Kôm and near Amaẓiah (Ḥorvat Loya = Khirbet Beit-Lei) in the Shefelah, also feature a large central hall leading to several burial chambers. The decorative cornice in the cave near Amaẓiah cut in the rock at the joint of the walls and the ceiling recalls that in the Tomb of the Royal Steward at Silwan.

Similar cornices appear in many of the Silwan caves. Headrests with recesses for the deceased's heads have been found at Khirbet el-Kôm and Silwan, and at Lachish and the necropolis in the Hinnom Valley in Jerusalem. The dimensions of the chambers in some of the caves are based on the long Egyptian cubit of 52.5 cm. which was in common use during the Iron Age, as is the case in the burial caves at Silwan. Additional, if indirect, support for dating these caves to the period of the Judean monarchy is the fact that none of them have any of the typical features of Jewish tombs of the Second Temple period in Jerusalem. Further evidence is provided by the pottery of the 8th–7th centuries B.C.E. found *in situ* in some of the burial caves and probably also in front of the Garden Tomb.

## Conclusion

The spacious caves on the grounds of the Monastery of St. Étienne are the largest and most carefully hewn burial caves known to date from the time of the kingdom of Judah. Their sophisticated layout and meticulous stone-dressing rank them among the finest examples of sepulchral architecture from the period of the monarchy. Apart from their exceptional size, these caves have several features as yet not seen elsewhere, such as recessed wall-panels, rock-hewn sarcophagi, and headrests shaped like Hathor's hairstyle.

The northern necropolis of Jerusalem, dating to the end of the kingdom of Judah, is of great importance to our knowledge of the topography of ancient Jerusalem. It seems that this necropolis, together with others of the same period, encompassed the residential quarters of Jerusalem, which was then at the height of its development. Presumably, there were several residential areas outside the city walls between the northern wall discovered by N. Avigad and the northern necropolis; this is the most probable explanation for the names "Goah" and "hill Gareb" mentioned by Jeremiah (31:39). The location of the northern necropolis may be explained by the expansion of Jerusalem toward the Western Hill at the turn of the 8th century B.C.E., which made it necessary to establish new burial grounds west and north of the city, in addition to the Silwan necropolis. On the other hand, the necropolis on the eastern slopes of the Western Hill, west of the southwestern corner of the Temple Mount, seems not to have been in use at that time.

# The Inscribed Pomegranate from the "House of the Lord"

## Nahman Avigad

The Israel Museum recently made an outstanding acquisition—a thumb-sized pomegranate carved in ivory bearing a paleo-Hebrew inscription. It is believed to be the only archaeological find known so far which in all probability can be associated with the Temple in Jerusalem built by King Solomon. No wonder, then that this acquisition has stirred public interest and gained worldwide publicity (Pl. IIb).

At the same time, queries have been raised regarding the authenticity of the pomegranate and its inscription. These doubts derive primarily from lack of sufficient information, notwithstanding the initial publication of the object. It is therefore essential to comment on this important find in order to provide additional data and promote scholarly discussion of this fascinating object.

## The Recent History of the Pomegranate
The exact provenance of the ivory pomegranate is unknown. Although not found officially in a controlled excavation, it may yet have come from such an excavation conducted in Jerusalem, possibly stolen by the workman who discovered it and sold to an antiquities dealer. It could also be either an accidental find or booty from an illegal dig.

When in 1979 the French biblical scholar A. Lemaire visited an antiquities shop in the Old City of Jerusalem, he was given the opportunity to examine an ancient inscribed ivory object in the shape of a pomegranate. Lemaire, being familiar with Hebrew paleography, recognized the significance of the inscription. He took photographs of the object and published the result of his investi-

gation, first in a scholarly journal[1] and then in a popular magazine.[2]

The object was later purchased in Jerusalem by an unknown person who took it out of the country illegally. In 1988, it was offered anonymously for sale and subsequently acquired and brought back home to Jerusalem by the Israel Museum, with the generous help of an anonymous donor from Basel, Switzerland. Hence this unique relic was redeemed and returned to its place of origin.

## Description of the Pomegranate
The shape of the pomegranate is reminiscent of a very small, gracefully designed vase with a rounded body tapering towards its flat bottom, and with a narrow, tall neck. This neck terminates in the form of six lengthy petals, two of them broken. The shape of the pomegranate represents the fruit in its blossom stage of growth. This form is less frequently depicted in ancient art than the globular body of the ripe pomegranate with its crown of short petals.

The total height of the pomegranate is 43 mm. (1.68 in.) and the diameter of the body is 21 mm. (0.83 in.). The body is solid but has a hole 6.5 mm. in diameter and 15 mm. deep cut into its bottom. This hole most probably served to insert a rod, stick, or shaft. Around the shoulder of the object is an incised inscrip-

[1] A. Lemaire, "Une inscription paléo-hébraïque sur grenade en ivoire," RB 88 (1981): 236–239.

[2] Idem, "Probable Head of Priestly Scepter from Solomon's Temple Surfaces in Jerusalem," BAR 10/1 (1984): 24–29; see also H. Shanks, "Pomegranate, Sole Relic from Solomon's Temple, Smuggled out of Israel, Now Recovered," Moment 13 (1988): 36–43.

**The inscribed pomegranate**

**Complete portion of inscription**

**Damaged portion of inscription showing fragmentary letter *tav***

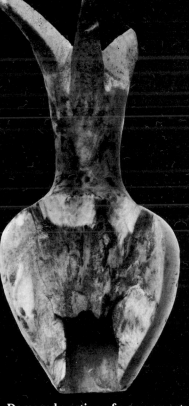

**Damaged portion of pomegranate**

129

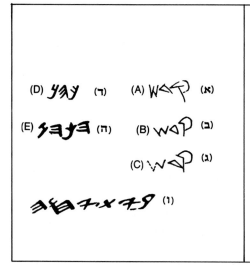

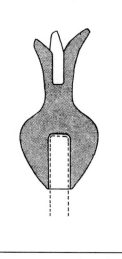

A. Inscription from Hazor; B. Inscription from Beer-sheba; C. Inscription from Arad; D, and E. Inscriptions on seals; F. Letter from Arad

Cross-section of pomegranate

Inscription: viewed from above

tion in paleo-Hebrew characters. A considerable part of the body is missing so that about one-third of the inscription is obliterated.

## The Inscription

The inscription is carefully engraved around the shoulder of the body in small but very clear letters. The preserved part of the inscription was deciphered by Lemaire:

לבי[. ...]ה קדש כהנם   *lby[. ...]h qdš khnm.*

Only the lower horizontal stroke of the *yod* and the upper horizontal stroke of the *he* remain. Lemaire proposed the restoration of the remaining letters and read the complete legend as follows:

לבי[ת יהו]ה קדש כהנם   *lby[t yhw]h qdš khnm:*
"Belonging to the Tem[ple of Yahw]eh, holy to the priests."

Dating the inscription on paleographic grounds to the late 8th century B.C.E., Lemaire advanced the hypothesis that the pomegranate had been used by the priests in the service of the Temple of Jerusalem.

## Discussion

Undoubtedly, the most important and enlightening aspect of the pomegranate is its inscription. Quite a number of pomegranates of this and other kinds have been found in excavations, but none of them were inscribed. Since the Israel Museum's acquisition of the pomegranate I have been able to reexamine the inscription and to elaborate on this matter. If my interpretation is correct, the inscription opens a new area of investigation in biblical archaeology related to the First Temple in Jerusalem.

First of all, the authenticity of the inscription must be established. Once this is proven, the genuineness of the pomegranate itself becomes self-evident. Lemaire, aware of the problem, had the inscription examined under a microscope. He found that traces of the ancient patina, which covered the surface of the pomegranate, could also be seen in the incisions of the letters. This is a recognized proof of the antiquity of such an inscription. The examination was later repeated in the chemistry laboratory of the Israel Museum, with the same results.

One might claim that forgers would be able to produce an artificial patina by chemical means. This may be true, but no forger in his right mind would deliberately break such an attractive item in a way that would efface the most important part of its inscription, or sell it

130

קדש ע[ן]לל ך ל[ל]ת א בלי[ ]קץ

Inscription presented in inverted order

for a low price in the Jerusalem flea market, as happened before the pomegranate reached the antiquities market in Switzerland.

In addition to the evidence of its patina, other distinctive features attest to the antiquity of the inscription. The edges of several of the lines making up the letters are rounded and worn, not sharp as they would be in new incisions. The broken surface of the object extends over its entire width and bears distinct signs of intentional destruction and of having been buried in the soil for many years.

Furthermore, a paleographic examination of the inscription leaves no doubt whatsoever concerning its genuineness. The script shows correct forms, well executed by a skilled engraver who was familiar with Hebrew writing. He successfully overcame the difficulty of engraving at such a small scale upon the uneven and rounded surface of the pomegranate's shoulder.

Lemaire compared the script with that of the Siloam Tunnel inscription and dated it accordingly to the late 8th century B.C.E. Actually, the pomegranate inscription is not of the elegant formal cursive script which characterizes the Siloam inscription. It diverges from the latter in various aspects, including the form of the letters *dalet*, *he*, and, especially, *mem*, with its irregular w-shaped head. Moreover, our inscription looks generally more archaic. Consequently, I am inclined to join F. M. Cross in dating it to the mid–8th century B.C.E.[3]

It is of interest to compare the word *qdš* with the same word incised on three contemporary bowls found in excavations at Hazor,[4] Beer-

sheba,[5] and Arad.[6] The script is extremely similar in all cases. The first two inscriptions are assigned to the second half of the 8th century B.C.E.; the third is unstratified. The word *khn* (*kohen*) was also found on two Hebrew seals, probably dating to the second half of the 8th century B.C.E.[7]

As mentioned above, Lemaire proposed a restoration of the broken part of the inscription by reading לבי[ת יהו]ה "belonging to the Temple of the Lord." If correct, then this restored part corroborates the interpretation of the inscription as associating the pomegranate with the Temple.

However, Lemaire provided no graphic evidence nor a detailed presentation of his arguments to prove the credibility of this restoration. Although the proposed restoration convinced some scholars, it left others in doubt and impelled them to look for an alternative text. My examination of the original inscription not only confirmed the proposed reading, but also added new evidence for its validity. I was able to discern traces of the last letter of the word *lbyt*, which Lemaire had apparently overlooked. As can be seen on the photograph, the upper two tips of the X-shaped letter *taw* are clearly visible to the left of the letters *lby*. The addition of this letter lends substantial weight to the proposed restoration of the inscription.

Having established the word *lbyt*, the restoration of the next word as *yhwh* becomes the more plausible. The name of no deity ending

[3] Lemaire, (see Note 2), p. 29, box.

[4] Y. Yadin, et al., *Hazor* III–V (Jerusalem, 1961), Pls. CCCLVII:4, CCCLVIII:4.

[5] Y. Aharoni, ed., *Beer Sheba*, I (Tel Aviv, 1973), p. 73, Pls. 42:4; 69:2.

[6] Y. Aharoni, *Arad Inscriptions* (Jerusalem, 1988), inscription no. 104.

[7] N. Avigad, "The Priests of Dor," *IEJ* 25 (1975): 101, Pl. 10:D; J. Elayi, "Le sceau de prêtre Hanan, fils de Hilqiyahu," *Semitica* 36 (1986): 45.

with *he* other than *yhwh* would fit here. In view of this, the only possible reading seems to be לבית [יהו]ה קדש כהנם *lbyt [yhw]h qdš khnm*. The inscription runs in a continuous circular line with irregular intervals between the individual letters and without separation marks between the words. The proposal to begin the inscription with the word *lbyt* is based upon the vacant space before (to the right of) that word.

In biblical Hebrew, the letter *lamed* preceding a noun without a verb means "of," "belonging to."[8] Hence לבית יהוה (*lbyt yhwh*) at the beginning of a sentence means: "belonging to the house of Yahweh." The phrase קדש כהנם (*qdš khnm*), to be pronounced *qodeš kohanim*, has met with much reservation and deserves a short comment. קדש (*Qodeš*), meaning "holiness," designates a thing set apart for worship; consecrated to the Lord; sacred donation for priests. Thus, for instance, the contents of the bowls from Hazor, Beersheba and Arad inscribed with the word קדש (*qdš*) (described above) were dedicated to priests or sanctuaries. *Qodeš kohanim* is but a regular shortened form of such phrases as: "...they are a holy portion for the priest"[9] (Numbers 6:20) or "...the holy portion of the land; it shall be for the priests, who minister in the sanctuary..." (Ezekiel 45:4). Compare similar formulations such as: "the things which David...had dedicated" (1 Kings 7:51; 2 Chronicles 5:1).

Accordingly, in our case, קדש כהנם should be translated "sacred donation for the priests." We should thus regard the pomegranate as a donation, an offering, to be used by the priests during their service in the Temple. With this in mind, the previously suggested order of the legend should be reversed to read:

קדש כהנם לבית [יהו]ה "sacred donation for the priests of (in) the house of Yahweh"

The vacant space, which after this amendment is located in the middle of the inscription and not at its beginning, may be ex-

plained by a miscalculation of space on the part of the engraver, or else by a need to skip a defect on the ivory surface, on the assumption that it is indeed an old defect. Such a change of the syntax would facilitate the interpretation of the legend.

In view of certain linguistic peculiarities in the Bible text, the expression לבית יהוה (*lbyt yhwh*) in this context may eventually be translated: "in the house of Yahweh"; compare הכהנים אשר לבית ה' "the priests of the house of the Lord" (Zechariah 7:3).

A few remarks on the term "house of Yahweh" are in place here. The question has been raised whether the term "house of Yahweh" or as rendered in English versions of the Bible, "house of the Lord," refers in our inscription to the Temple in Jerusalem, or rather to one of the sanctuaries outside of Jerusalem. Our knowledge of the latter is very limited. The Bible contains only indirect references to their existence at such places as Shiloh, Hebron, Bethlehem, Mizpah.[10] Some of them are referred to as "house of Yahweh" or "house of God."

However, all these sanctuaries were of an early date and preceded the Temple of Jerusalem. After Solomon's Temple became the central place of worship, no mention is made in the Bible of any other sanctuaries except that of Bethel, called the "king's sanctuary" (Amos 7:13). It served as the main temple of the northern kingdom of Israel and was the rival of the Temple in Jerusalem.

As for shrines or sanctuaries which continued to operate unlawfully, these could hardly be expected to be referred to as "houses of Yahweh." They were finally destroyed during Josiah's reform in 622 B.C.E. The only archaeological remains of what seems to be an Israelite temple dating to the monarchic period were uncovered at Arad.[11] This temple is not mentioned in the Bible. However, among

[8] Y. Yadin, "A Further Note on the *Lamed* in the Samaria Ostraca," *IEJ* 18 (1968): 50–51.

[9] Translation: *The Jewish Publication Society of America.*

[10] M. Haran, *Temples and Temple Service in Ancient Israel* (Oxford, 1978).

[11] Y. Aharoni, "The Israelite Sanctuary at Arad," in: D.N. Freedman and J.C. Greenfield (eds.), *New Directions in Biblical Archaeology*, (Garden City, 1969), pp. 25–39.

the many ostraca discovered in the fortress of Arad is a letter addressed to Elyashib in which he is informed about a certain person who "sits in the house of Yahweh."[12] It is generally believed that this letter was written in Jerusalem and that the term "house of Yahweh" refers to the Temple in Jerusalem, and not to the shrine at Arad, for two reasons: 1) Arad was the destination of the letter; thus the person and the temple must have been outside of Arad; 2) when the letter was written (late 7th or early 6th century B.C.E.) the shrine at Arad no longer existed: it was apparently destroyed during Josiah's reform.

It is beyond the scope of this article to discuss the term "house of Yahweh" in greater detail, but in view of the above arguments, it stands to reason that the pomegranate inscription indeed refers specifically to the Temple of Jerusalem.

The revised definition of the inscription as a dedicatory text is preferable to its interpretation as designating ownership. It seems unlikely that the Temple authorities would have taken the trouble of marking so laboriously the Temple's ownership on such a tiny and humble object, which at that time was not allotted any particular significance. Still it was important enough to serve as a donation on behalf of an anonymous donor.

How then, was our pomegranate used in the Temple? Does the Bible refer to the use of such objects by the priests? Does archaeological evidence provide any information in this respect? A short comparative study of the extant material may reveal some important data relevant to our subject.

The juicy pomegranate fruit with its multitudinous seeds was a popular symbol of fertility from earliest times.[13] It was widely used as a symbolic and decorative motif in sacred and secular art of various cultures throughout the ancient Near East. The pomegranate (*rimmon* in Hebrew) is frequently mentioned in the Bible and is counted among the seven kinds of

Tripod from Ugarit

Bronze pendants from Megiddo

Hebrew seal decorated with pomegranates

Coin depicting cluster of pomegranates, inscribed "Jerusalem the holy"

---

[12] Aharoni, (see Note 6), inscription No. 18.

[13] F. Muthmann, *Der Granatapfel, Symbol des Lebens in der alten Welt* (Bern, 1982).

fruit with which the country is blessed: "For the Lord your God is bringing you into a good land... a land of wheat and barley, of vines and fig trees and pomegranates, a land of olive trees and honey" (Deuteronomy 8:7–8). The *rimmon* became a favorite symbolic motif in Jewish art from its earliest beginnings and has remained so down to modern times.

In the sphere of art, ancient Israel was directly influenced by its Canaanite and Phoenician neighbors. In Israel, we meet the pomegranate motif, first of all, in the Temple of Solomon. The Bible describes the chains formed by hundreds of *rimmonim* which decorated the capitals of the two bronze columns, Yakhin and Boaz, in front of the entrance to the Temple (1 Kings 7:42; Jeremiah 52:23; 2 Chronicles 3:16).

This arrangement of pomegranates recalls the chains of pendants in the form of pomegranates which surround a Canaanite bronze cultic tripod from Ugarit, dating to the 13th century B.C.E.[14] We may assume that the Phoenicians who helped in building Solomon's Temple introduced this style of decoration in Jerusalem. Two isolated bronze pendants, of exactly the same kind as those at Ugarit, were found in Israelite Megiddo (8th century B.C.E.).[15] Moreover, they closely resemble the blossom shape of our ivory pomegranate.

The Bible also describes the robe of the high priest, which was embellished all along its hem with purple pomegranates and golden bells (Exodus 28:33–34). It makes no other mention of pomegranates in connection with priests which would attest to the purpose of our pomegranate. Divergent suggestions have been made in this respect: 1) it served as the head of the scepter-like object used by the high priest; 2) it was no more than a decorative piece on an altar, or a finial on a throne, a cultic box, or the like.

I am inclined to subscribe to the first alternative. According to our interpretation of the

inscription, the said object must have been used personally by the high priest during some ritual act performed in the Temple; otherwise it would not be termed קדש כהנם (*qodeš kohanim*). As the Bible refers neither to such a ritual object nor to such a ceremony, we must rely on external evidence.

The very use of pomegranate-shaped objects for cultic purposes is attested by a number of clay vessels in the form of globular pomegranates that were found in various excavations of sites in Israel dating to the 10th–8th centuries B.C.E. These are either individual vessels or attached to a bowl or to a *kernos* (a hollow ring base on which are mounted pomegranates and other objects believed to have been used for libation). The pomegranate also appears quite frequently as a decorative motif on Hebrew seals of the 8th–7th century B.C.E. Of a much later date is the cluster of pomegranates that adorns the Jewish *sheqel* coins of the 1st century C.E.

The closest and most significant parallel to our pomegranate comes from the British excavations at Lachish conducted in the 1930s.[16] In a Canaanite temple dating to the 13th century B.C.E., many cultic vessels and ritual artifacts were uncovered. Among them were two ivory scepters.[17] Each of these con-

---

[14] F.A. Schaeffer, "Les fouilles de Minet el-Beida et de Ras Shamra," *Syria* 10 (1929): Pl. 60:1.

[15] Y. Yadin, *Hazor: The Rediscovery of a Great Citadel of the Bible* (New York, 1975), p. 224 (bottom).

[16] O. Tufnell et al., *Lachish II, The Fosse Temple* (Oxford, 1940), p. 62; Pl. XX: 25–26.

[17] The term 'scepter' is arbitrary in this context, and the objects are not identified as such by the excavators. It is used here as a *terminus technicus* and does not attest a priori to the object's function. So far there is no evidence that objects of this specific kind were indeed used as scepters, and some of them certainly were not. The example cited by Lemaire of an Assyrian king holding such a scepter is vague and unconvincing. Looking for parallels among Assyrian reliefs one should not be misled by the globular head of the royal mace held by Assyrian kings as a symbol of their sovereignty, (see J.B. Pritchard, *The Ancient Near East in Pictures Relating to the Old Testament* [Princeton, 1954], Nos. 442, 576). It is therefore of special interest to point out a very rare example of a pomegranate scepter depicted on an Etruscan mirror of ca. 300 B.C.E. This long scepter is topped with a round pomegranate and held by Aphrodite (see Muthman, Note 13, p. 45, Fig. 32; with reference to E. Gerhard, *Etruskische Spiegel* I, 2 [1845], Taf. 181). This example, albeit late in date and of classic rather than Near Eastern origin, testifies to the use of pomegranate-headed scepters in ancient times.

sists of a pomegranate-shaped head mounted on a rod, 23 cm. long. One of the heads is very similar, both in shape and size, to our pomegranate; the other is more rounded and somewhat smaller. The function served by these scepters is unknown, but the very fact that such artifacts were used in the Temple is of the greatest importance for our attempt to verify the origin of the pomegranate now in the Israel Museum, its original shape, and presumed function. With the evidence from Lachish, we may be sure that such objects were used in temples and that our pomegranate was part of such a scepter. However, we are still left in the dark concerning its purpose.

It appears that these pomegranate scepter-heads are not as rare as one would expect, although ours remains the largest and most graceful among those unearthed so far. In Cyprus a number of such scepters were found in tombs also dating to the 13th century B.C.E. Their function is unknown. They are alternately termed spindles, pins for fastening clothing, and the like. Especially noteworthy are two ivory pins with heads in shape of a pomegranate which were found in Tomb 3 at Enkomi.[18] They are of the same length as those discovered at Lachish, while their shape is similar to that of our pomegranate. Other specimens, such as that from Kition, are of globular form.

Three ivory pomegranates, two of them attached to rods, were discovered in a Phoenician tomb at Akhziv north of Akko.[19] They are approximately contemporaneous with our pomegranate (8th century B.C.E.). A single scepter, smaller in size and made of bone, was uncovered in the excavations at Tel Seraʿ in the northwestern Negev.[20] It is dated to the

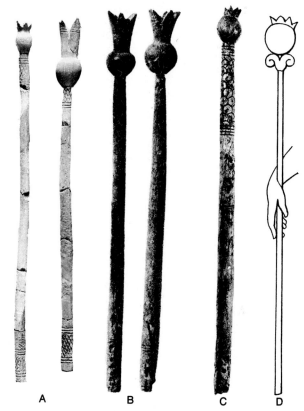

A. Two ivory scepters from Lachish; B. Two ivory scepters from Enkomi; C. Ivory scepter from Kition; D. Scepter depicted on an Etruscan mirror

late 7th–early 6th century B.C.E. We thus witness the continuation of a long tradition.

However, the most significant find of this kind after that of Lachish was made quite recently in a tomb a Tel Nami on the Mediterranean coast south of Haifa.[21] There, a skeleton was discovered with two pomegranate-headed scepters placed on top of it. Made of bronze, they measure approximately 30 cm. in length each. A group of exquisite bronze incense vessels was found in the same tomb, which dates to the 13th century B.C.E. The excavator, M. Artzy of Haifa University, suggested that the person interred in this tomb was a priest and that the tomb deposits represent cultic implements used by him when performing his office.

[18] E. Gjerstad et al., *The Swedish Cyprus Expedition*, II, *Plates* (Stockholm, 1935), Pl. LXXVIII: 240, 241; Idem, IV, Part 1D, L. and P. Åström, *The Late Cypriote Bronze Age* (Lund, 1972), pp. 550, 610, Fig. 74: 14; on specimen from Kition, see H. G. Buchholz and V. Karageorghis, *Prehistoric Greece and Cyprus* (New York, 1973), p. 479, No. 1746.

[19] Unpublished, courtesy of M. Prausnitz.

[20] Unpublished, courtesy of E. Oren.

[21] I am grateful to M. Artzy for an informative discussion and for her permission to make mention of the yet unpublished material.

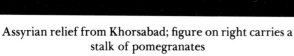

Assyrian relief from Khorsabad; figure on right carries a stalk of pomegranates

Assyrian relief from Nimrud

This find from Tel Nami, indicating that the pomegranate-headed scepters had probably belonged to a priest, supplements the find from Lachish, which, as we saw, attests to their being used in a temple. In combination, the two finds confirm the suggested interpretation of our inscribed pomegranate, namely: 1) that it was part of a pomegranate-headed scepter; 2) that it was destined for priests; 3) that it was used in a temple. What remains unanswered is the question of how and when this scepter was used in the Temple. It stands to reason that it served the priests during some kind of ceremony which took place in the Temple. The Bible, however, makes no mention of the use of such symbolic scepters in the Temple of Jerusalem.

Nonetheless, we must allow for the possibility that certain cultic rites performed in the Temple may have included some ceremonial customs of marginal significance and the use of auxiliary cultic utensils which are neither described nor listed in the Bible. Take, for instance, the offering of the first fruits—a major event in the cult of the Temple. The Bible relates very little about the ceremonies which were performed during these offerings, whereas the Mishnah (Bikkurim 3:2–8) describes the festive celebrations which took place at this event. They included processions of officiant fruit bearers proceeding to the Temple accompanied by music, songs, and prayers until the baskets containing the first fruits were handed over to the priests. The

136

choice first fruit belonged to the priests (Ezekiel 44:30).

Let us consider an imaginary scenario in which the priest, receiving baskets containing three kinds of fruit—grapes, figs, and pomegranates—and putting them on the altar, performed some kind of ritual act during which he made use of a symbolic pomegranate-headed scepter, such as the one discussed here. Such an assumption may perhaps find support in the customs of other ancient peoples. Of special interest are the sacral scenes depicted on the Assyrian wall reliefs of the 9th–8th century B.C.E. palaces of Nimrud, Nineveh, and Khorsabad. Some of these reliefs depict processions of offering-bearers with branches of pomegranates in their hands.[22] They are described as representing divinities, priests, and worshipers. One of the leading figures carries a kid to be offered up in one hand, and holds a stalk with pomegranates in the other. A second figure carries a goat and holds a stalk with lotus blossom. Both pomegranate and lotus have symbolic significance here, just as that which we would like to ascribe to our pomegranate scepter.

## Conclusions

My conclusions regarding the subject are two-fold—definitive and tentative. I am fully convinced of the genuineness of the ivory pomegranate, the authenticity of its inscription, and its use in a sacred service of the priests in the Temple of Yahweh. To this effect the epigraphic evidence alone, in my opinion, is absolutely convincing. It is also supported to some extent by archaeological evidence. The Temple of Yahweh was most probably that of Jerusalem. These conclusions determine the historical, religious, and cultural importance of our pomegranate.

I am less certain about the secondary issue: How, precisely, was the object used? The assumptions raised above are based on what appears to be relevant comparative material. At present, there is no decisive evidence from which final conclusions can be drawn regarding this particular point, but future finds or new suggestions may shed additional light on this intriguing ivory pomegranate whose inscription invests it with supreme significance.

[22] *Encyclopédie photographique de l'art. L'art de Mésopotamie ancienne au Musée du Louvre*, V (Paris, 1936), p. 307; R.D. Barnett and M. Falkner, *The Sculptures of Tiglath Pileser III (745–727 B.C.)* (London, 1962), Pls. CXXVI–CXXVII; E.A.W. Budge, *Assyrian Sculptures in the British Museum* (London, 1914), Pl. 48: 78.

# The "Governor of the City" Bulla

## Nahman Avigad

A large group of clay bullae bearing paleo-Hebrew inscriptions was recently discovered in Judah. The context in which these bullae were found is unknown. One particular bulla from this group differs considerably from the others and from the sizeable repertoire of known First Temple period Hebrew seals in both its iconographic and epigraphic attributes.[1]

The bulla, slightly broken at the top, presently measures 18 × 16 mm. The impression measures 13 × 11 mm. The clay is fired black. A deep groove surrounding the impression indicates that the seal-stone had been set into a metal bezel.

Within an oval linear frame is a depiction unique in the iconography of Hebrew seals;

two male figures, in pseudo-Assyrian style, stand opposite one another. Both are bearded, with long hair, and are dressed in long garments with a crosshatch pattern. The figure on the left is the larger of the two and holds in his outstretched left hand a bow and three arrows. The ends of the bow are curved outward like the head of a duck. His right hand rests on the hilt of a sword, shown jutting out behind his back. The lower end of what may be a quiver can be seen in the front, just below the waist.

The slightly smaller figure, on the right, stands at a somewhat higher level. His left hand hangs down at his side, while his right hand is raised toward the other figure in homage. He wears no sword. Beneath the feet

The bulla of the "Governor of the City", Sasson Collection; photo and drawing enlarged 4 × 1

[1] The bulla is in the possession of J. Sasson, Jerusalem, to whom I am greatly indebted for permission to publish it.

is a cartouche-like frame containing the inscription. The engraver of the seal appar-

138

ently considered the iconographic aspect more important than the script which is so small that it is difficult to read without magnification. Nevertheless, the script is very clear and the cartouche, a rare feature on Hebrew seals, serves to emphasize it.

The iconography of this bulla is influenced by Assyrian art. A king holding a bow and arrows (denoting power and rule) with one of his officials standing before him in a gesture of submission is a common motif in Assyrian reliefs and on cylinder-seals. However, the manner in which the smaller figure here holds out his hand, open toward the figure opposite, is Egyptian and can be seen in Phoenician art and elsewhere in the Near East. In Mesopotamian art the hand is held differently: open upward, or closed with one finger stretched out as a sign of blessing or prayer. The position of the hand and the schematic linear style of the figures point to the local workmanship of this seal.

The inscription within the cartouche is on a single line:

שר העד (sr hʿr) "governor of the city"

The minute script (the entire inscription is 4 mm. long), is very carefully executed. The defective orthography of the second word, which lacks the vowel *yod* may be compared to similar spellings of such words as אש for איש "man," and ים for יום "day," in the Siloam Tunnel inscription. In contrast, note the plene orthography of the same word, עיר "city," in the Lachish Letters (4:7) and in an Arad inscription (24:17).

This brief inscription, which omits the possessive *lamed* and lacks a personal name, comprises only the title of its owner, in sharp contrast to the personal seals of officials, which invariably bear the owner's name. Thus, we have before us a unique, anonymous, official seal that could have served successive office-holders bearing the title Governor of the City. The anonymous character of the seal leads us to assume that a city governor received the seal upon assumption of his office and that it was not made especially for him;

were this the case, it would surely have borne his name.

The title Governor of the City, otherwise unknown on seals, occurs in the Bible. It was held by senior officials appointed by the king who were responsible for a town. Several such title-bearers are noted in the Bible by name: "Zebul the ruler of the city" in the period of the Judges, (Judges 9:30); "Amon the governor of the city" of Samaria who imprisoned Micaiah the Prophet upon the order of King Ahab (1 Kings 22:26); "Maaseiah the governor of the city" who was ordered to repair the Temple by Josiah (2 Chronicles 34:8); and "Joshua the governor of the city" after whom a city gate was named, apparently in Jerusalem (2 Kings 23:8). One of the high officials of Samaria in the days of Jehu was entitled אשר על העיר "who was over the city," and another such personage אשר על הבית "who was over the house" but their names are not mentioned (2 Kings 10:5). It would seem that only capital cities were governed by officials bearing this title, and thus it is likely that our bulla was sealed by the governor of Jerusalem. One biblical passage has led some scholars to conclude that Jerusalem had more than one governor: "Then King Hezekiah rose early, assembled the שרי העיר ('governors of the city') and went up to the house of the Lord" (2 Chronicles 29:20). But the intention there seems to be not all those holding this title, but all the governors residing in Jerusalem.

As noted above, the seal with which our bulla was impressed is the first known Hebrew seal bearing this Assyrian motif. It is surprising that of all the officials' seals known to us, it is the seal of the governor of the city which bears a scene indicating royal authority—a most unexpected motif on an official seal in the kingdom of Judah.

The iconography of Hebrew seals generally employs Egyptian motifs common in Phoenician art. The use of an obviously Assyrian theme on the seal of a city governor may point to a period of Assyrian influence in Jerusalem. Such a time was the reign of Manasseh (698–642 B.C.E.), a loyal vassal of Assyria. But our assemblage contains sealings dating to the end of the 7th century B.C.E. However, if the archive to which these bullae belonged preserved documents over a period of several decades, we might ascribe the seal of the city governor to the mid–7th century B.C.E. and assume that it was used by a succession of officials, as suggested above.

The inscription is, of course, of particular interest. The title appears here for the first time on a seal and is, thus, a significant addition to the limited number of titles known from seals. Indeed, this bulla is the first vivid evidence of the administrative activities of an official responsible for a city administration in the days of the Judean monarchy. The city was surely the capital and not an outlying town of secondary importance, and the anonymous official was certainly the "mayor" of Jerusalem.

**Note.** After the preliminary publication of this bulla, G. Barkay published an identical one (see in this volume, pp. 141–144). No information as to its provenance was given, but, to the best of my knowledge, it cannot be associated with the present assemblage of bullae, for it was purchased from a Jerusalem antiquities dealer several years before the discovery of our bullae (by A. Kindler, Director of the Kadman Numismatic Museum of the Eretz-Israel Museum in Tel Aviv). I obtained a photograph of Barkay's bulla around the time of its acquisition. The two bullae were impressed from the same seal. This duplicate bulla is the clearer of the two in several aspects, such as the faces of the figures and the form of the bow. Barkay has interpreted the scene as a depiction of the installation ceremony of the seal's owner as governor of the city. He writes, *inter alia*: "Very likely, the ceremony was associated in some way with the owner of the seal, presumably the ritual in which the king vested his authority in the governor of the city. The latter reaches out to accept the bow and arrows from the king" (see below, p. 142). This interpretation, though very interesting, is entirely unconvincing. The scene is a standardized theme deriving from Assyrian reliefs, where the king holds a bow and arrows as symbols of his rule, while the other figure, a loyal official, raises his hand in submission—not to receive the weapons. We found no graphic expression in Mesopotamian art of a ceremony in which a king grants symbols of his authority to a subordinate. Moreover, if the owner of the seal had intended to commemorate such a ceremony on his seal, he would certainly have perpetuated his name as well.[2]

[2] See my response in "Responses and Notes: On 'A Second Bulla of a Sar Ha'ir'," *Qadmoniot* 41 (1978): 34 (Hebrew).

## Bibliography

Avigad, N., "The Governor of the City," *IEJ* 26 (1976): 178–182.
——— , *Hebrew Bullae from the Time of Jeremiah* (Jerusalem, 1986).
Barnett, R.D., *Assyrian Palace Reliefs* (London, 1960).
——— , *Sculptures from the North Palace of Ashurbanipal at Nineveh (668–631 B.C.)* (London, 1975).
Pritchard, J., *The Ancient Near East in Pictures* (Princeton, 1969).

# A Second "Governor of the City" Bulla

## Gabriel Barkay

By a rare coincidence, we are in the possession of two clay bullae of different provenance produced with the same seal. The bullae originally sealed two documents belonging to the same person. One bulla was published by N. Avigad (see in this volume, pp.138–140), the other is briefly described here.[1]

The bulla owes its survival to having been baked in a conflagration and has been restored from two fragments. Despite its small size the seal impression is very distinct and all the details of the design are clearly visible.

The bulla (actual size)

Indeed, some details are sharper on this bulla than on the other.

### Description of the Bulla

The impression depicts two standing bearded figures facing each other. The figure on the left is larger than the figure on the right. A cartouche under the right-hand figure contains the paleo-Hebrew inscription:

שר העיר (sr hʿr) "governor of the city."

Some details of the figures, both well exe-

cuted, deserve close scrutiny. Their beards are depicted with vertical lines, curled at the ends. Their hair also falls in straight, vertical lines, gathered together and curving upwards at the back of the neck. Both wear long robes, the fabric of which is represented by cross-hatching, partly of diagonal lines and partly of horizontal and vertical lines.

The figure on the left wears a sword on his left waist. His right hand rests on the hilt of the sword, which can be seen jutting out to the right of his waist. The slightly curved scabbard sticks out to his left. The sword is not shaped like the typical straight Assyrian sword, in which the scabbard ends in two lions' heads, giving it a cross-like shape; rather, it recalls the slightly curved swords wielded by the defenders of Lachish in the reliefs in Sennacherib's palace at Nineveh. Protruding to the right of the body under the belt is what looks like a small satchel—probably the end of the quiver hanging from the figure's left shoulder. The left hand holds out a triangular bow and a bundle of three arrows. The bow is slightly longer than the upper half of the body and its ends are curved in the shape of ducks' heads. The bowstring is on the side facing the figure itself. The form and relatively small size of the bow may indicate that it was a composite bow. Apart from the drawn bows of the defenders of Lachish depicted in the Assyrian Lachish relief, this is the only local bow known to us from the iconography of the period of the kingdom of Judah.

The right-hand figure holds out his right hand, almost touching the bundle of arrows in the left-hand figure's hand, as if reaching out to grasp the bow and the arrows.

[1] The bulla is now in the possession of the Kadman Numismatic Museum at the Eretz-Israel Museum, Tel Aviv. I am most grateful to Dr. A. Kindler for his permission to publish it here. The drawings of the bulla and of kings holding bow and arrows are by R. Barkay.

141

The Governor of the City bulla from the Kadman Museum: photograph of both sides and facsimile; note imprints of the papyrus fibers and the string that tied the document

## Discussion

Monumental reliefs from the Assyrian empire often feature the figure of a god or a king holding a bow and arrows, with worshipers or courtiers standing before him. The bow usually rests on the ground, with the bowstring turned away from the holder rather than toward him. Moreover, the king is generally shown holding the bow in one hand and the arrows—mostly two, not three—in the other. Depictions of a king holding a bow and a bundle of three arrows also appear on Phoenician metal bowls contemporary with the late Judean monarchy. Though discovered in Cyprus or Italy, these bowls, which are undoubtedly of Phoenician origin, reflect a combined Egyptian-Assyrian influence: the king himself is drawn in Egyptian style, but is accompanied by winged demons after the Assyrian manner.

Analysis of the parallels clearly shows that the larger left-hand figure in our bulla, obviously the dominant one, represents a king, most likely the king of Judah. The smaller right-hand figure, under which the inscription is engraved, probably represents the governor of the city. If the seal was cut by a local artisan he was certainly acquainted with Assyrian glyptic and monumental art. Although he created a scene similar in some details to those typical of Assyrian art, he gave it a somewhat different meaning, perhaps indicating some ceremonial occasion at the royal court of Judah. Very likely, the ceremony was associated in some way with the owner of the seal, presumably the ritual in which the king vested his authority in the governor of the city. The latter reaches out to accept the bow and arrows from the king.

In investiture scenes the senior figure hands over some symbolic object (a weapon, staff, scepter, orb, etc.) to the subordinate official. We have a detailed account of such a ceremony in the Bible with reference to Eliakim the son of Hilkiah, who was to replace Shebnah the steward "who is over the household" (Isaiah 22:15–22). The ceremony as described in this passage includes some symbolic and

A king depicted holding bow and arrows: left—from the Governor of the City bulla; center—from a Phoenician metal bowl from Cyprus; right—figure of Shalmaneser III of Assyria

142

ceremonial details, such as clothing the official in a robe and girdle, declaring: "I will commit...authority to his hand" and placing the key of the House of David on his shoulder. In the course of the ceremony, objects serving as symbols of authority were entrusted to the official. According to R. De Vaux, at a certain stage in the coronation of the kings of Judah the officials came to greet the new king; after the coronation they returned the symbols of authority to the king, who then renewed their authority over the kingdom in a symbolic ceremony. In the story of the coronation of Joash we read of "the spears and shields that had been King David's" conferred by the new king on the "captains" during the coronation ceremony as a sign of their authority (2 Kings 11:10; 2 Chronicles 23:9).

The Hebrew term for conferral of authority is מלוי יד (mlwy yd), literally: "filling of the hand."[2] This expression undoubtedly originated in the placing of a symbolic object in the hand of the person being given authority. It is particularly common in reference to priestly consecration ceremonies, the details of which are similar to the above-mentioned ceremony of the appointment of Eliakim the son of Hilkiah (Exodus 28:40–41; 29:8–9). Regarding David (1 Kings 8:15; 2 Chronicles 6:4), the original Hebrew text uses the expression "filling the hand" to denote giving of authority; and of Jehu the Bible relates that when he crowned himself and slew Joram the son of Ahab, he מלא ידו בקשת (ml' ydw bqšt), literally: "filled his hand with the bow" (2 Kings 9:24). A parallel phrase appears frequently in Akkadian: mullû[ana] qâtâ, to denote the delivery of an object in a ceremonial transfer of office. Thus, the stele of Hammurabi tells us that "the gods filled his hand with their scepter." The phrase thus seems to have been a common idiomatic expression in the ancient Near East, which probably derived from a ceremonial scene similar to that depicted in our bulla. Assyrian iconography and various

literary borrowings in the Bible seem to indicate that the bow was a symbol of power, so that the act of giving a bow symbolized delegation of the ruler's authority. Investiture scenes were a popular subject in the officially-inspired art of diverse civilizations in later periods as well.

The earliest biblical use of the title Governor of the City occurs in the story of Zebul, Abimelech's lieutenant in Shechem (Judges 9:28–30). It follows that the title was not necessarily confined to the kingdoms of Israel and Judah but was used before the establishment of the monarchy. Presumably the term is simply a Hebrew version of the ancient Ugaritic and Canaanite rb-qrt, known from the Ugarit documents of the 14th–13th centuries B.C.E. Quite possibly, therefore, the office and title of the governor of the city were part of the ancient Canaanite substratum in the administrative system at the time of the monarchy, as suggested by A. Alt.

Three incised inscriptions of the particle לשרער lsr'r were discovered on pottery vessels found at Kuntilat 'Ajrud, at the Sinai side of the Negev highlands.[3] There, too, the reference may be to an official title now known to us both from the Bible and from these two bullae.

The anonymity of the seal's owner and of the city which he governed is unusual in the context of Hebrew seals and seal impressions. This is the only parallel to the lmlk, or royal seals which are also inscribed with a title but without a personal name. Perhaps it was felt that because the official and his city—presumably Jerusalem—were commonly known, there was no need to be more specific; moreover, the main point of the seal was the scene depicted on it rather than the inscription, which was assigned very limited space. Despite the anonymity of the seal, it seems to be personal, the scene having been drawn as

---

[2] This subject was first pointed out to me by Dr. A. Demsky. I am grateful for his kind assistance.

[3] Z. Meshel, "Kuntillat 'Ajrud—An Israelite Site on the Sinai Border," *Qadmoniot* 36 (1976): 119–124 (Hebrew); *ibid*, *Kuntillet 'Ajrud, A Religious Centre from the Time of the Judean Monarchy on the Border of Sinai* Israel Museum Catalogue No. 175 (Jerusalem, 1978).

commissioned by the owner, referring to a ceremony which had significance for him. We have no knowledge of seals that were handed over together with an office. On the contrary, we possess several seals from Arad which were all used by one official.

The bulla published by Avigad seems to have been kept attached to a document several generations older than the other documents in the same archive, which were sealed with many other, probably later, bullae.[4]

The Governor of the City seal impressions contribute significantly to our knowledge of the bureaucracy of the Judean monarchy. Moreover, the scene depicted is quite unique in the art of Judah, referring as it does to a ceremony at the royal court, probably in the late 8th or early 7th century B.C.E.

[4] See: N. Avigad, *Hebrew Bullae from the Time of Jeremiah* (Jerusalem, 1986).

# JERUSALEM — SECOND TEMPLE PERIOD

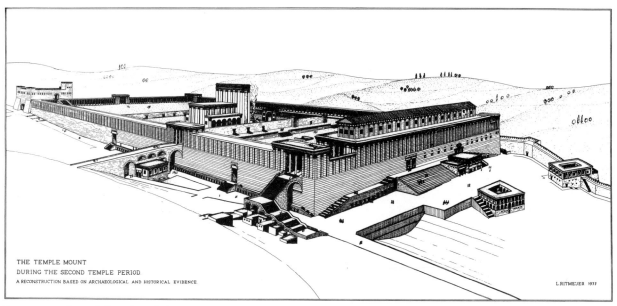

THE TEMPLE MOUNT
DURING THE SECOND TEMPLE PERIOD
A RECONSTRUCTION BASED ON ARCHAEOLOGICAL AND HISTORICAL EVIDENCE

L. RITMEIJER 1977

Reconstruction of the Temple Mount
precinct in the Herodian period

# Excavations Along the Western and Southern Walls of the Old City of Jerusalem

## Magen Broshi and Shimon Gibson

Between 1973 and 1978, the Mount Zion Archaeological Expedition conducted a series of excavations along the western and southern walls of the Old City of Jerusalem. The area extended some 700 m. (roughly one-sixth of the perimeter of the Old City) from the southern moat of the Tower of David Citadel to the vicinity of the Sulfur Tower (Burj Kibrit), the large tower in the southern wall east of the Zion Gate.* These excavations have added significantly to our understanding of the history of the Western Hill of ancient Jerusalem. Among the important discoveries were extramural Iron Age remains, substantial segments of the Hasmonean city wall, a gateway which led to Herod's palace on the western slope, and the remains of houses and of a Medieval gateway along the southern wall.

## The Western Wall of the Old City

Our work along the western city wall overlooking the Hinnom Valley aimed at clarifying the history of the fortifications in this area prior to the construction of the wall by Suleiman the Magnificent in the mid–16th century C.E. Earlier excavations by K.M. Kenyon and A.D. Tushingham in 1961–1967 and by M. Broshi and D. Bahat in 1971 in the Armenian

* The Mount Zion Expedition was directed by M. Broshi. Principal staff included N. Gershon, E. Braun, S. Gibson and J. Blumberg, with the participation of A. Segal and M. Stieglitz. Surveying was initially carried out by Y. Elder and later by S. Gibson, with the finds classified by Y. Sasson. E. Netzer and Y. Israeli were the expedition consultants. The excavations were sponsored by the Israel Department of Antiquities and Museums (now the Antiquities Authority), with the support of the Kress Foundation and the Jerusalem Foundation (along the western city wall) and the Jewish Quarter Reconstruction and Development Company (the area of the gate tower along the southern wall).

Garden, with soundings along the inner face of the city wall, had clearly shown that the foundations of the Ottoman wall there were built over an ancient line of fortifications. The discovery of significant stretches of ancient fortification walls by F.J. Bliss and A.C. Dickie in 1894–1897 along the southern slopes of Mount Zion, and later by C.N. Johns in the Citadel in 1934–1947, suggested that equally important ancient defensive walls could also be located along the western city wall.

## Remains of the Iron Age

The earliest remains found during the excavations are of the Iron Age (8th–6th centuries B.C.E), including signs of stone quarrying, three burial caves, an agricultural terrace with a small watchtower, and a building serving some manufacturing function.

Traces of stone quarrying were clearly visible in a number of places under the foundations of the later Hasmonean city wall. Although some of this quarrying may be of Hasmonean date, other parts are undoubtedly of the Iron Age. In one area, Iron Age sherds were found in a fill of limestone chips blocking a rock-cut channel between two partly quarried stones. This quarrying is now known to have been part of a whole system of quarries extending along the western slope of the hill and in the Armenian Garden, as far north as the Muristan and the Church of the Holy Sepulcher (see in this volume, pp. 82–84), and also south to the slopes of Mount Zion. Evidence from the excavations in the Armenian Quarter suggests that the quarrying dates to the 8th and 7th centuries B.C.E.

Two burial caves (3) were located in the rock scarp immediately below the line of the

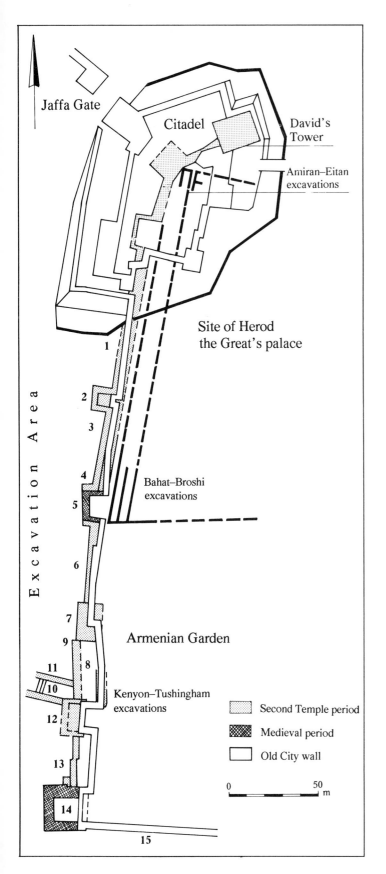

Jaffa Gate

Citadel

David's Tower

Amiran–Eitan excavations

Site of Herod the Great's palace

Excavation Area

Bahat–Broshi excavations

Armenian Garden

Kenyon–Tushingham excavations

Second Temple period

Medieval period

Old City wall

0          50
                m

Hasmonean-Herodian fortification wall. Both tombs were empty and had probably been cleared of their contents—perhaps for reburial elsewhere—at the time of the construction of the Hasmonean city wall in the late 2nd century B.C.E. The entrance to an additional third burial cave was found nearby. It had been blocked with mortar and rubble during the construction of a Medieval tower above it and except for the form of its entrance, nothing is known about the internal arrangements of the cave. A detailed study of these tombs was made in 1982 by the present authors in collaboration with G. Barkay. The caves differ from one another in the way they are hewn and in their internal layout. Tomb 1, which had been cut at a slightly later date than Tomb 2, has two entrances leading to a single chamber containing two trough-like burial spaces with carved headrests. Tomb 2 is the more impressive of the two caves. It has a smoothly chiselled entrance of very good workmanship that leads to a single chamber containing two broad benches at either side. Headrests are carved at the eastern end of the benches, two to each bench. Each bench was probably separated into individual burial spaces by the insertion of partition walls built of thin limestone slabs, some of which were found during the excavations. Neither of the two tombs has bone repositories which are so typical of family tombs dating to the Iron Age, suggesting that the tombs were used for the burial of only a limited number of individuals, perhaps for members of the Jerusalem aristocracy during the 8th century B.C.E.

General plan of the excavations at the western Old City wall: 1. sewage system of Herodian date; 2. Hasmonean tower reinforced by outer Herodian wall; 3. Iron Age burial caves; 4. line of Hasmonean First Wall with outer Herodian wall; 5. remains of Hellenistic watchtower under Herodian and Ayyubid towers; 6. line of Hasmonean city wall; 7. Hasmonean tower; 8. line of Hasmonean city wall; 9. line of Herodian city wall; 10. Herodian gateway approach; 11. Iron Age industrial structure; 12. Hasmonean tower reinforced by outer Herodian walls; 13. line of Herodian city wall; 14. Ayyubid tower; 15. locations of soundings along the southern wall of the Old City

Western wall of the Old City: the rock facade with the opening to the burial caves of the late First Temple period, looking east

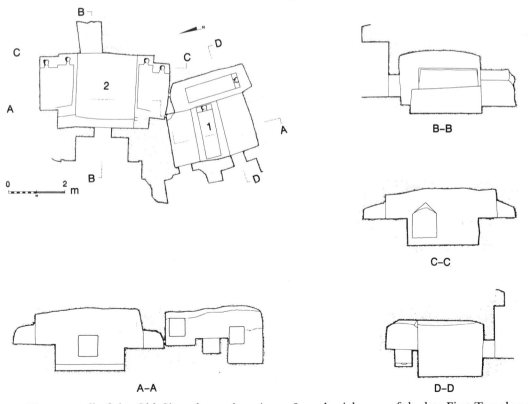

Western wall of the Old City: plan and sections of two burial caves of the late First Temple period

Western Wall of the Old City; the interior of Tomb 2; looking north

During the 7th–6th centuries B.C.E. an extramural suburb sprang up in the area of the abandoned (or partly abandoned) quarries in the present Armenian Quarter. Judging from a few agricultural terraces that were unearthed along the western city wall and in Tushingham's excavations further east, this suburb was semirural. One agricultural terrace was found in association with a small rectangular structure—perhaps a storage room similar to the agricultural watchtowers commonly encountered in the rural environs of Jerusalem. Further south, a six-roomed structure with plastered floors was unearthed (11). Various installations including fire-pits, raised plastered platforms, a rectangular bath and drains indicate that the structure served some manufacturing or agricultural processing function.

The extent of the walled Iron Age city on the Western Hill during the 8th–6th centuries B.C.E., is still a matter of dispute among scholars. Minimalists (K.M. Kenyon, A.D. Tushingham, D. Bahat) believe that the walled Iron Age city extended only as far as the present Jewish Quarter; the maximalist view (N. Avigad, H. Geva, G. Barkay) regards the course of the Iron Age city walls as almost identical to that of the later Hasmonean ones. This latter view would place the Iron Age wall along a line corresponding to the present western wall of the Old City. The discoveries made during our excavations, and by Kenyon and Tush-

ingham in the adjoining Armenian Garden, suggest that the western wall of the Iron Age city should perhaps be sought along the eastern limits of the Armenian Garden and not further west.

## Remains of the First Wall

The excavations revealed segments of ancient defensive walls of different periods, including a 200 m. section of the Hasmonean fortification line known as the First Wall, stretching from the southern moat wall of the Citadel to the southwest corner of the Old City. Parts of the inner face of this wall had previously been uncovered during excavations in the Armenian Garden—by Kenyon and Tushingham, and by Broshi and Bahat. Now, a considerable stretch of its outer face was exposed. It is built along an advantageous topographical course, at the top of the slope rising steeply from the bed of the Hinnom Valley. Since prior to the construction of the wall this slope had served as a quarry (and was probably the source of some of the stones used in the wall), the ascent was made more difficult. The advantages of this line were recognized and exploited by all subsequent builders of fortifications at this side of the city—from the time of the Hasmoneans (ca. 144–141 B.C.E.) to the Ottoman Turks (1538–1540 C.E.). Besides the favorable topography, the later builders had the benefit of using the earlier, ruined fortifications as foundations for their own walls—and as a source of building stone. The Ottoman wall was constructed directly over the surviving courses of the Hasmonean wall founded on bedrock, as well as over segments of walls dating from the Byzantine and Medieval periods.

The Hasmonean wall (4, 6, 8), which was up to 5 m. thick, was in part built of ashlars with bosses and chiselled margins occasionally laid in a header and stretcher arrangement, and partly of rough, undressed fieldstones. The variation in construction styles may be due to the work of separate groups of stonemasons assigned different sections of the wall. The remains of four towers (2, 5, 7, 12) were found along this wall, with no apparent uniformity in the spacing between the towers or in their dimensions. One of the towers (5), with a blocked gateway, clearly predates the wall itself and was probably a free-standing Hellenistic watchtower guarding the western approaches to the city which at that period was restricted to only the southeastern hill (the City of David). This would explain the discovery during the excavations, of stamped Rhodian wine amphora handles, some of them dating back to the middle of the 3rd century B.C.E.

The line of the First Wall is now well established owing to the excavations since the last century by H. Maudslay, F.J. Bliss and A.C. Dickie along the southern slopes of Mount Zion; by R.A.S. Macalister and J.G. Duncan, and K.M. Kenyon and Y. Shiloh along the eastern slope of the City of David; by N. Avigad along the northern stretch; and by C.N. Johns, H. Geva, R. Sivan and G. Solar in the Citadel. To these we can now add our own discoveries.

The construction of the First Wall was probably undertaken by Jonathan in ca. 144 B.C.E., and eventually finished by Simon in 141 B.C.E., following the destruction of the Seleucid Akra fortress. The building of this wall seems to have been a major political act—the first step towards the restoration of the previously destroyed Israelite city, its

Western wall of the Old City: view, looking south, of the excavations area south of the Citadel; note the line of the First Wall of the Second Temple period below the Ottoman Old City wall

Western wall of the Old City: below—the reinforcing revetment wall of the time of King Herod; above—courses of the Hasmonean city wall under the Turkish wall

ruins scattered for all to see over the Western Hill outside the Hellenistic city, which was restricted to the City of David. This would explain why parts of the Iron Age defenses were preserved by being incorporated into the northern stretch of the First Wall that was uncovered by Avigad in the Jewish Quarter excavations. It may also be the reason why the Western Hill was resettled only very gradually, from about 100 B.C.E. on.

## The Herodian Outer Rampart and the Palace Gateway Approach

Whatever the vicissitudes of the western stretch of the First Wall in the late 2nd and throughout the 1st centuries B.C.E., the archaeological excavations clearly show that

151

the Hasmonean defensive line underwent decisive modifications toward the end of the 1st century B.C.E. Most likely, this was the work of Herod the Great.

Our excavations revealed an outer rampart only along the northern section of the Hasmonean wall, as well as three remodelled defensive towers, a gateway approach leading into the area of the palace (the present Armenian Garden), and a major drainage tunnel extending from within the city. All these were clearly part of an integrated building program which can be linked to the construction of Herod's palace (ca. 25–22 B.C.E.) in the northwestern corner of the Upper City of Jerusalem. Previous excavations in the present Citadel by Amiran and Eitan, and in the Armenian Garden by Kenyon and Tushingham and by Broshi and Bahat have revealed the remains of a network of consolidation walls with massive earth fills between them which formed a raised platform (podium) for Herod's palace, including service buildings and gardens.

The Herodian outer rampart was traced along 70 m. immediately in front of the northern part of the Hasmonean city wall we discovered south of the Citadel (4). It was probably built to strengthen the defenses of this section of the city wall, forming an 8 m.-thick, solid barrier, and to help contain the outward static pressure of the fills in the podium of Herod the Great's palace against the inner face of the city wall. Parts of this outer rampart were built of ashlars with bosses and dressed margins, and others of large unhewn stones with plastered interstices. Nothing is known of the original height of this outer wall, but it may have stood as high as the inner one. On the other hand, it may have been only high enough to cover the foundations of the wall behind it, thus shielding the base of the wall against attempts at sapping. This is known in military terminology as a built scarp or vertical revetment. Such reinforcing may have been an adaptation of a technique common in Hellenistic military engineering, known as *proteichisma* in Greek and *agger* in Latin.

Of the four towers erected during the Hasmonean period, only three were remodelled

Western wall of the Old City: the reinforcing revetment wall of the time of King Herod

by Herod. Two of them were rebuilt in connection with the construction of the outer rampart along the city wall. The northernmost tower (2) was encased by a wall built of ashlars with dressed margins and bosses, and of headers and stretchers in no specific arrangement. Further south, the Herodian tower (5) was built of ashlars of a different style, with comb-picked margins and smoothed bosses, laid in alternating courses of headers and stretchers. The third tower (12) was connected with the Herodian gateway approach. It was a substantial reconstruction of the earlier, dismantled Hasmonean tower of which only a portion has survived.

Unlike the northern section of the First Wall which had an outer rampart, the southern section had a separate free-standing Herodian wall about 10 m. to the west of the original Hasmonean wall.

A small portion of the inner face of the Hasmonean First Wall was excavated by Kenyon and Tushingham; the outer face and two sections of the outer Herodian wall were found in our excavations. A gateway approach (10), consisting of paved steps bordered on either side by walls, was found leading up to the Herodian outer wall. Unfortunately, the stones belonging to the threshold of the gate had been robbed down to the foundations of the wall during the Byzantine period. The gate was probably a private entrance to Herod's palace rather than a public thoroughfare.

An substantial tunnel system (1), 1.45 m. wide and 6.5 m. high from floor to ceiling, was unearthed immediately south of the present Citadel. It extends for 27 m. from east to west, from a point within the city below the Turkish army barracks (the Kishle) down toward the Hinnom Valley. A gray silt from the rock-hewn channel in the floor of the tunnel was found to contain pottery and coins of the 1st century C.E. This tunnel, which can only have been used for carrying off sewage—perhaps only from the palace area—may be connected with the intriguing Bethso (interpreted as *beth şo'a* or "place of sewers") mentioned in Josephus' description of the western stretch of the First Wall (*War* V, 145).

## The Western City Wall During Later Periods

Following the destruction of Jerusalem by the Romans in 70 C.E., the First Wall was largely dismantled, except for the western stretch which was left standing as a protection for the Tenth Legion garrison, whose camp was located in the area of the present Citadel and the northern part of the Armenian Garden. However, Josephus (*War* VII, 1–2)—our primary source of information on the fortifications of Second Temple period Jerusalem —does not mention which part of the western city wall was preserved. Our excavations seem to indicate that only the northern half of the exposed line of wall was left standing. Large quantities of rooftiles, many impressed with the stamp of the Roman Tenth Fretensis Legion (LEG · X · FRE), were found in layers of debris along the line of the Herodian city wall. A small quantity of Byzantine pottery from these layers indicates that much of the

Roman Legion camp within the Armenian Garden was razed during this period and the rubble thrown over the wall.

The western city wall apparently remained in a semiruined state until it was restored in the Byzantine period, probably by the Empress Eudoxia in the mid–5th century C.E. We discovered several sections of wall, 2.4–2.7 m. thick, built in a manner similar to the masonry of Bliss and Dickie's Byzantine wall along the southern slope of Mount Zion.

This patched-up fortification line continued in use to Medieval times. An enormous corner tower (14) measuring 24 × 24 m. was exposed below the present southwest corner of the Old City, its internal space measuring 14 × 12.5 m. with the foundations of a wide, square pier in the center. The 5–7 m.-thick walls of this tower, built with a mortar core, are faced with courses of large ashlars having narrow margins dressed flat with a pointed drafting tool. Many fallen ashlars were found around this tower. Further north, another, smaller Medieval tower (5) built in a similar fashion was exposed. In front of this tower was a pile of fallen ashlars and a dated Ayyubid inscription mentioning the erection of the tower for 'al-Malik al-Mu'azzem 'Isa in A.H. 599 (1202–1203 C.E.).

The evidence from the excavations suggests that since the destruction of the towers in 1219 C.E. (see below), the line of the western city wall remained in ruins until the present Old City wall was constructed by Suleiman the Magnificent in the mid–16th century C.E.

## The Southern City Wall

Excavations were conducted at two locations along the southern Old City wall: at a site some 100 m. east of the Zion Gate, and near the southwest corner of the Old City (15), where the stairway leading up from the western city wall towards Zion Gate was to be constructed.

In both these excavation areas remains of ancient buildings were uncovered. In the area east of the Zion Gate, in front of the later Medieval tower, the excavations revealed a series of structures with cisterns and drainage

153

channels, dating to the late Byzantine and the Umayyad periods. These were located above the well-preserved remains of a Herodian building with an intact vault. Soundings undertaken near the southwest corner of the Old City, though limited in area, revealed the fragmentary remains of superimposed structures dating to Hasmonean (early 1st century B.C.E.), Herodian (1st century C.E.), and Byzantine (6th century C.E.) periods. A glass weight with the bust of the emperor Justinian was found with an assemblage of pottery vessels on the floor of the Byzantine structure.

One important result of these excavations is the discovery that the earliest fortification line in this area does not predate the Crusader period. Additional excavations by Avigad in the Jewish Quarter have confirmed this conclusion.

### The Ayyubid Gate Tower

A trial trench excavated outside the Ottoman city wall in the area east of the Zion Gate revealed the southern outer face of a Medieval tower, 23 m. long. In front of this tower were fallen ashlars and two fragments of an Ayyubid inscription, mentioning the erection of the tower for 'al-Malik al-Mu'azzem 'Isa in A.H. 609 (1212 C.E.) The inscription, 2.75 m.-long, was carved in relief with traces of a

Southern wall of the Old City: the Ayyubid gateway; the man stands on its outer wall

Southern wall of the Old City: the inscription of 'al-Malik al-Mu'azzam (left-hand part)

red-painted background still visible. Among the ashlars were jambstones and voussoirs which clearly belonged to a gateway. Judging from the position of these architectural fragments, with jambstones lying one in front of the other, the gateway was apparently located in the southern wall of the tower. Most probably, the inscription was originally inserted into the wall beneath a relieving arch, over the lintel of the gate. Excavations within the city by Avigad revealed the rest of the tower in 1977. It measured 23 × 23 m. with an internal space 13 × 12 m. and a central, built square pillar supporting its ceiling.

The fallen ashlars found alongside this tower, and also beneath towers along the western stretch of the present Old City wall (see above), confirm what we know from historical sources: In 1219 C.E. 'al-Malik al-Mu'azzam 'Isa, the Ayyubid ruler of Damascus and nephew of Salaḥ a-Din (Saladin), razed the walls of Jerusalem—after having had a major role in rebuilding them seven years before. This destruction, part of a considered

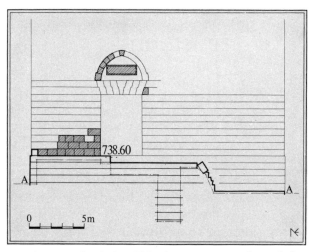

Southern wall of the Old City: reconstruction of the Ayyubid gateway

scorched-earth policy, was to prevent invading Crusaders from gaining a well-fortified city which the sultan had no means of garrisoning effectively. In the words of a Muslim historian:

When the Crusader siege on the port of Damietta tightened, and it was about to surrender, 'al-Malik al-Mu'azzam sharf al-Din 'Isa ibn al-Malik al-'Adil, ruler of Damascus, feared lest great Frank forces arrive by sea upon hearing of the strength of their comrades and of their success within Egypt; and that 'al-Malik al-Kamil was engaged by the war against the Franks within Egypt; that then they would turn toward Jerusalem (for it was now fortified), and that they would gain control over it and he would not be able later to wrest it from their hands. Then he ('al-Malik al-Mu'azzam) began to dismantle the towers of Jerusalem and its walls which were of the mightiest and most powerful. And Jerusalem, since it had been wrested from the Franks by 'al-Malik al-Nasr Salah al-Din (Saladin), stood built, and every one of its towers was planned as a fortress. And he gathered the masons and sappers and undermined the walls and its towers, and destroyed them—except David's Tower, which he left. And when the walls were destroyed, most of the inhabitants left, for there had lived within (the city) an innumerable population and now but a few people remained. After these events, 'al-Malik al-Mu'azzam began to transfer the armories and weapons, and the like, and its (Jerusalem's) destruction was a hard blow to the Muslims and they sorrowed greatly. (Ibn Wasl, *Mufarij el-Kurub* IV, 32)

Indeed, in the year 1229 C.E. the undefended city was delivered to Frederick II. From the time of their destruction in 1219 C.E., the walls of Jerusalem lay in ruins until Suleiman the Magnificent rebuilt them some 320 years later. Several Muslim rulers had previously suggested rebuilding the defenses of the city, but none had done so. Numerous Jewish, Christian and Muslim accounts tell of the undefended state of the city during these centuries. In the words of Obadiah of Bertinoro (1488 C.E.): "The greater part of Jerusalem is destroyed and desolated, not to mention that it has no walls".

## Bibliography

Bahat, D. and Broshi, M., "Excavations in the Armenian Garden," in: Yadin, Y. (ed.) *Jerusalem Revealed* (Jerusalem, 1976), pp. 55–56.

Broshi, M., "Al-Malek al-Muazzam—Evidence in a New Inscription," *Eretz Israel* 19 (Jerusalem, 1987), pp. 299–302 (Hebrew).

Broshi, M., Barkay, G. and Gibson, S., "Two Iron Age Tombs Below the Western City Wall, Jerusalem and the Talmudic Law of Purity," *Cathedra* 28 (1983): 17–32 (Hebrew).

Gibson, S., "The 1961–67 Excavations in the Armenian Garden, Jerusalem," *PEQ* 119 (1987): 81–96.

Tushingham, A.D., *Excavations in Jerusalem 1961–1967*, I (Toronto, 1985).

# Excavations at the Citadel of Jerusalem, 1976–1980

## Hillel Geva

The Citadel of Jerusalem, better known as the Tower of David, is located just south of the Jaffa Gate—the northwestern corner of the Western Hill of ancient Jerusalem. Its commanding topographical situation overlooking the city gave the place great strategic importance, as reflected by the construction there of successive series of fortifications and citadels in the course of two thousand years.

The ancient remains of the Citadel aroused scholarly interest already at the beginning of the 19th century. The Tower of David was identified with one of three towers constructed by King Herod (*War* V, 161–175) at this point along the line of the First Wall north of his palace.

The first to undertake an archaeological study of the Citadel was C. Schick, at the end of the 19th century. He recorded measurements of architectural features of the Tower of David and proved that the tower was constructed of a solid mass of large stones.

Excavations in the Citadel were conducted initially by C.N. Johns between 1934 and 1947. In the Citadel courtyard Johns revealed a long, curved section of the city wall dating to the Second Temple period. He correctly identified it as the northwestern angle of the First Wall of Jerusalem which encompassed the entire Western Hill during the Hasmonean and Herodian periods. He traced the line of this wall by excavating down to bedrock in several places along its outer face. Johns identified four periods in the wall's construction, beginning with the First Build, dated to the early Hasmonean period, through the Fourth Build of the end of the 1st century C.E. Johns also cleared the upper strata in the area inside this wall down to Roman and Byzantine levels.

In 1968–1969, R. Amiran and A. Eitan excavated an area located inside the city wall opposite (east of) Johns' Middle Tower *d–e–f*. They revealed there an Inner Tower in the city wall, and Hasmonean building remains beneath Herodian-period construction which they later identified as part of the foundations of Herod the Great's palace.

Extensive excavations were resumed in the Citadel courtyard in 1976–1980.[1] In order to obtain more evidence of the architectural history of the First Wall we dug a stratigraphic trench against its outer face (Area C–2) and a limited sounding was dug against its inner face (Area C–3). An additional trench was cut against a later fortification wall (Area C–1). The main area of excavation was the entire southern part of the Citadel's courtyard (Areas A–B). We commenced our work here by locating and clearing the remains of the lowest stratum reached by Johns, which had been covered up again, and then continued downward. A series of massive towers forming part of the city's defenses, each built on the

---

[1]  The new excavations in the Citadel of Jerusalem are part of the overall reconstruction of the site which has been planned as the permanent home of the Jerusalem City Museum. The excavations were sponsored by the Jerusalem City Museum in cooperation with the Institute of Archaeology of the Hebrew University in Jerusalem and the Israel Exploration Society. The Jerusalem Foundation financed the excavations and the study of finds. The excavations were directed by the author with the assistance of M. Adato, D. Gottlieb and A. Rochman. L. Ritmeyer served as surveyor. Y. Harlap took the photographs and V. Mashali helped in administrative matters. R. Sivan, curator of the Jerusalem City Museum at the time, was most helpful in advising the expedition. From 1980–1988 additional excavations were conducted at the site by R. Sivan and G. Solar (see in this volume, pp. 168–176).

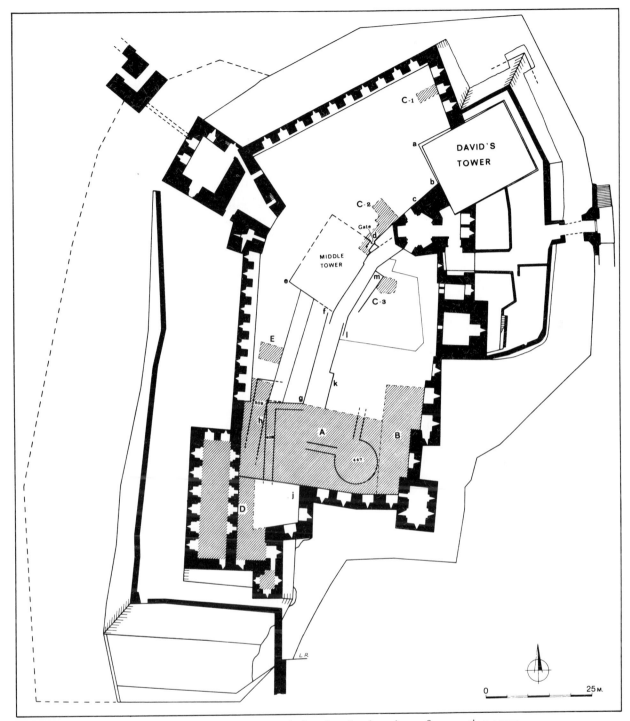

Tower of David Citadel: general plan showing locations of excavation areas

foundations of its predecessor, were exposed. Area E is located along the outer face of the massive wall which, according to Johns, was added to the city's defenses during the Medieval period. We also excavated under the floor of the southwestern tower of the present Citadel (Area D).

## The Iron Age

The recent excavations on the Western Hill of ancient Jerusalem have demonstrated that during the 8th century B.C.E. the settlement of the city expanded from the City of David up to this hill. The topography of the hill, the discovery by N. Avigad of the Broad Wall in the Jewish Quarter, and Josephus's statement (*War* V, 143) that the First Wall originated during the monarchic period, all seem to support the theory that the preexilic fortifications extended westward as far as the Hinnom Valley. It may be assumed, therefore, that the entire Western Hill already lay within the city limits by the end of the Judean monarchy (8th–6th centuries B.C.E.). The remains of this city wall were later buried below the Hasmonean city wall (2nd–1st centuries B.C.E.). In order to gather more archaeological evidence we excavated in two places along the inner side of the Second Temple period city wall.

In Area C–3 excavation of a layer of large fieldstones below the Hasmonean stratum exposed by Amiran and Eitan showed that it had been subjected to an extensive fire. The few pottery sherds found among the stones are identical with the types commonly found on the Western Hill, which date the layer to the late Iron Age (8th–7th centuries B.C.E.). The appearance of the stone layer and its having been burned in a conflagration suggest that the stones had collapsed and fallen from the city wall of that period, or possibly, that these stones had been part of the core-fill of the city wall. Indeed, slightly to the west, a small section of an earlier wall was exposed by Johns under the outer face of the Hasmonean First Build. It is constructed of large field-stones laid in courses, and was incorporated into later city walls. We believe that the remains of this earlier construction may represent the preexilic city wall, the upper part of which collapsed eastward into the city during the destruction of Jerusalem in 587/6 B.C.E.

In Area A, underneath 7 m. of loose debris and under an early Hasmonean floor, a layer of large fieldstones (W. 520) was revealed. Its appearance and stratigraphic position allow us to assume it to be another section of the preexilic city wall.

Although the results of our excavations did not yield conclusive proof, they do appear to add more evidence in support of the view that the city wall of Jerusalem, known as the First Wall of the late First Temple period (8th–7th centuries B.C.E.), extended westward from the Temple Mount to the Hinnom Valley and turned south along the western slope of the Western Hill toward Mount Zion.[2] This city wall was succeeded by a later wall built by the Hasmoneans along the same line.

## The Hasmonean Period

The archaeological finds show that the Western Hill, after having been abandoned for hundreds of years following the Babylonian destruction of 587/6 B.C.E., was reoccupied at the beginning of the Hasmonean period (second half of the 2nd century B.C.E.) and refortified shortly afterward.

Area C–2 is located at the junction of Johns's Middle Tower *d–e–f* and the city wall *c–d* northeast of the Tower. Johns excavated the earth debris at this point to elevation 766.5 m. above sea level and noted that Wall *c–d* had been constructed later than Tower *d–e–f*. He had considered these two structures to belong to the Second Build which he dated to the late 2nd–early 1st centuries B.C.E.

As we dug down it became apparent that the northern side of the Middle Tower is built directly upon the bedrock at elevation 765 m. On the other hand, the southwestern corner exposed by Johns (at *e*) is founded on earth-fill at elevation 766.5 m. The construction of the foundations and superstructure are the same in this tower. The outer northern face of the tower, which was revealed by us, is constructed of large ashlars, carefully dressed with protruding unworked bosses framed by flat margins.[3] The stones are laid in alternating courses of headers and stretchers. The inside of the tower is filled with large, rectangular, roughly-worked stones. The preserved eastern doorjamb enabled Johns to reconstruct a small opening in the tower's northern

[2] See also in this volume, pp. 147–155, on the discovery of another section of fortifications of the late First Temple period by Sivan and Solar in the Tower of David Citadel.

[3] This wall turned out to be the northern side of an earlier Hasmonean tower discovered by Sivan and Solar under the foundations of Middle Tower *d-e-f* which was uncovered by Johns. See above pp. 170.

face—possibly a postern—although the stones of the rest of the reconstructed opening had been robbed to a level of about 3 m. below its assumed threshold.

Northeast of the tower, a new wall (c–d) was added to the western outer face of the city wall. Its lower part was assigned by Johns to the First Build. Consequently, the city wall was now approximately 6 m. wide. The lower part of the outer face of this later wall is composed of large, rectangular, roughly-worked stones laid in alternating courses of headers and stretchers with small stones in the interstices between the larger stones. This lower part of the wall is undoubtedly the foundation of the upper part, and did not, as Johns assumed, belong to the earlier city wall of the First Build. Its upper part is built of large ashlars with dressed margins on four sides and protruding rough bosses. As Johns noted, many of these stones bear masons' marks which do not appear on the stones of the Middle Tower (d–e–f). The straight joint between this tower and the added wall (c–d) was formed by fitting the stones of the wall to the bossed stones of the tower's northeastern face. The wall is recessed at this point to provide access to the opening Johns reconstructed in the tower. We assume that the Middle Tower (d–e–f) was constructed no earlier than the beginning of the 1st century B.C.E. wall c–d which is later than this tower. It certainly predates the construction of the Tower of David which Herod the Great added to this wall by at the beginning of his reign.

In Area A we continued the exposure of Johns's Southern Tower g–h–j. Its reconstructed outlines are based on a small section of the western face cleared by Johns at h. In recent excavations of the northern wall (W. 508) and western wall (W. 509), sides of the earlier phase of this tower have been revealed. These walls consist of ashlars with dressed margins and protruding rough bosses laid in courses. Of the inner eastern side of the tower, a small section of wall (W. 493) was exposed. This was beneath 2 m. of earth-fill below the foundations of a later tower erected above it during the 1st century C.E. The east-

Tower of David Citadel, Area C-2: outer face of the Hasmonean First Wall in section c-d; the northern side of the Middle Tower d–e–f is at the lower right-hand side

west width of the Southern Tower is 18.5 m.; its length, north-to-south, is over 20 m. The inside of this tower, too, is solidly filled with layers of large, roughly-dressed stones. In view of the stratigraphy, features of construction and the pottery analysis, we tend to date its origin to the Hasmonean period, generally contemporary with Middle Tower d–e–f and Wall c–d.

In Johns's excavations, as in our areas west of the line of the First Wall, a very extensive accumulation of debris had been dug about 8 m. down to bedrock. This is undoubtedly the city's refuse which over the centuries was thrown outside the wall and piled up along its outer face on the slope of the Hinnom Valley, thus covering part of the wall. This thick layer of debris contained a large quantity of pottery, coins and remains of organic material. Most of the pottery which appears alongside the city wall, from the present ground level down to bedrock, dates to the 1st century B.C.E. Especially surprising is the general absence here of pottery clearly dated to the 1st century C.E., which is usually present in large quantities in ceramic assemblages of the Second Temple period found on the Western Hill. This may be due to large-scale earth-

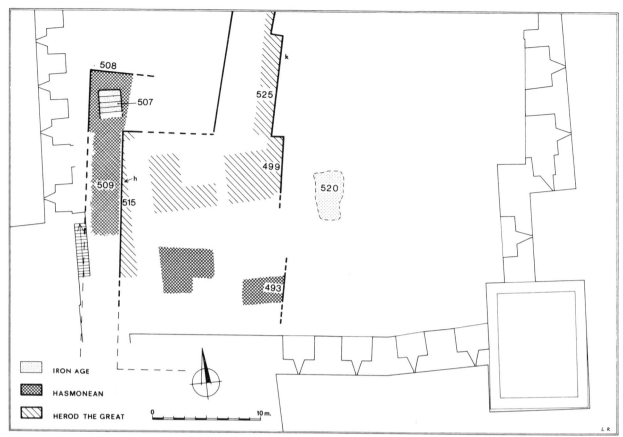

Tower of David Citadel: the Southern Tower in the courtyard during the Hasmonean and early Herodian periods, 1st century B.C.E.

works carried out during the Medieval period before the line of the defenses was moved westward. Consequently, all the upper part of the accumulated debris, containing 1st-century C.E. pottery, was moved down the slope into the valley. Another possible explanation is that the construction of the palace of Herod the Great at the end of the 1st century B.C.E. put an end to the dumping of refuse here.

Archaeological finds from various excavations conducted on the Western Hill, and historical testimony, indicate that the First Wall was restored along the same line as the preceding one of the end of the First Temple period in the second half of the 2nd century B.C.E., during the reigns of the Hasmonean kings Simon (142–134 B.C.E.) or Hyrcanus I (134–104 B.C.E.). In the course of the Hasmonean period, and in particular during the 1st century B.C.E., this wall underwent several phases of repair.

## The Period of Herod the Great

During the time of Herod the Great, the fortification system was strengthened by adding three large towers—Hippicus, Phasael and Mariamne—which were incorporated in the line of the old First Wall. Of these, only the tower known today as the Tower of David is preserved. As shown by Amiran and Eitan in their excavations, a long section of the inner face of the city wall was rebuilt at that time. The area inside the city wall was radically changed by the construction of a system of foundation walls intended to raise the ground level and creating the raised platform upon which the palace of Herod the Great was built.

A new tower was erected at this time above the earlier Hasmonean Southern Tower, remains of which were revealed in Area A. This is Johns's reconstructed tower g–h–j, of which only a small section of the western side (h, our Wall W. 515) was exposed by him. Only the northern part of the tower was revealed in our excavations. The eastern wall (W. 499), the two northern corners, and the inner face of the city wall from this tower-northward (W. 525, Johns's *k*) are built of large ashlars with precise, comb-picked margins on four sides and flat, chiselled bosses. The western outer wall of the tower (W. 515), preserved only to a very low level of its foundations, is constructed of dressed stones of various shapes laid in courses. The inner space of the rebuilt Southern Tower is filled up with large stones of various shapes, many reused from the Hasmonean period. The new tower is orientated like the preceding Hasmonean tower, but its width was reduced to 14.5 m.

Stratigraphy and the masonry of its large ashlars date the rebuilt tower to the time of Herod—in contrast to Johns's identification of this tower (*g–h–j*) as belonging to the Fourth Build, of the end of the 1st century C.E.

In the northwestern corner of the earlier tower Johns discovered a stepped pool (507), now identified by its form as a typical Jewish ritual bath (*miqveh*) of the Second Temple period. Its surprising location, at the outer side of the fortification line, has not been sufficiently clarified, although in the area of Mount Zion and the City of David identically situated *miqva'ot* were uncovered in towers of the First Wall.

The renewed building of the Southern Tower of the Citadel was part of the general reconstruction of the First Wall during the days of King Herod. Its northwestern corner was also fortified with three great towers—Phasael, Hippicus and Mariamne—described in detail by Josephus Flavius (*War* V 163–175). Various considerations led us to believe that the identification of the Tower of David with Hippicus is to be preferred over its generally accepted association with Phasael. According to our view, the two additional towers, Phasael and Mariamne, were situated in the line of the First Wall east of the Tower of David.

## The Later Herodian Period

At the beginning of the 1st century C.E. the Southern Tower went out of use and a new tower was erected on its foundations. The new tower differs in plan, dimensions and orientation from the preceding Hasmonean and Herodian towers. The width (north-south) of the tower is 17 m. Its southern wall (W. 496), which was traced for 13 m. eastward from the eastern edge of the earlier tower. The orientation of the new tower is due north.

The northern part of the exposed tower is composed of two rooms, 121 and 149, and a larger room, 93, to the south. The walls of the tower are preserved to a maximum height of 2 m. on the northern side, and only to the top of its foundations and floor-level on the southern side. The western wall no longer exists. A later wall (W. 402) was built on its assumed line during the Byzantine period. The exterior walls of the tower are 1.5 m. wide, while the internal walls are only 1 m. in width. The rooms are connected by well constructed openings. Except for Walls 472 and 496, which rest on new, massive foundations as a result of the change in dimension and orientation from the previous tower, the walls of the new tower were built directly on the stone-fill of the earlier tower. Ashlars of earlier periods were used in the foundations. They are laid in courses, with the dressed margin faces set indiscriminately in all directions. The interstices are sometimes filled with white mortar and small stones.

All the walls of the tower are built of large ashlars, their masonry features closely resembling those of Herod's tower. The largest among them were certainly reused from this earlier tower. The stones are laid in courses of various heights, with white mortar between the stones. Small sections of smooth, white plaster are preserved on the walls of Room 149. Other sections in Room 121, of gray plaster, show the builders' handprints. Only small parts of the original floor remain. The floor of fine, white beaten gravel in the northern rooms is laid directly over the stone-fill of the earlier tower, while the same type of floor in the southern room is laid on 2 m. of earth-fill containing many small fragments of painted plaster. On a small section of the floor preserved in Room 121, a thick destruction

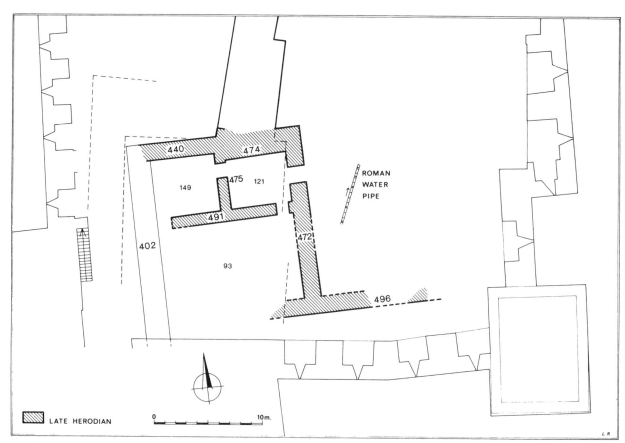

Tower of David Citadel: Southern Tower in the courtyard during the later Herodian period, 1st century C.E.

layer was discovered which contains building materials such as stones, a large quantity of broken ceiling plaster and charred wooden beams. This indicates that the tower was destroyed in a large conflagration, which caused the upper parts of the tower to collapse on the floor below.

Tower of David Citadel: Southern Tower in the courtyard, looking south; the two northern rooms in the tower of the 1st century C.E.

The pottery finds under the floors of the tower, and particularly the numismatic evidence, indicate that the tower was erected during the 1st century C.E., possibly at the initiative of Agrippa I or one of the Roman procurators. The advantages of this tower are obvious. It was massive enough to withstand enemy attack and could have served as a storehouse and living quarters for a garrison of soldiers.

On the basis of the pottery found on the floors and the stratigraphic evidence, the destruction of the tower can be assigned to the fall of Jerusalem in 70 C.E. Totally demolished, it was never rebuilt—except perhaps for its northern wall, which was incorporated into the later Byzantine defenses.

The uncovering of this tower is of great importance for our understanding of the different stages in the rebuilding of the First Wall of Jerusalem during the last two centuries of the Second Temple period. The study of the construction of the First Wall made it

Tower of David Citadel: heaps of fallen plaster fragments of the ceiling of the Southern Tower—evidence of the destruction in 70 C.E.

are set below this floor. Of special importance is a water pipe built above the eastern part of the 1st-century C.E. tower. It was found *in situ* and consists of fifteen sections of red clay pipe. Most of the sections are impressed with a round-frame stamp of the Tenth Roman Legion, "L(egio) · X · F(retensis)." A large quantity of Roman rooftile fragments, impressed with rectangular Tenth Legion stamps in several variants of size and text, was found in the present excavations. Most of the rooftile fragments come from the debris which had accumulated along the northern outer face of the Tower of David. This evidence, added to the finds from other excavations carried out on the Western Hill, confirms the presence of living quarters of the Tenth Legion here. However, there is still insufficient information as to the plan, dimensions and features of the Roman camp in Jerusalem during the 2nd–3rd centuries C.E.

clear that several types of towers were incorporated along its line as a result of the many repairs. The evidence from our excavations showed that the 1st century B.C.E. Southern Tower was destroyed at the end of the Second Temple period and that the Roman Tenth Legion built upon its foundations during the 2nd–3rd centuries C.E. This contradicts in some ways the testimony of Josephus Flavius (*War* VII, 1–4) that the western section of the city wall was not dismantled by the Romans after the conquest of Jerusalem in 70 C.E.

**The Roman Period**

The Roman Tenth Legion, which was stationed in Jerusalem after the city's destruction in 70 C.E., encamped, according to Josephus (*War* VII, 1–5), on the Western Hill. So far, only scattered and unremarkable building remains clearly identifiable with the encampment period have been found on this hill, mainly in the course of past excavations in the courtyard of the Citadel.

In Area A, a few fragmentary walls attributed to the late Roman-early Byzantine periods (3rd–4th centuries C.E.) have been exposed. They consist of reused ashlars trimmed to smaller dimensions and laid with their dressed-margin surfaces facing in all directions. The walls are built in some places above the floor-level of the 1st-century C.E. Southern Tower, and at one spot their foundations

Tower of David Citadel: sections of Roman drain pipe impressed with the stamp of the Roman Tenth Legion

**The Byzantine Period**

Area C–1 was opened against the western outer face of a massive city wall, partly exposed by Johns, under the northern fortification of the existing Citadel. He identified it as the extension of the city wall stretching northward from the Tower of David, and dated it to the late 3rd–early 4th centuries C.E.

Our sounding here was excavated to a depth of 6 m., revealing the wall to its maximum preserved height. We concluded that it

Tower of David Citadel; Area C-1; Byzantine City wall under the northern fortifications of the present Citadel; looking east

is not possible to identify, as Johns did, several phases of construction in this Byzantine city wall. On the contrary, we saw that it was built in one period of construction, and that its lower, stepped part is merely its foundation. It was built in this manner in order to strengthen the wall which is constructed on the loose debris of the Second Temple period. The pottery evidence seems to date the construction of the wall to the beginning of the Byzantine period.

A new Southern Tower was erected during the Byzantine period in Area A, over the remains of the earlier towers of the Second Temple period. It apparently combines earlier walls (W. 440, W. 474) on the northern side which was originally part of the 1st century C.E. tower, and a new wall (W. 402) on the western side. Together they form a massive tower protruding westward from the line of the earlier city wall. The width of the new western wall is 2.25 m.; it was exposed for a length of 18 m. Six courses are preserved to a total height of 3.3 m. We believe that it was erected on the same line as the western wall of the 1st-century tower and replaced it.

Johns dated this tower to the Medieval period. The stratigraphy indicates that the tower's western wall (W. 402) was erected later than the tower of the 1st century C.E., since its foundation trench intersects Wall 491 and Floors 93 and 149 of the earlier tower. The pottery evidence, though scanty, leads us to assign the construction of the new tower to the beginning of the Byzantine period (4th century C.E.).

In Areas A and B, three construction phases of Byzantine domestic structures were revealed. The upper phase, which comprises several small rooms with plain white mosaic floors, is especially noteworthy. These rooms, which adjoined the inner face of the tower in the west, were exposed all over Areas A and B.

The archaeological evidence from our excavation clearly shows that at the beginning of the Byzantine period the western section of the old fortification system of Second Temple period Jerusalem—the First Wall—was reconstructed, and that a new city wall was erected north of the Citadel on a line east of the Jaffa Gate. This fortification project may be assigned to the period of the emperor Constantine, who restored to Jerusalem its religious importance. The rebuilding of the fortifications of Jerusalem may also be connected with the transfer of the Roman Tenth Legion to Aila at the northern end of the Gulf of Elat (Aqaba) at the end of the 3rd century C.E.

**The Early Arab Period**

The Muslim conquest did not immediately alter the architectural features of the Citadel complex. Byzantine constructions remained in use, and several rooms were even rebuilt by the addition of new, white-plastered walls and floors of beaten earth. Shortly afterward, a new fortification system was built there. In Area A a round corner tower (447) was completely exposed, together with its two extension walls (426 and 431). A small section of the southern side of the tower had previously been revealed and identified by Johns. The diameter of Tower 447 is 9.8 m. Its outer face is built of small, slightly curved ashlars with dressed margins and flat bosses. The tower is solidly filled with stones of all kinds, many of which were taken from earlier buildings. These are laid in courses and bound with gray mortar. Wall 426, northward from the round tower, was excavated by us for a length of 13 m.; Johns had earlier traced an additional few meters of this wall. Wall 431 extends westward to the inner face of the earlier Byzantine tower, at which point it becomes much wider. Two walls (412 and 468) were constructed to reinforce the inner side of the tower; they may have supported a staircase which led to the upper part of the tower. To the outer sides of extension Wall 431, a reinforcing wall (456) was added later in the Early Arab period. Wall 420 was already partly founded on the tower, which apparently was severely damaged by that time. The walls are 4 m. wide on the average. The outer faces of the walls are built of small, well dressed stones, while small fieldstones were employed for the construction of their inner faces. The cores of the walls are filled with small stones bound with gray mortar.

The ground-level between the extension walls was raised by about 2 m. during the years of occupation. Several stone-lined pits are dug into the occupation level here. One contained two bronze tools and pottery vessels such as juglets, cooking pots, glazed bowls and oil-lamps typical of the Early Arab period (8th–9th centuries C.E.). Of special interest is an Abbasid gold coin dated to 819/20 C.E. found in Area A. Outside the new fortifications, refuse and debris thrown outside the walls accumulated to a height of 2 m. above the Byzantine level.

These impressive remains of the round corner tower with its extension walls may be identified as the southern part of the Early Arab citadel. The new fortification system was erected east of the previous city wall, the First Wall of the Second Temple and the Byzantine periods. It incorporates a section of this early city wall in the west, with a new round tower at the southeastern corner, and its walls in the south and east. The complete plan of this

Tower of David Citadel: the round corner tower of the Early Arab period in the southern part of the courtyard

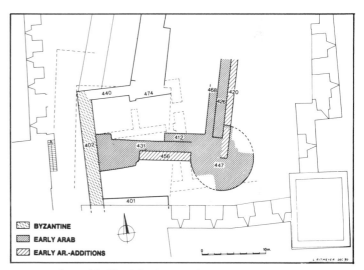

Tower of David Citadel: the Southern Tower in the courtyard during the Byzantine period and the round corner tower of the Early Arab period

Tower of David Citadel: assemblage of pottery including two glazed bowls found in a pit in the courtyard of the Early Arab citadel

165

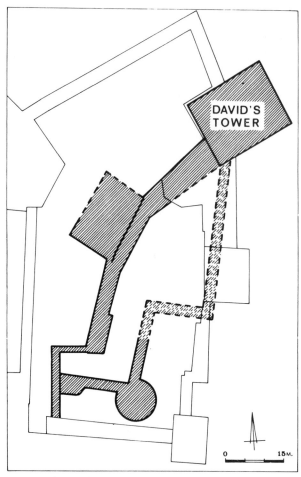

Tower of David Citadel: tentative reconstructed plan of
the Citadel in the Early Arab period

citadel is difficult to reconstruct because the continuation of its eastern wall northward was not found in Johns's nor in Amiran and Eitan's excavations. We assume that the eastern wall of the Early Arab citadel turned eastward, and then northward toward the Tower of David in order to provide a maximum width for the new citadel. The evidence clearly shows that the Early Arab citadel was smaller than either the earlier citadels or the later ones built in this spot.

The stratigraphy and the large quantities of pottery which accumulated along the inner and outer faces of this citadel indicate that it was built during the Early Arab period. Round towers are typical mainly of Early Arab fortification architecture and are known elsewhere in Israel and the region.

Based upon these considerations, we are inclined to believe that the Early Arab citadel was erected by one of the Umayyad rulers of the late 7th–early 8th centuries C.E. to control the still overwhelmingly Christian city of Jerusalem. With few changes, the Citadel continued to exist until the 10th–11th centuries C.E.

## The Crusader, Mamluk and Ottoman Periods

As already demonstrated by Johns, a new citadel, larger than the previous one, was built at this site by the Crusaders. The line of fortification was extended beyond those of the Early Arab citadel which fell into disuse and was buried under the courtyard of the new citadel. The Crusader citadel was enlarged, particularly toward the west and north, to encompass an area that until then had been outside the city limits. This had become necessary because the large accumulation of debris outside the city wall covered the slope of the valley at the western entrance to the city and tended to nullify the original, dominant topographical advantage of the fortress. In our excavations only a small section of the southern defence line (W. 401) was exposed under the southern wall of the present citadel. The corner is built of large ashlars with dressed margins on their two outer faces. This section is identified as an inner corner in the southern defenses of the Crusader citadel, or is of somewhat later date.

Above the remains of the Crusader citadel the present Citadel was erected during the Mamluk and Ottoman periods. Its plan generally follows the preceding one. Even the southern part of the eastern wall of the present Citadel, which Johns attributed to the Crusader citadel, is now proven to be later.

In our Areas A an B, remains of walls, stone pavements and water channels were exposed and identified as parts of the buildings which existed in the later citadels. The remains of the stable located in the southeastern corner of the present Citadel, assigned by Johns to the Crusader period, should now be regarded as part of the Ottoman citadel.

Tower of David Citadel; Area A; Buildings of the Crusader, Mamluk and Ottoman periods; looking west

## Bibliography

Amiran, R. and Eitan, A., "Excavations in the Courtyard of the Citadel, Jerusalem, 1968–1969," *IEJ* 20 (1970): 9–17.

Bahat, D., "David's Tower and its Name in Second Temple Times," *Eretz Israel* 15, (Jerusalem, 1981), pp. 396–400 (Hebrew).

Geva, H., "The Western Boundary of Jerusalem at the End of the Monarchy," *IEJ* 29 (1979): 84–91.

——— , "'The Tower of David'—Phasael or Hippicus?" *IEJ* 31 (1981): 57–65.

——— , "Excavations in the Citadel of Jerusalem, 1979–1980, Preliminary Report," *IEJ* 33 (1983): 55–71.

——— , "The Camp of the Tenth Legion in Jerusalem: An Archaeological Reconsideration," *IEJ* 34 (1984): 239–254.

——— , "The 'First Wall' of Jerusalem During the Second Temple Period. An Architectural-Chronological Note," *Eretz Israel* 18 (Jerusalem, 1985), pp. 21–39 (Hebrew).

Johns, C.N., "The Citadel, Jerusalem—A Summary of Work Since 1934," *QDAP* 14 (1950): 121–190.

Schick, C., "Der Davids Turm in Jerusalem," *ZDPV* 1 (1878): 226–237.

# Excavations in the Jerusalem Citadel, 1980–1988

## Renée Sivan and Giora Solar

Many of the Western travelers, including scholars and theologians, who visited Jerusalem since the early 19th century in search of remains of the biblical city have also described the ancient tower in the Citadel popularly known as the Tower of David. Although this tower has often been dated to the Herodian period, E. Robinson, Ch. Wilson, Ch. Warren, C.R. Conder and others disagreed on whether it represents the Hippicus or the Phasael towers—a controversy which persists to this day.

Aerial view of the excavations in the courtyard of the Jerusalem Tower of David Citadel; looking south

In 1898, C. Schick carried out the first extensive survey of the ancient remains in the Citadel precinct. Between the years 1934 and 1947, C.N. Johns conducted the first archaeological excavation of the site on behalf of the British Mandatory Department of Antiquities, uncovering a section of the First Wall of the Second Temple period. Johns exposed the outer north and west faces of the First Wall, comprising four phases of construction. On the eastern, inner side of the wall, he only uncovered the upper strata down to the Roman period.

During the years 1968–1969, R. Amiran and A. Eitan conducted new excavations in the Citadel's courtyard. They excavated along the inner side of the city wall and uncovered Hasmonean buildings overlaid by a complex of walls which they interpreted as part of the foundations of Herod's palace. During the years 1976–1980, H. Geva excavated the southern part of the Citadel courtyard, and conducted surveys in various areas of the courtyard (see in this volume, pp. 156–167).

Following this work, we excavated the entire northern and western parts of the courtyard northwest of the First Wall, in addition to carrying out surveys of a number of halls of the present Citadel and a comprehensive excavation of the eastern and southern sides of the Citadel's moat.[1]

[1] The excavations, conducted on behalf of the Tower of David Museum and the Department of Antiquities and Museums (today, the Antiquities Authority), with the financial support of the Jerusalem Foundation, were part of the site restoration project in conjunction with the preparations for the Museum of the History of Jerusalem. The work was directed by R. Sivan and G. Solar. D. Kaufman supervised the excavations in the moat.

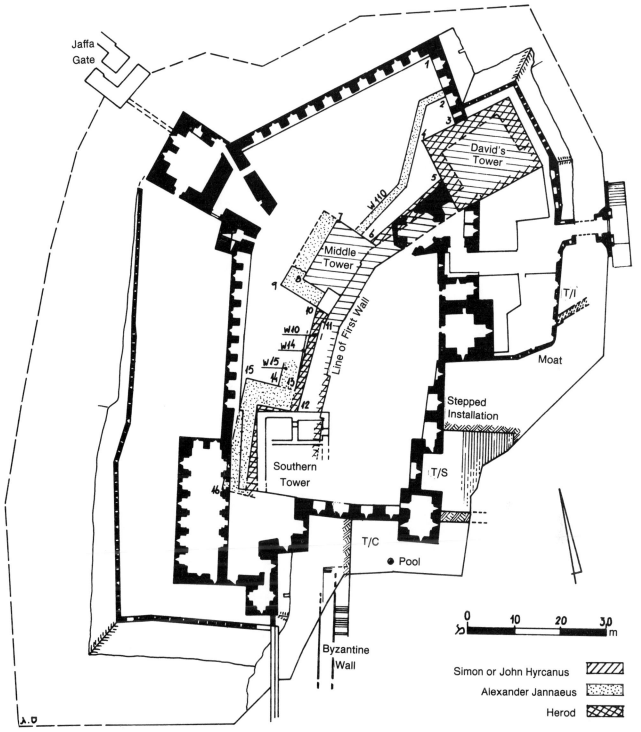

Jaffa
Gate

David's
Tower

Middle
Tower

W10

T/I

Moat

Line of First Wall

W10

W14

W15

Stepped
Installation

Southern
Tower

T/S

T/C

Pool

Byzantine
Wall

0   10   20   30
                    m

Simon or John Hyrcanus

Alexander Jannaeus

Herod

Tower of David Citadel: general plan of the excavations

## The Second Temple Period Fortifications

Our excavations along the city wall between Points 3 and 12 (see plan), complemented those conducted by Johns. We uncovered additional sections of the ancient fortifica-tions which shed new light on the various construction phases of the Second Temple period fortifications.

AREA A. THE NORTHWESTERN CORNER OF THE TOWER OF DAVID (POINTS 3-5). The northern side of the

Tower of David was exposed down to bedrock, showing that the entire tower was founded on bedrock—except for its northwestern corner (4) which was built on small stones and debris. The rock surface is 766.65 m. above sea level and contains natural pockets of terra-rossa soil. Northwest of the corner of the tower an artificial trench, 7 m. long and 1.8 m. deep, was found cut in the rock. In it were accumulations of ballista stones and bronze arrowheads. A lead sling projectile was found in fill material from the foundations of the Roman-Byzantine city wall (1–3) below the eastern wall of the Citadel adjoining the Tower of David (see below).

AREA B. JOHNS'S MIDDLE TOWER (6–10). At this point we dug 7 m. to reach bedrock and exposed a tower of ashlar construction, 14.35 m. long and 8.9 m. wide (Tower 6-7-8). At the corner (7), eleven courses survived, each 55 cm. high. The outer faces of the tower are built of ashlars with dressed margins and rough, unworked bosses, laid in alternating courses of headers and stretchers. Two different methods were employed in building the tower core: with layers of closely set, roughly dressed stones; and layers of unhewn stone construction (Pl. IIIa).

A 3.5 m. massive, reinforcing revetment wall (9–10) was added along the western and southern sides of this tower. Unlike the earlier tower (6-7-8), this added construction was founded on an earth fill. Johns had already uncovered this section, as well as a small part of the earlier tower's northern wall (6–7), and he considered them all as part of one Hasmonean tower (Johns's Middle Tower *d–e–f*). Geva reexamined the northern side of the earlier tower.

Our excavations along the northern wall (7–8) of the early tower and around its northwestern corner (7) uncovered additional concentrations of ballista stones and arrowheads.

Tower of David Citadel: view of the First Wall and the Middle Tower of the Second Temple period; looking southeast (and see Pl. IIIa)

170

These, and other finds, clearly indicate that the original tower dates to the beginning of the Hasmonean period, while its reinforcing revetment uncovered by Johns should be attributed to Herod's time and not to Alexander Jannaeus as Johns thought.

**AREA C. WALL 5–6 BETWEEN THE TOWER OF DAVID AND THE MIDDLE TOWER.** Scholars have noted in the past that this section actually reinforces an earlier city wall. This addition along the outer face of the wall is built of ashlars with dressed margins and rough bosses laid in alternating header and stretcher courses. Underneath, five foundation courses constructed of roughly dressed stones laid by the same method were revealed. The thickness of the later wall was ascertained where it adjoins the towers (5 and 6).

At the juncture (6) of the reinforcing revetment of the city wall (5–6) and the Middle Tower (6–10), a number of foundation stones were removed from the wall to expose behind it, 1.6 m. from the outer face, the original construction of the First Wall of the Second Temple period. The extension of this wall behind (east of) the Middle Tower is partially built of unhewn stones. This led to the hypothesis that these are remains of a First Temple period wall; however, the finds do not support. It seems that the wall was constructed with rough stones because the building of the tower against this section was planned from the outset.

We also removed foundation stones from the joint (5) between this revetment wall (5–6) and the Tower of David (3–5) with the aim of locating the early wall and determining its relation here to the Tower of David. However, the ancient wall proved inaccessible due to the thickness of the reinforcing wall (3.5 m.) at this point.

Until now, the reinforcement (5–6) of the city wall had been attributed to the days of Alexander Jannaeus, i.e., after the construction of the Middle Tower and before that of the Tower of David. Between the Tower of David and a "seam" identified by Johns some 6.5 m. to its south, repair work of different masonry can be seen in the upper part of the revetment wall. This section was generally considered to be stone construction filling up the wide foundation trench of the Tower of David that dated to Herod's reign.

Excavation of the city wall (5–6) and its foundations down to bedrock at the point (5) where it meets the Tower of David facilitated a reassessment of their mutual relation. We were able to ascertain that two of the lower ashlar courses, and all the courses of the foundation of the reinforcing revetment wall below, extend uninterruptedly from the Middle Tower to the Tower of David. This proves that the wall does not predate the Tower of David, as originally believed, and can also be attributed to the Herodian period. The repair of the reinforcing revetment wall (Johns's "foundation trench") was carried out at an indeterminate, later date.

West of the city wall, Wall 110 was uncovered extending from the Middle Tower and disappearing from sight beneath the Roman-Byzantine city wall (2). It is composed of small

Tower of David Citadel: the joint at Point 5 of the reinforcing revetment of the city wall (right) and the Tower of David (left)

171

Tower of David Citadel: view to northeast of the outer face of the First Wall to the right, Tower of David in the center, and Wall 110 in front of them

unhewn stones, is 1.6 m. thick, and was partly founded on bedrock and in part built upon earth fills. Wall 110 runs northeastward from the northeastern side of the Middle Tower (6–7), parallel to the city wall for 13 m. north of the Tower of David, where it veers slightly northward, passing approximately 50 cm. from the northwestern corner of the Tower of David (4). Six meters from the tower the wall once again turns eastward. The stratigraphy shows that Wall 110 is earlier than the Tower of David and the reinforcing revetment (5–6) of the First Wall. The ballista stones incorporated in its construction indicate that it is later than the mid–2nd century B.C.E. (see below).

**AREA D. THE WALL BETWEEN THE MIDDLE AND SOUTHERN TOWERS (10–13).** The excavations in this area uncovered three additional fortification lines west and lower than the line of the First Wall discovered earlier by Johns (11–12).

**Wall 10.** Three foundation courses with stones in secondary use were found in this wall, as well as two upper courses, built of stones

resembling the ashlar courses of the Herodian reinforcing revetment between the Tower of David and the Middle Tower.

**Wall 14.** The course of this wall, deviating slightly westward from Wall 10, was preserved 2.9 m. below the latter. Only three courses of roughly dressed stones without margins survived.

**Wall 15.** The outer side of this wall was uncovered 3.5 m. west of Wall 14. Only a short section of its construction was visible since a wall of the early Medieval period was superimposed on it. Wall 15 consists of stones with dressed margins similar to those found in the reinforcing revetment of the Middle Tower (9–10).

In the Byzantine period repairs were made along the line of the First Wall of the Second Temple period with additional courses at the northern end of the wall (11–12).

**THE SOUTHERN TOWER (14–16).** A massive tower was uncovered south of the three walls described above. Part of its core, exposed by Johns, was reexcavated by Geva. In our excavations we uncovered the northern side of the tower (14–15) and most of the western side (15–16). The tower is approximately 24 m. long and 11 m. wide. It is built of roughly dressed stones. Twelve courses of the northern side were exposed, each 52–55 cm. high.

Previous excavations uncovered two later towers dating to the Herodian period built above this one. A *miqveh* (ritual bath) was found built into the core of the earlier stage of the Southern Tower. The evidence indicates that the large Southern Tower described above was originally built before Herod's reign and thus should be dated to the Hasmonean period. The similarity of its construction to that of the later stage of the Middle Tower (9–10) suggests that it was built by Alexander Jannaeus. Wall 15 was built at the same time, while Wall 10 is later, perhaps dating to the Herodian period. The available data do not permit a more precise dating of Wall 14.

## The Assemblages of Military Projectiles and their Significance

The accumulations of weaponry discovered in well-defined contexts outside the fortification systems in Areas A–C constitute a unique find. These comprise ballista stones and arrowheads, ferrules of spear hafts, and lead sling-projectiles.

A large concentration of ballista stones was found near the Tower of David; two of the stones had been covered up by the foundation of the northwestern corner of this tower (4). An additional assemblage lay along the northern side of the Middle Tower and near its northwestern corner (7). Scattered ballista stones were also found under and within Wall 110. The ballista stones, approximately 200 in number, are smoothly dressed. They are 10–30 cm. in diameter and, with the exception of two basalt ones, all are made of hard limestone.

Dozens of typical Hellenistic arrowheads were found together with the ballista stones. The largest group was discovered near the Middle Tower. All the arrowheads are of bronze and most are marked with the device

Tower of David Citadel: view over the northwestern corner (4) of the Tower of David and the rock-cut trench containing a concentration of ballista stones

illustrated in the photograph. This may have been the emblem of a military unit, the initials of a ruler, or markings for a shooting range.[2] Many hollow, conical iron objects about 5–7 cm. long—apparently ferrules of spear hafts, some of them still containing wooden fragments—were found together with the ballista stones and the arrowheads. In addition, two lead sling-projectiles were uncovered, weighing 36 and 59.5 g. Each was marked with a winged lightening device. One bears a fragmentary Greek inscription and the representation of an arrow of a type similar to the arrowheads found at the site. These finds, dating to the 2nd century B.C.E., clearly

---

[2] This was suggested to the writers by V. Tzaferis.

Tower of David Citadel: group of bronze arrowheads of the Hellenistic period

Tower of David Citadel: Hellenistic period arrowheads marked with device

belonged to an attacking army—perhaps at the siege of Jerusalem by Antiochus VII Sidetes during the reign of John Hyrcanus (133–132 B.C.E.).

The location of this assemblage of projectiles leads us to conclude that the Tower of David was actually built above a smaller, earlier Hasmonean tower. As described above, the ballista stones were found in two separate concentrations, one against the corner of the Hasmonean Middle Tower and the other near and beneath the corner of the Tower of

Tower of David Citadel: lead sling projectile marked with arrow device similar to that on the arrowheads found in the excavations

David, at some distance from the city wall of that period. This suggests that the ballista stones and arrowheads were actually shot at an earlier tower. This conjecture is also supported by the irregular course of Wall 110 here which originally antedated the Herodian Tower of David.

## Chronological Conclusions

In the fortifications system of the Second Temple period uncovered in the Citadel courtyard, three main periods of construction entailing six building phases can be distinguished. In the initial construction period, the city wall (the First Wall) including the early Middle Tower (6–8) and the tower surmised to be beneath the Tower of David were built. This period preceded the siege by Antiochus VII Sidetes, and perhaps coincided with the time of Simon the Hasmonean and John Hyrcanus I. The second period of construction included the building of Wall 110, the later stage of the Middle Tower (9–10), Wall 15, and the early stage of the Southern Tower (14–16). This construction followed Antiochus VII Sidetes's siege and predated Herod's intensive building activities, and should perhaps be ascribed to the time of Alexander Jannaeus. In the third period of construction—the time of Herod—the Tower of David and the reinforcing revetment of the city wall (5–6), and Wall 10 were built.

## The Moat
Three parts of the moat were excavated:

THE SOUTHERN SECTION T/C. This section of the moat extends from the southwestern corner of the Citadel to the southeastern tower, including the area within the Kishle police station south of it. The southwestern part of this area was excavated down to bedrock. We reexposed here the Second Temple period *miqveh* (ritual bath) first discovered by Johns. Part of the western side and several plastered steps of the *miqveh* were revealed. It was damaged, presumably during the Roman-Byzantine period, when the entire area was converted into a quarry. Various quarrying stages can be identified. Traces of the contours of stone blocks are still visible in the quarry face and two partly quarried blocks remain attached to the rock.

Tower of David Citadel: base of Herodian column uncovered in the southeast section of the Citadel moat

Over the quarry, a late Byzantine period city wall, 3.1 m. thick, was exposed running north-south to a length of 13 m. in the Kishle area. Plastered steps, about 3 m. wide, were discovered adjoining the wall on its eastern side. The upper steps were built-up, while the lower ones were hewn in the rock. The eastern edge of the steps abuts on a long, deep artificial escarpment cut in the rock, marking the western side of a large pool. Part of the pool's northern side under the southern wall of the Citadel was also uncovered. The full dimensions of the pool could not be determined since it extends south and east under the Kishle. The date of the pool is undoubtedly Byzantine. In the late Byzantine period, a deep, large water cistern was dug under its floor. A large base of a Herodian column, 1.1 m. in diameter, in which an opening was cut, covered the narrow mouth of the cistern. Buildings were constructed around the cistern during the Early Arab period, and a plastered trough was installed.

Tower of David Citadel: the monumental staircase of the 1st century B.C.E. uncovered at the southeastern section of the Citadel moat

THE SOUTHEASTERN SECTION T/S. This section of the moat extends from the southeastern tower to the eastern tower. The entire area was excavated down to bedrock. A very large, 17 m.-wide recessed installation hewn vertically in the rock and oriented east-to-west was uncovered, including a broad flight of nineteen steps leading into it from ground level at the eastern side. The lower steps, each 25 cm.

175

Tower of David Citadel: section of massive wall of the 8th century B.C.E. built of large unhewn stones uncovered at the eastern side of the Citadel moat

survived, since most were subsequently removed for secondary use. Along the seventh step from the bottom of this installation, and turning westward along its northern scarp-wall toward the Citadel, is a rock-cut, plastered channel.

On the basis of coins found in the plaster used to fill holes and to level the rock surface at the bottom of the installation, and associated finds, we were able to date it to the Hasmonean period. This stepped installation probably pertained to a monumental building, possibly connected with the royal Hasmonean palace which, we believe, extended over the area of the present-day Citadel. The installation was in some way utilized also in Herod's royal palace.

THE EASTERN SECTION T/I. In this area along the northeastern section of the moat the discoveries included a fragment of a wall built of large, unhewn stones and several small fragments of walls built of small, unhewn stones. These walls were constructed over former stone quarries. Associated ceramic finds are dated to the 8th–7th centuries B.C.E. The limited area excavated did not provide sufficient evidence for determining the function of the structure constructed of large stones. Perhaps it was part of the city wall or of another fortification in the northwestern corner of the city dating to the end of the First Temple period.

high, are hewn in the rock; the upper steps were built of stones only a few of which have

## Bibliography

Amiran, R. and Eitan, A., "Excavations in the Courtyard of the Citadel, Jerusalem, 1968–1969," *IEJ* 20 (1970): 9–17.

——— , "Excavations in the Jerusalem Citadel," in: Y. Yadin (ed.), *Jerusalem Revealed* (Jerusalem, 1976), pp. 52–54.

Bahat, D., "David's Tower and its Name in Second Temple Times," *Eretz Israel* 15 (1981): 396–400 (Hebrew).

Geva, H., "The Tower of David—Phasael or Hippicus?" *IEJ* 31 (1981): 57–65.

——— , "Excavations in the Citadel of Jerusalem, 1979–1980, Preliminary Report," *IEJ* 33 (1983): 55–71.

Johns, C.N., "The Citadel, Jerusalem—A Summary of Work Since 1934," *QDAP* 14 (1950): 121–190.

Sivan, R. (ed.), *David's Tower Rediscovered* (Jerusalem, 1983).

# The Western Wall Tunnels

## Dan Bahat

After the Six-Day War, the Ministry of Religious Affairs began to expose parts of the Western Wall of the Temple Mount along its entire length of 488 m. The section of the Western Wall accessible to the public at the prayer plaza (2) is less than 60 m. In the area south of it, the excavations conducted by B. Mazar exposed the Western Wall along about 70 m. The northern stretch of the Wall, about 320–340 m. long, is hidden beneath the buildings of the Muslim Quarter; hence work from the prayer plaza northward required tunneling under the existing structures of Old City.[1]

The excavations followed the underground explorations begun in 1867–1870 by Ch. Warren, whose discoveries included what he called the Secret Passage (3) and the Giant Causeway (4). During the first stage of the work, the large space under Wilson's Arch (5) was cleared, and a wall, built in 1866 by the inhabitants of the houses above to form an immense water cistern under part of this vaulted structure, was removed. Tunneling then proceeded northward along the Western Wall, exposing about two courses out of its entire height. The long, narrow tunnel extended to the vicinity of the Prison—or Inspector's—Gate (Bab el-Nādir) in the Western Wall of the Temple Mount above.

## The Bridge

Widespread interest in the large bridge complex (4) adjacent to the Temple compound was aroused already at the time of its discovery in 1853 by T. Tobler, one of the outstanding 19th-century explorers of Jerusalem. Ch. Wilson, who worked in the city within the framework of the 1864 Survey of Jerusalem, described it, and since then it became associated with his name—although he himself heard about it from Tobler. Wilson's Arch (5), which is about 12.8 m. wide, is the easternmost of the complex of vaults supporting the bridge. Above Wilson's Arch is the Gate of the Chain (Bab es-Silsileh) (9), and next to it, the Gate of Peace (Bab es-Salām).

Warren dated Wilson's Arch to the Roman or Byzantine periods rather than to the time of the Second Temple. From Wilson's Arch west to Ha-Gai (El-Wad) Street, a complex of vaults supports what Warren called the Giant Causeway. All the vaulting consists of two adjoining, staggered series of vaults, alternating between the southern one overlapping the northern, and vice versa. Warren attributed these constructions to the Roman period, or later to the 4th–5th centuries C.E. R.W. Hamilton, who in 1931 excavated at the western end of this vaulted complex, proposed an Early Arab period dating (7th–8th centuries C.E.) for the entire construction. Archaeological excavations above these vaults in 1991 suggested a Roman-period dating for the street pavement beneath the modern Street of the Chain and over the vaults.[2]

---

[1] Archaeological supervision of the Western Wall project was initially entrusted (until 1978) to the Southern Wall Expedition under B. Mazar, directed by M. Ben-Dov. After an interruption of several years, work was resumed in 1985, under the direction of the present writer. Today, the site is administered by the Western Wall Heritage Foundation. It has been necessary periodically to close it in order perform maintenance work because the antiquated water and drainage networks above the tunnel break down frequently and require repair.

[2] R. Abu-Riya, "Jerusalem, Street of the Chain (A)," and L. Gershuny, "Jerusalem, Street of the Chain (B)," *Excavations and Surveys in Israel 1991* 10 (1992): 134–136.

I prefer and accept Hamilton's Early Arab period dating for the construction of this complex of vaults—not only because in my view the archaeological data are indecisive in this case, but also because it fits in well with the historical evidence concerning Jerusalem at that later period: the Temple Mount was rebuilt in a new form—the walls were repaired, mosques erected on it, and the immediate surroundings became an important Muslim center. Apparently, the large bridge, which according to Josephus Flavius was destroyed at the beginning of the First Jewish

Revolt against Rome (66–70 C.E.), was reconstructed as part of the restoration of the water supply system from Solomon's Pools to the Temple Mount during the Early Arab period. The double, overlapping form of the supporting bridge vaults may be explained by the foundations of the new bridge built by the Muslims onto partly surviving Second Temple masonry, which must still have been very impressive at that time. These dictated to the Muslim architects the rhythm and height of the vault spacing. The integration of the old remains was facilitated by splitting the width of the supporting vaulting in two.

This can be demonstrated by examining the vaulted structure filling the space between Wilson's Arch (5) and the Herodian "Masonic Hall" (7) west of it. (Warren proposed this hall as a gathering place for Freemasons who convened in the Holy City at the time of his exploration work.) The hall is known today colloquially—but incorrectly—as the Hasmonean Hall. Since the Muslim architects found no earlier structural remains upon which they could build in this space, they erected a new lower vault on the occupational level of the Second Temple period, and above this constructed an additional vault to bring it up to

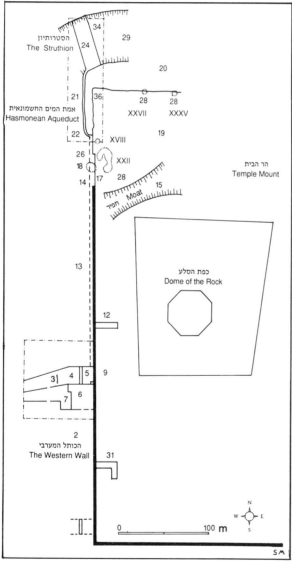

Plan of the Western Wall and the early remains adjacent to it

1. Western Wall; 2. Western Wall prayer plaza; 3. Secret Passage; 4. Giant Causeway; 5. Wilson's Arch; 6. Warren's shaft under Wilson's Arch; 7. Herodian ("Masonic") Hasmonean Hall; 8. stairway of the Second Temple period; 9. Gate of the Chain; 10. area of Crusader construction in the bridge complex; 11. large hall; 12. Warren's Gate; 13. narrow part of Western Wall tunnel dug in 1967–1982; 14. beginning of bedrock in line of Western Wall; 15. fosse on earlier Temple Mount; 16. Herodian street; 17. ancient foundation trenches; 18. Hasmonean water cistern; 19. conjectured site of Baris fortress; 20. site of Antonia fortress; 21. large aqueduct; 22. earlier water channels cut through by the large aqueduct; 23. early dam across the large aqueduct; 24. Strouthion pool; 25. engaged pilasters in Western Wall; 26. el-Madrasa al-Manjakiyya; 27. turning in Western Wall—tower; 28. cisterns on Temple Mount (Roman numeration is that of Warren and Wilson); 29. moat of the Antonia fortress; 30. Pool of Israel; 31. Barclay's Gate; 32. Ghawanima Gate; 33. Via Dolorosa; 34. Lithostrotos; 35. Sisters of Zion Convent; 36. Ghawanima minaret

178

Schematic view to the north in the area of Wilson's Arch and the Hasmonean Hall

the height of the entire complex supporting the bridge. The lower Muslim vault thus abuts the Masonic Hall, dating to the Second Temple period, on one side, and the western pier of Wilson's Arch, the lower part of which is also of Second Temple date, on the other. In one of the halls (used today for the audio-visual presentation), stairs (8) can be seen ascending from the street level of the Second Temple period to the contemporaneous hall (7). The lower Muslim vault is built over them. There is also no connection—as was thought when Warren published his findings—between the bridge complex and the First Wall of Jerusalem of the Second Temple period.

On entering the bridge substructure complex, we first come to the Secret Passage (3).

This name was given by Warren to a long barrel-vault adjoining the vaults of the bridge to the south. He identified it with the tunnel described by the 15th-century C.E. historian Mujir ed-Din who writes that it was King David's secret passage between his palace (the Tower of David!) and his place of prayer on the Temple Mount. Mujir ed-Din also mentions that anyone digging beneath his house in the Street of the Chain in order to construct a private water cistern meets up with this secret passage. It is very hard to date this passageway which was constructed by breaking through several vaults of the bridge—that is, after the Early Arab period. In one of the walls of the passage there is even a stone in secondary use with a broken inscription of the Roman Tenth

179

Legion. The passage was thus most probably constructed in the Mamluk period (14th–15th centuries C.E.) when the entire area of the Western Wall again underwent architectural reorganization (see below). Above the Masonic Hall are several particularly narrow vaults (10) which undoubtedly date to the Crusader period. Contemporary sources tell of a Church of St. Gilles in this area. It is difficult to establish a link of these narrow vaults with the church, although some such connection is certainly a possibility.

## Supporting Structures along the Western Wall

Adjoining the entire length of the Western Wall at the present street level are buildings of the Mamluk period (14th–15th centuries C.E.). These are well known from the historical sources and from the survey conducted there during the past two decades by the British School of Archaeology in Jerusalem.[3] Our tunneling work did not interfere with these structures but only penetrated into the water cisterns beneath them. This was possible because during the Mamluk period the buildings were erected upon vaults and arches constructed to raise them high above the

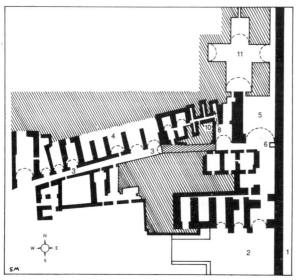

Plan of the Giant Causeway and Wilson's Arch

[3] M.H. Burgoyne, *Mamluk Jerusalem* (London, 1987).

occupational level of the city here, so as to bring the floors to the level of the adjacent Temple Mount. Under the Mamluks, Jerusalem became an important Islamic religious center, and the new buildings along and above the Western Wall, all of religious import, were designed to communicate directly with the Temple Mount. All the area between the Temple Mount and present-day Ha-Gai (El-Wad) Street was elevated in this way. Until now, only one complete vault of this type, the large hall (11)—the supporting structure of the Madrasa el-Baladiyya—has been cleared. (This substructure is now an exhibition hall in which a model of the Temple Mount in the Second Temple period is on display.)

Since the Madrasa el-Baladiyya is a building with four iwans, the large hall beneath it has a corresponding cruciform plan (11). In other words, the supporting structures determined the plan of the buildings above. This large building is entirely constructed of stones with rough margins typical of the Ayyubid period in Jerusalem. It may be, therefore, that formerly this was an Ayyubid madrasa known today only from historic sources to have stood in this vicinity. The supporting structure of the Madrasa al-Manjakiyya (26) is also known to us and is built entirely on the Herodian street that was discovered in the northernmost part of the excavations (see below). As it progressed along the Western Wall, the tunneling work passed through many such supporting structures. These served in part as water cisterns for the buildings above; others filled all sorts of other purposes and their existence was completely unknown to the people who lived in the houses over them. This is probably why there is no mention of these supporting structures in the historical sources that describe Mamluk Jerusalem.

## The Large Hall

As indicated above, the large hall (11), which is the supporting structure of the Madrasa el-Baladiyya building above it, was completely cleared of debris and several new details were revealed. Sometime after the destruction of the Second Temple in 70 C.E., a large water pool was built up here against the outside of the Western Wall of the Temple Mount. This entailed the construction of a thin wall onto the Western Wall. It was held in place by being built up around stone pegs that had been forced into rectangular holes cut in the Temple Mount wall and secured by means of an extremely hard binding cement. The pool was lined on the inside with impermeable plaster. The pool measures 30 m. along the Western Wall; its width westward could not yet be established. A probe dug in the earth fill of the pool reached a depth of 5 m. below the upper edge of the plaster on the walls, but we were unable to reach the bottom at the time. As to the date of this pool, it clearly could no longer have been used when the Ayyubid building of the 13th century C.E. was constructed, and it postdates the Second Temple period.

## The Large Stone—the "Master Course"

Several stages of construction can be detected in the Western Wall of the Temple Mount north of Wilson' Arch. At the bottom of the section uncovered in the large hall can be seen a 1.3 m.-high course of large stones typical of the Herodian masonry in the walls of the Temple Mount. Above this, four giant cut stones form a remarkable course in the Wall. The longest of these stones measures 13.7 m. and the second 12.05 m.; the two others are much smaller. This course is 3.5 m. high. Ground-penetrating radar tests by experts from the Haifa Technion showed the course to be 4.2–4.9 m. wide at this point. Thus it seems that each of the stones occupies the entire width of the wall. The weight of the largest of these ashlars can be calculated at 570 tons! Apparently, when the Temple was destroyed by the Romans in 70 C.E. the walls were dismantled, and this immense course of masonry was even partly chiselled away in an attempt to topple it, as was done to the courses above it. Only a little of the marginal dressing on the upper part of the huge stones in this course remains intact. Evidence of this deliberate destruction of the Western Wall turned up in the shaft dug by Warren down to the

Herodian street (6) and in B. Mazar's excavations of this street further south along the Western Wall of the Temple Mount.

Why was the outer Temple wall built of these huge stones in this particular place? A course in the walls of the Temple Mount built intermittently of stones twice the height of the average ones can be seen also along the southern wall. This course has become known as the Master Course. But since stones of the tremendous proportions discovered in the excavated tunnel appear only in this section of the western Temple Mount walls, there must have been a local engineering reason for their placement here. And indeed, the electronic probes showed that behind these stones is an empty space under the esplanade of the Temple Mount. The mammoth stones were laid here in order to counterbalance the static outward pressure of the vault that was built over this void to support the paved surface above it. We dubbed also these gigantic stones the Master Course, after the huge, but smaller, stones in the southern wall.

Above the Master Course of Herodian construction there remain a few of the courses laid down during the Early Arab period when the Wall was reconstructed. The earthquakes that shook Jerusalem in 747 (or 749 C.E.), and in 1033 C.E., necessitated repeated repairs to the Wall. That is why the stones are of many types and sizes, giving the Wall an uneven appearance here.

## Warren's Gate

The Master Course ends in the north, at Warren's Gate (12). This was one of the entrances of the Temple Mount mentioned by Josephus as the gate leading to the Mount from the suburb west of it. The sealed-off structure of Warren's Gate, which nowadays serves as a water cistern of the Temple Mount, was discovered by Warren (No. XXX in his list of the cisterns on the Temple Mount) and since then bears his name. He surveyed the cistern and described its position as perpendicular to the Western Wall, identifying it as a gateway to the Temple Mount. Of course, Warren did not see the exterior part of the

Arch of Warren's Gate in the Western Wall of the Temple Mount

was called in the 11th century C.E.—and certainly from the time Jews were permitted to live again in the Holy City following the Muslim conquest. Among the Genizah documents are some which relate that as a result of the 1033 C.E. earthquake, the Cave Synagogue was destroyed and was afterwards restored with money raised by a special appeal undertaken by the Jews of Jerusalem in Diaspora communities. Near Warren's Gate—actually slightly north of it—we are now directly west of the Stone of Foundation under the Dome of the Rock, the traditional site of the Holy of Holies near which Jews strove to pray.

## The Narrow Tunnel

From Warren's Gate northward, the underground passage narrows to permit only one person at a time to proceed (13). At first the tunnel crosses a disused water cistern that

Section of construction of the Western Wall as uncovered in the water cistern of the Mamluk period

gateway that was found in the present tunneling excavations along the wall. The southern jamb of the gateway is the northernmost monolithic edge of the Master Course; the northern jamb was built up of smaller stones at some later time. The stones of the arch over the gateway are worked in a very similar manner to those of the Triple and the Single Gate of the southern wall of the Temple Mount, both of which are dated, mainly on historic grounds, to the 11th century C.E. It seems, therefore, that Warren's Gate as it is now should also be dated to that period. This fits in well with information gleaned from the Cairo Genizah, which suggests that this gateway structure can be identified with the Cave, as the main synagogue of the Jews of Jerusalem

182

Southern part of the Western Wall tunnel; the wall of the Herodian Temple Mount is on the right side

belongs to the Mamluk building above (Ribat ez-Zamani). Beyond the place in the Wall that was repaired after the 1033 C.E. earthquake some of the finest Herodian masonry begins to appear. Each course is set back about 2 cm. from the face of the one beneath it, and the bosses of the ashlars are framed with three bands of carved edging—an unusual form of stone dressing typical of the construction of the Temple Mount.

Proceeding north, the narrow tunnel reveals the natural rock cut to form a kind of stepped surface upon which the courses of the Western Wall are laid (14). The point where the natural rock first appears is northwest of the fosse (15) discovered by Warren, north of the raised platform inside the Temple Mount.

This area north of the fosse was beyond the limits of the earlier Temple Mount (the one built before King Herod's) and was incorporated into the complex by Herod. The quarrying at this part of the Western Wall was the work of Herod to permit the passage of the street (16) along the Wall (see below).

## The Baris Fortress
Near the northern end of the tunnel, remains of well-hewn trenches (17), that were cut through by the Herodian quarrying, can be distinguished in the worked natural rock beneath the Herodian courses. These trenches are too wide to have served as water conduits and most probably were foundation trenches for earlier walls from which the stones had

183

Steps in the Hasmonean water cistern

Stone in the process of being worked found near the northwestern corner of the Temple Mount; its far end is roughly hewn and the fore part is finely finished

been removed. A little to the north of these trenches we found remains of a water cistern (18) that was also cut through by Herodian quarrying. Only the western part of this cistern can be seen now; its eastern part probably still exists under the Temple Mount platform. The very rough rock-cutting in this cistern suggests that Herod's builders did not have the time to smooth the quarrying marks as they did elsewhere. The cistern was originally at least 10 m. in diameter. The steps we found leading into it were integral with the central pier of living rock that had been left in place to support the ceiling. When the Herodian street along the Western Wall was paved (see below), it circumvented the cistern on its western side. It is the only known section of this street that does not closely hug the wall. In order to keep passers-by from falling into the open cistern and to keep the paving stones of the street from gradually sliding into it, a

large stone, with a slightly convex side, was placed there as a permanent barrier and balustrade. The upper, rounded part of this stone, facing the Western Wall, is polished from being constantly handled.

Once we understood that the large aqueduct (21; see below) reaches only as far as the northwestern Herodian addition to the earlier Temple Mount precinct, we realized that its only function was to supply the cisterns cut into the rock there. The construction of the stone-cut water conduit was a major public works project. We know from the sources that the only building that antedated the Herodian construction in this area was the Baris fortress (19). Therefore, the above-mentioned water cistern, the large aqueduct, all the rock-cut trenches described above, as well as Cisterns XVIII, XXII, XXVII, XXXV on the Temple

Mount must have been connected with the Baris fortress that was destroyed when Herod integrated the hill on which it stood in his expanded reconstitution of the Temple Mount.

The Baris fortress was probably founded already in the First Temple period, or perhaps it was built by the returnees from Babylonian exile. In any case, already in the days of Nehemiah, a governor was put in charge of it (Nehemiah 7:2). Nehemiah saw to the repair of its gate (Nehemiah 2:8). The Baris reached the zenith of its fame in the days of the Hasmoneans. Josephus relates that it was the Hasmoneans who built it (*Ant.* XV, 403). It is possible, as also Warren suggested, that the large aqueduct permitted access to the Temple Mount from the Baris fortress (*War* V, 75; *Ant.* XIII, 307). Josephus also mentions that Herod had a secret passageway made from the Antonia (20) fortress facing the eastern gate of the interior Temple platform (*Ant.* XV, 424). Elsewhere, he refers to an event that occurred at the time of Aristobolus I (104–103 B.C.E.) in the Baris: "...Antonia...was a fortress adjoining the north side of the temple, which was formerly called Baris, but afterwards took this new name under Antony's supremacy" (*War* I, 118). Thus, Josephus equates the Baris with the Antonia fortress. But in another passage (*Ant.* XV, 409) he explains that the Antonia was built in place of the Baris, and that Herod rebuilt the Baris in a stronger manner and renamed it Antonia. The site of the Baris is inside the northwestern corner of the Herodian Temple Mount (19) where the southern scarp of the hill formerly sloped toward the northern end of the earlier Temple Mount platform. This entire southern part of the hill was subsequently removed by Herod when he integrated this area in the Temple precinct and it was levelled to conform with the rest of the Temple Mount surface. As mentioned above, in the Western Wall tunnel project remains that may be ascribed to the Baris fortress were discovered for the first time. Among these are the aqueduct (21), cistern (18), and indirect evidence of wall sections of which only the foundation trenches (17) survive. A study of the existing water cisterns (28; Wilson-Warren Nos. XXVII and XXXV) in the northwestern corner of the Temple Mount, which were surveyed by Warren, shows that their upper parts had been severed when the rock was levelled at this spot in the course of Herod's construction. They may originally have been part of the Baris water system supplied by the large aqueduct along with Cisterns XVIII and XXII.

Today, the view from the school built on the highest remaining point of the Antonia hill attests the dominating topographic position of the Baris and Antonia fortresses as guardians of the Temple. The elevation here is 7 m. above the natural rock—the Stone of Foundation—under the Dome of the Rock.

### The Large Aqueduct

The large, deep, trench-like aqueduct (21) cut in the rock was first discovered by Warren on 28 October 1867, and was later investigated also by other explorers of Jerusalem in that period, such as C.R. Conder and C. Schick. According to Warren, the aqueduct flowed with sewage to a depth of 1.8 m. and he floated on these effluents on a raft made of old doors. When we rediscovered the aqueduct in 1985 it was almost dry. Water percolating through the rock-cut walls and collecting in a narrow channel (about 30 × 30 cm.) along the bottom of the western side of the aqueduct, drains into a natural karstic fissure located midway in the aqueduct. The rock walls of the aqueduct are about 10 m. at their highest, and it is 1.2 m. wide. Its floor slopes gently downward from north to south to allow the water to flow by gravity. Despite its appearance, it is not a tunnel but a deep channel cut into the rocky surface of the ground and covered with stone slabs, among which is even a fragment of column in secondary use. In some of the places, where the surface of the rock does not come up to the required level, the walls are built up with stones. In this way, by being covered with stone slabs, the aqueduct became a tunnel over a distance of about 80 m. between the Strouthion pool (24) and the

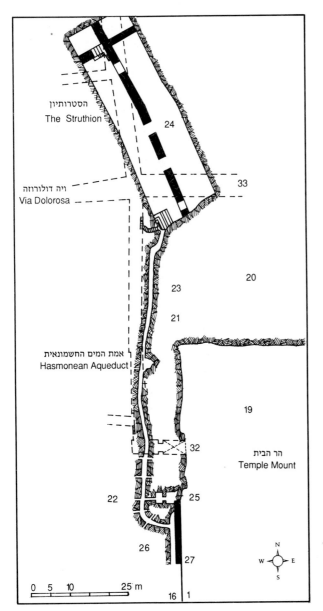

הסטרותיון
The Struthion

ויה דולורוזה
Via Dolorosa

אמת המים החשמונאית
Hasmonean Aqueduct

24

33

20

23

21

19

הר הבית
Temple Mount

32

22          25

26

27

N
W · E
S

0  5  10        25 m

16  1

Western Wall. About 20 m. south of the pool, during the Herodian period, a 3 m.-high dam (23) was built across the aqueduct leaving only a small opening at the bottom leading to the narrow channel and the karstic fissure. The dam is built near the point where the aqueduct channel was cut by the Western Wall to keep rainwater in the aqueduct from flooding the foundation trench of the Wall during its construction. The general direction of the aqueduct is from due north to south; its southern part parallels the Western Wall, but then it turns eastward toward the Wall. At this point it intersects five narrow, rock-cut water channels (22) at about 1 m. above the bottom of the aqueduct. The channels seem to be of earlier date and were cut through when the large aqueduct was hewn in the rock. In the southern stretch of the aqueduct there still are Medieval supporting vaults, as in the southern part of the entire system.

Where did the large aqueduct receive its water? Warren traced its course north of the Strouthion pool and conjectured that it began at a point a little northeast of the Damascus Gate. He identified this aqueduct as one of the conduits that brought water to the Temple

◁ Left: plan of the northwestern corner of the Temple Mount, the large aqueduct and the Strouthion pool; below: north-south section and view east along the large aqueduct

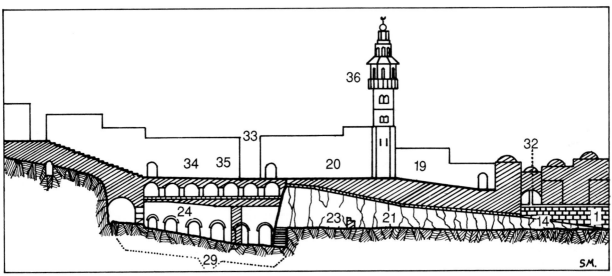

36

33

34    35        20        19        32

24

29

23  21            14    1

S.M.

Mount from a source north of the city. We cannot agree with this assumption because the aqueduct antedates the Herodian period and was cut through and became inoperative when the Western Wall was built. Moreover, the aqueduct did not reach the Temple Mount precinct as it was before Herod extended its limits northward. At the time of writing the northern stretch of the aqueduct has not yet been investigated, but it apparently collected surface runoff water from the higher ground to the north and west of the Baris and conveyed it to the cisterns beneath the fortress. Warren believed that the aqueduct went as far as Cistern XXII—one of the Temple Mount cisterns. The ancient bisected cistern discovered by us in the Western Wall tunnel (18), and Cisterns XVIII and XXII on the Temple Mount, can be dated to before the Herodian period because of their location. Since the two latter have a rounded form, it may be that other rounded cisterns on the Temple Mount—Nos. V, XXVIII, XXXIV and others—can also be dated to the pre-Herodian period.

## The Date of the Large Aqueduct

Since it was cut through by the foundation trenches of the Western Wall of the Temple Mount, the large aqueduct must have been hewn in the rock and constructed earlier—probably in the Hasmonean period—as part of the installations of the Baris fortress. It is generally agreed that the Baris was built in the place of the Tower of Hananel of First Temple times (Jeremiah 31:38; Zechariah 14:10) which survived into the early Second Temple period (Nehemiah 3:1; 12:39). But the Tower of Hananel cannot be identified with the Baris: The Book of Nehemiah mentions both fortifications—the Baris, and the city wall of which the Tower of Hananel was part—without making any connection between them (Nehemiah 2:8). We therefore have no evidence of a First Temple period construction, north of the pre-Herodian Temple Mount, that would have required such an elaborate water supply system.

There is much similarity between this aque-

The large Hasmonean aqueduct near the northwestern corner of the Temple Mount

duct and the Iron Age water system of Gibeon, which was also cut in the rock from ground level and was covered with stone slabs. Although this would support a First Temple period dating for the large Jerusalem aqueduct, there are differences in construction and in the way the two systems functioned.

I suggested in the past that the "channel of the Upper Pool" is the one passing from today's Bethesda (Bethzetha) pools to the northern part of the City of David,[4] and possibly it also provided water to the lower eastern slope of the Western Hill. Recently uncovered archaeological evidence points to First Temple remains in the Bethesda pools.[5] Thus,

[4] D. Bahat, "The Fuller's Field and the 'Conduit of the Upper Pool'," *Eretz Israel* 20 (Jerusalem, 1989), pp. 253–255 (Hebrew).

[5] M.J. Pierre and I.M. Rousée, "Sainte Marie de la Probatique. États et orientations de recherches," *POC* 31 (1981): 23–42.

The quarry near the northern end of the Western Wall
of the Temple Mount

the suggestion of some scholars that the large aqueduct at the northwestern side of the Temple Mount is the First Temple period channel of the Upper Pool does not seem justified.[6] Perhaps the water supply system described here is the one mentioned in the Letter of Aristeas of the 3rd century B.C.E. according to which a subterranean water conduit brought water to the Temple and its surroundings. If this is indeed so, the large aqueduct can be assigned to the Hellenistic-Ptolemaic period. Although no archaeological evidence emerged to permit a definitive dating for the cutting and construction of the aqueduct, it seems reasonable that it was part of the establishment of the Baris as the residence of the Hasmonean kings.

## Engaged Pilasters in the Western Wall
Between the southern section of the large aqueduct and the Western Wall, Conder, in 1867–1870, discovered a room at a higher level in which two rock-cut and built-up engaged pilasters (25) could be seen in the Western Wall. This suggested that the entire upper part of the Temple Mount's outer face

[6] This opinion was expressed by some of the scholars visiting the site.

was built with engaged pilasters—as in the construction of the Herodian Cave of the Patriarchs in Hebron. Recently, in his survey of Mamluk buildings, M.H. Burgoyne discovered an additional engaged pilaster in the northern wall of the Temple Mount, in the Madrasa el-Isa'ardiyya. These architectural features, not seen since Conder discovered them, are an important contribution to establishing the outer form of the Temple Mount walls.

## The Herodian Street
The existence of a paved street (16) along the Western Wall is known from the shaft dug by Warren (6) near the southern corner of Wilson's Arch and from the excavations of B. Mazar at the southwestern corner of the Temple Mount. Since the street ascends from south to north, and the tunnel dug along the Western Wall is on the whole horizontal, it was clear that it would intersect the street at some point. This indeed happened, the Herodian street was exposed and can be followed today for about 20 m. at the northern end of the tunnel. The eastern side of the street is contiguous with the Western Wall and is there actually cut into the rock. Further digging at this spot is restricted by the Mamluk substructures of the building above, which rest upon Second Temple period remains. The paving stones of the street are of impressive dimensions, some of them over 1.5 m. wide and over 20 cm. thick. The upper side of these paving stones has marginal dressing, but a rough surface to prevent slippage. Every paving stone is carefully cut and closely matches its neighbors. On the western side of the street two columns were found standing. The columns are made up of several sections and have Doric capitals typical of burial structures around Jerusalem of the Second Temple period, the Bene Ḥezir (Zechariah's) tomb in the Kidron Valley. For lack of historic sources and the limited area exposed, we could not determine whether the pillars formed part of a colonnade along the street, or if the area in which they were found was part of a plaza surrounded by columns. In describing the

destruction of Jerusalem, Josephus (*War* V, 331) mentions workshops and markets in this vicinity, and perhaps that is what we uncovered here.

At this point the street ends, as do all signs of stone-cutting connected with the construction of the Western Wall. Having cleared every possible place where there was the slightest chance of tracing additional construction of the Western Wall, we must conclude that it was never completed and did not extend further north. The cessation of work here can probably be related to the death of Herod in 4 B.C.E.

## The Northwestern Corner of the Temple Mount

The rock at the base of the Western Wall here was cut in imitation of bossed masonry ashlars that characterize the construction in other parts of the Temple Mount, making it difficult to distinguish between actual construction and the expert stone cutting of the same forms in the living rock. What has remained here is a quarry which most probably was one of the sources for the stones used in the Temple Mount walls. The traces of quarrying in the rock reveal the dimensions of the stones that were removed. Each of the stones extracted there measured about 1.3 m. on one side—the average height of a regular masonry course of the Temple Mount walls. Our discovery that Herod planned to remove large parts of the hill to the west of the Wall for use as

The Herodian street with the two columns as found near the northern end of the Western Wall of the Temple Mount

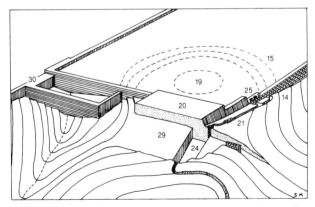

Schematic reconstruction of the ancient remains at the northern part of the Temple Mount

building material, and to level the northwestern part of the Temple Mount, attest to the stones for the building of the Wall having been quarried in the immediate vicinity. This quarry must have been one of the most important, if not the only, source of building stone for the Western Wall.

Before disappearing further north, the Western Wall turns west to form a kind of projecting tower (27). In the northeastern corner of the Temple Mount there is an identical protuberance that forms a kind of tower which Warren named the "tower of the Antonia." We have no unequivocal explanation for this eastern tower. Perhaps the corner of the Temple Mount above the very deep Kidron Valley was reinforced there by additional massive construction. The foundations of the tower at the northwestern corner of the Temple Mount are mainly cut into the rock. A few building stones that were integrated in the Wall, and which show the typical stone-dressing techniques, have been preserved. The stones were built into the Western Wall in a roughly-hewn state and the edges framing the boss were outlined with a flat chisel. This preliminary stone work was done in the quarry, and the stonemasons finished shaping the face of the stone after it was built into the Wall, working with a broad chisel in a crescent-like movement. At its southern end, this stone already has the final appearance of the other stones in the Wall. The Western Wall disappears entirely somewhat to the north, where it cuts through the aqueduct.

## The Strouthion Pools

The northern end of the large aqueduct (21) is at the western edge of the rock-cut Strouthion pool (24) north of the Antonia fortress that was divided into two barrel vaulted parts. The northern part of this pool, which is today beneath the Sisters of Zion Convent (35), is located northwest of the Temple Mount. It is now possible to visit the southern part of this pool from the Western Wall tunnel. The southern wall of the Strouthion pool is the rock scarp that protected the Antonia fortress (20) from the north, as described in detail by Josephus (*War* V, 238). At the side of the pool can be seen the bottom of the rock-cut moat (29) that separates the Antonia from the elongated hill extending north from here. The pool roofed with the twin barrel vaults was initially hewn as an open pool during the Second Temple period and was only covered in the Roman period (2nd century C.E.). Since it was too wide to be roofed over with stone slabs, a thick wall was constructed down the middle of the pool to support two adjoining barrel vaults. In its lower part the supporting wall incorporates large, open arches, so that what appears as twin pools is in effect one large pool.

## In Retrospect

Revealing a narrow strip along the Western Wall is all we have been able to do so far. Although the excavations do provide several answers to problems connected with the Western Wall, questions remain. Since it is not possible to dig in the Temple Mount proper, continued excavation along the tunnel can add many details and new insights to Warren's explorations. Indeed, without his pioneering work we would know much less about the Temple Mount and its surroundings than we do.

# Ossuaries and *Ossilegium* (Bone-Gathering) In the Late Second Temple Period

## Levi Yizḥaq Raḥmani

Much of our knowledge of Jewish funerary rites and practices toward the end of the Second Temple period derives from ancient literary sources as well as from modern archaeological research. However, specialized studies of this subject are few; some of the most important and accessible ones are listed in the short bibliography below. To these might be added several excavation reports on tombs, mainly in Jerusalem and its surroundings, but also at Jericho and some sites in Judea and Galilee.*

For a better understanding of these practices in the late Second Temple period it is well to summarize briefly the funerary customs in the country during earlier periods as seen against their social and religious backgrounds.

From very early times natural caves, but mainly caves hewn in the rock for the purpose, were used for burial. Each cave would contain the remains of members of one family or family-group; personal possessions—raiment, jewelry, arms, sometimes even furniture—were laid beside each body, according to the deceased's standing in life. Lamps to light the way of the dead in the nether world were always provided, as was food and drink in ceramic or more costly vessels. When all the space in the cave was taken up, additional chambers might be added, or the remains from earlier burials were moved to the sides of the cave together with the accompanying objects—be they whole or broken. The re-

mains of those buried in the cave were never removed from the family tomb.

Such practices are still in evidence in Jewish burial caves of the First Temple period, though the tombs were now more carefully planned and executed. The burial caves of the more affluent families feature rectangular walls lined with well-carved benches, often having special headrests. The shrouded body was laid out on such a bench, along with grave goods very similar in character to those in contemporary or earlier Canaanite burials. When full occupancy of a family tomb necessitated its enlargement, more chambers were added and provision was made for preserving the remains of earlier burials in a communal charnel: a cavity hewn in the rock in a corner or under one of the benches where remains of bones and funerary objects would be deposited. Such repositories became integral parts of family tombs.

This form of burial is reflected in the biblical text: "And all that generation also were gathered to their fathers" (Judges 2:10), and with expressions constantly recurring in Kings and Chronicles concerning the deceased, who were "laid down with their fathers," "buried with their fathers," and the like. Their fate was understood to be one of descent to the nether world: "But you are brought down to Sheol, to the depths of the Pit" (Isaiah 14:15). The dead were conceived as those "who go down to the dust" (*yordey 'afar*, Psalms 22:29). Since the descent was considered one of no return, the living members of the family group provided the deceased in the afterlife with some of the basic necessities: food and drink, light, covering for the body, weapons —caring for their relatives as they might

---

* I am grateful to the Director of the Israel Antiquities Authority for permission to reproduce the photographs in this article.

Ossuaries, as found in a Jerusalem tomb

expect to be cared for when their turn came to rest with their fathers in the family tomb.

In such a concept of life and death, there was as yet no place for the idea of physical and individual resurrection. It is only in later biblical texts (Ezekiel 37:1–14, and also Isaiah 26:19) that there is mention of resurrection, mainly allegoric, which refers to the fate of the nation as a whole rather than to that of any individual. The earliest biblical passage that clearly alludes to physical and individual resurrection is Daniel 12:2, which most probably should be dated to the 2nd century B.C.E.

## Jewish Funerary Customs in the Second Temple Period

It is in the early Hasmonean period that the first clear indications of a Jewish belief in individual physical resurrection appear, as stated explicitly by a woman and her sons whom Antiochus urged to renounce their faith: "The King of the World shall raise up us, who have died for His laws, unto an eternal renewal of life...From Heaven I possess these

[tongue and hands]; and for His laws' sake I contemn these and from Him I hope to receive these back again...that we shall be raised up again by Him, for as for thee [Antiochus] thou shalt have no resurrection unto life...." The mother finally addresses her sons: "The Creator of the World...in mercy giveth back to you again both your spirit and your life." (2 Maccabees 7, 9–23) It is a belief most clearly expressed in the dying words of the martyred Razis, an elder of Jerusalem, "when as his blood was now well nigh spent, he drew forth his bowels through the wound, and taking them in both his hands he shook them at the crowds; and calling upon him who is Lord of life and spirit to restore him these again, he thus died" (2 Maccabees 14, 46).

According to this concept of resurrection, the wicked would have no part in it. Indeed, even for those Jews who had given their lives for the Lord's laws in a fight against the enemy, but had at that stage been in a state of sin, a sacrifice in propitiation was offered by Judas and the army "in that he took thought for a resurrection" (2 Maccabees 12, 39–45).

This belief of the Hasidim, members of a pious sect in early Hasmonean times, was eventually rejected by the Sadducees, who insisted that such a belief had no scriptural foundation (see Mishnah, Sanhedrin 10:1 and Matthew 22:23; Luke 20:27; also Josephus, *War* II, 165, and Bab. Tal., Sanhedrin 4b). Indeed, the Sadducees, like their forefathers, found it sufficient to ascertain the well-being of their relatives who had descended into the nether world, within the confines of the ancestral tomb. They thus fashioned their tombs in accordance with Hellenistic esthetic principles, as developed in Egypt and found locally in tombs of Sidonian settlers at Marissa in the Shephelah.

A good example is Jason's Tomb in Jerusalem, which seems to have belonged to a wealthy family, using in their inscriptions both Greek and Aramaic. Some of its members were seafaring people of the first half of the 1st century B.C.E. who laid their deceased relatives to rest in a burial chamber with ten loculi, and eventually transferred their remains, including each one's grave goods, to a large communal charnel that adjoins the loculi-chamber at a right angle. Both were separately closed by stone blocks, but together formed a single family tomb with a sumptuous porch surmounted by a pyramidal monument (*nefesh*) and entered through two forecourts, the outer one via an arched gate. Inscriptions on the wall of the porch emphasize the belief of this family in the enjoyment of life by the living, prior to their eternal descent. Rather than representing any notion of resurrection, the only reason for preserving the remains of former burials was to vacate loculi for further use while retaining these remains within the family tomb in a common charnel. This practice is thus not to be included within the concept of individual bone-gathering (*liqut ʿaẓamot*) in the sense discussed below, but should be considered as a continuation of ancient customs, the sole change being a more satisfying architectural expression of the tradition.

## *Ossilegium* (Bone-Gathering) in the Late Second Temple Period

E.M. Meyers's thesis that individual *ossilegium* is no more than a continuation of such ancient practices is thus unacceptable. Such a view disregards the fundamental difference between not removing a deceased's remains from the ancestral tomb, and the gathering of such remains and their preservation within a special chest—a well-closed ossuary. In the present writer's view, the latter practice, novel at the time, was founded in the belief in individual, physical resurrection, which was then taking deep root in Pharisaic circles, being based, as has been noted, on concepts of the early Hasidim. L. Finkelstein rightly argued that these beliefs were well suited to the conditions of the life of artisans, scribes, scholars and many others who belonged to this socio-economic element. These were people who had to earn their daily livelihood, without the possibility of relying on their family group in times of need. Though a final resting place within a family tomb still continued to be desirable for tradition's sake and out of a deep psychological need, the individual could no longer depend on being provided for by a family unable to do so. Having had to fend for himself in this world, such a person deemed it more desirable to regain life. The preservation of one's remains for a physical resurrection thus became a dominant concern. In accordance with eschatological ideas of that period, such an event seemed near at hand. Belief in resurrection thus became one of the explicit credos among Pharisees, whose practices were finally assimilated by the great majority of people in Jerusalem prior to its destruction. Its dogmatically binding formulation is to be found in the second of the Eighteen Benedictions of the daily prayer. The use of a separate receptacle—the ossuary—where remains of an individual in their entirety might attend the resurrection, can thus be seen as a logical solution.

Moreover, such gathering of an individual's bones, after decomposition of the flesh had taken place, appears also to have been conceived as attesting to the atonement of sins

Vaulted loculi in Sanhedria Tomb 14

presumably committed by any mortal; such sins, as we have noted, were believed to impede resurrection (see also Josephus, *Ant.* XVIII, 14). We may gather as much from the law-court procedure of those days concerning capital punishment: "They used not to bury him (the executed) in the burial place of his fathers, but two burying places were kept in readiness by the court...When the flesh had wasted away they gathered together the bones and buried them in their own place (i.e., the ancestral tomb)" (Mishnah, Sanhedrin 6:5–6).

It is thus evident that execution itself was not considered sufficient atonement: "judgement of the unrighteous in Gehenna shall endure twelve months" (Rabbi Akiba in the Mishnah, Nezikin 2:10). The indication of such a way of atonement seems to have been the disintegration of the sinner's body (Bab. Tal., Sanhedrin 47b; Shabbat 152a; cf. also Rosh Hashana 17a). Thus the very pious, considering themselves sinners whose resurrection might be in jeopardy, would wish to ensure it in similar a way: the collection, after a minimum period of twelve months, of their

remains in a special receptacle, to rest until resurrection in the confines of the ancestral tomb (cf. Semaḥot 12:7, 9). This linking of ideas of atonement, decay of the flesh and collection of bones in an ossuary is clearly expressed in a contemporary source: "And further said Rabbi Meir: A man collects the bones of his father and mother, because it is a gladness unto him...When the flesh had decayed, they collected the bones and buried them in an ossuary. That day (the son) kept (again) full mourning rites, but the following day he was glad because his forbears rested from judgment" (Jer. Tal., Mo'ed Katan 1:5; 80c).

The words of this 2nd century C.E. sage make reference to an earlier custom and its motivation, which reflect Jerusalem rites and their motivation in late Second Temple times. This is further attested in a detailed description of such a gathering of remains in the family of Rabbi Eleazar ben Zadok. Even though he may be the second of two members of this family having the same name, this tradition dates back to the first, who still lived in Jerusalem before its destruction: "Just as he (Eleazar ben Zadok's father) attended his father, so I attended him" (Bab. Tal., Semaḥot 12:9).

Such an innovation in burial practice is borne out by finds in Jerusalem's rock-cut tombs, which contain, in addition to ossuaries, pottery and oil-lamps dating from the days of King Herod (ca. 20–15 B.C.E.) to the destruction of the Second Temple (70 C.E.). Tombs containing only earlier pottery lack ossuaries.

Once the flesh of the deceased had decomposed in the loculus or—in much rarer cases —in sarcophagi and occasionally also in wooden coffins, the bones were collected into an ossuary, usually made of stone, though sometimes clay was used. In many cases the remains are those of an individual, even an infant; but often the bones of several people were collected in one ossuary. Inscriptions identify them as close relatives: man and wife; mother and infants; brothers; sisters. Anthropological research has provided proof of this. Such an inclination seems at odds with the tendency to preserve each individual's remains separately. It was, however, dictated by a strong natural urge, which seems to have convinced the sages. They finally formulated their ruling in the mid–2nd century C.E.: "Whomsoever a person may sleep with when he is living, he may be buried with when he is dead" (Bab. Tal., Semaḥot 13:8).

The actual remains within the ossuaries often reveal much negligence in adhering to such rules. This is far from surprising considering the darkness and extreme unpleasantness of these tombs when still in use, and the natural slovenliness even of members of the *ossilegium* society of Jerusalem (Bab. Tal., Semaḥot 12:5).

The closed ossuaries were deposited within the family tomb. At times, and in better furnished tombs, they were placed within a special chamber, often the hindmost and lowest one. Once such a chamber was filled up to its ceiling with ossuaries stacked one on top of the other, they were pushed into loculi or placed on the benches in front of them, as well as in the central pit. This has been encountered even in tombs which show no sign of ancient or more recent robbery—a fate which, however, overtook many of these tombs from Roman times on.

## Geographical Distribution of Jewish Ossuaries at the End of the Second Temple Period and Thereafter

The great majority of the ossuaries discovered come from tombs in the necropolis of Jerusalem at the time—a belt surrounding the city, 200 m. to 3 km. distant from the city walls. Those tombs nearest the walls are on the slopes of the hills east and south of the city. To the north they are situated farther away, and those to the west are located at the greatest distance from the city walls. With few exceptions, people seem to have adhered to rulings which postulated a distance of at least 50 cubits between the city walls and tombs, refraining especially from establishing tombs to the west, the direction of the prevailing winds. Indeed, during this period very few cave tombs seem to have been hewn on that side of Jerusalem, up to the western slopes of the hills, west of the city wall. Apparently the Rephaim Valley southwest of the city was completely excluded from this necropolis, probably because in it was Jerusalem's only arable land and there were no rock-scarps which might first serve as quarries and then be utilized for hewing out a tomb with its facade in the vertical rock-face.

Within a far wider radius from the city walls, a much smaller number of such tombs containing ossuaries was discovered, and these are few and far between. These seem to be the tombs of land-owning families, perhaps living nearby.

Tombs containing ossuaries contemporaneous with those of Jerusalem have been discovered in other parts of the country. A number of them have been excavated at Jericho; others, in more remote sites of Judea, the Coastal Plain and Galilee date mostly to the period between 70 and 135 C.E.; indeed some groups of tombs are as late as the mid–3rd century C.E. Except for a unique find at Nebo, no Jewish ossuaries are known from the

Negev or Transjordan. A few such finds have also been reported from the Alexandria and Carthage regions, although identification of Jewish ossuaries from other sites in North Africa and Spain has proved erroneous.

## The Ossuary and Its Ornamentation

The ossuaries here discussed are rectangular chests, with or without low feet. They thus copy in all details chests whose size would be adapted to the functions they served in the households of the whole ancient Mediterranean world, from very early times on.

The dimensions of an ossuary were determined by its intended use: its length by that of thigh bones (femur); its width by that of the pelvis; its height by the pile of bones with the skull on top. Thus smaller ossuaries might be prepared for children, while especially large ones would be made for several closely related members of a family.

Inscriptions, which in some cases bear witness to such contents, appear both in Hebrew and Aramaic, indiscriminately used on one and the same ossuary, at times together with Greek or else replaced by it. The inscriptions, most of them shallowly incised into the soft local limestone and some written on it in charcoal, are usually very negligently executed. They may appear on any side of the chest or on the lid, in all sizes, often running with complete disregard over a previously incised ornament. It seems that such inscriptions were added by relatives or friends, after the deposition of the deceased's remains in the chest. It is thus only very rarely that one comes across a carefully executed and well-spaced inscription, seemingly the work of the artisan who ornamented the ossuary, or at least someone who took the decoration into full account.

More recent excavations have shown that decorated ossuaries constitute a minority of all those known. Earlier excavators tended to retain or mention mainly ornamented or inscribed ossuaries, and extant collections contain comparatively few plain and uninscribed ossuaries.

The lids of the ossuaries also reproduce the forms of lids of common household chests: they are gabled, vaulted or flat, the latter often sliding in grooves. Much thought and effort seem to have been devoted to firm closure of the ossuary: pairs of matching marks on the lid and the side or rim of the chest indicate the direction in which the lid is to be positioned in order to achieve such a closure, or how a sliding lid is to be inserted into the grooves. A pin or nail might be inserted through the edge of the lid into the rim, or a piece of string drawn through holes bored for the purpose—all in order to ensure such closure.

In addition, or alternatively, protection of the remains was sometimes further attempted through inscriptions that warned against opening the chest or removing its contents. During the period in question such admonitions could still be read on tombs in Jerusalem of the First Temple period; eventually they were given expression also in the slightly later inscriptions in the Beth She'arim necropolis.

Most of the ossuaries are fashioned of local soft limestone; only a small minority were made of the hard limestone quarried for building in the city. Clay ossuaries are rare, though more may have existed. All of the tombs around Jerusalem have yielded only one such ossuary, probably from before 70 C.E. but more likely dating to 70–135 C.E. Ossuaries fashioned of clay and found mainly in the north of the country can be dated from the late 1st century until well into the 2nd century C.E., while a further group dates to the late 2nd century and to the first half of the 3rd century C.E. Some of the clay ossuaries belonging to the above-mentioned Carthage group are contemporaneous with the latter.

The ornamentation of ossuaries shows two different trends, dictated by the material employed and the craftsmanship of the artisans. The smaller group of ossuaries, made of hard limestone, was the handiwork of the local stonemasons, who embellished them with ornamental elements from their work on buildings, tomb facades and sarcophagi of the same material. They employed mallet and chisels and the usual measuring instruments.

The vast majority of the decorated soft limestone ossuaries, however, have chip-carved or thin-line incised designs. The former technique being common in European woodwork, scholars from that part of the world took it for granted that chip-carved wooden ossuaries served as a prototype. Moreover, researchers held that the term 'arazin, used for ossuaries in Talmudic literature, indicated cedar wood. Further evidence for the assumed existence of wooden ossuaries, which were claimed to have disintegrated in the tombs, was seen in the finds of nails within the tombs. In Jerusalem. however, such finds are narrowed down to some two or three: mainly groups of tiny nailheads, very likely remnants of a box or leather belt. All wooden coffins subsequently discovered in tombs at Jericho and En-Gedi proved to have been fastened with wooden pegs only, many featuring dovetail joints. None of these tombs yielded any but soft limestone ossuaries, nor do the wooden coffins or any other wooden objects or fragments from this region show any trace of chip carving.

As to the Aramaic term 'arazin and its many variants, it is clearly a foreign word, unrelated to the Hebrew term for cedar ('erez). S. Lieberman and D. Zlotnik interpreted the word to represent a metathesis of the Greek (σὸρος) meaning burial urn, box or coffin. This was finally confirmed by the discovery of this word in an inscription on an ossuary at Jericho, where it indeed stands for ossuary. It seems that the use of wood (or other perishable materials) for ossuaries was actually avoided as a rule:

> The *ossilegium* of two corpses may take place at the same time, as long as the bones of the one are put at one end of the sheet and the other at the other end of the sheet. Thus Rabbi Johanan ben Nori. Rabbi 'Akiba says: "In the course of time the sheet will waste away; in the course of time the bones will intermingle. Let them rather be gathered and placed in ossuaries." (Bab. Tal., Semahot 12:8.)

Since stone was thus regarded as preferable, it was the local variety of soft limestone that was mainly used in ossuary manufacture. It was already widely employed in the city's workshops, which fashioned out of it household goods ranging from tabletops to containers for liquids and solids and could thus easily meet a demand for such ossuaries. Quarries of this stone have been discovered in caves in the vicinity of Jerusalem, at Abu Dis, Beth Sahur and Ḥizma; manufacturing waste, in one case from ossuaries, found there proves such quarries to have been the first station in the manufacturing process of these goods (see in this volume, pp. 244–256).

The artisans who worked on such vessels used tools well suited to the ornamentation of ossuaries. Besides mallets, chisels, and rulers and compasses, they employed augers, gouges and veining-tools with rounded and V-shaped cutting edges—all familiar from finds in the Roman world and indeed still used by modern chip-carvers.

The local artisans were not only able to provide stone copies of household chests in the sizes needed for bone-gathering, but could also quickly and cheaply adapt the much more elaborately executed metopes and rosettes of tomb facades. Less gifted artisans might incise such ornamentation on the chest front or sides, at times also on the lid. They heightened the effect by first covering the white stone surface with a red or yellow wash, the incision appearing white on the tinted surface. Very simple red wash strips were added to those sides which lacked incisions. Such washes must have been widely applied, but have long since faded away. Similar strips were also added to the backs, mainly of chip-carved ossuaries, which represent the work of the more skillful artisans of such workshops.

Around fifteen percent of the ornamented ossuaries show work that is only partly finished, e.g., one rosette completely chip-carved, the other remaining with only one finished petal or with only the marked-out guidelines. This holds true even for elaborately carved, hard limestone chests where details remain unfinished. Perhaps this was due to the purchaser's urgency, or to disagreement over the price for the work.

Restored facade of the Tombs of the Kings, Jerusalem:
frieze showing metopes and triglyphs

The common ossuary ornamentation: geometric
rosettes in metopes, as on a tomb frieze

Ossuary with schematic ornamentation of rosettes
within metopes

Since the first ossuaries were reported, scholars have sought for prototypes in different countries. Comparisons were made with Etruscan ash urns, which are appreciably earlier, and with Roman ones, which are contem-

porary. However no urns of these types have been found in Jerusalem, or indeed anywhere in the country; nor is it likely that any of Jerusalem's humble artisans visited Rome, its workshops or its funerary installations prior to 70 C.E. Iranian ossuaries (*astodâns*) are Sassanian, and thus later than ours; nor can any connection be suggested with those from Khwarazm in Central Asia, also too late. Thus these Jewish ossuaries can only be a local creation, meeting a local demand.

## Motifs of Ossuary Ornamentation

The obvious sources for motifs depicted on ossuaries are to be sought in Jerusalem's necropolis. A detailed study of some 1,500 ossuaries in the various collections and in publications reveals that the absolute majority of such ornaments have their parallels in Jerusalem's tombs of the period, some of which have survived to the present day.

Some of these tombs retain their ornate facades, including a porch with columns and antae supporting an entablature with metopes, each containing a disk or rosette. In some cases the rock-face is worked to resemble an ashlar wall of the kind erected in Jerusalem's buildings of the period. One or even several forecourts precede the porch, the former often entered through an arched gate. Above the tomb or at its side a monument (*nefesh*) may appear, cube- or obelisk-shaped, capped by a pyramid or a cone. Within the tomb are loculi hewn into the walls of the chamber, often with benches in front of them. Most of the loculi are vaulted, and some are gabled.

In addition to copies of metopes—usually two—each containing a compass-drawn rosette, the ornamentation of ossuaries portrays all such elements of the local tombs. in some cases these are depicted in their entirety, e.g., on an ossuary from the Mount of Olives where details include an entrance similar to the one surviving at the Tomb of the Grapes. The *nefesh* on the side of this ossuary features details very similar to actual finds at the Tombs of the Kings in Jerusalem and in a contemporary tomb in Jericho. On another ossuary of this type is a fairly exact image of the *nefesh* known as Zechariah's Tomb in the Kidron Valley or that on Jason's Tomb, both in Jerusalem.

Classical as well as ancient Jewish sources mention flowers and trees, growing or planted near the tombs. Thus the Mishnah (Tohorot 3:7) refers to the lily. This plant—the Madonna lily (*Lilium candidum*; Hebrew: *shoshan zahor*)—grows wild in shady and moist earth pockets in the hilly parts of the country. Shade trees are also mentioned in connection with tombs, explicitly in the Tosefta (Niddah 6:16); the New Testament (John 19:41) refers to a tomb in a garden and tells of palm trees growing in Jerusalem (John 12:13). Presumably, these were planted there for their beauty

Cave of Jehoshaphat and Absalom monument in the Kidron Valley

Central ornamentation on the front panel of an ossuary from the Mount of Olives: left—gabled tomb entrance; right—*nefesh*

Jason's Tomb, Jerusalem: view from outer court

Pyramid-capped *nefesh* on the narrow side of a Jerusalem ossuary

Pyramid-capped *nefesh* on the front panel of the same ossuary, narrowed to fit into central triglyph

Gable over entrance to the Tomb of the Grapes, Jerusalem

and shade; in the colder climate of Jerusalem their fruit—unlike that of the date palms at Jericho—is unfit for consumption (Mishnah, Bikkurim 1:3). Ossuary ornamentation thus incorporated motifs seen near the tombs, depicting such plants, at times rather natural-

Palm tree in front of tomb gate on an ossuary from Jebel er-Ras, Jerusalem

200

Palm tree reduced to a single branch, the trunk is indicated by two vertical lines and the roots by small triangles—on front side of an ossuary from Jerusalem

Palm tree motif turned into a representation of a sword, the lines suggesting tree trunks are still indicated in center of an ossuary from Bet Zayit near Jerusalem

istically, even down to the exposed roots of the palm. More often these motifs were stylized beyond easy recognition—suggesting that the artisan copying previous designs no longer understood the meaning of the motifs and gave it his own interpretations. After

chip-carving certain parts in the traditional stylized form, he added naturalistically conceived details—in one case, the representation of a bone handle—to give the whole the appearance of a sword. Only the two short lines descending from the rosettes to the base

Palm trees flanking *nefashot* incised on the lid of an ossuary from the Judean foothills, ca. 70–135 C.E.

Representation of an Ionian column with base and capital on an ossuary from Jerusalem

Amphora as the central decorative element on an ossuary from Jerusalem

frame, here a meaningless detail remaining from the outlines of the tree's trunk, connect this representation with its source: the single-branched palm-tree motif.

In doing so the local artisan followed the practice of many folk-artists in various places and periods: using, combining or separating details culled from their environment; enlarging a minor detail or reducing a major one. Thus one column of a row—originally appearing on a tomb facade—can be detached from its normal context and added to steps taken from the representation of a *nefesh* base. Such expressions of free play abound: an amphora from the top of a tomb pediment or a *nefesh* pyramid (as on contemporary Nabatean tombs), might be portrayed independently and copied almost out of recognition.

Petra: upper part of the rock-cut Khazne tomb crowned by an urn

A local tomb facade, carved to resemble an ashlar wall, is portrayed on the sides and lids of several ossuaries, as on one from Mount Scopus. The same ornamentation appears on all sides, and on the lid where this motif replaces a representation of rooftiles. This, as well as the absence of any windows or doors in the "ashlar wall," and the superimposition of rosettes on this image, make it very clear that no representation of a temple, actual building, or Eternal House (*beth 'olam*) was intended. Indeed the concept of the latter gained acceptance in Judaism only toward the end of the period during which ossuaries were used, well after the destruction of the Temple and the manufacture of the specimens discussed here.

Such free use of details from local tombs is most evident in the common motif of rosettes within a metope scheme. In one rare example, the ossuary front displays more than the usual two metopes: to the extreme left appears part of an additional one with part of a rosette, and on the right side there is at least a portion of

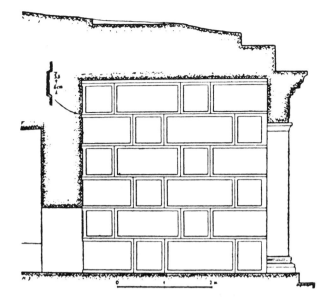

Rock-cut porch of the Um el-'Amad Tomb, Jerusalem, showing imitation ashlar dressing

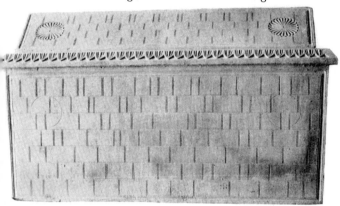

The ashlar motif on an ossuary from Mount Scopus

another. Such motifs, which were much more elaborately carved on tomb facades (and on a few hard limestone sarcophagi and ossuaries) are here executed very simply, as are the triglyphs that are represented by vertical lines or zigzags.

## Interpretation of the Ornaments

Two scholarly interpretations have attempted to ascribe to this ornamentation deep symbolic significance—even to minor details. E.R. Goodenough and, with some variations and a slightly different approach, P. Figueras, represent the one while the other was given expression by E. Testa and B. Bagatti. Goodenough seeks to present these ornaments as "repressed symbols...of hope of another life" for the deceased, "...perhaps direct aids to its fulfillment." However, he fails to furnish any

proof from the rich contemporary literature of a people wont to discuss each and every detail of life, death, ritual and belief. Thus, in various parts of his work he does occasionally admit the difficulty in establishing—as far as ossuaries are concerned—such symbolic "values," which in the last resort are defined by him as unchanging within his own psyche.

In fact, however, the motifs on ossuaries are found to change constantly in form, size, application and composition—in absolute contrast to standardized symbols that convey a concept or idea to a given group of people and thus are clearly understood by them. The most common motif on ossuaries—the rosette —appears in many different forms, often unfinished, constantly changing, as do all the other motifs. Moreover, it served as a decorative element in contemporary homes of the living, on objects ranging from cosmetic spoons and sundials to tabletops in kitchens and dining rooms, or mosaic floors in the bath—all surely unconnected with the supposed bliss of the dead in afterlife. Nor is it reasonable that pious and loving sons would bestow such symbols, perhaps even regarded as amulets, on some members of their family and deny them to others. Ossuaries with these common decorative motifs appear side by side with many ossuaries totally lacking ornamentation, some of which bear inscriptions identifying them as the property of the most important and cherished members of the family. Thus Goodenough's interpretations may be rejected as subjective and unconvincing.

Taking up where Goodenough left off, Figueras attempted to link the various motifs of this ornamentation, and thus the whole complex of burial practices, to a belief in afterlife because they appear on receptacles located within the darkness of the tomb. While assuming that "decoration (on ossuaries)... would be symbolic only at times," he nevertheless concluded that it was "a sign of *bene volens* from the relatives, an expression of their wish for the peace of the dead person, which includes their hope for the everlasting life and perhaps for the bodily resurrection." In support of these assumptions Figueras quotes for each motif a long list of passages ranging from the Bible to Jewish and Christian literature, some much later than the ossuaries in question. All are cited to express an association of ideas in the mind of the compiler of these lists, without offering any evidence regarding the intent of the artisans who made the ossuaries or the customers who ordered them. In the final analysis, all of the aforementioned objections to Goodenough's assumptions apply here as well.

Testa and Bagatti sought to present all ornamentation on ossuaries as an expression of the faith of early Judeo-Christians. In their view, all these ossuaries belonged to Jews believing in Jesus and his teachings. With no more concrete proof than was adduced by Goodenough and Figueras, they interpreted the guidemarks on lids, rims or sides—some of which are in the form of crosses—as Christian symbols, and eventually extended such an interpretation to all known ossuaries.

While this second view seems to claim that the majority of the Jews of Jerusalem in the period under discussion were believers in Jesus, both interpretations disregard the simple fact that we are dealing with a highly literate and normative society, which at that time and subsequently, in rulings and anecdotes, dealt with all details of life and death, opinions and beliefs—permissible, doubtful or totally inadmissible. Such treatment, fully available in religious as well as secular writings of the period, includes ample passages concerning death and burial practices, including bone-gathering in ossuaries. Any such practices known or even suspected to be pagan or those of Judeo-Christians would have been roundly condemned in such writings and not, as is actually the case, dealt with in detail and in a natural and approving manner. Inasmuch as Jerusalemites of that period wished to add a protective formula to ornamented or undecorated ossuaries of their forebears, they did so in fairly clear language, in Hebrew, Aramaic or Greek. Beliefs or hopes connected with their dead would surely have been expressed, at least in some cases, in a similar manner. The only example known to us is the inscription, in just the opposite vein, in the earlier Jason's Tomb, and such intents are less forcefully conveyed once only in an Aramaic epigram on a Jerusalem ossuary. A few instances of *shalom* "peace" written on an ossuary may be added to this. Such expressions become more plentiful only in the slightly later tombs at Beth She'arim, where there are indeed several representations of the Menorah (the seven-branched candelabrum) as a distinctly Jewish symbol. However, this motif appears on only two of the approximately 1,500 known ossuaries, these being practically the only cases of anything resembling a symbol as part of an ossuary ornamentation (see in this volume, pp. 00–00). Two or three additional specimens also feature pagan motifs; probably reflecting the influence of Jewish customs on the pagan inhabitants of the Hebron foothills.

## Summary and Conclusions

The custom of preserving the bones of an individual in a receptacle specially prepared for that purpose—the ossuary—began in Jerusalem in the twenties of the 1st century B.C.E. It was spread by Jerusalemites to other parts of the country, and eventually fell off around the mid–3rd century C.E. Most ossuaries, and virtually all of the chip-carved ones, were made in Jerusalem and its surroundings, but sometimes in places as far removed as Jericho. The practice ceased with the destruction of the city in 70 C.E., which must have entailed the death or captivity of practically all artisans sufficiently skilled to produce them. The devastation following the Second Revolt in 135 C.E. probably eliminated any surviving artisans—apprentices or less skilled workers—who were still able to make ossuaries with the traditional ornamentation, though employing the less demanding technique of shallow incision.

A number of ossuaries appearing toward the end of the 2nd and in the first part of the 3rd century C.E. are already made of clay. Sometimes they are found—mainly in Galilee, but occasionally also south of Jerusalem—together with clumsily executed stone ossuaries, some of which are attempts at copying contemporary coffins with gabled lids and acroteria.

By the end of this timespan Jewish theological thought had undergone significant changes concerning the fate of the deceased. It was now generally accepted that "there is no eating and no drinking in the Future World" (Bab. Tal., Berakhot 14a). Jewish martyrology and the growing dispersion of Jews, with the ensuing instability and insecurity of their economic, social and personal situation, gave rise to the belief that preserving the bones of the deceased was not relevant to their personal and physical resurrection. At any rate, frequent changes in everyday life made the implementation of such bone-gathering by the surviving generation of a family impractical, if not actually impossible. This situation led to an adjustment of thought that eventually negated the necessity of such remains for future resurrection. A legend of the 4th–5th centuries C.E. summarizes this attitude clearly enough: A group of Jewish boys and girls being shipped into shameful captivity to Rome are urged by the eldest of their group to commit suicide by throwing themselves into the sea; he assures them that the Lord could and would resurrect even those torn asunder by lions' teeth or lost in the depths of the sea (Bab. Tal., Gittin 57b; Lamentations Rabbah 1:16).

Consequently, Jewish tombs from the 3rd century C.E. on contain less and less grave goods, which are finally reduced to the oil-lamps only. Such provision of light remains a symbolic act to the present day.

The use of ossuaries for bone-gathering in the ancient sense of preserving such remains in their sinless state, as considered necessary for a personal and physical resurrection, thus came to an end during the 3rd century C.E. Some ossuaries—apparently made of wood—were now used to transport the bones of Jews from abroad for reinterment in the Holy Land, often within a family vault as at Beth She'arim, the seat of the Sanhedrin, or on the Mount of Olives, opposite the Temple Mount. This, however, must be seen as a new and different custom with different motivation, unrelated to the *ossilegium* of the Second Temple period.

## Bibliography

Avigad, N., "The Rock-Carved Facades of the Jerusalem Necropolis," *IEJ* 1 (1950–51): 96–106.

Bagatti, B., *The Church of the Circumcision, History and Archaeology of the Judeo-Christians* (Jerusalem, 1971).

Figueras, P., *Decorated Jewish Ossuaries* (Leiden, 1983).

Finkelstein, L., *The Pharisees: The Sociological Background of Their Faith* (Philadelphia, 1946), pp. 146–159.

Gafni, Y., "Reinterment in the Land of Israel," *Jerusalem Cathedra* 1 (1981), pp. 96–105.

Goodenough, E.R., *Jewish Symbols in the Greco-Roman Period, 1: The Archaeological Evidence from Palestine* (New York, 1953), pp. 110–139; *ibid. 4: The Problem of Method* (1954), pp. 3–33, 111–112, 120; *ibid. 12: Summary and Conclusion* (1965), pp. 24, 64–77, 106.

Hachlili, R., "The Goliath Family in Jericho," *BASOR* 225 (1979): 31–66.

Klein, S., *Tod und Begräbnis in Palästina zur Zeit der Tannaiten* (Berlin, 1908).

Meyers, E.M., *Jewish Ossuaries: Reburial and Rebirth* (Rome, 1971).

Naveh, J., "An Aramaic Consolatory Burial Inscription," *'Atiqot* 14 (1980): 55–59 (Hebrew).

Rahmani, L.Y., "Jason's Tomb," *IEJ* 17 (1967): 61–100.

——— , "Ancient Jerusalem's Funerary Customs and Tombs III/IV," *BA* 45 (1981/2): 43–53, 109–119.

——— , "Chip-Carving in Palestine," *IEJ* 38 (1988): 59–75.

——— , *Catalogue of the Jewish Ossuaries in the State and Israel Museum Collections* (Jerusalem, in press).

Sukenik, E.L., *Jüdische Gräber Jerusalems um Christi Geburt* (Jerusalem, 1931).

Testa, E., *Il simbolismo dei Giudeo-Christiani* (Jerusalem, 1962), pp. 426–573.

Zlotnik, D.Z., *The Tractate "Mourning" (Semahot)* (New Haven & London, 1966).

# Three New Burial Caves of the Second Temple Period in Aceldama (Kidron Valley)

Gideon Avni, Zvi Greenhut, Tal Ilan

The area around the confluence of the Kidron and Hinnom valleys is unique for the dense concentration of rock-cut burial caves of the Second Temple period. Among these are some of the most sumptuous tombs of the Jerusalem necropolis. The tombs in this vicinity attracted the attention of travelers and explorers already in the 19th century: several caves were examined and recorded by E. Pierotti, Ch.W. Wilson (in the Ordnance Survey of Jerusalem), C. Schick and others. In a survey of the area in 1900, R.A.S. Macalister systematically examined and described several caves, and additional ones were recorded later in the 20th century in the course of clearing and construction operations in the nearby Aceldama convent and its environs. Most of the tombs reported in this area were found to be robbed and empty; only the rock-cut facades and rich interior architecture attest to their former splendor.[1]

In the summer of 1989, when the road from the Abu Tor quarter to the village of Silwan was being widened, several additional burial caves were accidentally discovered at the foot of the western slope of the Kidron Valley, near the walls of the Aceldama convent.[2] The road-building operations exposed a rectangular, rock-cut court open to the east, in whose sides are two openings, each 60 cm. square. The openings were sealed with flat stones having margins recessed to fit into corresponding profiles carved around the entrances. Removal of the sealing stones revealed entrances to two large burial caves: Caves 1 and 2, each comprising several chambers hewn in the rock. Unlike many other tombs in the vicinity, these caves had never been robbed and contained an abundance of finds.

## The Burial Caves

BURIAL CAVE 1. This cave consists of three burial chambers, including a total of twenty-one loculi (kokhim), as well as an inner chamber containing three arcosolia and burial troughs. The first chamber (A) is 3.3 m. square and approximately 2.3 m. high. Three steps descend from the entrance to the floor of the chamber. Flanking the entrance are two loculi, one on either side, sealed with flat stone slabs affixed to the wall of the chamber with mortar. Another loculus is hewn in the northern wall of the chamber. The chamber itself was partly silted up. Among the finds were a large quantity of pottery, including deep bowls, jars and oil-lamps, and a few glass bottles. In one corner of the chamber were the remains of a wooden coffin, near which were many glass vessels and clay oil-lamps, as well as

[1] For a survey of the finds in burial caves in this area see: A. Kloner, "The Necropolis of Jerusalem in the Second Temple Period." Ph.D. dissertation (Hebrew University, Jerusalem, 1980), pp. 60–66 (Hebrew).

[2] The excavation was directed by G. Avni and Z. Greenhut on behalf of the Israel Antiquities Authority; the participants were B. Zisu, I. Dahari, D. Weiss, R. Birger, R. Abu Riya and student volunteers from the Hebrew University Department of Archaeology. Surveying operations were carried out by G. Solar and B. Arobas. The photographer was D. Adar. Anthropological data were assembled by J. Zias; coins were identified by D.T. Ariel. Teams of the Unit for Prevention of Antiquities

Robbery helped to guard the site during the excavation. Technical assistance was rendered by the Supervision Office of Y. Gadish and the contractor H. Fares. We offer our thanks to L.Y. Rahmani for his comments concerning the ornamentation of the ossuaries.

a few gold earrings. These remains should probably be ascribed to the later stages of the tomb's use during the late Roman and the Byzantine periods (3rd to 6th centuries C.E.).

A passage leads from this chamber to Chamber B through a small, square opening. This opening is at some height above the floor, and is reached by two rock-cut steps. Chamber B is 2.8 m. long and 2.75 m. wide. Five loculi are hewn in its walls. Flanking the opening are two loculi, one on either side. The southern loculus contained two ossuaries *in situ*. In the wall opposite the opening are three additional loculi, two elongated and a third (the southernmost) only 1.2 m. long. No loculi were hewn in the southern wall of the room; an attempt made to cut a new loculus there was discontinued as it penetrated into the adjoining Cave 3. Another accidental breach of the wall into Cave 3 occurred at the corner of the western wall of the room. These breaches show that Cave 1 was hewn later than Cave 3, and that the proximity of the

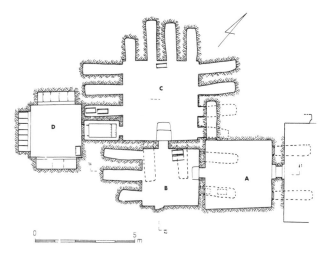

Aceldama: plan of Burial Cave 1

latter prevented the hewing of additional loculi on this side.

Chamber B was completely free of silt. Numerous glass vessels and lamps were found on the floor. In the southeastern corner is a repository for bones that were most probably

Aceldama, Burial Cave 1: selection of glassware of the candlestick-bottle type

Aceldama: Burial Cave 1, Chamber C

Aceldama: Burial Cave 1, Chamber D

collected from the nearby loculus. Two ossuaries lay side by side near the northwestern wall of the chamber. Remains of charred bones and ash residues were found on the floor and in some of the ossuaries in the chamber—evidence of a later stage, when the tomb was used to inter cremated remains. Near the concentrations of charred bones were many glass bottles together with a few coins of the 3rd century C.E.

An opening in the northern wall of the chamber leads to Chamber C, a square burial chamber (3.8 × 3.8 m.) larger than the other chambers, with fourteen loculi cut into its walls. Three ossuaries were discovered in this chamber. Scattered over the floor were oil-lamps and glassware, and the loculi contained remains of bones.

The loculus at the southern corner of the room had been expanded to create a passage, 1.7 m. high and 95 cm. wide, ending in a small square opening leading into Chamber D, the innermost burial chamber of the tomb. Chamber D is 2.5 m. square. In its walls are three arcosolia, each containing a burial trough. The troughs were covered with rectangular stone slabs, fitted to one another and cemented with mortar to the edges of the troughs. Some of these stone covers have depressions affording a grip on the slabs when raising them to deal with the bodies or collect

Aceldama, Burial Cave 1: glassware and glazed amphoriskos from bench in Chamber D

the bones. Found *in situ* in one of the troughs were two glass bottles and with them, a green-glazed pottery amphoriskos, most probably of Parthian origin. Clay lamps and glass vessels were found on the chamber floor. A single ossuary stood in the eastern corner.

**BURIAL CAVE 2—TOMB OF THE EROS FAMILY.** This tomb consists of a central burial chamber (A) with loculi cut in the walls. An opening in the floor leads to two chambers on a lower level: a repository for ossuaries (B) and an additional burial chamber (C) with loculi and arcosolia. Access to the tomb is by way of the court which it shares with Cave 1. The entrance, in the upper part of the wall of the burial chamber, was sealed with a square stone. Stone-cut steps descend to the floor of Chamber A. The chamber itself is 4.3 m. long and 3.9 m. wide. Ten elongated loculi are cut in the walls. Judging from the finds in this chamber it was used in two different periods: at its earliest in the Second Temple period, when the deceased were laid in loculi and the bones later collected in ossuaries; and at a later stage in

the Byzantine period, when the tomb was used for multiple burials, some in wooden coffins. Accumulated on the floor of the chamber was a layer, 50–60 cm. deep, consisting mainly of crushed bones and fragments of wooden coffins. In this layer were several complete ossuaries which had been covered by the late burials. The upper level of the layer contained several skeletons, lying side by side in wooden coffins. Remains of wooden coffins from the late phase of the tomb were also found in some of the loculi. Beside the skeletons were clay oil-lamps, coins and glass vessels.

Hewn in the floor near the southern corner of Chamber A is a square shaft, about $1 \times 1$ m. in cross-section. This shaft leads by way of a flight of stone-cut steps to the small, 2.15-meter-square Chamber B in which ossuaries were stored. About fifteen stone ossuaries were found in this chamber, piled one on another. In the western corner is a cell, 1.1 m. long and 90 cm. wide, containing three decorated ossuaries, and in the southern corner is a loculus, 1.7 m. long, in which a stone sarcophagus decorated in relief with rosettes and wreaths was found. On and beside the ossuaries were several large *mortaria* bowls and a few oil-lamps and glass vessels.

Most of the ossuaries found in Chamber B are of characteristic Second Temple period types. Some are decorated with rosettes carved in metopes, surrounded with zigzag-like frames. One relatively large ossuary in the chamber, made of soft limestone, bears a schematic relief depiction of a horned animal,

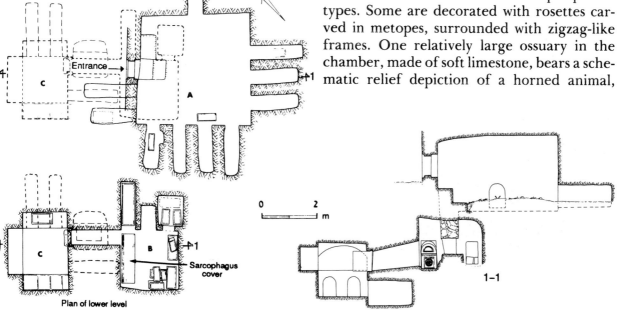

Aceldama: plan and sections of Burial Cave 2

209

Aceldama, Burial Cave 2: ox-head decoration on ossuary

perhaps the head of an ox seen frontally. Above this pattern is a fine, deeply incised Greek inscription, specifying the name and origin of the artist who carved it:

ΠΕΠΟΙΗΚΕΝ ΛΖΑ ΒΕΡΟΥΤΟC
"(E)le(a)za(r) of Beirut made it"

The broad front of the ossuary bears a relief consisting of two stylized rosettes. On the rear of the ossuary, in cursive script similar to the usual mode of incision on ossuaries, appears the name of the deceased, Eros in the inscription:

ΕΡΩΤΑC
"belonging to Eros"

This Greek name, though not unknown, has not been found hitherto in this country in a Jewish context of the Second Temple period. It appears three more times in this burial cave, among others on the fine sarcophagus found in Chamber B. The decoration of the ossuary and the inscriptions are quite unique. As far as

we know, this is the only ossuary depicting a bull's head, in contravention of the spirit of contemporary Jewish art. Perhaps the artisan who made the ossuary was not a Jerusalem-born Jew; alternatively, he may have learned his trade in his home city of Beirut, on the Phoenician coast.

The name Eros appears several more times in various forms in inscriptions on ossuaries from this cave. Most probably, therefore, this was the tomb of a family in which Eros was a common name. The inscription on one ossuary mentions a woman named Eiras of Seleucia—the Syrian city that served as the port of Antioch.

Another notable inscription, also in Greek, refers to a woman entitled "priestess," that is to say, the daughter of a priestly family married to a priest:

ΜΕΓΙCΤΗC ΙΕΡΙCΗC
"belonging to Megiste the priestess"

A similar title was found at Beth She'arim, but this is its first appearance on a Jerusalem ossuary. This ossuary contained the remains of one woman.[3]

A narrow passage, 60 cm. wide, cut in the southern wall of ossuary Repository B leads to Chamber C, the outermost burial chamber in the tomb. This is a small, square (1.7 × 1.7 m.) chamber, 1.6 m. high. In its walls are three arcosolia, with burial shelves and troughs. The entrance to the chamber is a small opening sealed with a rectangular stone door opening inward by pivoting in a hinge socket. The height of the door is 67 cm., its width 64 cm. and it is 10.5 cm. thick. At the top and bottom of one side are 5–8 cm.-long rounded hinge-pin projections that fit into the hinge sockets carved into the lintel and the doorsill. In the middle of the door, on the side opposite the hinge-pin projections, is an iron bolt secured by loops that are affixed to the stone with lead.

[3] For a discussion of the title "priestess," see B. Brooten, *Women Leaders in the Ancient Synagogue*, (Chico, 1982) pp. 73–99. Brooten concluded that the use of the title "priestess" always denotes a woman who had officiated in the holy service. This conclusion may be somewhat far-fetched and should be reconsidered.

Aceldama, Burial Cave 2: general view of innermost Chamber C; note stone door with iron bolt at right

The bolt is 30 cm. long and 2.5 cm. wide, with parallel vertical grooves along its length. Fifteen centimeters above the bolt, a hole, for inserting a key, was pierced in the door.

Hewn in the western wall of the chamber is a 60 cm.-wide arcosolium containing a burial shelf on which a decorated stone ossuary was found *in situ*. Beneath the arcosolium two parallel loculi are hewn. A similar arcosolium is hewn in the southern wall; the eastern wall has an arcosolium with a burial trough covered with flat stone slabs.

Underneath the entrance, at floor level, there is a square opening sealed with a square stone. Removal of the stone revealed a small cell, 1.2 m. long and 95 cm. wide, in which rested a magnificent ossuary, made of hard limestone and decorated with floral patterns in relief. Ossuaries of this type are rare in burial caves of the Jerusalem area. A few ossuaries of similar shape and ornamentation are known from Second Temple period tombs in the Franciscan precincts on the slope of the Mount of Olives (Dominus Flevit) and from a tomb in Ruppin Road. Inside the ossuary were bones arranged carefully at one side.

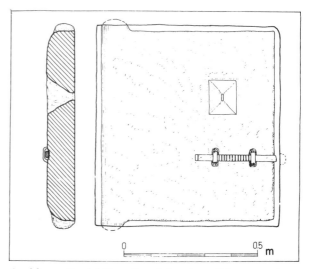

Aceldama, Burial Cave 2 and drawing of the stone door

Aceldama, Burial Cave 2: sumptuous ossuary of hard limestone

Among the more noteworthy finds from this chamber are glass vessels, particularly candlestick-bottles, clay oil-lamps and coins of the 3rd century C.E. All the finds were scattered around the chamber and at the openings of the loculi. This chamber, too, was probably used for burial at the late phase of the tomb's use, during the late Roman period.

**BURIAL CAVE 3—THE ARISTON FAMILY TOMB.** This cave comprises four chambers two of which (A and B) contain loculi; Chamber C is an elaborate burial chamber with arcosolia and burial shelves; and the inner Chamber D was used to store ossuaries.

As mentioned previously, Burial Cave 1 was hewn later in close proximity to Burial Cave 3 with only a thin stone partition between them. The original entrance to the cave is now blocked by silt and debris; we penetrated it by way of Cave 1, through a narrow breach in the partition wall.

The central Chamber A is square, measuring 2.85 × 2.85 m. and 2 m. high. Hewn in the

walls are six loculi, sealed with flat stones. The sealing stones had been removed and were found discarded in the middle of the room. On the floor were also several stone ossuaries, near which were broken clay oil-lamps and a few glass vessels. The scattered state of the finds probably indicates that the original burial arrangements were disturbed in antiquity.

South of the central chamber, on a lower level, is burial Chamber B, 1.96 m. long and 1.92 m. wide. Here, too, there are six loculi, four of them elongated and two shorter ones, perhaps used as repositories for bones. Once again, a few stone ossuaries were found in this chamber, some smashed, and near them heaps of bones, clay oil-lamps and glass vessels.

North of the central burial chamber, opposite the tomb entrance, a passage leads to Chamber C, the most elaborate in the tomb. The passage is shaped like a tall, arched doorway, consisting of a rectangular frame, 1.4 m. high and 70 cm. wide. Within this frame is a stone door, 70 cm. high and 48 cm. wide, which pivots inward on a hinge. The front of the door is decorated with a recessed relief of four rectangular frames, probably imitating a panelled wooden door. Within the upper right frame the craftsman carved a knocker, held in place by hooks (Pl. IIIb).

The passage leads to the rectangular Chamber C, 1.92 m. long, 1.48 m. wide and 2 m. high. Three of its walls contain arcosolia, each 1.8 m. long and 60 cm. wide, with shallow (about 10 cm. deep) burial shelves. Each shelf was designed for a single body, with a rounded headrest carved at the end. The walls of this chamber are finely decorated with incised and painted geometric designs. Above the entrance is a delicate pattern of lozenges in decorated frames, the lines incised in the rock and painted dark red (Pl. IIIc). Beneath the arcosolia, in the western and eastern walls of the chamber, the wall is carved to represent rectangular frames in sunken relief, similar to those ornamenting the main door. In each wall are two such "doors," each consisting of four rectangular frames incised and painted dark red. Alongside the "doors" and in the corners of the chamber are delicate columns,

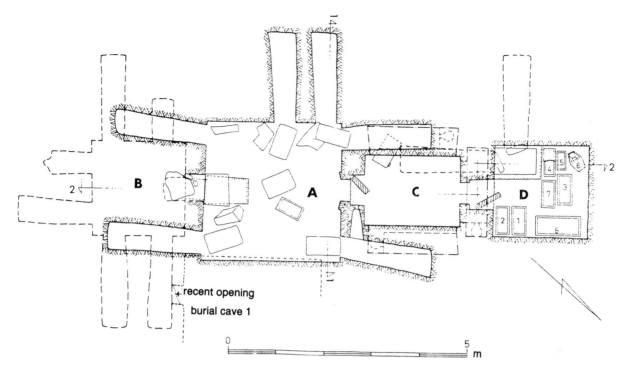

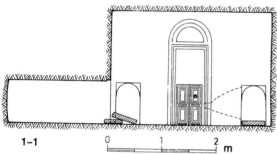

Aceldama: plan and section of Burial Cave 3

1–1

A total of about twenty-five ossuaries, and fragments of others, were found in Cave 3. Eleven ossuaries bear inscriptions in Hebrew and Greek. The decorations are of the standard type, featuring various rosette motifs within metopes, some painted red.

molded in relief, with bases and capitals in Doric style. Bones, fragments of ossuaries and clay oil-lamps were scattered on the burial shelves and on the floor of the chamber.

A passage in the northern wall of this chamber leads to inner Room D, which was used as a repository for ossuaries. The passage was also sealed by a hinged stone door, similar to that in the southern wall of the arcosolia chamber. This inner room is almost cubical, measuring 1.96 × 1.9 m. and 1.9 m. high. It contained some fifteen ossuaries piled one on another. In the southwestern corner of the chamber there is a rectangular depression in the floor. In the sides of this depression are two long loculi, which were sealed with rectangular stone slabs secured in place with mortar. Inside the loculi were found remains of collected bones.

Aceldama, Burial Cave 3: hinged stone door at entrance to arcosolia room

Aceldama, Burial Cave 3: the decorated arcosolia room (C)

An examination of the inscriptions found in this cave indicates that most of the deceased whose names are given belonged to one family named Ariston. One ossuary, found broken in pieces, bears several names in Greek and Hebrew, among them what was probably the name of the family patriarch:

Aceldama, Burial Cave 3: inner Chamber D used as repository for ossuaries

APICTΩN אריסטון אפמי "Ariston of Apamea"

Beside this inscription was another name, incised in Hebrew only:

יהודה הגיור "Judah the proselyte"

This ossuary apparently contained the collected bones of two persons: Ariston, whose name was written in both Hebrew and Greek (the Hebrew version also including his provenance, "of Apamea," referring to the city of that name in Syria); and Judah, who declared himself a proselyte.

Ariston seems to have been a fairly common name among Jews during the Second Temple period and later in the Diaspora, although less so in Roman Palestine. One of the Bar-Kokhba letters from Wadi Murraba'at refers to one "Jehoseph son of Ariston." The name Aristion also appears in a document from the archive of Babta, found at En-Gedi, and Josephus mentions a faithful servant of King Agrippa named Ariston (*Ant.* XIX, 2). However, it is not entirely certain that the last two mentioned were Jews, as the name was also used by non-Jews, one example being the early Christian author Ariston of Pella.

Aceldama, Burial Cave 3: ossuary of Ariston of Apamea

A Jew from Apamea named Ariston is mentioned in the Mishnah:

> Nitai of Tekoa brought *ḥallot* from Betar, but they were not accepted. The people of Alexandria brought their *ḥallot* from Alexandria, but they were not accepted. The people of Mount Zevo'im brought their first fruits before Shavuot, but they were not accepted, because it is written in the Torah: And the Feast of the Harvest, of the first fruits of your work, of what you sow in the field. The son of Antinos brought firstborn from Babylonia, but they were not accepted. Joseph the Priest brought first fruits of oil and wine, but they were not accepted. He also brought up his sons and the members of his household to celebrate the Small Passover in Jerusalem, but he was ordered to return, so that the practice should not be considered obligatory. *Ariston* (our italics) brought his first fruits from *Apamea* (our italics) and they were accepted, for it was said: Whosoever purchases in Syria, it is as if he purchased in the environs of Jerusalem (Ḥallah 4:10–11).

It seems that the editors of the Mishnah recalled a famous pilgrim of Second Temple times named Ariston, from the Syrian city of Apamea, who had properly observed the precept of bringing first fruits to the Temple. Of course, we cannot be absolutely certain that the person whose bones were collected here was the Ariston of Apamea mentioned in the Mishnah, but there are several indications in support of this conjecture: both had the same name; both are mentioned in different sources assigned to the Second Temple period; both hailed from Apamea in Syria; and both came to Jerusalem. This is the only tomb of a Jew from Apamea found in Jerusalem to

date. Moreover, the name Ariston was not common among the Jews in the Land of Israel, and it is hard to imagine that two persons of this name, both originally from Apamea, lived in Jerusalem during the Second Temple period—though we have no information about the currency of the name among Apamean Jews. If the identification is correct, this ossuary would recall that of Nicanor the "gate-maker," another Diaspora Jew mentioned in the Talmudic literature of Second Temple times whose tomb was discovered in Jerusalem in the past.

The second individual whose remains were interred in this ossuary is also intriguing: a self-declared proselyte. The usual Hebrew noun for a convert to Judaism is *ger*, or in Aramaic *giyora*, whereas the word used on this ossuary is a Hebraized form of the Aramaic, *giyor*. The proselyte whose bones were collected in the ossuary received the Hebrew name Judah upon conversion; presumably this name was commonly given to male converts to Judaism in Second Temple times. Indeed, in all known cases of conversion from this period the Hebrew name given to the convert is Judah. The Mishnah refers to Judah the Ammonite proselyte (Yadayim 4:4), and the Sages mention "Judah, son of the proselytes" (for example, Bab. Tal., Mo'ed Katan 9a). Judah, as a proselyte's name, also appears in inscriptions on two other ossuaries found in Jerusalem. At present we know of ossuaries of three proselytes in the region of Jerusalem. One of them, Diogenes, retained his non-Jewish name, while the other two, Judah Leganion and Judah Tyropoeien (cheesemaker), took the same Hebrew name as our "Judah the proselyte."

Additional inscriptions from this chamber feature names of members of Ariston the Apamean's family, such as his daughters' names on two ossuaries:

СЕΛΑΜΨΙΝ ΑΡΙCΤWΝΟC
"Selamzion daughter of Ariston" and
CΑΛWΜ ΑΡΙCΤWΝ(ΟC)
"Salome daughter of Ariston"

Until the discovery of these ossuaries it was

Aceldama, Burial Cave 3: ossuary of Selamzion daughter of Ariston

believed that these two names were interchangeable, one being an abbreviation of the other.[4] However, we know of no case of Jewish sisters bearing the same name; and it is unlikely that such a situation could arise. We may therefore state on the basis of the finds in this chamber that Salome and Selamzion were two distinct names.

Another ossuary inscription found here includes the name Shabbetai son of Nehemiah. Shabbetai does not occur among the known Jewish names of Second Temple times, except in the fictitious list of the translators who prepared the Septuagint, where it occurs twice, as related in the Letter of Aristeas (48:49). It was, however, a popular name in the Diaspora, identified with the unique phenomenon of the "venerators of heaven"— gentiles who adopted certain Jewish customs but did not actually convert.

The three persons mentioned on the ossuaries in this cave—Ariston the Apamean, Judah the proselyte and Shabbetai the son of Nehemiah—indicate that those interred in Cave 3 were recent arrivals in Jerusalem from the Diaspora or recent converts to Judaism. The use of Hebrew in the inscriptions may testify to their attempts to penetrate Jewish society in Jerusalem.

[4] See: T. Ilan, "Notes on the Distribution of Jewish Women's Names in Palestine in the Second Temple and Mishnaic Periods," *JJS* 40 (1989): 191–192.

## Architecture and Decoration of the Burial Caves

Two of the burial caves described here have architectural and ornamental features unique for burial caves of the Second Temple period in Jerusalem. One prominent element, appearing in both Caves 2 and 3, are the hinged stone doors sealing the entrance to some of the burial chambers. In Cave 2 the stone door of the innermost chamber also has an iron bolt surviving *in situ*. The date of this door and its intact locking device could not be determined. As the cave contained evidence of secondary use during the late Roman and the Byzantine periods, the door and bolt could well belong to this later stage rather than to the original phase of the tomb's use in the Second Temple period. Cave 3 has two hinged stone doors, sealing the sumptuous arcosolia chamber in the center of the cave. In this case the doors may definitely be assigned to the original, Second Temple stage, as nothing of later date was found in the chamber.

Hinged stone doors are rare in tombs of the Second Temple period; they are mostly found in the largest and most sumptuously appointed tombs, such as the Tombs of the Kings. This method of sealing burial chambers became more common in the late Roman period and was used in many of the burial caves of the Beth She'arim necropolis. However, to the best of our knowledge, nowhere have such doors been discovered complete with their locks *in situ*, as in Cave 2 here. Artistic representations of decorated doors appear in some of the facades of sumptuous burial caves reported in the Kidron Valley at the beginning of the 20th century by Macalister, but this is the first discovery of a stone door with a locking device.

In Caves 1 and 2 are a combination of burial in loculi and in arcosolia with trough-like burial benches. In most cases the arcosolia and burial troughs are located in the innermost chamber of the tomb. This practice is relatively uncommon in burial caves of the Second Temple period, being found in a small number of caves of the 1st century C.E. discovered around the Kidron Valley, as well as in the

216

Tombs of the Sanhedrin. From the 3rd century C.E. on, arcosolia chambers became fairly common; at Beth She'arim, for example, they are the most frequent mode of burial.

Stylized architectural ornamentation appears mainly in the central burial chamber of Cave 3. Besides the decorations of the door frames, the inner walls of the chamber are also adorned with lozenge patters, made by a combination of incision and red painting which is unparalleled in other burial caves of the Jerusalem necropolis. The sides of the arcosolia are decorated with sunken reliefs fashioned in imitation of columns and Doric capitals, as in the ornamentation in the facades of the largest cave tombs of contemporary Jerusalem. The wealth of decoration and the finely carved frames around the stone doors, probably in imitation of wooden doors, testify to the close attention devoted to nonfunctional details. The sole purpose of such details was to ornament the tomb and impress visitors, as was the case in the magnificent facades of Second Temple period tombs found elsewhere in Jerusalem.

## Periods of Use

The findings of the excavations indicate at least three phases of use of these burial caves:

ORIGINAL PHASE: LATE SECOND TEMPLE PERIOD. All three caves were undoubtedly hewn and fitted out for burial during the 1st century C.E. The appearance of burial troughs and arcosolia, encountered for the most part in Jerusalem burial caves only in the mid–1st century C.E., indicates that these caves may be counted among the latest of that period in Jerusalem. Possibly, burial in the upper part of the Kidron Valley reached its peak in this period, during which the most elaborate caves in the region were hewn.

REUSE DURING THE LATE ROMAN PERIOD. Caves 1 and 2 presented clear evidence of reuse for the interment of cremated remains. Some chambers contained glassware of the candlestick-bottle type, together with clay oil-lamps and coins of the 3rd century C.E. A most surprising find was ossuaries from Second Temple times that had been reused as receptacles for cremated remains: several ossuaries discovered in Cave 1 contained the remains of charred bones, together with clay oil-lamps, glass vessels, jewelry and coins of the late Roman period. Similar evidence was provided by bones scattered around the loculi and in corners of the burial chambers. The late reuse of Second Temple period tombs for the burial of cremated remains is unknown elsewhere in Jerusalem, with the sole exception of the Tombs of the Kings. F. De Saulcy, excavating there in the mid–19th century, found pottery vessels of the late Roman period containing the remains of burned bones in some of the inner chambers.

In contrast to some cave tombs of the Second Temple period in Jerusalem and its environs, where the finds point to continued use of the tombs after the destruction of the Temple in 70 C.E., the evidence from the Kidron Valley caves seems to indicate that there were no further burials after that year. Use of the caves was resumed only in the 3rd century C.E.—for pagan burials. Cremation being prohibited by Jewish law, it seems fairly certain that the new users of the tombs were non-Jews. It is therefore rather surprising that the remains of the earlier burials were left undisturbed. Other than using ossuaries as receptacles for burned bones, no changes were made in the burial chambers, and ossuaries that were not reused were left untouched.

No evidence of secondary use was unearthed in Cave 3. It most probably ceased to be used after the destruction of the Temple.

FURTHER REUSE OF PART OF THE CAVES IN THE BYZANTINE PERIOD. Evidence of multiple burials during the 5th–6th centuries C.E. was found in Cave 2, where many bodies were crowded together in the upper chamber, some buried separately in wooden coffins placed side by side. Some bodies were laid close together without coffins in the middle of the room. A few clay oil-lamps and glass vessels were placed alongside. Here again, the reuse of the tomb had no effect on the burial remains from the Second Temple period, and efforts were made to arrange the wooden coffins among the ossuaries without damaging them.

Judging from finds in other caves surveyed in this region in the early years of the 20th century, many of the ancient burial caves in the Kidron Valley were used by hermit monks during the Byzantine period. Some of the First and Second Temple period tombs in the area were enlarged and used as living quarters, and Christian inscriptions and decorations were added. It is not inconceivable, therefore, that the upper chamber of Cave 2 was used for the collective burial of monks who inhabited the Kidron Valley caves.

On the basis of this chronology, it would appear that Caves 1 and 2 were in use between the 1st and 6th centuries C.E. for the burial of different populations. They began as unmistakably Jewish tombs, fitted out in accordance with traditional Jewish burial customs of the late Second Temple period. In the late Roman period the remains of cremated pagans were interred in them; and in the 5th–6th centuries C.E. they served as graves for Christian monks, some buried in wooden coffins.

## Conclusion

The three caves discovered in the Kidron Valley constitute further evidence of the importance of this region in the late Second Temple period necropolis of Jerusalem. Like other caves previously reported in the vicinity, they show evidence of excellent workmanship, a wealth of decorative motifs and architectural characteristics almost unparalleled in contemporary burial caves in Jerusalem. The considerable labor invested in the cutting of the caves, and the careful attention to the creation of nonfunctional decorations—all

indicate that these were probably the tombs of rich Jewish families of Second Temple period Jerusalem.

A unique feature of these caves, in comparison with others discovered in the vicinity, was that they had not been significantly disturbed since their latest use; neither were they robbed in modern times. The rich finds of ossuaries, pottery and glassware give us an idea of the social standing of the persons buried here and have made it possible to map the different phases of the caves' use during the 1st to 6th centuries C.E.—about half a millennium.

The many inscriptions on the ossuaries enable us to reconstruct a rough sociological profile of the individuals interred in these caves in Second Temple times. The two tombs in which inscribed ossuaries were found contained the remains of members of two Jewish families. The unique names, which recur frequently, indicate that Cave 2 was the tomb of the Eros family, probably of Syrian origin. Cave 3 contained the remains of the family of Ariston the Apamean, also originally from the Syrian Diaspora. However, the caves do not divide clearly between the two families. The ossuaries found in the caves indicate that members of the Eros family were also buried in one of the chambers in Cave 3. The inscriptions found there feature unique Greek names, unknown in Jewish onomastics of the Second Temple period, which also appear in inscriptions from the adjoining Cave 2; this applies, in particular, to the name Eros. We may surmise, therefore, that both tombs originally belonged to the Eros family who sold or rented part of Cave 3 to the family of Ariston, which came to Jerusalem from Apamea. As the Eros family was also of Syrian origin, this may be evidence of continued social contact among Jews who came from Syria and who found a common language in their new home.

# The Caiaphas Tomb in North Talpiyot, Jerusalem

## Zvi Greenhut

A rock-hewn tomb with loculi (*kokhim*), typical of the Second Temple period in the Jerusalem region, was discovered in 1990 in the course of development work in the Peace Forest in North Talpiyot, south of the Old City.[1] The tomb was cut into the characteristic soft, friable limestone of the eastern slopes of the Judean Hills. Over the years, dozens of similar tombs have been discovered in the vicinity, which was part of Jerusalem's necropolis during the Second Temple period.

The tomb comprises an irregular burial chamber containing four loculi with arched ceilings. Three of the loculi were cut into the western wall of the chamber and contained scattered bones. The fourth loculus, in the southern wall, contained two ossuaries *in situ*. The cave entrance, on the east, was found sealed with earth and stones. In the center of the chamber floor is a rectangular pit, deep enough to have permitted the burial attendants to stand erect. Nearby, on the right-hand side, is a depression cut in the floor, probably a repository for bones.

A total of twelve ossuaries were found in the tomb. Four were found intact but not *in situ*, resting on piles of fragments of other ossuaries, as well as a mixture of sherds and broken bones. (They were most probably removed by

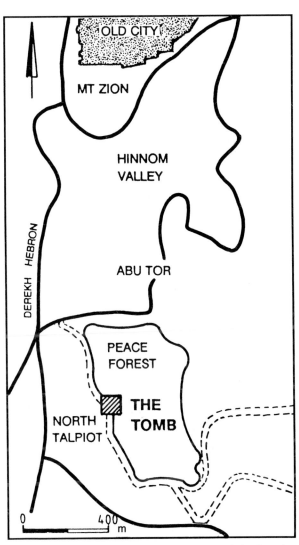

Map of the southern area of Jerusalem and the location of the Caiaphas tomb

the workmen before the excavation began.) Near some of the ossuaries were broken stone slabs that originally served to seal the loculi. The broken fragments of some ossuaries

---

[1] Development work in the Peace Forest has been conducted by the Jerusalem Foundation. The discovery of the tomb was reported by S. Feldman, the site foreman, to the Israel Antiquities Authority. The site was excavated on behalf of the Authority by the author, with the participation of J. Zias and Z. Cahana (anthropology), A. Hajian (surveying and drafting) and Y. Shaked (administration). Another Second Temple tomb, with a collapsed ceiling, found nearby contained no artifacts.

219

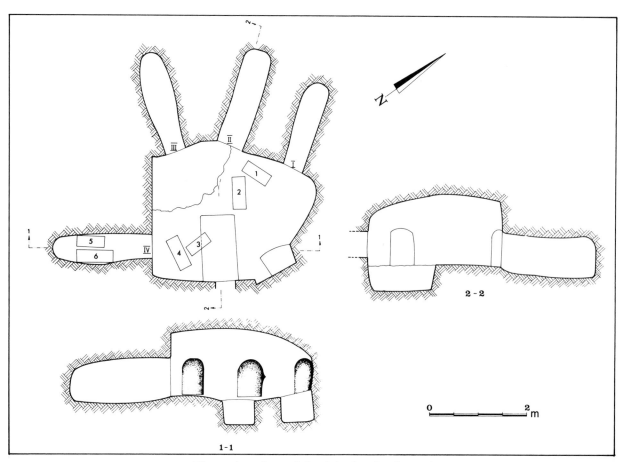

Plan and sections of the Caiaphas family tomb

Caiaphas Tomb: some of the upside-down and broken
ossuaries in the burial cave

indicate that the tomb was robbed in antiquity. The robbers removed the ossuaries
from the loculi, smashed them and removed
their contents. For some reason, the two
ossuaries found *in situ* in the southern loculus
escaped damage.

Judging from the small number of loculi,
the tomb probably belonged to a small family,
though the number of ossuaries is indicative
of use over a relatively long period of time.
The pottery found in the tomb is characteristic of the Second Temple period, from the 1st
century B.C.E. to the 1st century C.E.

Some of the ossuaries are decorated with
patterns featuring rosettes, zigzags and division into metopes, all typical of Jerusalem
ossuaries of the Second Temple period. One
panel of Ossuary 2 is decorated with an architectural pattern representing a fluted column
set on a three-stepped base and surmounted
by a stylized Ionic capital. Flanking the column are six-petaled rosettes, with ivy leaves
among the petals. The rosettes are set in a
frame of two concentric circles, separated by a
zigzag line. Around the edges, on both sides of
this panel, is a frame consisting of a zigzag
within double lines. Along the top of the panel
are two parallel lines, between which is an egg-
and-dart pattern.

220

Caiaphas Tomb: Ossuary 6, decorated front side

Caiaphas Tomb: Ossuary 2, decoration with architectural and floral motifs

Ossuary 6, the most richly decorated one in the tomb, features a pattern of two large concentric circles, separated by a symmetrical floral motif, clasped at the center by a ring or ribbon tying the long leaves together. Within each circle are six small rosettes—a central rosette surrounded by five others. The uppermost of the small rosettes has six petals, the three odd ones are painted orange. The other many-petaled rosettes are not colored, but the field between them is painted orange, showing a symmetric floral motif like that separating the two large circles. At the outer edge of the large circles are palmettes, one in each corner. Another, smaller, six-petaled rosette, its petals also alternately painted orange, is incised above the central floral motif. The decorated front panel of the ossuary is surrounded on three sides by a frame of stylized leaves—a pattern typical of the period.

Incised on the sides of Ossuary 6 are the inscriptions יהוסף בר קיפא "Yehosef bar (son of) Qafa (Caiapha)." Some of the other ossuaries also bear inscriptions, including the names קפא "Qafa'," שלום "Shalom," שם "Shem," and מרים ברת שמעון "Miriam barat (daughter of) Shim'on" (see in this volume, pp. 223–225).

The word קפא, קיפא "Caiapha" on two of the ossuaries in the tomb appears here for the first time in an archaeological context. It is probably the name of the family of the High Priest Caiaphas, mentioned both by Josephus (*Ant.* XVIII, 35, 95) and in the New Testament (Matthew 26:3, 57; Luke 3:2; John 11:49; 18:13–14, 24, 28; Acts 4:6) it was from his house in Jerusalem that Jesus was delivered to the Roman procurator Pontius Pilatus.

Another notable find is a coin of Agrippa I of the Year Six (42/43 C.E.), found in a woman's skull.[2] The skull was found in an ossuary inscribed "Miriam daughter of Shim'on." This is clear-cut evidence of the practice of a pagan custom—placing a coin in the mouth of the deceased as payment to Charon for ferrying his or her soul across the River Styx. It is the first concrete evidence of the practice in a Jewish tomb of Second Temple period Jerusalem. Hitherto, the only other possible example of the practice in a Jewish context was from Jericho.

[2] The coin was found by J. Zias while the bones were being removed from the tomb.

## Bibliography

Greenhut, Z., "The 'Caiaphas' Tomb in the North of Jerusalem," *'Atiqot* (English Series) XXI (1992): 63–71.
——— , "Burial Cave of the Caiphas Family," *BAR* 18/5 (1992): 28–36, 76.
Hachlili, R. and Killebrew, A., Jewish Funerary Customs during the Second Temple Period, in the Light of the Excavation at the Jericho Necropolis," *PEQ* 115 (1983): 109–132.
Kloner, A., *The Necropolis of Jerusalem in the Second Temple Period* PhD. dissertation (Jerusalem, Hebrew University, 1980) (Hebrew).
Rahmani, L.Y., "Jewish Rock-Cut Tombs in Jerusalem," *'Atiqot* (English Series) III (1961): 93–120.
——— , "Ossuaries and Bone-Gathering in the Late Second Temple Period," *Qadmoniot* 11 (1978): 102–112 (Hebrew). And see also in this volume, pp. 00–00).
Reich, R. "Ossuary Inscriptions from the 'Caiaphas' Tomb," *'Atiqot* (English Series) XXI (1992): 72–77.
——— , "Caiaphas Name Inscribed on Bone Boxes," *BAR* 18/5 (1992): 38–44, 76.

# Ossuary Inscriptions of the Caiaphas Family from Jerusalem

## Ronny Reich

In 1990 several inscribed ossuaries were excavated by Z. Greenhut in a burial cave south of Jerusalem (see in this volume, pp. 219–222). The inscriptions were incised with a sharp instrument into the soft chalky limestone of which the ossuaries are made, probably by the relatives of the deceased. The language of the inscriptions is Aramaic and the script is the Jewish cursive typical of ossuary inscriptions of the 1st century C.E.

## The Inscriptions

**ON OSSUARY 5:** שלום (*Šlwm*) "Shalom"

**Shalom** is the common personal name and not the greeting or benediction. In this case it is a woman's name, equivalent to the Greek name Salome, or a short version of the name שלומציון "Shlomẓion."

**ON OSSUARY 7:** מרים ברת שמעון (*Mrym brt Šm'wn*) "Miriam daughter of Shim'on"

**Miriam**, or in its other version: מריה "Miriya", was a common woman's name. The most recent statistical study of private names of the Second Temple period by T. Ilan found that 25 percent of the women who are mentioned by name in the literary sources and inscription bore the name מרים "Miriam" or מריה "Miriya;" while another 25 percent represented one of the versions of the name שלום "Shalom" or שלומציון "Shlomẓion." These findings imply that half of the women were called by only two names![1]

**Shim'on**, שמעון (*Shim'on*) "Simon" is the most frequently encountered male name in the Second Temple period.

**ON OSSUARY 4:** שמ (*Šm*) "Shem"

**Shem** was one of Noah's sons (Genesis 6:10) but most probably this is not the case here, as Jews usually did not use this group of names—the progenitors of mankind. The Mishnah (Shabbat 12:3) mentions that names were occasionally abbreviated. The example cited is actually שמ "Shem" for "Shim'on." Abbreviated names in burial inscriptions seem meaningless, unless Shem was indeed the interred person's nickname used by his relatives and friends. Or, perhaps, Shem is the incomplete beginning of the name Shim'on.

**ON OSSUARY 3:** קפא (*Qp'*) "Qafa"

Caiaphas Tomb: Ossuary 3 with the name "Qafa"

**ON OSSUARY 6:** יהוסף בר קפא (*Yhwsp br Qp'*) "Yehosef son of Qafa" on the narrow side, and יהוסף בר קיפא (*Yhwsp br Qyp'*) "Yehosef son of Qaifa (or Qofa)" on the long rear side of the ossuary.

**Yosef** (Joseph) or in its versions Yehosef, Yoseh or Yosi is the second most frequent

[1] T. Ilan, "Notes on the Distribution of Jewish Women's Names in Palestine in the Second Temple and Mishnaic Periods," *JJS* 40 (1989): 186–200, especially pp. 191–192.

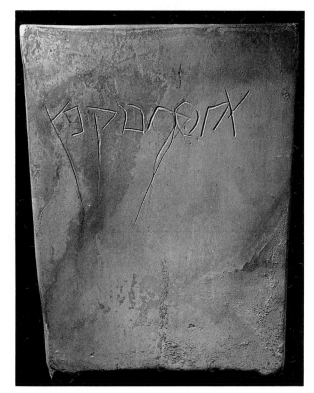

Caiaphas Tomb: Ossuary 6, the inscription "Yehosef son of Caiaphas" on a narrow side of the ossuary

Caiaphas Tomb: Ossuary 6, the inscription "Yehosef son of Qafa" on the back of the ossuary

name encountered in the Second Temple period.

**Qaifa** or **Qofa** is an Aramaic name here encountered for the first time on an inscription. At first glance it seems that the person buried in Ossuary 3, Qafa', was the father of Joseph buried in Ossuary 6. However, since Qafa' is not a name but rather a nickname, it is more likely that both persons were related to a common forefather of the family known by this nickname, and which became a sort of family name passed on to his descendants. Since the male population also used a limited number of names,[2] a nickname was a good way to distinguish among people. Persons were sometimes called only by the nickname given to one of their forefathers. Thus, in the present case the meaning might be: "Joseph (of) the Caiaphas."

This epigraphic discovery draws attention

to the high priest in Jerusalem in the years 18–36 C.E. The New Testament gives only his nickname: Caiaphas (Matthew 26:3, 57; Luke 3:2; John 11:49; 18:13–14, 24, 28; Acts 4:6). Josephus Flavius mentions the man twice and calls him "Joseph 'who is called' Caiaphas" (*Ant.* XVIII, 35, 95). Both sources give only the Greek version of the name. The present inscription has established the correct Semitic transcription קיפא *Qyp'*. This rules out the transcription כיפא *Kyp'* which in the past was occasionally used by scholars. Now that the archaeological find has established the form קיפא additional literary sources can be considered for a historical study.

The first such source (אליועיני בן הקוף (הקייף) mentions "Elio'eynai the son of Qayaf (Caiaphas)." הקוף "HaQof" was one of the few high priests in Jerusalem who burned a red heifer (Mishnah, Para 3:5). הקייף "Ha-Qayaf" is the Hebrew version of the Aramaic form קיפא. The identity of this person with Joseph Caiaphas mentioned by Josephus and the Gospels has been suggested by several scholars. Some propose that Elio'eynai was the son of Joseph,[3] others, such as D. Schwartz, believe that they were brothers.[4] Another source mentions the family of Qifai (or Neqifai, Qifa) from Bet Meqoshesh (Tosefta, Yebamot 1 10; Jer. Tal., Yebamot 1 6, 3 [1]; Jer. Tal., Ma'asrot 52a), a priestly family some of whose members became high priests. The Talmud mentions also a certain Menahem son of Maxima,

[2] See for example: T. Ilan, "Names of Hasmoneans in the Second Temple Period," *Eretz Israel* 19 (Jerusalem, 1987), pp. 238–241 (Hebrew, with English summary on p. 79*).

[3] M. Stern, "The Politics of Herod and Jewish Society Towards the End of the Second Commonwealth," *Tarbiz* 35 (1966): 235–253 (Hebrew).

[4] D.R. Schwartz, *Agrippa I, The Last King of Judaea* (Jerusalem, 1987), pp. 129–130 (Hebrew).

brother of Jonathan Qaifa (Jer. Tal., Ma'asrot 52a), in a passage which clearly indicates Qaifa to be a nickname, Maxima being Jonathan's father.

Two studies published before this discovery attempt to reconstruct the history of the Caiaphas family in the Second Temple period and even earlier. R. Brodi[5] focusses on the passage in Mishnah, Para 3:5, and attempts to demonstrate that Elio'eynai son of HaQof (HaQayaf) and Elio'eynai son of Qantheras (*Ant.* IX, 342) are very probably the same person. He shows that the different names Qantheras and Qayafa, Qayaf are etymologically related since the Hebrew הקיי(ו)ף (Aramaic קיפא) and Latin Cant(h)erius (Greek κανϑηριος) have the same two meanings: 'basket' and 'carrying' (i.e., wooden pole used either for roofing or for the support of grapevines). B.Z. Rosenfeld[6] focusses on the mention of the family of Qifai in Tosefta, Yebamot 1:10. While Brodi devotes great efforts to proving that קנתרס = הקייף. קיפא, through the double etymological identity; Rosenfeld takes this equation, in its version קנתרס = קיפא "Qaifa" = "Qatros" for granted.

What do the inscriptions presented here contribute to the history of the family? They point to the name in its Aramaic version קיפא "Qaifa" being common in the mid–1st century C.E. It shows that the Qaifa family had a burial place in the necropolis of Jerusalem.

This quite ordinary burial cave might have belonged only to a certain branch of the family, perhaps that branch which left the original settlement of the family in Bet Meqoshesh and moved to Jerusalem. If this was indeed the case, it probably happened during the early days of Herod's reign when certain priestly families were promoted by him over those that held power during the preceding Hasmonean period, and as a consequence were encouraged to move to Jerusalem.[7]

## Summary

We have mentioned three family names in Jerusalem of the Second Temple period: קיפא (הקיף), קתרס "Cantheras." Are all of these different versions of the same family name? The equation קנתרס (the Semitic version of "Cantheras") = קתרס appears reasonable. It seems unlikely that two different families would have names that are so close phonetically. The equation Canteras = קיפא (הקיף) is based on the fact that a certain private name: אליועיני "Elio'eynai" is related to both. As this name is rare for this period (it is, in effect, known only from this instance) it is reasonable to believe that this equation is also valid.

These inscriptions, and especially the name, or nickname קפא, קיפא (הקיף) might be related directly or indirectly to one of the priestly families that lived in Jerusalem in the 1st century C.E. This family was known by the nickname of one of its ancestors who probably acquired it through his occupation. A certain branch of this family, and especially several of its members, achieved high positions in Jerusalem.

---

[5] R. Brodi, "Caiaphas and Cantheras," in: D.R. Schwartz, *Agrippa I, The Last King of Judaea* (Jerusalem, 1990), Appendix 4, pp. 190–195.

[6] B.-Z. Rosenfeld, "The Settlement of Two Families of High Priests During the Second Temple Period," in: Y. Katz, Y. Ben-Arieh and Y. Kaniel (eds.), *Historical-Geographical Studies in the Settlement of Eretz-Israel* II (Jerusalem, 1991), pp. 206–218 (Hebrew).

[7] Stern, see Note 3.

## Bibliography

Flusser, D., "Caiphas in the New Testament," '*Atiqot* 21 (1992): 81–87 (Hebrew).
Greenhut, Z., "Burial Cave of the Caiaphas Family," *BAR* 18/5 (1992): 28–36, 76.
——— , "The 'Caiaphas' Tomb in the North of Jerusalem," '*Atiqot* (English Series) XXI (1992): 63–71.
Reich, R. "Caiaphas Name Inscribed on Bone Boxes," *BAR* 18/5 (1992): 38–44, 76.
——— , "Ossuary Inscriptions from the 'Caiaphas' Tomb," '*Atiqot* (English Series) XXI (1992): 72–77.
Zias, J., "Human Skeletal Remains from the 'Caiaphas' Tomb," '*Atiqot* (English Series) XXI (1992): 78–80.

# A Jewish Burial Cave on Mount Scopus

## Varda Sussman

A Second Temple period burial cave was discovered and excavated in 1989 on Mount Scopus in the burial ground known as Auguste Victoria.[1] The cave consists of one rather small rock-hewn burial chamber with two loculi (*kokhim*) in each of its four walls. The poor quality of the limestone at the site dictated the chamber's asymmetrical shape and probably also contributed to the collapse of its roof in antiquity. The entrance to the burial cave, on its northern side, was partly blocked with roughly hewn stones. One steep, hewn step leads down into the 2.5 × 2.5 m. chamber which has a central depression only 15 cm. deep.

The loculi of this burial cave are typical of those found in contemporary Jewish tombs in Jerusalem. Loculus II was extended and

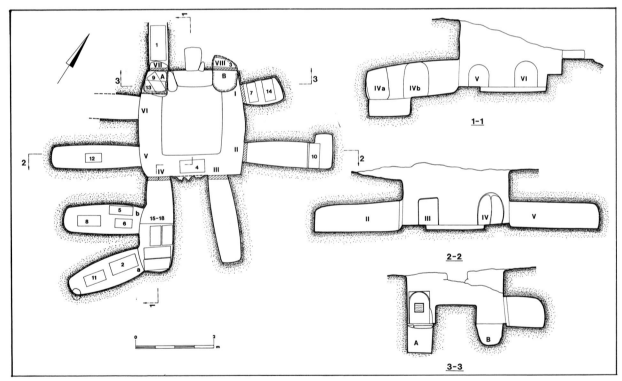

Mount Scopus: plan and sections of the burial cave

[1] The cave, located near the entrance to Brigham Young University on the southwestern slope of Mount Scopus, was excavated by the Israel Antiquities Authority in February 1989 with the assistance of B. Ziso. The bones were removed and studied by J. Zias. For the final excavation report of the burial cave, see: V. Sussman, "A Burial Cave on Mount Scopus," *'Atiqot* . 21 (1992): 89–96 (Hebrew).

divided into two sections by a slab, behind which an ossuary was found. Two sub-loculi were annexed to Loculus IV and its interior was deepened so that it could hold four additional ossuaries with flat lids. Loculus VIII is a short oval cavity sunk below floor-level, large enough to hold an ossuary placed across its width. The entrances to all the loculi were found blocked by stone slabs which were adapted to the shape of the openings. Some of the slabs were reinforced with plaster. Two repositories, Pits A and B, flank the entrance to the cave. Pit A, located in front of the sealed entrance to Loculus VII, has a rectangular opening and is 1 m. deep. Pit B, of irregular oval shape, is connected to Loculus VIII.

The burials in the loculi were of two types: primary burials of individuals in a fully extended position with heads facing to the east; and secondary burials in ossuaries. The ossuaries were sometimes placed upon skeletal remains. Each ossuary contained bones of two to six individuals. Only three ossuaries were found empty. One of these, made of hard limestone, was found broken on the bench in the eastern part of the chamber, perhaps as a result of the ceiling collapse. Two additional ossuaries were found next to each other, covered with one lid in a diagonal position, on the cover of Pit A. The contents of these two ossuaries were scattered around them. They appear to have been moved from Loculus VII prior to the placing of Ossuary 1 there, and were placed in such a way as to hide the entrance to Loculus VII with their decorated panels facing the loculus.

Eighteen ossuaries were found in the burial cave. Sixteen of the ossuaries are of soft limestone; twelve of these are decorated with the common incised and chip-carved designs, some cut into a red painted background. In one case, dots were added with black paint to the centers of the rosettes. Of the two ossuaries made of hard limestone, Ossuary 1 is large and fully decorated. Three types of covers were used: gabled, vaulted and flat, the latter often sliding in grooves. Bases are either flat or raised upon four short feet.

## The Repertoire of Incised Decoration on the Ossuaries

The ossuaries are ornamented with the characteristic multiple-petalled rosettes and whorl rosettes with pointed or heart-shaped petals.

Mount Scopus: view of the burial cave from above

Many of the front panels are divided into two metopes, each with a central rosette. Some have an additional motif between the two metopes, examples of which include: a *nefesh* (burial monument) or obelisk erected on a high pedestal; a tomb facade; and a prayer-shawl-like pattern.

Ossuary 1 from Loculus VII which contained the remains of six adult males, is unique. It is made of hard limestone of poor quality and was repaired inside with plaster. The ossuary measures 85 × 39.5 by 45 cm. high, and its gabled lid is 23 cm. high. The base is flat. Three of the panels of the chest are decorated in high relief surrounded by a raised frame, as are the two sloping panels of the lid. The designs combine natural and schematic floral motifs, several of which are known from facades of large, sumptuous burial caves, ossuaries and coffins from Jerusalem cemeteries of the same period. The rear panel of this ossuary has the appearance of a single-framed Herodian ashlar, with rough chisel marks.

On the front panel of Ossuary 1 is a central, five-branched acanthus plant with small knobs (fruits?) at the ends of some of the leaves. The plant is flanked by two large, tripartite grape clusters suspended from a horizontal staff, with symmetrically arranged tendrils above

227

Mount Scopus: group of decorated ossuaries found in the burial cave

the clusters. The elongated fruit of the right-hand cluster suggests the renowned Hebron grapes. Suspended from a stem on either side of each of the large clusters are small clusters of grapes corresponding in form to those of the large clusters—five elongated grapes on the right, and six rounded grapes on the left. On the front panel of the lid, five vine leaves form a central cluster from which tendrils sprout outward, each with two additional leaves and one small grape cluster. The tendrils pointing toward the corners open into ivy leaves which enclose a five-petalled flower, echoing the design of the front panel. On one short end of the lid is a flower with six drop-shaped leaves within a stepped, rounded, triangular frame.

Within a recessed rectangular frame on one of the narrow sides of the chest is a heavy wreath composed of a myrtle, berries and a ribbon ending below in a knot, with a long bow at the bottom and its two ends flanking a lanceolate leaf. The other narrow side has a raised, ornate blossom, also composed of several elements—an egg-and-dart pattern encircling a six-petalled rosette with a central, small, four-petalled bud interspersed with ivy leaves.

## Inscriptions

Above the frame of the elaborately decorated front panel of Ossuary 1, the name of the deceased is engraved in square Aramaic letters:

יהוסף בר חנניה הספר (yhwsf br ḥnnyh hsfr) "Jehoseph the son of Hananiah the Scribe."[2]

[2] The last word of the inscription is virtually illegible. The reading "the scribe" was proposed by L.Y. Rahmani.

228

**Mount Scopus: decorated Ossuary 1 with inscription "Jehoseph the son of Hananiah the Scribe" (Pl. VIIb)**

Mount Scopus: square frame with Aramaic inscription
in the center of the door to Loculus VII

An illegible five-line inscription written with black ink or carbon in square Aramaic characters was found on the blocking stone that sealed Loculus VII in which this ossuary was found.

## Finds

Only fragmentary pottery vessels typical of the Herodian period in Jerusalem were found at or near floor level, mainly in the central chamber. These include sherds of Herodian-type oil-lamps, cooking pots and piriform bottles as well as a fragment of a ladle of a type known from Qumran and dated to 50–31 B.C.E. A unique find from Loculus VI is a broken iron finger-ring with an engraved carnelian gem set in a bezel. The engraved gem depicts a bust of the young Apollo, facing left, with short-cropped hair held by a laurel sprig. The lower part of the neck is divided. While Apollo was a popular motif on amulets, such amulets were not commonly used by Jews and this type of ring is rare in Jewish burials. Similar gems dating to the 1st century C.E. are known from Caesarea.[3] The gem found here lacks Apollo's attribute—the palm, per-

haps, as L.Y. Rahmani has suggested, intentionally eliminated for use by Jews.[4]

## Summary

The burial cave is typical of Second Temple period tombs. The plan of the cave is almost identical to a burial cave in the nearby Dominus Flevit burial ground published by B. Bagatti, perhaps indicative of having been planned for use by the same family.

The decorated ossuary described here has close parallels in these tombs[5] It must have been quite expensive and probably belonged to a wealthy and prominent person. The name of the deceased, *yhwsf*, is extremely common during this period and is also known from the Dominus Flevit burial ground. It is possible that the Yehosef Bar Ḥananya of this tomb may be the son of Ḥananya bar Menaḥem, buried nearby in the same burial ground.[6]

Placing many of the ossuaries in the tomb so that their decorated panels are hidden from view suggests the hope of averting the attention of grave-robbers.[7] No complete ceramic offering vessels were found in this tomb, suggesting that such vessels, frequently encountered elsewhere, were not commonly placed in Jewish tombs until after the destruction of the First Temple.

Despite its small size, the cave contained rather a large number of individuals—eighty-eight. Half of these, according to J. Zias,[8] were children under eighteen years of age. The finds in Loculus IV indicate unplanned, perhaps hurriedly executed burials in unornamented ossuaries. This suggests an episode of high and unexpected mortality over a short period of time.

[3] A. Hamburger, "Gems from Caesarea Maritima," *Atiqot* 8 (1968): Pl. 1:16 (Hebrew).

[4] L.Y. Rahmani, "A Jewish Rock-Cut Tomb on Mt. Scopus," *Atiqot* (English Series) XIV (1980): 54.

[5] B. Bagatti, "Nuovi apporti archeologici al 'Dominus Flevit' (Oliveto)," *LA* 19 (1969): 194–236; Fig. 19, Tomb 2, pp. 225–232.

[6] P.B. Bagatti and J.T. Milik, *Gli scavi al "Dominus Flevit" (Mont Oliveto, Gerusalemme) I. Le necropoli del periodo Romano* (Jerusalem, 1958), Pl. 14–16.

[7] V. Sussman, "A Burial Cave near Augusta Victoria," *Atiqot* 8 (1982): 46 (Hebrew).

[8] J. Zias, "Human Skeletal Remains from the Mount Scopus Tomb," *Atiqot* (English Series) XXI (1992): 97–103.

# Sarcophagi of the Late Second Temple Period in Secondary Use

## Levi Yizḥaq Raḥmani

Visitors to the Temple Mount may have noted a decorated sarcophagus and a plain ossuary displayed together on the large platform between the Al-Aqsa Mosque and the Islamic Museum. Another decorated sarcophagus can be seen at the foot of the fine Qayatbay fountain (*sebil*) west of the Dome of the Rock. Holes cut into the lower facades of these and two other sarcophagi attest to their sometime use as watering troughs. All the sarcophagi (but not the ossuary) were studied about a century ago by Ch. Clermont-Ganneau and others, and were mentioned occasionally in guide books since then.

### A. The Sarcophagus in Front of the Islamic Museum

This sarcophagus is made of hard limestone. It is 2.02 m. long, 55 cm. wide, and 51 cm. high. The facade and narrow sides have recessed panels with carved frames. The panel on the facade is decorated with five rosettes carved in relief, each having a smaller rosette in the center. The rosettes, which are separated by small disks, are of three different designs: the petals of the two large rosettes at

Temple Mount; the sarcophagus and the ossuary in front of the Islamic Museum

either end are rounded and abut their neighbors; the petals of the two inner rosettes are heart- or ivy-shaped with lanceolate leaves between them; while instead of petals, the large central rosette has stylized lily blossoms that are also separated by sharp, narrow leaves. Each of the small rosettes in the centers of the larger ones differs from the others. At each of the narrow sides of the sarcophagus are crude carvings of wreaths. Within one of these is an eight-petaled rosette.

The sarcophagus was used as a water trough in the small plaza in front of the Gate of the Chain. For this purpose a hole was made at the bottom of the central rosette, and the interior

Temple Mount; the sarcophagus in front of the Islamic Museum

The sarcophagus in the Louvre Museum, Paris

Side of the lid in the Louvre Museum, Paris

Side of the lid in the Louvre Museum, Paris

of the sarcophagus was plastered. The sarcophagus was removed from that location in 1871 to a private building nearby. It was brought to its present place only recently.

## B. The Sarcophagus in the Louvre Museum

The sarcophagus is made of hard reddish limestone. It is 2.02 m. long, 49 cm. wide, and 50 cm. high. It is very similar to the one described above, except for minor details in the design of the rosette petals and the narrow sides. Several holes pierce the facade—three on the left side and two on the right.

The sarcophagus served as a watering trough in the Madrasa el-Tankiziyya. This is a Mamluk structure dating to 1328/9 C.E. which later housed the Muslim Shariyya court. In 1866 the sarcophagus was removed from there at the orders of the Turkish governor of Jerusalem and given to the French explorer F. de Saulcy. Along with fragments of a lid decorated with similar motifs, it is now in the Louvre Museum.[1]

The lid of this sarcophagus is 2.02 m. long, 49 cm. wide, and 27 cm. high. A large disc is carved on one side of the lid, while on the other are two symmetrical lily blossoms with a fruit (pomegranate?) between them.

## C. The Sarcophagus at the Foot of the Qayatbay Fountain

This sarcophagus too is made of hard limestone. The dimensions are 2.07 m. long, 62 cm. wide and 34 cm. high. The sarcophagus is set into the lower part of the Mamluk structure dating to 1482 C.E., at its southern side. Presumably it was higher originally.

Only the facade of the sarcophagus is decorated. Under an egg-and-dart frieze are six rosettes, each of a different design. The rosette at the left is whorl-like. The others, from left to right have six, seven, six, four,

[1] I am grateful to Dr. A. Coubet, the Curator of the Oriental Antiquities Division of the Louvre Museum in Paris for providing me with information about this sarcophagus and for allowing me to reproduce the photographs she kindly supplied.

232

Temple Mount; the sarcophagus at the base of the Qayatbay fountain

and thirteen petals respectively. The petals also differ in form. In this sarcophagus too, the petals of one of the rosettes are replaced by lily blossoms.

The small rosettes in the centers of the large ones also differ from one another. Some of them were reduced to small buds or buttons. The large rosettes are separated by a decorative motif composed of vertically symmetrical pairs of lily blossoms. Clermont-Ganneau noted that the interior of the sarcophagus was rounded on the end where the head was placed. The lower part of the facade into which the holes are cut was plastered or cemented over in a rather crude manner, partly obliterating the carved decoration. Nevertheless, even from the photograph it is still possible to make out the holes at the bottom of the second and fourth rosettes from the left. These holes can also be seen in Clermont-Ganneau's drawing.

### D. The Sarcophagus in Ha-Gai Street
The sarcophagus is made of reddish limestone; 1.9–2 m. long, 55–60 cm. wide, and 54–56 cm. high. On its facade is a bossed panel on which are three protruding, smooth disks.

The sarcophagus is still in place as the trough of the fountain that was constructed in 1536/7 C.E.—part of the city's water supply system commissioned by Sultan Suleiman the Magnificent. The sarcophagus was moved from its setting at Clermont-Ganneau's request in order to study it. He found the same decorative pattern on the other side and a large disk on each of the small ends. The disk at the head end is concave with a protruding button in the center. Inside the sarcophagus, at that end, is an elevated ledge used as a headrest.

Most probably, after Clermont-Ganneau examined the sarcophagus it was replaced with its facade to the wall. In any case, the hole at the bottom now faces in that direction.

### E. The Ossuary in Front of the Islamic Museum
The ossuary made of hard limestone is 96 cm. long, 41 cm. wide, and 48 cm. high and stands

Ha-Gai Street; the sarcophagus as part of the fountain

on four short feet. At each end is a recessed, smooth panel. A recess was cut into the inner sides of three of the top edges to receive the lid. At the bottom of the front facade a large hole is pierced.

## Summary

According to Clermont-Ganneau, all the sarcophagi described above were removed from the Tombs of the Kings in the 15th century C.E. The site has been identified as the ornate family tombs of Queen Helena of Adiabene, which date to the end of the Second Temple period. Clermont-Ganneau relied on the book by Mujir ed-Din of 1496 C.E. who described the construction of the basin (al-fiskiyya) next to the Gate of the Chain in 1483 C.E. And indeed, Clermont-Ganneau makes sense: The style of the sarcophagus from Ha-Gai (El-Wad) Street is very similar to that of Queen Helena—the sarcophagus discovered by de Saulcy in the Tomb of the Kings and brought to the Louvre. The form of the rosettes on Sarcophagi A and B resembles those on the broken fragments removed by de Saulcy from these tombs, as well as the rosettes on the fragments of the lid that was shipped to Paris together with Sarcophagus B.

The style of Sarcophagus C differs from that of the others. It represents an extreme expression of *horror vacui*, for the design of most of the rosettes is similar to the decorative elements on other sarcophagi from the Tombs of the Kings. They also resemble those on the facade of the Frieze Tomb in north Jerusalem. Thus, R. Jacoby may well be right in suggesting that this object was originally part of a frieze of the Second Temple period.[2] As such, it may have been brought to its present place from one of the tombs north of the city.

The ossuary could have come from any other Jewish tomb of the period in the Jerusalem area, but ossuaries were also found in the Tombs of the Kings. One of these—with decorations—is preserved in the Louvre.

If, sometime in the mid-15th century, Jerusalem construction workers and stonemasons indeed came upon Jewish sarcophagi and ossuaries of the end of the Second Temple period, this may be of some significance. For from that time on, simple rosettes with six petals and other characteristic rosette designs, sometimes chip-carved, began to appear on various buildings—first in Jerusalem and later throughout the country. Perhaps it was not a new invention but a fashion of copying local examples at a time when such sarcophagi were being removed from ancient tombs in the city.

[2] R. Jacoby, "The Ornamented Stone Near the Fountain of Qayatbay: A Sarcophagus or a Frieze?" *IEJ* 39 (1989): 284–286.

## Bibliography

Clermont-Ganneau, C. *Archaeological Researches in Palestine*, I (London, 1899), pp. 129–131, 138–139, 232–233.

Dussaud, R. *Les monuments palestiniens et judaïques* (Paris, 1912), pp. 42–46, No. 30; p. 50, No. 43.

Musée du Louvre, *Félix de Saulcy (1807-1880) et la Terre Sainte* Exhibition Catalog (Paris, 1982), pp. 101–102, Nos. 49–53; p. 203, No. 246.

Rahmani, L.Y., "Chip-Carving in Palestine," *IEJ* 38 (1988): 59–75.

Saulcy, F. de, *Voyage autour de la Mer Morte* (Paris, 1853), Pl. 31–33.

———, Jérusalem (Paris, 1882), p. 283.

Vilnay, Z., *Jerusalem the Capital of Israel. Vol. I. The Old City* (Jerusalem, 1970), p. 266 (Hebrew).

# An Ossuary from Jerusalem Ornamented with Monumental Facades

## Amos Kloner

More than eighty burial caves dating to the two centuries preceding the destruction of the Second Temple have been discovered on Mount Scopus and on its eastern and western slopes. During construction of the Humanities Building of the Hebrew University, a large burial complex consisting of two caves, interconnected since ancient times, was exposed.[1]

Both caves have south-facing entrances. One of the caves contains three burial chambers, while the other has two. In Chamber E of the western cave, loculi (*kokhim*) for primary burial, and eighteen ossuaries for secondary burial were revealed. Seven of these ossuaries were found in niches and loculi hewn in the walls of the chamber while the others were found on the floor.

Ossuary 14 was situated near the eastern wall, on top of a 7-cm.-thick layer of earth which probably accumulated during the time the cave was in use.

This ossuary is outstanding in the quality of its ornamentation, its form and its dimensions. The ossuary broadens a little toward the top and its edges are slightly broken. The lid is somewhat longer and better preserved than the ossuary itself, and may have been added to the chest when the latter was utilized, rather than at the time of its manufacture. The chest is 84 cm. long, 43.5 cm. wide and 47 cm. high.

[1] The excavation was carried out in May–June 1974 by the Department of Antiquities and Museums (the present Israel Antiquities Authority). The caves were exposed by a mechanical tool when digging the southern foundations of the Humanities Building on Mount Scopus. For more details, see: A. Kloner, "Burial Complex and Ossuaries from the Second Temple Period," *S. Safrai Jubilee Volume* (Jerusalem, in press) (Hebrew). The ossuary is numbered 74.1508 in the records of the Israel Antiquities Authority and is on permanent display in the Israel Museum.

The side walls are 8–9 cm. thick and the bottom 12 cm. The lid, 86 cm. long, 46.5 cm. wide and 20 cm. high, has a barrel-vault form and is ornamented on top with a rosette carved in relief. The ossuary is carved of a harder limestone than the usual chalk of which most ossuaries in Jerusalem are made.

The context indicates that the ossuary may have previously been used elsewhere and later moved to our cave. The earth layer on which the ossuary stood shows that the cave had been already in use for some time when it was placed inside. The remains in the cave and the condition of the ossuary lead us to assign its manufacture to around the mid–1st century C.E.

## The Ornamentation

All of the decoration on the sides of the ossuary is carved in relief. The front panel has six square pilasters with capitals supporting an architrave, In the center is an entrance with doorjambs and lintel and a triangular pediment topped by a large, unfinished acroterion featuring a floral motif. Although the outlines of the acroterion are marked out, the craftsman did not complete the carving. Two entrance-like niches with round arches flank the central entrance on each side. The spaces inside these niches are filled with different vegetal designs, including leaves and flowers closely related to ornamental masonry motifs of Jerusalem tombs of the Second Temple period—such as the bottom of the lintel over the entrance to the Tomb of the Grapes cave, the sides of the hewn burial platforms in Sanhedria Cave 7, the ornamentation on an internal wall of Sanhedria Cave 16, and the corpus of ossuary ornamentation. The vegetal

The four sides of the decorated ossuary from Mount Scopus, Jerusalem.

motifs on the front of this particular ossuary replace the human figures in raised relief occurring on monumental facades outside of Judea, such as the Khazneh at Petra and monuments in Greek and Roman cities. The relief ornamentation in the niche on the extreme left is damaged.

A similar relief facade was left incomplete on the rear panel of the ossuary chest. Here too, the artist intended to execute a central entrance with a pediment topped by an acroterion and two niches on either side. However, due to an error in spacing the pilasters, the decoration of this panel was apparently abandoned. The panel gives good insight into the process of creating relief decorations on ossuaries: first, the surface was laid out into sections, the design was then sketched in, and finally, the panel was carved in relief.

One of the narrow side panels has a relief showing a building facade with four pilasters surmounted by capitals, architraves and a broken pediment. As on the other side panel, the capitals on the pilasters are not identical in form and design (see below). Similar differences between pairs of column capitals flanking entrances may be seen in various contemporaneous Jerusalem monuments. In front of the two middle pilasters, the artist fashioned a monumental entrance with a pediment and a door having four recessed panels. The tetrastyle facade probably indicates that the door was meant to be located behind the two central pilasters, but the artist was apparently unable to execute this and instead depicted the doorway in front of the pilasters. The acroterion on top of the pediment features a stylized vegetal motif: three leaf stalks growing out of a single stem. As depicted, the door would have opened inward. Stone doors are quite rare in the Jerusalem necropolis of the Second Temple period. One such door is represented on the facade of a tomb in the Kidron Valley area. Likenesses of stone doors in relief are carved in burial caves in the lower Hinnom Valley at Aceldama (see in this volume, pp. 206–218). We also find stone doors on the inside of monumental tombs in Jerusalem, as in the so-called Tombs of the Kings.

On the other narrow panel, a facade is depicted in relief consisting of two columns surmounted by a segmental (gently curved) arch. Such arches are familiar from monumental structures and residential buildings of the Herodian period and later. Examples may be seen on the facades of two burial caves in the area of Armon Hanaẓiv in Jerusalem and in numerous arcosolia inside burial cave chambers. In the middle of the facade is an entrance with a lintel extending beyond the lines of the doorposts. This type of entranceway was rather common in monumental facades of Second Temple period tombs in Jerusalem and in later facades at Beth She'arim and in Galilean synagogues. Above the entrance is a pediment with a tympanum. The ornamentation includes a circle with a knob in the middle. To the right is a strip in the shape of a coil or snake; its counterpart on the left was apparently effaced. In the entranceway, a door with four recessed panels is depicted. The door itself is recessed 1.5 cm. from the surface of the doorframe, indicating that it also opened inward—like the door on the other narrow side panel of the ossuary chest. The space between the pediment over the entrance and the curve of the arch at the top of the facade is filled by four circles with knobs at their centers. This facade was fashioned like a monument with a protruding entranceway: the main facade, consisting of pilasters bearing the arch, stands behind this entrance.

Many of the ornamented Jerusalem ossuaries, which make up less than half of the known items, are decorated on one, two, or three panels only, leaving the long panel at the rear unadorned. In the ossuary described here, the rear panel remained incomplete due to an error by the artisan. That the work was not completed apparently attests, as suggested by L.Y. Rahmani, to the esthetic rather than religious or ideological significance of the ossuary ornamentation.[2]

[2] See in this volume, pp. 196–197; and L.Y. Rahmani, "Ancient Jerusalem's Funerary Customs and Tombs," *BA* 43 (1982): 109–119.

The motif of the broken pediment found on one of the narrow panels of the ossuary appears in monuments at Petra including ed-Deir, the Khazneh and the Corinthian Tomb,[3] as well as at Boscoreale, Herculaneum, Pompeii and other localities where Roman wall frescoes have been found. The various styles of wall frescoes found at sites destroyed by the eruption of Vesuvius in 79 C.E., especially the Fourth Pompeii Style, were influenced by the art of Alexandria, which was a center for arts and crafts from the Ptolemaic period on. It is possible that Alexandrian rather than local artists designed the facade of the Khazneh and other monuments at Petra, as these feature purely classical elements and lack characteristic Nabatean mofits. Moreover, the facades depicted on our ossuary display elements with parallels in the Alexandrian funerary style of the Hellenistic period. We may thus assume an Alexandrian influence.[4]

Central entrances topped by triangular pediments, similar to the one depicted on our ossuary, appear in monumental burial caves in Jerusalem, such as Jehoshaphat's Tomb, Cave 14 of the Sanhedria Tombs, and the Tomb of the Grapes. A central entrance of this type, with side entrances or arched recesses like the ones depicted—or at least planned—on the long panels of our ossuary, can be seen on the facade of ed-Deir at Petra.[5] This rock-cut monument has a facade of columns with entrances between them. The middle entrance features a triangular pediment, and arched entrances flank it on either side. The Palace Tomb in Petra, also known as the Multistoried Tomb, has four entrances separated by pilasters—two rectangular entrances with triangular pediments above them in the middle flanked by two arched entrances.

The design of the two long sides of the ossuary is, in general, similar to that of the inner walls of the Triclinium Tomb at Petra. The front panel is similar both in conception and details to the tomb of Sextius Florentinus at Petra.[6] The circular motif with a snake-like coil on its right on the tympanum of one of the side panels of the ossuary suggests the tympanum adorned with a Medusa, or a mask with snakes emerging from it at this same Petra tomb.

The artist who fashioned our ossuary depicted facades that he may have seen himself, although, more probably, he worked from pattern books. We may safely assume that he saw and was inspired by similar structures in the Jerusalem necropolis. Since no complete facades of this type are known in Jerusalem until now, it is also possible that the artist based his work on what he had seen in Alexandria—the capital of Egypt and the center of culture at the time. There can be little doubt that the man who fashioned this ossuary knew of the monuments at Petra, the Nabatean capital, and that—directly or indirectly—its facades were the main inspiration for his work.

[3] A. Negev, "Petra and the Nabateans," *Qadmoniot* 27–28 (1974): 71–93 (Hebrew); and idem., "The Nabateans and the Provincia Arabia," in: G. Hasse and H. Temporini (eds.), *Aufstieg und Niedergang der Römischen Welt, II Principat* 8 (1977), pp. 520–686.

[4] J. McKenzie, *The Architecture of Petra* (Oxford, 1990).

[5] Ed-Deir has been dated to the period between the 1st century B.C.E. and the early 2nd century C.E. Recently, A. Negev advanced the theory that it is the tomb of Rabel II (76–106 C.E.), and should be dated to around 100–106 C.E. In any event, our ossuary could not have been made after 70 C.E.

[6] The tomb was that of one of the Roman governors at Petra, as indicated in the inscription carved above its entrance. It is known that he served in 127 C.E., but the date of his burial is uncertain. Because of its Latin inscription, this tomb served as a point of reference for the dating of graves of the Roman Temple type at Petra. See: A. Negev, *Qadmoniot* 8 (1975): 84–85 (Hebrew); and idem, Note 3 (1977), p. 597.

# Representations of the Menorah on Ossuaries

## Levi Yizḥaq Raḥmani

A study of Jewish ossuaries of the Second Temple period by the present writer has shown that decorative motifs appearing on these funerary chests reflect the general aspect and various details of contemporary tombs and of the vegetation near these. These motifs were apparently treated as purely decorative elements of no particular symbolic significance (see in this volume, pp. 191–205). Two of the very rare exceptions to this rule are representations of the Menorah.

Both appear on ossuaries kept in the Israel Museum collections. Although these ossuaries were acquired locally, their exact provenance remains unknown. By style and workmanship they may be ascribed to the area south or southwest of Jerusalem and to the period between 70 and 135 C.E.*

Ossuary A with a representation of the Menorah on its lid

### Ossuary A.

The form of a Menorah lacking a foot or base, executed in shallow zigzag incision, appears along the length of the vaulted lid of this ossuary. Two branches arch out on either side of the stem of the Menorah. Two short, additional branches, issuing from the outer branch on each side as if by afterthought, raise the total to seven.

On one of the long sides of the ossuary is an ordinary decorative motif: a central metope with a large six-petaled rosette, and two flanking metopes containing half and quarter circles and a lattice pattern. One narrow side of the ossuary again features lattice patterns, here applied to frame a six-petaled rosette.

* I am grateful to the Chief Curator, Archaeology, The Israel Museum, Jerusalem for permission to publish photographs of Ossuaries A and B.

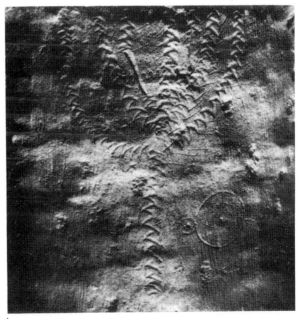

Lid of Ossuary A: detail showing representation of Menorah

Above the frame is a cross mark, corresponding to the top of the Menorah, to indicate how the lid is to be placed for a proper fit.

A Greek inscription at the front, above the frames of the central and left metope, reads: ANANIAC K(AI) ANANAC. Flanking the central, upper petal of the rosette on the front appears an additional incised ANA. The two names Ananias (Ḥanania) and Ananus (here spelled Ananas—Ḥanan) are repeatedly mentioned by Josephus and other ancient sources as members of priestly families—even of high priests—of the 2nd century B.C.E. to the 3rd century C.E. and later; no identification with any of these is suggested here. "ANA" may be seen as an attempt to write one of these names in too small a space, or it could represent an abbreviated form, like that found in an inscription in the Jewish catacomb at Venosa.

## Ossuary B.

The second ossuary also has a vaulted lid decorated with an incised zigzag lattice pattern. On the back of the chest appears a large saltire executed in red wash, and such wash also covers the other sides. Into this, barely recognizable representations of amphoras are incised freehand in shallow zigzags. A large amphora is depicted in this fashion on each of the narrow sides, and two amphoras appear on the front of the chest. Of the latter, the round body of the right-hand amphora encompasses a six-petaled rosette. Between the

Ossuary B: five-branched Menorah flanked by highly stylized amphoras

two amphoras is a Menorah with five branches and a long stem on a triangular foot. It is executed in the same zigzag technique, as is also the border design framing the entire composition.

Jewish representations of the Menorah (as distinct from the Roman one on the Arch of Titus) of such antiquity are very rare. Of the nine known depictions of the Menorah dating to before the end of the Bar Kokhba Revolt, only four are earlier than 70 C.E.: 1) on a coin

Coin of King Mattathias-Antigonus, ca. 37 B.C.E.

of King Mattathias Antigonus, probably of 37 B.C.E.; 2) scratched into the plastered wall of a Jerusalem house uncovered in the Jewish Quarter, dated to the latter part of the 1st century B.C.E.; 3) scratched on a sundial dated to the Herodian dynasty that was found at the foot of the southwestern corner of the Temple Mount; and 4) scratched into the plaster of the porch of Jason's Tomb and dated earlier than 30/31 C.E. In the period 70–135 C.E., the Menorah appears as part of the decoration of five Darom-type oil-lamps, out of about one thousand such items found until now in the Judean Hills.

**The Foot.** The Menorah represented on Ossuary A lacks a foot, as do the ones on the sundial and most of the Menorahs in Jason's Tomb, though some are depicted with the stem emerging from a sort of rectangular

Menorah and other objects incised on plastered wall in
the Jewish Quarter of Jerusalem, Herodian period

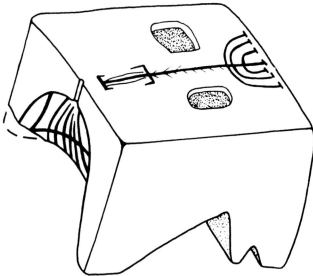

Sundial from the excavations south of the Temple
Mount, Jerusalem, Herodian period

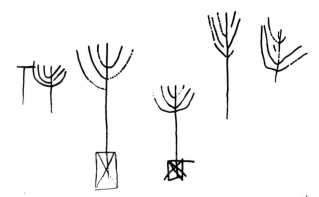

Representations of the Menorah, from the porch of
Jason's Tomb, Jerusalem, before 30/31 C.E.

Darom-type oil-lamp with representation of nine-
branched Menorah, ca. 70–135 C.E.

base. The Menorah on Ossuary B has a triangular base or foot, similar to the one from the
Jewish Quarter.

**The Branches.** While representations of the
Menorah antedating the destruction of the
Second Temple (1–4) all show the correct
number of branches—seven, the ones on the
oil-lamps, as well as the two on the ossuaries
described here, have either fewer or more
branches, though an attempt to redress this
was made on Ossuary A. This variation in
representation seems to be related to another
exceptional difference observed on the oil-
lamps: handles added to the lower part of the

outer branches, which give the body of the candelabrum the appearance of an amphora or krater. V. Sussman, who first noted this detail, suggests one of two explanations: either the artisans were disinclined to portray an exact image of this sanctified object, or such handles actually existed on the Menorah in the Temple. The second explanation is hardly acceptable: no other representations of the Menorah show such handles, nor are they mentioned in texts describing it.

The first assumption is indeed well founded in an ancient ruling laid down in a discussion involving Rabbi Yosi ben Yehuda, a sage living toward the end of the 2nd century C.E., that prohibits making an exact replica of the Menorah out of any metal or even wood (Bab. Tal., Menaḥot 28b = Rosh Hashana 24a). It seems that this interdict on the making of a three-dimensional copy of this sacred object was extended, at least by some, during the time-span from the destruction of the Temple in 70 C.E. until after the suppression of the Bar Kokhba Revolt of 135 C.E., to include also an exact two-dimensional representation. Thus, observance of the ancient ruling led to depictions of the Menorah with five, six, eight, or even more branches.

Menorahs on the oil-lamps have up to ten branches, and are further differentiated by the addition of rather incongruous handles. On the two ossuaries are candelabra with five branches, though two shorter branches were added, rather ingenuously, to the one on Ossuary A, apparently out of some conflicting urge to have this representation as close as possible to the hallowed object.

## Discussion

The tendency to safeguard the realm of holiness in form, gesture or word, permissible only at some appropriate place, by specially appointed persons and under exactly specified circumstances, finds expression in an interesting contemporary Jewish parallel: the interdict on uttering the Tetragrammaton—the Divine Name—as it appears in the Holy Writ (Mishnah, Sanhedrin 10:1). This ruling, quoted in the name of Abba Sha'ul (first half of

2nd century C.E.), did not apply to the high priest in the threefold confession of the Day of Atonement (Mishnah, Yoma 3:8; 4:2; 6:2) or to the priests pronouncing their blessing in the Temple. In the provinces, and even in synagogue services in Jerusalem proper, a substitute word was used instead of the Tetragrammaton (Mishnah, Sotah 7:6; cf. Bab. Tal., Kiddushin 71a). To this day this substitution takes the form of *Adonai* (Lord), in prayer or benedictions, and in secular use is often removed even further from the realm of the sacred by being pronounced *Adoshem*—from *Ha-Shem*, "The Name." In writing, this is further abbreviated to the letter *heh*, and the observant who regard even such usage to be a profanation of the sacrosanct, substitute for it the letter *dalet*.

Another interesting way of safeguarding the holiness and ineffability of the Tetragrammaton is to be found in the 1st century B.C.E. Dead Sea Scrolls, where it is inserted in paleo-Hebrew letters within texts written in the square Hebrew script of that period.

This masking of the Menorah on the oil-lamps and ossuaries is known to psychologists as a defense mechanism—conscious, unconscious or subconscious—intended to conceal the real intention of the perpetrator. In our case it seems to resolve conflicting interests: compliance with the interdict on a full and complete representation of the Menorah, and the wish to depict it as accurately as possible. The outcome is especially revealing on Ossuary A, where we find the still permissible representation, with only five branches, but with the addition of two ancillary branches, to be counted or disregarded at one's pleasure or peril, but still attaining the hallowed number of seven.

Possibly, many of the representations of the Menorah enumerated above—a total of eleven, counting Ossuaries A and B—are connected with priests and their activities. This is certainly the case with regard to the last priest-king's coin and the sundial found on the Temple Mount, an instrument most necessary to priests, whose duties called for frequent reference to time. There can also be little doubt that the Menorah from the Jewish Quarter was incised by a member of a priestly family. Not only does it feature details attested by contemporary literature and known at the time only to an insider, but to its right are representations of what apparently are parts of the Showbread Table and the Incense Altar, also familiar to priests (see in this volume, pp. 272–278). It was executed on plaster which once covered the walls of one of the houses in the quarter inhabited by affluent families, identified by other finds as members of the priesthood.

Admittedly, such a priestly connection can only be conjectured in the case of the Menorahs from Jason's Tomb, but it seems at least likely with regard to Ossuary A, because of the two names appearing on it. Indeed, the insistence on the seven branches, through the addition of two more and the positioning of the Menorah at the top, may suggest that this depiction was of special significance to the persons who incised it, perhaps even revealing the intention of providing some protection for the remains of the deceased.

Such attribution, though still possible, cannot be proven for Ossuary B or the group of Darom oil-lamps, all of which are strictly in compliance with the prohibition of exact representations of the Menorah. However, the remarkable fact that only five out of more than one thousand oil-lamps of this type show this motif, which appears even more rarely on the ossuaries, points to the use of the Menorah motif by a restricted group within the population—possibly, priestly families.

Representations of the Menorah which disregard such prohibitions, or masking, make their appearance in Roman Palestine in the late 2nd century C.E., at first in the Beth She'arim necropolis. There, as N. Avigad rightly pointed out, they seem to have been introduced by Jews from abroad, who, from the 2nd century C.E. on, often adorned their tombs in the Diaspora with a seven-branched candelabrum, probably as an expression of their faith. In Palestine, however, it seems likely that until the 2nd century C.E. the Menorah was regarded as an emblem or mark of priestly families. Only subsequently, probably under the influence of the Diaspora, did it acquire a wider meaning here as well, identifying the Jewish ownership of an edifice or object.

## Bibliography

Avigad, N., "Excavations in the Jewish Quarter of the Old City, Jerusalem, 1969/70 (Preliminary Report)," *IEJ* 20 (1970): 3–5.

————, *Beth She'arim* 3 (Jerusalem, 1976), pp. 268–274.

Negev, A., "The Chronology of the Seven-Branched Menorah," *Eretz Israel* 8 (Jerusalem, 1967), pp. 193–210 (Hebrew; English summary on p. 74*).

Siegel, J.P., "Palaeo-Hebrew Characters for the Divine Names at Qumran in the Light of Tanaitic Sources," *HUCA* XLI (1971): 159–172.

Sussman, V., *Ornamented Jewish Oil Lamps from the Destruction of the Second Temple through the Bar Kokhba Revolt* (Warminster, 1982), Nos. 1–5.

# Jerusalem as a Center of the Stone Vessel Industry during the Second Temple Period

## Yitzhak Magen

Vessels made of stone have always occupied a prominent position among the artifacts used by man. Such vessels were used mainly for grinding and pounding, and were fashioned of hard limestone or basalt. The material culture of the Second Temple period was marked by the appearance of a different type of stone vessel, made of chalk (a soft limestone). The presence of these vessels mainly in characteristically Jewish areas, such as Jerusalem, Judea and the Galilee; their absence generally from non-Jewish areas; and their sudden disappearance after the destruction of the Second Temple and the Bar Kokhba Revolt suggests that the stone vessel industry during the Second Temple period was a distinct Jewish phenomenon connected with Jerusalem and the Temple, Jewish religious law, and the Jewish population (Pl. VIf).

### Materials and Workshops for the Production of Stone Vessels

Stone vessels were made of both white and bituminous chalk. The former type of stone is abundant in the eastern part of Jerusalem, from Ḥizma in the north to Beit Sahur in the south. Local *kakula* and *nari* limestone was also used at times for the production of stone vessels such as ossuaries. Bituminous chalk quarried in the Nebi Musa area in the Judean Desert was used mainly for the manufacture of stone tables.

Workshops for the production of stone vessels were concentrated in Jerusalem and its environs. Evidence of such workshops was found on the slope of the Ophel south of the Temple Mount and in the City of David in Jerusalem. Apparently these workshops employed heavy-duty lathes for the production of such items as large vessels and stone tables.

The manufacture of small vessels, mainly "measuring cups," (see below) was carried out at the stone quarries outside the city. Such a workshop for the production of stone vessels was discovered in 1968 in the Abu Dis area, east of Jerusalem. In this workshop small vessels were produced on a lathe. Vessels that had been discarded as faulty while they were being made, as well as cores—the material removed from inside the vessels by turning—were found in Bethany. This discovery on the Mount of Olives attests to the presence of a stone vessel industry there as well. A workshop for the production of stone vessels was also discovered in Galilee, near Reina, on a chalk dome 6 km. north of Nazareth where measuring cups, and apparently also other small vessels made on a lathe, were produced.

The largest quarry-based workshop found until now is located in the village of Ḥizma, the biblical Azmaveth, north of Jerusalem. A number of caves used as stone quarries, and a workshop for making stone vessels were discovered on the northern slope of the village. The dimensions of two of the caves are, respectively, $38 \times 26$ m. and $33 \times 8$ m.; another cave, used as a water cistern, measures $8 \times 7.5$ m. In the early 1980s, two excavation seasons were conducted under the direction of the present author in one of the Ḥizma caves. The excavations revealed archaeological deposits, 5–6 m. thick, containing stone chips. Tens of measuring cups that had been damaged in the various stages of working, stone cores extracted on a lathe, and various small lathe-turned vessels were uncovered. Also found were metal vessels and iron cutting tools such as knives and chisels for separating stone blocks,

Cave at Ḥizma where a Second Temple period workshop for the manufacture of stone vessels was discovered

and a large quantity of pottery vessels of the 1st century C.E.—jars, cooking pots, many oil-lamps, and painted bowls. The pottery vessels are of good quality and were probably made in Jerusalem.

## Methods of Manufacturing Stone Vessels

Two main methods of production can be discerned in the stone vessel industry: manual and lathe work. The manual manufacture of vessels obviously predated the latter, although vessels made entirely by hand continued to be produced also after the introduction of lathes. Mallets, chisels and gouges—tools used for making wooden vessels—were employed in the production of varied types of stone vessels, fashioned both manually and on a lathe.

### Stone Vessels Made Entirely by Hand

Working the stone by hand gave the crafts-man a great deal of freedom and therefore this group of vessels comprises a broad range of shapes. Three main types of objects were

produced in this way: ossuaries; tables; and small vessels of which the most prominent are the measuring cups.

The methods of making and decorating ossuaries for secondary burials were identical to those of the other stone utensils. The ossuaries were fashioned manually with mallet and chisel from preshaped rectangular blocks, and ornamentation was chip-carved or incised in the stone—techniques obviously derived from woodcarving since the chalk lends itself to similar treatment (see in this volume, pp. 191–205).

The tables are rectangular with a single, central leg in the form of a column, that was sometimes turned on a lathe. The ornamentation on the edges of these tables, which imitated imported stone, marble, and metal tables, in some cases resembles that on the ossuaries. Among the stone used for making tables is white chalk, gray-black bituminous chalk, and harder limestones.

Measuring cups in various stages of working were found in all the workshops discovered so

245

A group of measuring cups in process of manufacture found in the cave at Ḥizma

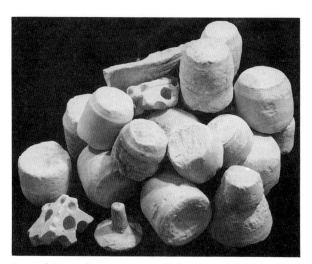

Assemblage of cores extracted from stone vessels, from Ḥizma

far in quarries. In the Ḥizma caves we found dozens of measuring cups that had been damaged while being worked, enabling us to reconstruct the production process. After the chunk of stone to be worked was detached from the rock, it was given the basic shape of the vessel with mallet and chisel. The next stage entailed hollowing out the vessel with mallet, gouge and chisel. Judging from the finds, many vessels must have been damaged at this stage of the manufacturing process. Finally, the outer surface of the vessel was fashioned with a fine chisel, no effort being made to smooth the chisel marks on the sides of the vessels. Vessels other than measuring cups made in this way include mainly square bowls with rounded corners and ledge-handles in the rim.

## Stone Vessels Made on a Lathe

Finds of complete stone vessels, vessels damaged while being worked, and turned stone cores extracted from the vessels, enabled us to reconstruct the two main methods by which stone vessels were made on a lathe: turning small vessels on a simple lathe, and producing large vessels on a massive, technologically more advanced lathe.

The small stone vessels were made mainly in the quarry on a simple bow lathe of a type still used in some traditional societies. Such a lathe consists of a sturdy, adjustable wooden frame having two centers between which the work is held laterally. As in all lathes, the center which holds the work rotates in a fixed headstock; the opposite center or spindle, in an adjustable "loose" headstock, is set to support and align the work. A wooden spool or pulley is firmly affixed—usually with hot tar—to the end of the work on the rotating center, and the string of the bow is looped around the spool. The other side of the work is aligned by means of the non-rotating, adjustable center; or sometimes, if the work is held strongly enough by the tar, it remains unsupported on the other side. By a back-and-forth motion of the bow the artisan rotates the spool with the work affixed to it, and shapes it with the appropriate cutting tools.

Finds dating to the Second Temple period of stone chunks prepared for working and

Manufacture of stone vessels on a lathe; right: before separation of the core; left: the detached core (found at Ḥizma)

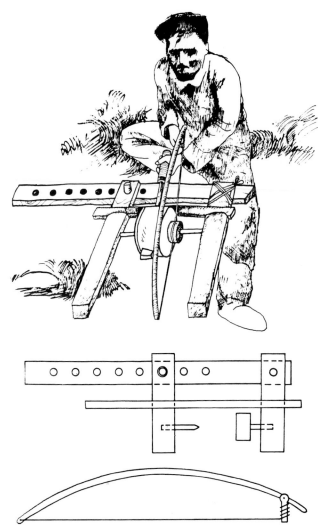

Method of turning small stone vessels on a traditional bow lathe in Mashhad, Iran

vessels damaged in the course of being worked seem to indicate that the small vessels were made by this method. At first, the chunk of stone was shaped roughly to the desired form and probably soaked in water to soften the chalk and keep it from cracking. The outer and inner faces were worked by hand with a chisel to a closer approximation of the desired form. The spool was then firmly affixed to what was to be the bottom of the vessel and the work was mounted laterally in the lathe. After the outer face of the vessel was roughly turned, the inside was removed by deep cutting, and the core detached. In the final stage, the outside of the vessel was smoothed with a sharp knife to obtain extremely thin, fine walls, and ornamented. Stone stoppers and lids have a small center hole into which the tip of the movable aligning and support center was inserted to hold the work steady.

Large vessels, sometimes made from stone blocks weighing more than 400 kg., were manufactured by means of massive, heavy-duty lathes with a rapid-drive mechanism. Due to the great weight of the work, the roughly shaped vessel could not be turned by the spool-and-bow method. All of the large stone vessels have a specially carved, shaped recess and socket in the base into which a heavy wood or metal center was introduced to rotate the work; at the top side of the vessel that was to be hollowed out, an adjustable pole or spindle serving as the aligning or support center steadied the work as it turned.

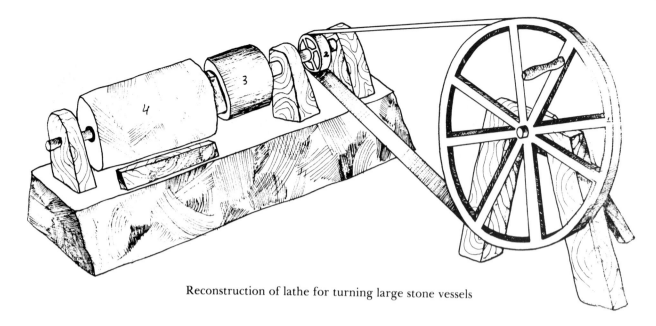

Reconstruction of lathe for turning large stone vessels

## Stone Vessels: Categorization and Description

Stone vessels of the Second Temple period were intended to replace materials that had become ritually impure (see below). The great variety of forms stems from the many attempts to imitate, in stone, utensils in common usage such as imported ceramic ware and metal, glass, or wooden vessels. Our classification of stone vessels into groups is based mainly on the method by which they were made. Vessels made entirely by hand are different from the large and small vessels turned on a lathe. Small vessels produced on a bow lathe differ in outline, form, and ornamentation from those of the large vessels produced on large, technologically more sophisticated lathes. The manner of working also reflected the models copied: turned stone vessels usually were imitations of metal and wooden vessels also made on a lathe and of imported pottery vessels thrown on a wheel; stone vessels made manually strove to imitate hand-crafted wooden vessels and items of furniture.

### Types of Handmade Stone Vessels

The handmade stone vessels comprise a large and diverse group. As mentioned above, three distinct types of stone objects were made by hand: ossuaries which constitute one of the dominant types of products in the entire stone utensils industry; measuring cups; and rectangular stone tables with a single central leg (*monopodia*).

The measuring cups are of unique shape, probably in imitation of wooden cups, and appear in different sizes—with one, but sometimes also with two handles. Scholars have

Stone measuring cup

Decorated stone vessel and its lid, discovered in Tubas in the Samaria mountains

Stone table of hard limestone of the *monopodium* type from the Burnt House in the Upper City of Jerusalem (the Jewish Quarter) of the Second Temple period

Stone table reconstructed from fragments discovered in the Temple Mount area, Jerusalem; the table leg is made in two sections

regarded them as measuring vessels, hence the name "measuring cup." However, this determination is erroneous; a few such vessels may possibly have been used for measuring, but basically this was the common household cup in use during the Second Temple period —also for the ritual washing of the hands. To this group of handmade stone vessels may be added square, handmade bowls with ledge-handles in the rim of the vessel.

The Roman rectangular *monopodium* table was commonly used in the patrician houses of Rome and Herodian Jerusalem. The Roman tables were made of stone, marble, or a combination of a bronze stand and a marble top. We surmise that the stone tables discovered in Jerusalem imitate mainly the latter. Among the many fragments of stone tables ornamented with various patterns found in Jerusalem is one of rarer form that was discovered in the excavations south of the Temple Mount: the blackish bituminous chalk table-top is inlaid with a mosaic of white, gray, and black tesserae characteristic of the Second Temple period.

### Types of Lathe-Turned Stone Vessels
Small, lathe-turned vessels constitute one of the richest and most diverse groups of stone vessels that includes bowls and cups of various sizes and shapes, inkwells, and imitations of glass vessels, wooden bowls, and pottery vessels of the *terra sigillata* type. In this group are also goblet-shaped vessels of which examples were found in the excavations in Jerusalem. Being produced on a lathe, most of the vessels lack handles. Another group of objects in this category consists of assorted plates, platters, and round tabletops. The ornamentation of these small vessels is relatively simple: a fine ridge incised around the wall.

Many lids were discovered, some of which served to cover the large vessels. One of the more interesting discoveries was the many stoppers found in various excavations. The absence among the finds of stone vessels with narrow mouth and stem showed that these stone stoppers were not intended to close stone vessels, but were made to fit pottery

Fragment of a table-top of blackish bituminous stone with mosaic inlay, from the Temple Mount, Jerusalem

pottery vessels from becoming defiled "through their air-space"—an ingenious solution. Apparently stone stoppers were used only by those especially strict in their observance, since lids in general were considered ritually clean (Mishnah, Kelim 2:5).

A large and diverse group of stone utensils turned on a lathe are large vessels. Most of the items of this type were discovered in Jerusalem, and only a few outside the city. Apparently, these large vessels are the *kalal* mentioned in Tosefta, Parah 3:4 which may have been imitations of bronze *kalal*, or calyx-kraters—large bronze and marble vessels common in the Greco-Roman world. There are three main types of large, lathe-turned stone vessels: The first type consists of barrel-shaped vessels, sometimes also with handles, having a trumpet base. The rims, and occasionally also the foot, are decorated with a scale-like ornamentation. Some are well executed while a few exhibit inferior workmanship. This is the dominant type among all the large vessels which are very widely distributed and were found in most of the excavations in Jerusalem and in many sites throughout the country. The second type resembles the first, but has a tall base like that of a column, apparently in imitation of the *labrum* stone vessel in common use in Roman patrician homes and bathhouses. The third type consists of small vessels with a hole-mouth rim, a narrow base and two handles at the upper edge, that may have served for diluting and

jugs, juglets, and jars. According to the halakhah, pottery vessels "contract uncleanness and convey uncleanness through their air-space" i.e., if they are defiled through the opening of the vessel, the contents become ritually unclean (Mishnah, Kelim 2:1). Thus stone stoppers, which are not susceptible to becoming ritually unclean, were used to keep

Group of small lathe-turned vessels from the Jewish Quarter, Jerusalem

Stone stoppers of various sizes turned on a lathe, from the Temple Mount area, Jerusalem

Stone lid turned on a lathe; note the support and rotation point in the knob of the lid

Large *kalal*-type vessel made on a lathe, from the Temple Mount area, Jerusalem

Rim of large, goblet-shaped stone vessel incised with the name יהוסף "Yehosef" from the Temple Mount area, Jerusalem

pouring wine. The narrow base enabled these vessels to be tilted to the side. Variants of this type are rare, and only single items have been found occasionally.

Among the larger lathe-turned utensils are also round tables of white or bituminous chalk, 50–60 cm. in diameter. Three carved wooden ornamental legs were inserted into recesses at the underside of the tabletop (Pl.

251

Stone table and large vessels from the Jewish Quarter excavations, Jerusalem

VIIa). This type of table was exceedingly common in the Greek world, and became popular during the Roman period. It is probably the *delphica* mentioned in the Jewish sources (Mishnah, Kelim 22:2; Abodah Zarah 5:4–5) which was a wood or marble table.

## Stone Vessels in Jewish Halakhah

During the Second Temple period strict attention was paid to the laws of ritual purity. According to the Tosefta, "purity broke out among Israel." Strictness regarding ritual cleanness was not limited solely to the bounds of the Temple, but spread throughout the Jewish communities. The laws of ritual cleanness had far-reaching influence over daily life and on the material culture. Definitions of cleanness and uncleanness are of biblical ori-

Stone vessel with short leg and two handles from Qalandiya, north of Jerusalem

gin (cf., Leviticus 11:33 ff.) and during the Second Temple period they were expanded and discussed in detail in the Order of Tohoroth in the Mishnah. Due to the strictures governing ritual cleanness it was more worthwhile to purchase a vessel which could not become unclean, for once a vessel became ritually unclean it had to be taken out of use—especially a pottery vessel, which had to be broken. As a consequence of this halakhic precept of strict observance of the purity laws both in and outside the Temple, a stone vessel industry began to develop in the Second Temple period. According to the halakhah, stone and earth do not become ritually unclean: "All the utensils that were in the Temple required immersion, excepting the altar of gold and the altar of bronze, for they were reckoned as like to the ground. So R(abbi) Eliezer. But the Sages say, Because they were plated (with metal)" (Mishnah, Hagigah 3:8).

The Mishnah lists groups of vessels which were not susceptible to becoming ritually unclean: cattle-dung vessels, stone vessels, and earthen vessels (Kelim 10:1; Oholoth 5:5; Parah 5:5; Yadayim 1:2). This group of vessels was made of materials originating in the earth. Dung vessels were made of a mixture of animal dung and clay, dried in the sun. They were used mainly for the storage of dry materials: wheat, barley, lentils, etc. Earthen vessels were made of unfired clay. The Mishnah defines an earthen vessel as one which had not been fired in an oven, and determines: "After what time does an earthenware vessel become susceptible to uncleanness? From the time that it is fired in the furnace, for that is the completion of its manufacture" (Kelim 4:4). Stone vessels were thus included among unfired vessels i.e., natural material.

Stone vessels also appear as a separate group connected with water: "...they may render (unclean) water clean by (surface) contact in a stone vessel, but they may not immerse it" (Mishnah, Betzah 2:3); and similarly in the Tosefta: "A person may not immerse water on a Festival, nor may he make surface contact of water in a stone vessel to purify it on the Sabbath; the opinion of Rabbi.

Assemblage of stone vessels of the Second Temple period, with large goblet-shaped vessel, bowls, stoppers and lids, platter, and fragments of rectangular stone table tops from the Temple Mount area, Jerusalem

But the Sages say, A person may immerse water on a Festival, and he may make surface contact of water in a stone vessel to purify it, but he may not immerse it" (Tosefta, Shabbath 17:1; Betzah 2:9).

These laws stress the great importance of stone vessels in the purification of water on a festival or on the Sabbath. Water kept in a stone vessel could be made ritually clean on a festival or on the Sabbath, while water kept in a pottery vessel could not be made clean, since the instant the water became unclean, it imparted this uncleanness to the vessel as well, thus preventing the purification of the water it contained. This leads us to the assumption that the large stone vessels were used to store ritually clean water for the washing of the hands, etc., as illustrated in the New Testament in the story of the transformation of water into wine by Jesus, at Cana in Galilee:

253

"Now six stone jars were standing there, for the Jewish rites of purification..." (John 2:6). These stone vessels, according to the King James version, held "two or three firkins"—or 44–66 liters—approximately the capacity of the large stone vessels of the Second Temple period. (Firkin is the ancient Hebrew bath, a liquid measure equivalent to 21.83 liters.)

There is a clear preference in the Mishnah for stone objects as being ritually clean, over objects made of other materials. If an oven is made of stone and metal it is not susceptible to uncleanness as is a pottery oven, and if the metal becomes unclean it may be made clean; a stone oven, however, is not susceptible to uncleanness at all (Kelim 5:11). The Mishnah asserts that a stone bathhouse bench is not susceptible to uncleanness (Niddah 9:3).

Since stone vessels are not susceptible to becoming ritually unclean, they were used extensively in the Temple. The burning of the red heifer required flawless ritual cleanness. The priest who burned the heifer stayed for seven days in the House of Stone (Parah 3:1). In his commentary on the Mishnah, Maimonides explains that the chamber was given this name because all the vessels used in it during his stay there were of stone, which are not susceptible to uncleanness. After the heifer was burned, it had to be finely crushed; to this end, stone mallets were employed, and the ashes were sifted with stoneware sieves (Parah 3:11). The drawing of water from the Shiloah for the consecration of the ashes of the heifer and its transport to the Temple Mount entailed a long and complicated process which required the strictest attention to ritual purity. The water from the Shiloah was drawn up in stone cups (Parah 3:2–3), and the ashes of the heifer would be placed in large stone vessels of the *kalal* type (Tosefta, Parah 3:4). The consecration of the ashes was also performed with vessels of cattle-dung, stone, and unbaked clay (Parah 5:5).

The Mishnaic sources, especially regarding the burning of the red heifer, emphasize the great importance of stone vessels for the maintenance of a high level of ritual cleanness in the Temple and in daily life. In that period,

the first pair of Sages (Jose ben Joezer and Jose ben Johanan) ruled that glass vessels can become ritually defiled even though they are clean by Torah law (Tosefta, Kelim Baba Batra 7:7). Similar strictures regarding the ritual cleanness of metal vessels were introduced by Shimon ben Shetah (Bab. Tal., Shabbath 14b; 16b). The susceptibility of pottery vessels to becoming unclean had already been established in the Bible. Consequently, all materials could now become ritually unclean—except for stone vessels, cattle-dung vessels, and earthen vessels.

The Mishnah does not explain or substantiate these matters, and we can only speculate about them. Two main reasons come to mind for limiting the purity of glass and metal vessels, and for the ritual cleanness of stone vessels. One is a matter of principle connected with the essential nature of the materials, and the second reflects the harsh Pharisee-Sadducee social conflict. Due to the severe strictures

Small, cylindrical stone object from the Temple Mount area, Jerusalem (two sides) incised with the word קרבן "offering" over two doves; below: impression of the entire design

regarding ritual purity during the Second Temple period, a principle had to be established for defining the states of ritual cleanness and defilement. This principle stated that natural materials that had not been fired—stone, earth, and anything connected with earth—do not become unclean. The attribution of uncleanness to glass vessels, metal vessels, and to the "lands of the gentiles" (from which luxury pottery was imported), all of which were expensive items, contrasted with the elevation of cheap, local products —dung, earthen and stone vessels—to a high level of ritual cleanness. Thus, all strata of society, and not only the wealthy classes in Jerusalem, were able to maintain a high degree of ritual purity, especially as it pertained to their contact with the Temple. This led to the increased use of stone vessels by all who were strict in their observance. Stone thereby became a common material for imitating vessels which were liable to become ritually unclean—mainly luxury and other imported vessels which filled the homes of the upper classes in Jerusalem.

## Distribution of the Stone Vessels

As we have shown, the development of the stone vessel industry had its source in the halakhah. This assumption is confirmed by the distribution map of stone vessels in the various regions of the Land of Israel.

The largest quantity of stone vessels was discovered in Jerusalem in the excavations in the City of David, in the Upper City, on the Ophel south of the Temple Mount, and in tombs around Jerusalem. The city was the center of production, distribution, and consumption of stone vessels during the time of the Second Temple. The most diverse range of vessels was found there, and some items, such as stone tables, were discovered mainly in the city. Similarly, most of the large stone vessels were found in Jerusalem. Another area rich in stone vessels was the territory of Benjamin, north of Jerusalem, where dozens of ancient settlements are known; in almost all of them miqva'ot (ritual baths) were discovered. Stone vessels were found in the region of

Benjamin at sites such as Shiloh, Gibeon, Ḥizma, Beit Iksa, and also in many ancient farmsteads. In the farmstead at Qalandiya, where wine was produced, two miqva'ot and a large selection of stone vessels were discovered. Stone vessels were also found in settlements east of Jerusalem, such as Bethany, and south of the city as in the 'Arrub caves. Only a few stone vessels were discovered in Herodium, notwithstanding the size and importance of the site. Almost no stone vessels are recorded from the Hebron hill country. But on the other hand, stone vessels were discovered at sites on the western slopes of the Hebron hills, among them Khirbet Ramamin (Rimon), and in Khirbet el-Muraq.

A few stone vessels were found at several sites in the Jordan Valley and the Judean Desert: the palace of Herod in Jericho and the Kypros fortress above it, Qumran, the Cave of the Scrolls, the Treasure Cave, Wadi Murabba'at, and En-Gedi. The small number of stone vessels at these sites is surprising considering that the area was a distinctly Jewish region. However, many stone vessels were found in Masada, apparently belonging to the final phase of occupation and not to the Herodian period. Some of the stone vessels from the Judean Desert caves belong to the period preceding the First Jewish Revolt, and others to the time of Bar Kokhba.

In the Samaria mountains, as in the Hebron hill country, very few stone vessels were found at sites such as Sebastia (Samaria) and Shechem, but it is not clear whether they belong to the Second Temple period. In the Coastal Plain a few vessels were discovered at Antipatris (Rosh ha-'Ayin) and in Ashdod. A wealth of stone vessels are known from Jaffa—the Jewish port of Judea, and therefore the quantity of stone vessels there is not surprising. Stone vessels were also discovered in Galilee —Nazareth, Capernaum, and in the above-mentioned stone vessel manufacturing workshop at Reina. Stone vessels were also discovered on the Golan Heights in sites such as Gamla.

This survey shows that stone vessels were common in Jewish regions and settlements.

The Samaritans in Samaria and the Idumeans in the Hebron hill country—Herodium was apparently inhabited by Idumeans in this period—did not observe the laws of ritual purity related to stone vessels, and therefore it is not surprising that such vessels are almost entirely absent from these regions. Stone vessels are very rarely present in non-Jewish regions, and obviously not in the lands and cities beyond the area of Jewish settlement in the Second Temple period. The presence of a large quantity of stone vessels in the villages of Benjamin, north of Jerusalem, and their virtual absence in Herodium and Sebastia implies that the use of stone vessels was not a matter of fashion among the wealthy Jews and in these regions in general, but rather was connected with concern for a high level of ritual purity, among all classes of Jewish society.

## The Date of the Stone Vessels Industry

Determining the beginnings of the stone vessel industry poses a difficult problem; their disappearance is easier to establish, due to its connection with the destruction of the Temple in 70 C.E. In sites clearly belonging to the Hellenistic period, no stone vessels were discovered, nor were stone vessels found in the Hasmonean palace in Jericho. We may thus assume that stone vessels first appeared in the second half of the 1st century B.C.E., while their main distribution occurred in the 1st century C.E.

## Conclusion

The fine quality and relative cheapness of the stone vessels contributed to their extensive use. However, the main reason for the development of the stone vessel industry is to be sought in the halakhah and the strict observance of the Temple purity rites. When, in 70 C.E., the Temple and Jerusalem were destroyed, and the Jewish population in Judea, Galilee and the Golan suffered severe reverses in the aftermath of the defeat, many laws connected with ritual cleanness of the Temple lapsed and the stone vessel industry declined and disappeared almost completely.

The discovery of a few stone vessels in the caves connected with the Bar Kokhba Revolt seems to indicate that the standard-bearers of the Revolt, those who anticipated the speedy rebuilding of the Temple, strove to observe the laws of ritual cleanness as practiced before the destruction of the Temple. But in effect, this industry ceased after the destruction of the Temple and did not survive among the Jews who continued to dwell and to thrive in the Land of Israel in the Roman-Byzantine period. Clearly, the stone vessel industry was connected with the Temple and the mandatory purity for its rite.

The diffusion pattern of the stone vessels throughout the Jewish areas of the country, and the dates of their appearance and disappearance correspond to those of the ossuaries. Together, they constitute a unique Jewish phenomenon.

## Bibliography

Avigad, N., *Discovering Jerusalem* (Nashville, 1983), pp. 165–183.

Cahill, J.M., "Chalk Vessel Assemblages of the Persian/Hellenistic and Early Roman Periods," in: De Groot, A. and Ariel, D.T. (eds.) *Excavations at the City of David 1978–1985 Directed by Yigal Shiloh* III *Qedem* 33 (Jerusalem, 1992), pp. 190–274.

Magen, Y., *The Stone Vessel Industry in the Second Temple Period in Jerusalem and a Traditional Workshop in Bethlehem* (Tel Aviv, 1976) (Hebrew).

————, *The Stone Vessel Industry in Jerusalem in the Days of the Second Temple* (Tel Aviv, 1988) (Hebrew).

Mazar, B., "The Excavations in the Old City of Jerusalem near the Temple Mount—Second Preliminary Report 1969–70 Seasons," *Eretz Israel* 10 (Jerusalem, 1971), Fig. 12 (Hebrew).

Macalister, R.A.S. and Duncan, J.G., "Excavations on the Hill of Ophel 1923–1925, Jerusalem," *PEFA* IV (London, 1926), pp. 147–164; Figs. 138–141, 144–146, 152, 156, 164.

The Jewish Quarter: a. the Broad Wall of the end of the First Temple Period; b. corner of the Israelite tower

c. The central entrance hall in Cave Complex 1 at the St. Étienne Monastery

a. Clay fertility figurine of the end of the First Temple period found in the Jewish Quarter excavations

b. The inscribed ivory pomegranate: "Sacred Donation for the Priests of (in) the House of Yahweh"

c. Bulla No. 2 of the end of the First Temple period from the City of David bearing inscription "(belonging) to Gemaryahu son of Shaphan"

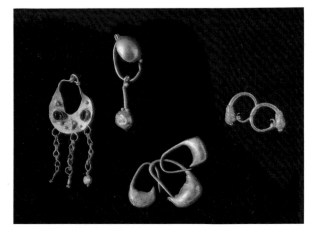

d. Two glass amphoriskoi of the 7th–5th century B.C.E. from Burial Cave 34 at Ketef Hinnom

e. Gold jewelry of the end of the First Temple to Roman periods from Ketef Hinnom

a. View of the early Middle Tower of the Hasmonean period in front of the First Wall uncovered in the courtyard of the Tower of David Citadel

Aceldama, Burial Cave 3: b. wall decoration in Chamber A; c. wall decoration in Chamber C

Remains of the palatial mansions of the Second Temple period uncovered on the eastern slope of the Jewish Quarter, looking southeast

a. Remains of the Burnt House destroyed in 70 C.E. uncovered in the Jewish Quarter

The Jewish Quarter, Burnt House destroyed in 70 C.E.: b. remains of the kitchen; c. stone table and vessels after reconstruction

a. Stucco wall of the Second Temple Period uncovered in the palatial mansion in the Jewish Quarter

b. Wall fresco depicting panels and architectural motifs of the Second Temple period, uncovered in the palatial mansion in the Jewish Quarter

c,d. Mosaic floors with rosette motif of the Second Temple period, uncovered in the Jewish Quarter

-e. Mosaic pavement with meander fret pattern in reconstructed room of the Second Temple period uncovered in the Jewish Quarter

f. Assemblage of stone vessels of the Second Temple period from the Jewish Quarter

a. Round stone table of the Second Temple Period uncovered in the Jewish Quarter

b. Corinthian capital of the Second Temple period from the Jewish Quarter

c. Decorated stone ossuary with the inscription "Jehoseph the son of Hananiah the Scribe" from Mount Scopus

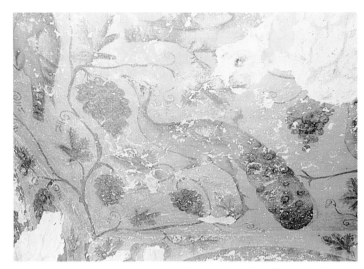

a,b.    Mount of Olives: colored ceiling painting in the Cave of the Birds of the Byzantine period

c.    The vaulted cistern of the Nea Church of the Byzantine period uncovered in the Jewish Quarter

d.    The southern section of the Byzantine Cardo uncovered in the Jewish Quarter

# Two Bullae of Jonathan, King and High Priest

## Nahman Avigad

The two clay bullae stamped with the seals of a Hasmonean king and priest discussed here were probably found in Jerusalem and have been acquired by the Israel Museum.

### A Bulla of King Jonathan

The bulla is of reddish clay and is roughly round in shape. It is slightly broken at both ends and measures 12 × 11 mm. in its present state. The bulla originally sealed a papyrus document the imprints of which are preserved on its reverse. At the center of the bulla is a relief of a palm tree. Its knobby trunk is thin

The bulla of "Jonathan (the) King" (actual size)

at the top and thick and rounded at the bottom, reminiscent of a club in shape. Two branches of the palm are preserved, one on each side; the top is broken away. A group of short lines beneath the right branch is apparently meant to represent a cluster of fruit. A line of inscription extends around both sides of the tree. On the left side of the bulla the remains of a herring-bone pattern are preserved, and on the edge are fingerprints.

The inscription runs from the upper left down around the tree to the upper right and reads:

יהונתן מלך (yhwntn mlk)
"Yehonathan (the) King"

The letters, in the paleo-Hebrew script, are bold and clear. The second *nun* in the first word, just below the tree, is broken away, but

The bulla of "Jonathan (the) King" (enlarged)

its lower stroke is preserved, touching the following *mem*. Thus the word מלך "king" lacks the article *he*. However, the article is also missing in the legend יהונתן כהן גדל "Yehonathan (the) High Priest," which appears on the second bulla and on many Hasmonean coins.

The legend יהונתן מלך "Yehonathan (the) King" and in Greek, ΒΑΣΙΛΕΩΣ ΑΛΕΞΑΝΔΡΟΥ occurs on one of the coin types minted by the most powerful Hasmonean king, Alexander Jannaeus (103–76 B.C.E.), whose Hebrew name was יהונתן "Yehonathan." Alexander Jannaeus was probably also the owner of this bulla. Another type of coin bears the title of the high priest, for which see below.

The paleo-Hebrew script of our inscription displays three noteworthy features: the *he* with its three horizontal strokes, which appears only on the last Hasmonean coins of Mattathias Antigonus; the *waw*, which is not of the standard type; and the classical three-pronged *kaf*, which never appears on Hasmonean coins.

The palm tree is a well-known motif in Jewish numismatics and is a standard Jewish symbol. On Hasmonean coins, however, it is still absent, and is represented by a palm branch only. Alexander Jannaeus borrowed

257

the symbols for his coins (anchor, cornucopias and flower) from contemporary Seleucid coinage, and may have drawn the symbol for his seals from the same source. The palm tree of our bullae thus makes here its first appearance in Jewish symbolic art.

## A Bulla of Jonathan the High Priest

The bulla is of reddish-brown clay and is roughly oval in shape, 13 mm. long, 12 mm. wide and 2–3 mm. thick. The impressed area is slightly smaller, forming a rounded shape 10 mm. wide with undefined straight ends on two sides. The bulla originally sealed a rolled papyrus document tied with a string. On its reverse are imprints of the papyrus fibers and of the string to which it was attached. On the right edge of the seal-impression are remains of what seems to have been a beaded border line. In the center is a relief of the knobby trunk of a palm tree, as on the previous bulla. The branches of the tree are obliterated. On each side of the tree are two lines of writing. The inscription reads as follows:

ינתן כֹהן גדל ירשלם מ (*yntn khn gdl yršlm m*)
"Jonathan High Priest Jerusalem M"

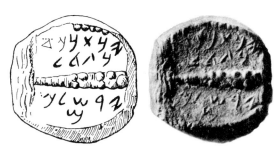

The bulla of "Jonathan the High Priest" (1:2.5 scale)

The script is very minute but quite distinct. The only letters which are badly blurred and difficult to discern are the last two in the first line; however, careful examination reveals unmistakable traces of *kaf* and *he*. The script is clearly to be associated with the paleo-Hebrew script of Hasmonean coinage (2nd–1st centuries B.C.E.). It is, however, much more carefully executed than the average coin inscription.

The letters display the following paleographic characteristics: *dalet*, with its large triangle and the upper line extending far beyond the vertical, is characteristic of one of the coin types; *he* is the key letter of the Hasmonean coin script; it is badly blurred but its characteristic triangle can still be discerned; *yod* shows a cursive trend with its bottom stroke turning back up at a very sharp angle; *kaf* is faint, but seems to be of the current developed type; *lamed* is short and does not extend above the line; *mem* has a broad and rounded w-shaped head; *nun* has a tall head; *resh*, *shin* and *taw* are archaic. The first part of the inscription gives the name of the seal's owner, Jonathan, and his title, high priest. The second part indicates the seat of the high priest, Jerusalem, and terminates with an enigmatic letter *mem*.

As all Hasmonean rulers, King Alexander Jannaeus held the prestigious office of the high priesthood. He also minted a series of coins bearing the legend

ינתן הכהן הגדל וחבר היהודים

"Yonathan the High Priest and the Council(?) of the Jews."

The defective orthography ינתן "Yonathan" on these coins is most unusual in its strange deformation of the theophoric element of the name. It also occurs in the present bulla inscription:

ינתן כהן גדל "Yonathan High Priest,"

thus favoring the full identification of the first part of the bulla's legend with that on the coins (the indefinite status כהן גדל "High Priest" also occurs on many coins).

It is very unusual for an ancient seal to specify the place of residence of its owner. Obviously, Jerusalem has here a further meaning. It was the seat of the high priest, the Holy City and the capital of Judea. It may be compared with the paleo-Hebrew seal impression *Yršlm* "Yer(u)salem" found on jar handles of the 2nd century B.C.E. and on coins of the two revolts. The tripartite bulla inscription consisting of name, title and place name, may be compared with the stamped jar handles of the Persian period bearing the legend: "Yehud, Yeho'ezer, the Governor."

Why did Alexander Jannaeus have two different seals, one with his royal title and the other with his high priestly rank, just as on his coins? Obviously he required them for different functions, secular and religious.

An interesting contemporary example of the use of such a seal is referred to in the Talmudic story of how the Maccabees, when entering the desecrated Temple, found only one jug of oil sealed with the "seal of the high priest" (Bab. Tal., Sabbath, 21b).

## Summary

Thus, our two bullae bear the first known impressions of seals belonging to a Hasmonean high priest and king, or to any other Jewish ruler. We do not possess any actual seals belonging to such personages. This is also one of the very few archaeological examples of the use of inscribed personal seals in the Hasmonean and Herodian periods. Apparently only members of the ruling class and officials had inscribed seals. Common seals were mostly ornamented, after the Greek custom, with human and animal representations and were rarely inscribed.

## Bibliography

Avigad, N., "A Bulla of Jonathan the High Priest," *IEJ* 25 (1975): 8–12.
——— , "A Bulla of King Jonathan," *IEJ* 25 (1975): 245–246.

# The Structure of the Second Temple
# A New Reconstruction

## Joseph Patrich

For generations, numerous commentators and scholars have attempted to reconstruct the appearance of the Second Temple built in Jerusalem by Herod the Great toward the end of the 1st century B.C.E. Particularly well-known are drawings attached to the commentaries of Maimonides (13th century C.E.), R. Yom Tov Lipmann Heller (17th century), R. Jonathan b. Joseph of Ruzhany (early 18th century) and R. Israel Lipschutz (19th century). We will not concern ourselves here with drawings of the Temple which took their inspiration from the Dome of the Rock standing on the site of the ancient Temple, and will focus on reconstructions based upon ancient literary sources. As regards modern scholarship, we must mention the reconstructions and plans proposed by M. De Vogüé, G. Dalman, F.J. Hollis, C. Watzinger, L.H. Vincent, M. Avi-Yonah, S. Shefer and E. Eybeschütz, and, of course, the monumental work of T.A. Busink. Among the more important discussions of this question are those of I. Hildesheimer, who compared the descriptions of the Temple in the Mishnah with those in Josephus's works, and that of O. Holtzmann.

The reconstruction proposed here[1] includes two innovations: the structure of the *mesibbah* (Stepped Passageway) and the Golden Vine above the portal of the Sanctuary and the columns over which it hung; and the attention to detail, particularly the scale drawings of the various Temple components. I have attempted to remain as faithful as possible to the literary sources, avoiding conjectures unsupported by written material. I shall therefore discuss the two new features mentioned, and present a detailed description of the Temple and its components based upon the present reconstruction.

The most detailed description of the Temple is that in Tractate Middot of the Mishnah. One of the oldest tractates in the Mishnah, it is attributed to R. Eliezer b. Jacob, a Tanna who lived during the last years of the Second Temple and had first-hand knowledge of the building before its destruction. His description is generally considered as a realistic one, though some scholars claim it to be idealized. The Temple described in Middot is the one built by Herod the Great in 20–19 B.C.E., completed, according to Josephus, over a period of one year and seven months. There are several discrepancies between Tractate Middot and Josephus's description of the Temple, and there are even differences in certain details reported in Josephus's two works *The Jewish War* and *Antiquities of the Jews*. The discrepancies relate mainly to the dimensions of the doorways and a few parts of the Temple. However, the sources agree as to the overall structure. Thus, both Middot and Josephus describe the Portico ('ulam), the Sanctuary (heikhal) and the Holy of Holies (qodesh ha-qodashim) as constituting the core of the Temple. Both also refer to the Upper Chamber ('aliyah), Cells (ta'im) and Stepped Passageway (mesibbah). The discrepancies are minor; moreover, wherever one of the sources omits some detail, I have completed the missing data from another source. Many scholars, including E. Schürer, C. Watzinger, A. Schalit and M. Avi-Yonah, favor the Mishnah's description over that of Josephus.

---

[1] The drawings reproduced in this article are by L. Ritmeyer, who also conceived some of the graphic solutions. The drawings are reproduced by the kind permission of *Eretz*.

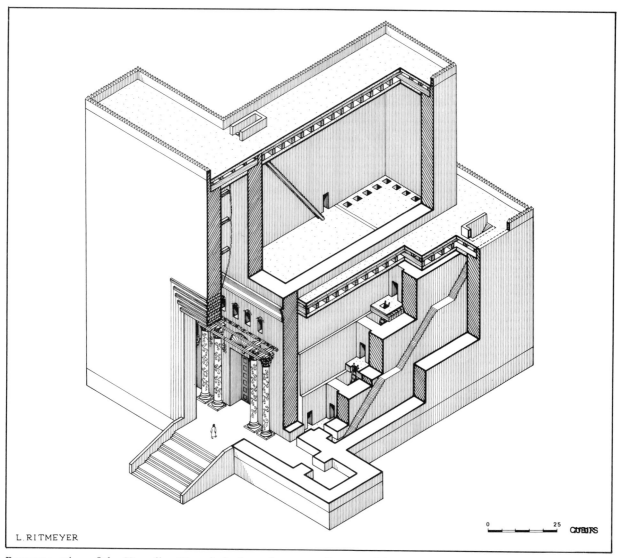

Reconstruction of the Herodian Temple in Jerusalem according to Mishnah Tractate Middot

## The Splendor of the Temple

The Temple made a profound impression on all who saw it: "Our Masters taught: Whosoever has not seen Jerusalem in its splendor has never seen a beautiful city; and whosoever has not seen the Temple standing has never seen a magnificent building" (Baraita, Bab. Tal., Sukkah 51b); "Whosoever has not seen Herod's Temple has never seen a beautiful building" (Bab. Tal., Baba Batra 4a).

What was the essence of the Temple's splendor? The Talmud states that it was built of "stones of yellow and white marble" or "stones of yellow, black and white marble" (Bab. Tal., Baba Batra 4a) We are also told that Herod intended to plate the Temple with gold, and

Josephus relates that its entire facade, which faced east, was covered with heavy gold plates. At sunrise, the reflection of the sunlight was so brilliant that it could blind unwary onlookers. The other walls were also plated with gold, though only in their lower parts; their upper parts were the pure white color of the stone of which they were built, perhaps whitewashed each year before Passover, causing the Temple to resemble a snow-clad mountain from afar. The parapets around the edges of the roofs were fitted with golden spikes.

Such was the external appearance of the Temple. No mention is made of columns, capitals or friezes adorned with reliefs in the facade of the building or on its other sides.

## Dimensions and General Form of the Temple

"The Sanctuary (the Mishnah uses the word here in its general sense, as a synonym for the Temple, which consisted of the Portico, the Sanctuary proper and the Holy of Holies) was a hundred cubits square and a hundred cubits high" (Mishnah, Middot IV:6) Above the Sanctuary and the Holy of Holies was the Upper Chamber, and these were surrounded on the north, west and south by three tiers of Cells. Along the northern side of the Temple, beyond the Cells, was the Stepped Passageway, and parallel to it on the south was the Water Drain (bet horadat ha-mayim).

The Portico was wider than the other parts of the Temple: "The Sanctuary (= Temple) was narrow behind and wide in front, and it was like to a lion" (Middot IV:7).

The Cells encompassed the walls of the Sanctuary and the Holy of Holies only, but not the Upper Chamber; in this area, therefore, the lower level of the Temple was wider than its upper level, making it rather similar to the royal stoa at the southern side of the Temple Mount.

Thanks to the exact measurements specified in the Mishnah, we can draw a scale plan of the Temple, together with cross-sections. All the dimensions are in cubits.[2] The measurements of the Temple from east to west and from north to south are given at the level of the second tier of Cells; hence the plan drawn according to these figures depicts the situation at that level.

## The Portico

THE STEPS. Twelve steps led up to the entrance of the Portico. Since each step was half a cubit high, the floor of the Portico was 6 cubits higher than that of the Court of the Priests (the exterior courtyard surrounding the Temple). Therefore, this was also the height of the solid substructure or foundation ('otem, in the Mishnah) which supported the Temple walls.

FACADE OF THE TEMPLE AND ENTRANCE OF THE PORTICO. Aside from the gold plating of the facade and the ornamentation of the lintel, we have no information about additional decoration. The entrance of the Portico was 40 cubits high and 20 cubits wide. This large portal was provided with neither doors nor a curtain. The doorposts were gilded, and the lintel was made of five oak beams (called mal-tera'ot in the sources—a word deriving from the Greek μελαυρον), each 1 cubit thick. Each beam was separated from the one beneath it by a course of stones 1 cubit high. The lowest beam was 2 cubits longer than the width of the portal, that is to say, 22 cubits long, extending 1 cubit on either side of the entrance. Each of the following beams was 2 cubits longer than those beneath it, extending 1 cubit on each side. Thus the length of the uppermost beam was 30 cubits.

Summarizing, we see that the facade of the Portico was a plain, unadorned surface, 100 cubits wide and 100 cubits high. At its center was a portal of impressive dimensions, topped by a lintel with diagonally stepped ends. A similar portal is depicted on some rather rare silver didrachm coins of the Bar-Kokhba Revolt. I agree with the suggestion that the design on these coins depicts the entrance to the Portico.[3] The two columns flanking the entrance in the coin are not mentioned in the sources and therefore have no place in our reconstruction. The Mishnah describes the structure of the lintel in considerable detail but says nothing of the doorposts. It seems doubtful, therefore, that the doorposts were actually fashioned in the form of columns.

It was above this portal—the entrance to the Portico—that Herod affixed the golden eagle, which pious Jews removed only at the end of his reign.

MEASUREMENTS OF THE PORTICO. The wall of the Portico was 5 cubits thick. As the Portico measured only 11 cubits from east to west, it

---

[2] One cubit = 52.5 cm. = 20.7 inches.

[3] I am grateful to D. Barag who called my attention to these rare coins; see his article in this volume, pp. 272–276.

# Dimensions of Architectural Elements of the Temple as Recorded in Middot

(all dimensions are in cubits: 1 cubit = 52.5 cm = 20.7 inches)

| Vertical dimensions | | North-south measurements | | East-west measurements (in cubits) | |
|---|---|---|---|---|---|
| Substructure | 6 | Stepped passageway wall | 5 | Portico wall | 5 |
| Sanctuary | 40 | Stepped passageway | 3 | Portico | 11 |
| Sanctuary roof: | | Cell wall | 5 | Sanctuary wall | 6 |
| Molding (coffers) | 1 | Cell | 6 | Sanctuary | 40 |
| Water Drain | 2 | Sanctuary wall | 6 | ʾamah ṭraqsin (dividing square) | 1 |
| Ceiling | 1 | Sanctuary | 20 | Holy of Holies | 20 |
| Plasterwork | 1 | Sanctuary wall | 6 | Sanctuary wall | 6 |
| | | Cell | 6 | Cell | 6 |
| Total: | 5 | Cell wall | 5 | Cell wall | 5 |
| | | Water Drain | 3 | | 100 |
| Upper Chamber | 40 | Drain wall | 5 | | |
| Roof of Upper Chamber: | | | 70 | | |
| Molding (coffers) | 1 | | | | |
| Water Drain | 2 | | | | |
| Ceiling | 1 | | | | |
| Plasterwork | 1 | | | | |
| Total: | 5 | | | | |
| Parapet | 3 | | | | |
| Spikes | 1 | | | | |
| | 100 | | | | |

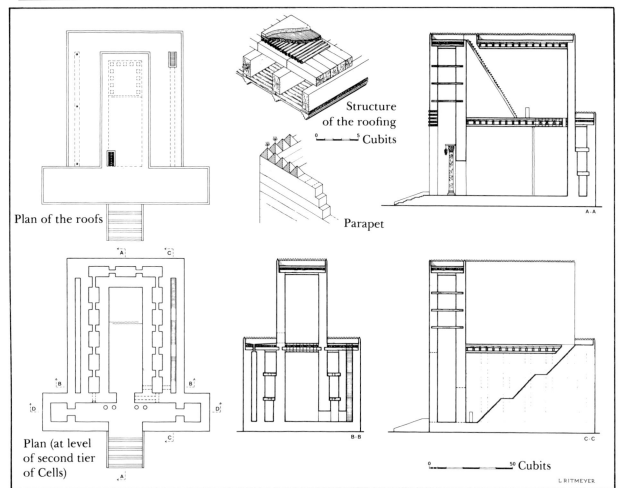

Structure of the roofing

0 — 5 Cubits

Parapet

Plan of the roofs

A-A

Plan (at level of second tier of Cells)

B-B

C-C

0 — 50 Cubits

L. RITMEYER

Plans and sections of the Herodian Temple in Jerusalem

was actually little more than a narrow antechamber built across the entire width of the Temple (from north to south) and rising to the latter's full height. It was 30 cubits wider than the rest of the Temple, extending for an additional 15 cubits on either side of the Sanctuary. In the protruding sections of the Portico were two rooms, known as the Chambers of the Slaughter Knives (*bet ha-ḥalifot*) and used, as their name implies, to store the knives used in the sacrificial service. Thus, assuming that the inner walls of the Chambers were 5 cubits thick like the outer walls of the Temple, the length of the Portico between the two rooms was 60 cubits. The full height of the Portico, from floor to ceiling, was 85 cubits. To prevent possible collapse of its wall, which together with the parapet rose to a height of 94 cubits above the substructure, it was buttressed with cedar beams set between it and the wall of the Sanctuary.

## Facade and Portal of the Sanctuary

THE WINDOWS. Fixed in the Portico ceiling were gold chains which young priests used to climb in order to inspect the ornaments above each of the window lintels. These decorations, referred to in the Mishnah as "crowns," were made of silver or gold fashioned into wreaths or crowns. They commemorated the four crowns made of silver and gold collected from the returnees from Babylon and placed on the head of Jehozadak the High Priest (Zechariah 6:9–14). On the basis of this biblical reference, I have reconstructed four windows; the sources contain no other indication of windows anywhere in the Temple.

PORTAL OF THE SANCTUARY. The portal of the Sanctuary was 20 cubits high and 10 cubits wide. On each side was a small wicket. The southern (i.e., left-hand) wicket was sealed and never used. The northern wicket led into a Cell from which the Sanctuary itself could be entered. In addition, this wicket provided access through a passage in the wall to the gap between the two sets of doors to the Sanctuary. The thickness of the wall containing the portal was 6 cubits. The facade of the Sanctu-

ary around the entrance, the frame of the portal itself and the doors were all overlaid with gold. Altogether there were four door panels, two inner and two outer. Each panel was 5 cubits wide. The outer doors opened inward, almost covering the thickness of the wall, while the inner doors opened into the Sanctuary, folding back onto the inner side of the Sanctuary wall (this part of the wall was known as "behind the doors"). A dissenting opinion cited in the Mishnah holds that each of the four doors folded in half, thus occupying a width of 2.5 cubits. When open, all of the door panels folded inside the entry; their combined width, together with that of the wooden doorposts (half a cubit each), covered the entire depth of the entrance, 6 cubits in all.

THE GOLDEN VINE. A vine is commonly used in the Bible as a metaphor for the people of Israel, e.g., "I planted you a choice vine, wholly of pure seed. How then have you turned degenerate and become a wild vine?" (Jeremiah 2:21; cf. Psalms 80:8–12; Ezekiel 17:5–10). The sources describe the Golden Vine in the Temple as follows:

> "A Golden Vine stood over the entrance to the Sanctuary, trained over posts" (Middot III:8); "Above the gate (of the Sanctuary) there was a Golden Vine, from which hung grape clusters as tall as a man" (*War* V, 210).

The text of *Antiquities* provides us with additional details (the Latin version in this case is better than the rather corrupt Greek one):

> He (Herod) decorated the doors of the entrance and the sections over the opening with a multicolored ornamentation and also with curtains, in accordance with the size of the Temple, and made flowers of gold surrounding columns, atop which stretched a vine, from which golden clusters of grapes were suspended (*Ant.* XV, 394–395, translated by Leah Di Segni).

My reconstruction relies on this description. Although the number of columns is not specified, there would appear to have been four, based upon the depiction on Bar-Kokhba's tetradrachm coins, as well as in the fresco

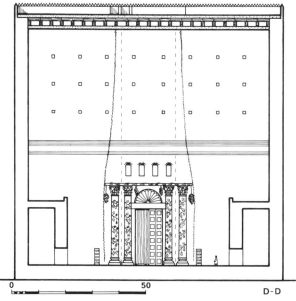

Section through the Portico (D-D), looking west

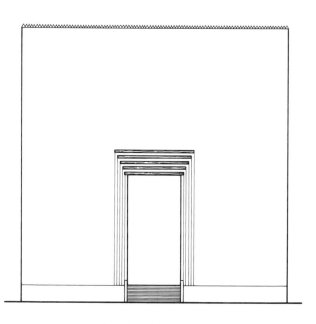

Facade of the Portico

Tetradrachm of Bar-Kokhba

Didrachm of Bar-Kokhba

above the Ark of the Law in the synagogue at Dura-Europos, which dates to the 3rd century C.E. While other scholars such as C. Watzinger, M. Avi-Yonah, Y. Meshorer, L. Mildenberg and D. Barag believe that these depictions portray the outer facade of the Temple, none of our written sources say anything about any columns or pilasters flanking the entrance to the Temple. On the other hand, the Golden Vine above the Sanctuary portal is explicitly described as suspended from columns; accordingly, I suggest that the above illustrations do indicate these columns. Bar-Kokhba's coins thus feature two portals. The less sacred portal of the Portico is portrayed on the didrachm, while the holier portal of the Sanctuary appears on the tetradrachm.

Some of the tetradrachms of Year Three of the Bar-Kokhba Revolt feature a wavy decoration running over the horizontal beams spanning the columns, which may well represent vine tendrils. The grape clusters and vine leaves, not depicted on these coins, form a central motif on some of the smaller denominations of the Bar-Kokhba coinage. The semicircles at the top of the facade in the Dura Europos fresco represent a degenerate version of the wavy line on the Bar-Kokhba tetradrachms.

The quantity of gold hanging over the portal was further increased by voluntary donations and vow-offerings which the contributors would hang upon the Golden Vine. The Mishnah may be exaggerating when it states that the gold was so heavy that three hundred priests were needed to remove it, but Josephus tells us that the grape clusters were man-high. Clearly, a massive structure was necessary to support the "tendrils" and "grape clusters," which trailed over the 20-cubit-high

265

portal. The columns mentioned in *Antiquities* must, therefore, have been very high.

The Golden Vine made a great impression on foreigners as well; it is mentioned in the works of Tacitus and Florus (late 1st to early 2nd century C.E.) in their accounts of Pompey's conquest of Jerusalem in 63 B.C.E.

## The Veil, Golden Lamp and Tables at the Entrance to the Sanctuary

Suspended in the Sanctuary portal was a Veil of Babylonian tapestry, woven of four different colored materials: azure, light brown, scarlet and purple. These colors were symbolic. The scarlet fabric symbolized fire; light brown, the natural color of fine linen, represented the earth from which the fiber grew; azure represented the sky; and purple, a dye extracted from a marine snail, stood for the sea. On the Veil was depicted a panorama of the heavens and the heavenly bodies, excluding the signs of the Zodiac. The historian Florus also alludes to this design on the Veil. The Veil hung outside the Sanctuary and was thus constantly visible, even when the doors to the Sanctuary were closed. During the Hellenistic period, before the erection of Herod's Temple, the Veil was suspended on a long golden rod concealed in a wooden beam. In 53 B.C.E. the priest responsible for the Veils handed this rod over to Crassus, who succeeded Gabinius as procurator of Syria, as a ransom in a vain attempt to avert the sacking of the other Temple treasures (*Ant.* XIV, 105–109).

Also hanging in the Sanctuary portal was a Golden Lamp—the gift of Helena, queen of Adiabene.

Two Tables stood at the entrance to the Sanctuary, one of marble and the other of gold. Both were used for the Showbread: the priest bringing the new Showbread to the Temple placed it on the marble Table, while the old Showbread was placed on the golden Table.[4]

---

[4] See in this volume, pp. 272–276.

The decorations adorning the Sanctuary portal and its appurtenances were visible to the people through the broad portal of the Portico.

## The Sanctuary and the Holy of Holies

The length of the Sanctuary was 40 cubits, and of the Holy of Holies 20 cubits. Both were the same width and height: 20 cubits wide by 40 cubits high. Separating the Sanctuary from the Holy of Holies were two curtains, 1 cubit apart. This gap of 1 cubit has a special name in the Mishnah, 'amah ṭraqsin; the meaning of the word ṭraqsin, probably of Greek derivation, is obscure. The eastern curtain was slightly open at its southern end, the western curtain at its northern end. Anyone desiring access to the Holy of Holies had to pass between them. The beautifully worked curtains were displayed to the public before being hung in the Temple. As the Mishnah tells us:

> The veil (curtain) was one handbreadth thick and was woven on (a loom having) seventy-two rods, and over each rod were twenty-four threads. Its length was forty cubits and its breadth twenty cubits; it was made by eighty-two young girls and they used to make two in every year; and three hundred priests immersed it [to purify it before hanging] (Sheqalim VIII:5).

The curtains were embroidered with lions and eagles.

The interior of the Sanctuary was overlaid with gold, except for the area "behind the doors." The overlay consisted of gold panels 1 cubit square. It was customary to remove these panels from the walls during the three pilgrimage festivals and display them for all to see at the ascent to the Temple Mount.

Standing in the Sanctuary were the seven-branched Candelabrum (*menorah*), the Showbread Table and the Incense Altar, all made of gold. The seven branches of the Candelabrum recalled the seven planets known in antiquity, and the twelve loaves of Showbread on the Table symbolized the signs of the Zodiac and the months of the year.

On the altar were thirteen different kinds of

incense, from the sea, the desert, and the earth.

The Holy of Holies was devoid of furnishings, and it was forbidden to enter or even look into it. The only exception to this rule was the High Priest, and he too was permitted entry only one day a year—on the Day of Atonement, when the sacred service required him to enter the Holy of Holies just four times (Tosefta Kelim, Baba Qama 1, 7). The artisans responsible for the maintenance of the Temple were lowered into the Holy of Holies in special cages, through openings (*lulin*) in the floor of the Upper Chamber; the cages were closed on three sides and open only to the walls, so that the artisans would not be tempted to steal a glance into the Holy of Holies. In the Holy of Holies was a stone, three fingerbreadths high, known as *even ha-shetiyah*, on which the High Priest would make incense offerings.Contributions of gold made to the Temple in fulfillment of vows were used exclusively to fashion beaten gold sheets for covering the walls of the Holy of Holies.

Above the Sanctuary and the Holy of Holies was the Upper Chamber surrounded by Cells, as we have stated, which encompassed the most sacred parts of the Temple.

## Structure of Ceiling and Roofs

The description of the structure of the roofs of the Sanctuary and the Upper Chamber, as given in the Mishnah, is sufficiently detailed to permit a precise reconstruction. The innermost level of the ceiling, facing the interior of the Upper Chamber, was fashioned with molded coffers; it was 1 cubit high. Above it were the main roof beams, which spanned the entire width of the building from north to south—a total of 20 cubits. Each beam was 2 cubits thick; possibly, two beams, each having a square 1 × 1 cubit cross-section, were placed on top of one another. In the reconstruction proposed here, each beam was 1 cubit wide and gaps of 3 cubits each were left between the beams. These gaps could collect and perhaps even drain the water dripping in from the roof; therefore, this part of the roof was known as *bet dilfah*, "dripping place." Resting

on these beams at right angles were additional beams, each 4 cubits long and 1 × 1 cubit in cross-section. This rectangular network of crisscrossing beams formed the ceiling. The plaster work (*ma'azivah*) above the ceiling consisted of several layers. The lowest was a layer of rods, above which, on a suitable bedding, the roofing was laid. The total height of the plaster work was 1 cubit. The overall thickness of the roof of the Sanctuary and the Upper Chamber, allowing for all its various constituents, was thus 5 cubits.

## Building Materials

The Temple was built of large stones, some of them as much as 45 cubits in length, 5 cubits high and 6 cubits wide. Although the sages of the Talmud believed that different hues of marble were used—"stones of yellow, black and white marble"—it is more likely that local limestone was employed, as we have no evidence for the utilization of marble masonry in the Herodian period. Perhaps the stones were of different hues. However, Josephus stresses their pure white color, saying that from afar the Temple looked like a snow-clad mountain. Nevertheless, as we have already seen, this may have been achieved by whitewashing the upper parts of the building.

The facade of the Temple, the lower parts of its outer side walls and the inner walls were all plated with gold.

The structural use of wooden beams in the Temple at Jerusalem is paralleled in contemporary Nabatean temples, such as Qasr Bint Far'un—the main Nabatean temple at Petra, and the Temple of Allat at er-Ramm.

## The Cells

The Mishnah gives the following account of the Cells:

> And there were thirty-eight cells there, fifteen to the north, fifteen to the south, and eight to the west. Those to the north and those to the south were (built) five over five and five over them; and those to the west, three over three and two over them. And to every one were three entrances, one into the cell on the right, and one into the cell on the

267

left, and one into the cell above it. And in the one at the north-eastern corner were five entrances: one into the cell on the right, and one into the cell above it, and one into the passage-way (mesibbah), and one into the wicket, and one into the Sanctuary (Middot IV:3).

This last-mentioned Cell was of course the one in the lowest tier of Cells, whose floors were flush with that of the Sanctuary and the Portico, accessible through the wicket. Thus the Cells stood directly upon the solid sub-structure of the Temple, like the walls of both the Sanctuary and Portico.

Josephus, too, refers to Cells arranged in three stories, around the Sanctuary and the Holy of Holies only, not the Upper Chamber:

> Around the sides of the lower part of the sanctuary were numerous chambers, in three stories, communicating with one another; these were approached by entrances from either side of the gateway. The upper part of the building had no similar chambers, being proportionately narrower (War V, 220–221).

Although Josephus mentions neither the number of Cells nor their arrangement around the sides of the building, his description of Solomon's Temple refers to thirty Cells encompassing the building (Ant. VIII, 65)—a detail mentioned nowhere in the Bible. Perhaps he counted only the Cells to the north and south of the Temple of his own day.

Most probably, the Cells were used to store ritual vessels, materials needed for the ritual (e.g., oil and spices), and the Temple treasures. These functions could also have been filled by many of the chambers in the courtyards roundabout the Temple. There is an interesting parallel to these Cells in the crypts surrounding the Temple of Hathor at Dendera and the Temple of Horus at Edfu in Egypt. Both were erected in the Hellenistic period and were completed in the first half of the 1st century B.C.E.

The ceilings of the first and second tiers of Cells were not bonded with the walls of the Sanctuary; instead, they rested on 1-cubit-wide ledges. The outer face of the Sanctuary wall thus had a stepped appearance because of its varying thickness. At the level of the lowest tier of Cells the wall was 7 cubits thick; at the level of the middle tier it was 6 cubits thick; and at the level of the upper tier, 5 cubits thick. Accordingly, each tier of Cells had a different width, varying from 5 cubits on the lowest level to 7 cubits on the highest.

The length of the Cells is not specified in the Mishnah. Our reconstruction assumes that there was a dividing wall, 4 cubits thick, between adjoining Cells, and that the overall length of the Cells on the northern and southern sides was equal to the length of the building's interior, i.e., 61 cubits. The Cells on the west, however, were bounded on the north and south by the Cell walls, and their total length was 44 cubits. This would make the Cells 9 cubits long in the north and south, while the Cells on the lowest and second tier on the west would have been 12 cubits long. Just how the space available on the third tier in the west was divided into two Cells is unknown; Cells may have been of unequal size.

The height of the Cells is also unknown. We may infer from Middot IV:5 that the Cells encompassed the Sanctuary and the Holy of Holies to their full height, as the surface of the Cell roofs was flush with the floor of the Upper Chamber. In other words, the roof of the third tier of Cells formed an extension of the roof of the lower story of the Temple; hence it was 5 cubits thick. Assuming that each tier of Cells was separated from the one above by a ceiling 2 cubits thick, we deduce that the inner height of each tier was 12 cubits, as drawn in the reconstruction. These ceilings, which rested on the Sanctuary walls, were in all probability built of wooden beams spanning the width of the Cells.

## The Stepped Passageway and the Water Drain

Between the Cells and the outer wall on the northern side of the Temple there was a space, 3 cubits wide, known as the mesibbah. The corresponding space on the south of the building, also 3 cubits wide, was known as bet *horadat ha-mayim*, literally, the "place for bringing down (draining) the water" or simply the Water Drain. The *mesibbah* was a kind of staircase inside the wall. A similar staircase is mentioned by Josephus in his account of Solomon's Temple (*Ant.* VIII, 70); however there is no such reference in his description of Herod's Temple. On the other hand, there is no hint of any such structure in the biblical description of Solomon's Temple, so it seems quite likely that Josephus simply borrowed it from the Temple of his own times. In our reconstruction, the *mesibbah* is a Stepped Passageway leading from the ground floor to the roof above the top tier of Cells. It was 66 cubits long and reached a height of 45 cubits. Each step had a rise of half a cubit and a tread of half a cubit (based on Middot II:3). These figures enable us to introduce several horizontal landings, with a total length of 21 cubits. The structure of the Stepped Passageway as we envisage it is as follows: a landing 7 cubits long, a flight of stairs 14 cubits long, followed by another 7-cubit landing and another 14-cubit flight; finally, another landing 7 cubits long and a flight 17 cubits long. This arrangement places the three horizontal landings at the same level as the floors of the tiers of Cells.

Structures similar to the *mesibbah* are found in some of the largest and best known pagan temples of the Hellenistic and Roman periods, such as the Temple of Hathor at Dendera, the Temple of Horus at Edfu, the palace-temple at Hatra (Parthia), the Temple of Zeus at Baetocece (Hosn Soleiman in Syria) and Qasr Bint Far'un at Petra. Herod may have built a similar ascent in the Temple of Augustus at Sebaste (Samaria).

The Water Drain, which drained runoff from the Temple roofs, was most probably an inclined channel, receiving water from the surfaces of the Cell roofs. Considerations of symmetry would imply a channel sloping downward from west to east like the *mesibbah*; but it may have sloped downward from east to west. This moderate incline might also have facilitated bringing up of building materials by workmen during the installation of the roof of the lower story and the construction of the Upper Chamber, which was simply the second story of the building. They could have made similar use of the *mesibbah*. Moreover, the external walls and walls of the Cells, between which these ascents were built, could have served both as scaffolding and as the "curtains" in the courtyard, mentioned in the Mishnah ('Eduyot VIII:6), which concealed the work in progress upon the Sanctuary and the Holy of Holies from the people.

## The Upper Chamber

As we have seen, the Upper Chamber, which was 40 cubits high, formed a second story above the Sanctuary and the Holy of Holies. A strip of mosaic paving (*rashei pesifasin*) 1 cubit wide separated the part of the Upper Chamber above the Sanctuary from that above the Holy of Holies, like the *'amah traqsin* on the ground floor. Curtains hung here too, as in the Sanctuary. The entrance to the Upper Chamber, on the south, certainly opened into the area above the Sanctuary rather than above the Holy of Holies. Near the entrance stood two cedar posts that served as a ladder to the roof of the Upper Chamber, which was 45 cubits above its floor. Breached in the floor of the area above the Holy of Holies were the openings (*lulin*), mentioned above.

My reconstruction assumes that these openings were 2 cubits square. They were 1 cubit distant from the walls, and the openings were 2 cubits apart. These dimensions would have given the artisans enough room to work, with a slight overlap between the working areas of adjacent openings. This arrangement of the openings was also correlated with the layout of the primary beams of the "dripping place" and the secondary beams of the ceiling forming squares of 3 × 3 cubits, within which the openings could have been breached. In other words, the position, size and spacing of the openings, as implied by their special function, dictated the structure of the whole network of beams supporting the ceiling of the Sanctuary and the Holy of Holies; the solution proposed in our reconstruction is based upon this interplay.

## Temple Roofs, the Parapet and the Spikes

As stated, the Temple had roofs on two levels, the lower one over the Cells flush with the roof of the Sanctuary and the Holy of Holies, and the upper one comprising the roofs of the Upper Chamber and the Portico. Built around both levels of roofs was a parapet 4 cubits high. Installed on top of the parapet were golden spikes, 1 cubit high, intended to prevent ravens and birds of prey from perching there, soiling the walls and disturbing the sacrificial ritual. The Mishnah calls these spikes *kalah 'orev*, literally "keeping off the raven." The Sages were divided on the question whether the height of the spikes was or was not included in the 4 cubits of the parapet. Similar devices to ward off birds of prey are known from pagan temples in which sacrificial rites played a central part. In our reconstruction, the top of the parapet consists of stone pyramids 1 cubit square at the base and 1 cubit high. This shape of the parapet, combined with the golden spikes, would make it difficult for birds to find a foothold. The crenelation generally adorning temple roofs could not, to my mind, have effectively prevented birds from perching on them. As against Josephus's reference to golden spikes, the Babylonian Talmud (Shabbat 90a; Menahot 107b) seems to indicate that these devices were made of iron plates. Possibly, therefore, they consisted of iron plates and spikes which were plated with gold. We may assume that in order to keep birds away from the Temple precincts it was also necessary to install spikes near the altar, on top of the stoas and on the roofs of the various chambers in the courts.

## Literary Sources for Details of the Temple Reconstruction

**General:** Middot 3:6–4:7; *War* V,5,1–8 (184–247); *Ant.* XV 380–425.

**Splendor:** Sukkah 51b; Baba Batra 4a; Tosefta, Menahot 13, 19; Beraita in Pesahim 57a; *War* V,5,4 and 6 (208–213, 222–227).

**Whitewashing:** Middot 3:4; Sukkah 51b; Baba Batra 4a.

**Dimensions and External Form:** Middot 4:6,7; *War* V,5,4 and 5 (208–221); *Ant.* XV 391, 393.

**Portico Steps:** Middot 3:6; *Wars* V, 5, 4 (207).

**Facade and Portico Portal:** Middot 2:3, 3:7. In *War* V,5,4 (208) the height of the Portal is 70 cubits and its width, 25 cubits.

**Golden Eagle:** *War* I,33,2–3 (648–653); *Ant.* XVII 149–155.

**Portico Dimensions:** Middot 4:7. In *War* V,5,4 (207–209) the excess is given as 20 cubits on either side; the Portico measurements are 20 cubits (depth) × 50 cubits (width) × 90 cubits (height).

**Cedar Beams between Portico and the Sanctuary Walls:** Middot 3:8.

**Gilding of Portico Walls:** Tosefta, Menahot 13, 19.

**Window Crowns on Sanctuary Facade:** Middot 3:8. Windows are mentioned in *Codex Kaufmann*; *Cambridge*; *Parma-De Rossi 138*; *Paris 328–329*; as well as in the *Mishnah Commentary of the Rambam* (Kappah ed.); and I Maccabees 1:22 and 4:57.

**Sanctuary Portal:** Middot 4:1; *War* V,5,4 (211) (the height of the Portal is 55 cubits and its width, 16 cubits); *Ant.* XV 394 (Latin version); Eruvin 2b.

**Golden Vine:** Middot 3:8; *War* V,5,4 (210); *Ant.* XV 394–395 (Latin version); Tacitus, *Historiae* V. 5. 5; Florus, *Epitoma* I, 40:30.

**Wickets:** Tamid 3:7–8; Middot 4:2; Yoma 39b.

**Door Panels:** (Gilded) *War* V 208; Tamid 3:7; Eruvin 10:11; 102a.

**Veil:** *War* V,5,4 (212–214); *Ant.* XV 394 (Latin Version); *Letter of Aristeas* 86; I Maccabees 1:22; *Ant.* XIV 105–109; Tamid 7:1; Tosefta, Sheqalim 3, 13; Yoma 54a; Ketubot 106a; Matthew 27:51.

**Gold Lampstand:** Yoma 3:10 and parallels; Yoma 37a and Baraita (*ibid.* 37b; Jer. Tal.) Yoma 3, 8, 41a.

**Tables:** Sheqalim 6:4; Menahot 99a,b; Tamid 31b; Jer. Tal., Sheqalim 6,3.

**Sanctuary and Holy of Holies, Dimensions:** Middot 4:6,7; *War* V,5,5 (215) (60 cubits in height).

**Curtains of Holy of Holies:** Yoma 5:1; Sheqalim 8:4, 5 (for the correct version of Mishnah 5, see: J.N. Epstein, *Introduction to the Mishnaic Text* [Hebrew], p. 952); Tosefta Sheqalim 3,15; Jer. Tal., Sheqalim 51b; Yoma 51b–52a; *The Apocalypse of Baruch* 10, 19; *Pesikta Rabbati* 26 (ed. Ish-Shalom 131a); *Protoevangelium Iacobi* 10,1.

**Gold Overlay in Sanctuary:** Middot 4:1; Baraita in Pesahim 57a.

**Sanctuary Vessels:** *War* V,5,5 (216–218); Yoma 5:3; Tosefta, Yoma 2,12; Menahot 11, 5–6; Bab. Tal., *ibid.* 98b–99a; Yoma 21b; 33b; 51b–52a; Jer. Tal., Sheqalim 6,3.

**Holy of Holies:** Middot 4:5; *War* V,5,5 (215–219); Sheqalim 4:4; Tosefta Kelim, Baba Qama 1,7; Tosefta, Sheqalim 3,6.

**Even Hashtiya:** Yoma 5:1; Tosefta, Yoma 2,14.

**Structure of the Ceiling and Roofs:** Middot 4:6.

**Building Materials:** *War* V,5,4 and 6 (208–213; 222–224); Sukkah 51b; Baba Batra 4a; Middot 3:4.

**Cells:** Middot 4:3,4; *War* V,5,5 (220); *Ant.* XV 393.

**Mesibbah and the Space for Draining Away the Water:** Middot 4:5,7.

**Upper Chamber:** Middot 4:5,6; *War* V,5,4,5 (209, 211, 221); *Ant.* XV 393.

**Curtains of the Upper Chamber:** Tosefta, Sheqalim 3, 13–15; Jer. Tal., Yoma 42b; Yoma 54a.

**Parapet and the Spikes:** Middot 4:6; *War* V,5,6 (224); Shabbat 90a; Menahot 107b; Eruvin 6a.

# Bibliography

Avi Yonah, M., "The Facade of Herod's Temple—An Attempted Reconstruction," in: Neusner, J. (ed.), *Religions in Antiquity—Essays in Memory of E. R. Goodenough* (Leiden, 1968), pp. 327–335.

———, "The Second Temple," in: Avi Yonah, M. (ed.), *Sefer Yerushalaim* (Jerusalem and Tel Aviv, 1956), pp. 392–418 (Hebrew).

Busink, T. A., *Der Tempel von Jerusalem* II (Leiden, 1980).

Dalman, G. "Der Zweite Tempel zu Jerusalem," *Palästinajahrbuch* 5 (1909): 29–57.

Hildesheimer, I., *Die Beschreibung des herodianischen Tempels im Tractate Middot und bei Flavius Josephus* (Berlin, 1877).

Holtzmann, O., *Die Mischna Middot—Text, Übersetzung und Erklärung* (Giessen, 1913).

Patrich, J., "The *Mesibbah* of the Temple According to the Tractate *Middot*," *IEJ* 36 (1986): 215–233.

———, "Reconstructing the Magnificent Temple Built," *BR* IV/5 (1988): 16–30.

———, "The Golden Vine, the Sanctuary Portal and its' Depiction on the Bar-Kokhba Coins," *JJA* (in press).

Schürer, E., (Vermes, G. and Millar, F. eds.), *The History of the Jewish People in the Age of Jesus Christ* I (Edinburgh, 1973), pp. 308–309.

Simons, J., *Jerusalem in the Old Testament* (Leiden, 1950), pp. 381–436.

Vincent, L. H., "Le Temple hérodien d'après la Michna," *RB* 61 (1954): 5–35, 398–415.

Vincent, L. H. and Steve, A.M., *Jérusalem de l'Ancien Testament* II–III (Paris, 1956), pp. 432–525.

De Vogüé, M., *Le Temple de Jérusalem* (Paris, 1864).

Watzinger, C., *Denkmäler Palästinas* II (Leipzig, 1935), pp. 41–45, Pls. 6–7.

# The Table of the Showbread and the Facade of the Temple on Coins of the Bar-Kokhba Revolt

## Dan Barag

The largest and most important silver coins struck by Bar-Kokhba (132–135 C.E.) show the facade of the Temple and the legend *yerushalem* "Jerusalem" or *shim'on* "Simeon." On the reverse appear a lulav (palm-branch) and an ethrog (citron), with the legend *shenat aḥat le ge'ulat yisra'el* "Year One of the Redemption of Israel," later *she(nat) b(et) le ḥer(ut) yisra'el* "Year Two of the Freedom of Israel," and finally *le ḥerut yerushalem* "For the Freedom of Jerusalem." These coins are referred to in documents of Bar-Kokhba's time as *sela'im* (tetradrachms). The facade of the Temple depicted on these coins has four columns; in the center stands an object of uncertain identity. Clearly, this object, or perhaps symbol, was held in exceptional esteem, just as pagan coins of the Roman era frequently featured temples with a statue of a god or goddess in the center.

A coin of this kind was first described in a book by the Jesuit monk Athanasius Kircher in 1653. He attributed the coin to King Solomon(!). Kircher did not relate to the object in the center of the Temple facade, whereas the German scholar Johann Hottinger, who depicted Bar-Kokhba's silver tetradrachms in his books which were published in 1659 and 1662, described it as an entrance to the Temple. Until the beginning of the 19th century, scholars who addressed this question advanced various suggestions and interpretations, some even inverting the facade and defining the object as a lyre. The interpretations proposed since the beginning of the 19th century may be divided into three main categories: an entrance or door; the Ark of the Covenant; a Torah shrine or chest.

None of these seems likely. The object cannot be a door or entrance since the lower horizontal line, which would then represent the threshold, is too high and in the Year One tetradrachm it is a beaded line. Descriptions of the door between the Porch and the Sanctuary (Mishnah, Middot 4:1–2) indicate that it was divided down the middle into two wings, each flanked by a postern, suggesting an entirely different picture from that on the coin.

The object portrayed on the coin has legs like those of a piece of furniture. It is therefore hardly possible that the Ark of the Covenant was intended, for the description in the Bible (Exodus 25:10–22; 37:1–9) makes no mention of legs or feet. Moreover, by the time of the Second Temple the Tablets of the Law were no longer in existence, and for that reason the returnees from Babylon and their descendants did not make an Ark. Both the Mishnah and Josephus state quite definitely that the Ark of the Covenant was no longer in existence in the Second Temple period (Mishnah, Sheqalim 6:1–2 and elsewhere in Rabbinic literature; *War* V:219). Is it conceivable that Bar-Kokhba and his followers, who wished to renew the Temple ritual, would have presumed to restore the Tablets of the Law and the Ark to the Temple? This interpretation is untenable; and indeed, the sources provide no hint of any such intention.

Finally, might the object in question possibly be a repository for copies of the holy scriptures, i.e., a Torah shrine? Rabbinic literature and Josephus's works leave us entirely ignorant as to where holy books were kept in the Temple; there is no hint of any ark of this sort endowed with some special significance. Moreover, it is inconceivable that Bar-Kokhba and his men planned to rebuild the Temple

The Lipkin-Raffaeli didrachm:
"Simon / For the Freedom of Jerusalem"

just to place there a Torah shrine, and so turning it into a synagogue. This surely would not have justified a revolt which endangered the very existence of the nation. Would such a project have attracted popular support? There is no hint in the sources that this was a goal of the Revolt. On the contrary, it is quite clear from the Temple vessels and instruments portrayed on the coins—amphora, jug, trumpets, lyre, cithara—that the rebels intended to renew the Temple rites and ritual. Hence the object in the center of the facade can be neither a door, the Ark of the Covenant, nor a Torah shrine.

L. Mildenberg recently published a silver didrachm (termed a *sheqel* in Hebrew documents from the time of Bar-Kokhba), purchased around 1985 in Jerusalem. On the obverse he made out a representation of the facade of the Temple consisting of two columns on a stepped base. Between the two columns, he claimed, was the open Ark of the Covenant(!). Around the border of the obverse of the coin is the name *shim'on* "Simon." The reverse shows a lulav (without an ethrog) and the legend *le herut yerushalem* "For the Freedom of Jerusalem," which dates the coin to the third year of the Revolt. Mildenberg believed the coin to be unique and unknown until then, but that is not the case. In a Hebrew book entitled *Coins of the Jews*, by S. Raffaeli, published in Jerusalem in 1913 (the first Hebrew book in this field), we read:

◁

Tetradrachms of the Bar-Kokhba Revolt: 1. "Jerusalem / Year One of the Redemption of Israel" 2. "Jerusalem / Y(ear) Two of the Free(dom) of Israel" 3–4. "Simeon / For the Freedom of Jerusalem" of the third year

In the treasure of our townsman Mr. Hayyim Lipkin there is a didrachm... And the gates of the Temple are (represented by) two columns and the shape of the *vav* is as on the Hasmonean coins. According to Mr. Lipkin, three such coins have been discovered up to this time, all of which passed through his hands.

That year, the coin was examined in the British Museum, and rejected as suspect by G.F. Hill. He described the coin in his *Catalogue of the Greek Coins of Palestine in the British Museum*, which was published in 1914, pointing out the peculiar shape of the letters. A plaster cast of the coin was kept in the British Museum. The subsequent history of the coin is interesting. Shortly after the establishment of the Palestine Department of Antiquities in 1920 Raffaeli was appointed keeper of its coin collection, a post he held until his death in November 1923. He acquired many important coins for the collection, and in the winter of 1922 purchased the above coin from Lipkin. In an unpublished manuscript, now in the Department of Antiquities archives, Raffaeli explained why he believed the coin to be genuine—notwithstanding Hill's reservations. In 1927 the coin was sent to the British Museum for reexamination. Hill declared the coin to be a forgery, and until recently it was stored as such at the Rockefeller Museum. We now know that some of the genuine Bar-Kokhba coins bear inscriptions in corrupt or irregular letters. The didrachm recently discovered and published by Mildenberg was struck from the same dies as the Lipkin-Raffaeli coin, and both coins are undoubtedly genuine.

The object pictured on this coin is a table viewed from its long side and having raised ends. The only table we know of in the Temple was the Table of the Showbread. N. Avigad, in his excavations in the Jewish Quarter of Jerusalem, discovered in a Herodian level two plaster fragments bearing a graffito of the Temple Menorah (the seven-branched candelabrum); to the right was a piece of furniture which B. Narkiss identified as the Showbread Table. This stylized depiction from the end of the Second Temple period also shows the

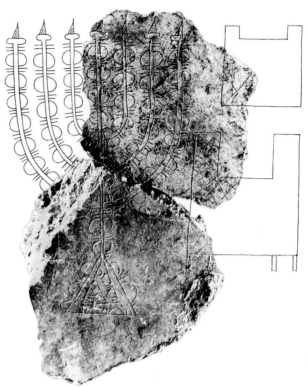

The Menorah and the Showbread Table incised on two plaster fragments from the Jewish Quarter excavations in Jerusalem

Table with its narrow sides elevated (see in this volume, pp. 277–278).

The biblical description is as follows:

> He also made the table of acacia wood; two cubits was its length, a cubit its breadth, and a cubit and a half its height; and he overlaid it with pure gold, and made a molding of gold around it. And he made around it a frame a handbreadth wide, and made a molding of gold around the frame. He cast for it four rings of gold, and fastened the rings to the four corners at its four legs. Close to the frame were the rings, as holders for the poles to carry the table. He made the poles of acacia wood to carry the table, and overlaid them with gold (Exodus 37:10-15).

Twelve loaves were placed on the Table, in two stacks of six loaves (Leviticus 24:6). The two lowest loaves were laid on the Table with the five others stacked above each of them. The loaves were separated by staves or rods which ensured ventilation to prevent the formation of mold (Mishnah, Menahot 11:6). Apparently the stacks stood higher than the Table itself; the sages of the Talmud disagreed as to whether the height of each stack was 12 or 15 handbreadths, i.e., two cubits or more (Bab. Tal., Menahot 11a). Possibly the raised ends of the Table were intended to prevent the stacked loaves from collapsing and falling off. If indeed the didrachm of the Bar Kokhba Revolt represents the Showbread Table, the depiction on the tetradrachms may also be explained: It shows the Table from its narrow side with its raised and arched ends; perhaps the two dots represent the ends of the poles by which the Table was carried. On the Year One coin of the Revolt, the Table was portrayed in a side view. But apparently this depiction was not satisfactory, and, from the beginning of Year Two, an additional arched strip was added to the top in order to impart some depth to the picture and give it a three-dimensional appearance, showing both the front, as well as the top of the opposite end.

Depicting the Table as seen from its narrow end on the tetradrachms conforms with the ruling that all the sacred utensils had to be placed along the length of the Temple—except for the Ark of the Covenant in the days of the First Temple (Mishnah, Menahot 11:6; Tosefta, Menahot 11:8). The artisan who prepared the design for the didrachm, however, placed the Table along the width of the Temple and omitted the two poles for carrying the table. At the upper part of the Table he indicated two parallel lines—perhaps also in an attempt to give the picture a three-dimensional aspect, that is, to show both the front side and the protruding part of the back.

The message Bar-Kokhba's warriors wished to convey on the tetradrachm and the didrachm should now be clear: their goal was to rebuild the Temple and renew the sacred service. The Showbread Table symbolized the restoration of the perpetual Temple ritual: "And you shall set the bread of the Presence on the table before me always" (Exodus 25:30; cf. Leviticus 24:6). The reverse of these coins bears a lulav and an ethrog (sometimes a lulav without an ethrog), symbolizing the yearning for the restoration of the three pilgrimage festivals, particularly Sukkoth.

The Showbread Table was first depicted on a coin of Mattathias Antigonus, the last Has-

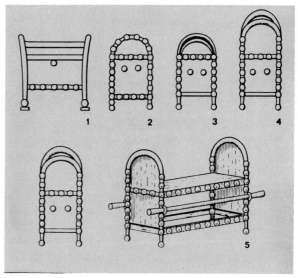

The Showbread Table: 1. Lengthwise view, on didrachm; 2. View of narrow end, as on Year One tetradrachm; 3. Same, on Year Two tetradrachm; 4. Same, on tetradrachms of second and third years; 5. Tentative reconstruction, based on tetradrachms of second and third years

monean king (40–37 B.C.E.). The Table was rendered in a highly stylized manner, without the raised ends, but in some of Mattathias's coins the two stacks of loaves are shown. The Table is struck on the obverse side of the coin—the side with the Hebrew inscription. The reverse, with the Greek legend, depicts the Menorah. The coin symbolizes Mattathias's control of the Temple—and perhaps also a passionate call to the people to join forces and defend the Temple was intended. Moses and the Israelites were commanded to make the Ark, the Table and the Menorah (Exodus 25:10–40). The biblical account of the Temple vessels describes them in this order, implying that the Table was considered more important than the Menorah; it is therefore obvious why the Table appears on the coins of Mattathias Antigonus on the side bearing the Hebrew legend. Moreover, in the description by Josephus of the Temple vessels paraded in the triumphal procession at Rome (War VII:148–150), as well as in the relief on the Arch of Titus, the Table of the Showbread is carried first, ahead of the Menorah. The relief on the Arch of Titus also shows the Table without raised ends, as in the Mattathias Antigonus coins. This may indicate that the raised

Facade of the Temple—tentative reconstruction, based on Bar-Kokhba coins and various details in Mishnah, Middot

ends were separate components which were attached to the Table by tenons or in some other way; perhaps they were not looted, or the gentile craftsman omitted them. It was only after the Bar-Kokhba Revolt, probably at the time of Rabbi Judah Ha-Nassi or later, that the Menorah became the main Jewish symbol.

But there is further information to be gleaned from the didrachm. Mildenberg suggested that the two-column facade was meant to indicate the denomination of the coin—two drachms (i.e., two dinars or two *zuzim*), whereas the four columns of the facade as portrayed on the tetradrachm indicated that it was a coin of four drachms. He interpreted the steps as representing the podium of the Temple. However, this must be rejected. Both the Mishnah and Josephus report that between the Priests' Court and the entrance to the Porch, i.e., the entrance to the Sanctuary, there were twelve steps (Middot 3:1; *War* V:206). I believe that the didrachm depicts the entrance to the Sanctuary, attesting that it

was flanked by single columns. The tetradrachms, on the other hand, portray the facade of the Temple and the Table of Showbread without the entrance—recalling the common representations on contemporary pagan coins in which the details of the entrance are omitted and the statue of a god or goddess occupies the center of the facade (see also in this volume, pp. 260–271).

On the Year One tetradrachm the Temple is shown standing on a base represented by a single horizontal line. This representation may have been considered inadequate, and when the Showbread Table was portrayed differently at the beginning of Year Two, the base was also changed with the addition of short vertical pilasters. This element too, has aroused scholarly controversy. Numerous conjectures have been advanced regarding a representation which seems to be merely the podium of the Temple without the steps in the center—perhaps to avoid too close a resemblance to pagan coins.

Although many questions remain unanswered, the didrachm recently discovered and published—together with the Lipkin-Raffaeli coin—has paved the way for the reconsideration of a most interesting problem. Thanks to coins of this type, it is now clear that the object in the center of the Temple facade on the tetradrachms of the Bar-Kokhba Revolt is the Showbread Table, and that the purpose of these coins was to proclaim the rebels' central goal: the rebuilding of the Temple and the restoration of the ritual and of the three festival pilgrimages. The representations on the tetradrachms and the didrachm give us the rebels' impression of the facade of the Temple they wished to rebuild, and convey an idea of the appearance of the facade of Herod's Temple.

## Bibliography

Barag, D. "New Evidence for the Identification of the Showbread Table on the Coins of the Bar Kokhba War," *Proceedings of the 10th International Congress of Numismatics* (London, 1986), pp. 217–222.

Hill, G.F., *Catalogue of the Greek Coins of Palestine* (London, 1914), p.cv, n.1.

Mildenberg, L. "A Bar Kokhba Didrachm," *INJ* VIII (1984–1985): 33–36; Pl. 28.

Raffaeli, S., *Coins of the Jews* (Jerusalem, 1913), pp. 160–161 (Hebrew).

# The Temple Cult Objects Graffito from the Jewish Quarter Excavations at Jerusalem

## Dan Barag

In the first season of excavations in the Jewish Quarter of Jerusalem, in 1969, a representation of the Menorah (the seven-branched candelabrum) incised on two plaster fragments, was found in Area A, in a large building of the Herodian period. N. Avigad has given us a dramatic description of how the fragment showing the base was first unearthed. Then, three weeks later, the other fragment turned up on which the central stem and the three right-hand branches are incised. News of the discovery aroused considerable interest, for depictions of the Menorah of the Second Temple period are extremely rare.

The two fragments, together with a large quantity of painted plaster pieces, were discovered in the fill between two floors. On the upper level were remains from the time of the destruction of the Second Temple (70 C.E.); beneath it, together with the plaster fragments, the excavators found coins of the time of Alexander Jannaeus (103–76 B.C.E.) and Herod (37–4 B.C.E) The plaster fragments, which Avigad ascribed to Herod's reign, must have been brought from some nearby building that had been destroyed or renovated. The fragments were undoubtedly discarded in Herod's time, but we cannot ascertain how long they adorned the walls of the building from which they were removed. Quite possibly, they should be assigned an earlier date, perhaps during the late Hasmonean period.

The Menorah was incised in the unpainted, wet plaster; it has a triangular base, and its U-shaped branches start rather low on the central stem. All parts of the Menorah, including the base, feature a pattern of ovals alternating with pairs of parallel lines—perhaps a schematic astragal pattern. Flames issue from

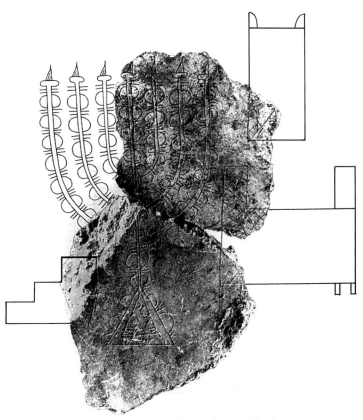

The incised plaster fragments from the Jewish Quarter in Jerusalem with the representation of the Menorah and proposed reconstruction of other cult vessels of the Second Temple

the flattened tops of the branches. The Menorah is 20 cm. high; its (reconstructed) width is 12.5 cm.

Two additional objects were incised to the right of the Menorah, but only small parts of these representations have survived. In 1974 B. Narkiss published an instructive paper in which he showed that the object on the right of the Menorah was the Table of the Showbread, although only a small part of its left side has been preserved. Just visible above the Showbread Table is the lower left corner of another object, possibly the Incense Altar.

Narkiss suggested that the plaster fragments from the Jewish Quarter were part of a schematic plan of the Sanctuary: the Menorah stood on the left (south), the Showbread Table on the right (north), and the Incense Altar above, in front of the *parokhet*—the Curtain of the Ark—(Exodus 26:35; 30:6). As drawn on the plaster fragments, the narrow end of the Showbread Table is appreciably higher than the tabletop proper. I have recently proposed that the object depicted in the middle of the Temple facade on tetradrachms from the time of the Bar-Kokhba Revolt, and in the entrance to the Temple on contemporary didrachms, is precisely the Showbread Table. The representation on the tetradrachms also shows the narrow end of the Showbread Table higher than the tabletop, but in this case it is arched (see in this volume, pp. 272–276).

Clearly visible to the left of the base of the Menorah is an incised vertical line, with a crack (not man-made) in the middle. A horizontal line abuts the vertical one near its lower end—apparently the lower right-hand corner of another object. Can this object be identified? In the Mishnah we read: "And there was a stone before the Menorah with three steps, on which the priest stands and lights the lamps" (Tamid 3:9). It seems likely, therefore, that the object whose lower right corner is visible to the left of the Menorah was this three-stepped stone.

The size of the Menorah is not specified in the Bible; neither is it mentioned in the Mishnah or in the works of Josephus. Rabbinic tradition (Bab. Tal., Menahot 28b) fixes the height of the Menorah at 18 handbreadths, i.e., 3 cubits (about 1.58 m.). This figure is plausible if one compares the height of the Menorah depicted on the Arch of Titus with the height of the soldiers carrying it. The Menorah was therefore so tall that the priest whose task was to light the lamps could not reach them without the aid of steps.

The tractate Tamid, one of the oldest in the Mishnah, was redacted—at least in part—soon after the time of the destruction of the Second Temple. The depiction of the Menorah and the three-stepped stone from the Jewish Quarter predates by at least a century the passage from the Mishnah in which the stone is mentioned, reinforcing the assumption that the tractate Tamid indeed preserves ancient, authentic traditions. This identification also corroborates Narkiss's suggestion that the sketch incised in the plaster was not a random combination of cult objects from the Temple, but a schematic plan f the Sanctuary. This plan was incised in oplaster by a person acquainted with the Sanctuary and its vessels before the destruction of the Temple. Narkiss suggested that the representation might have been sketched on the wall of a public building, or of the residence of a priestly family, to instruct children who might some day serve in the Temple. Since the picture is relatively small and schematic, and for lack of other evidence, this hypothesis of Narkiss cannot be confirmed. Whatever the case may be, this graffito is a unique testimony from a time when the Temple still stood.

## Bibliography

Avigad, N., "Excavations in the Jewish Quarter of the Old City of Jerusalem, 1969/70" (Preliminary Report) *IEJ* 20 (1970): 4–58.
———— , *Discovering Jerusalem* (Nashville, 1983), pp. 147–149.
Narkiss, B., "A Scheme of the Sanctuary from the Time of Herod the Great," *JJA* I (1974): 6–15.

# JERUSALEM — LATER PERIODS

General isometric view of the Byzantine Cardo uncovered in the Jewish Quarter

# Excavations at the Damascus Gate, 1979–1984

## Menahem Magen

The Damascus Gate in the northern wall of the Old City of Jerusalem is the largest and most elaborate of all the city's gateways. According to an inscription above this gateway, it was built by Sultan Suleiman the Magnificent in Hegira year 947/1538 C.E. Since that time, no substantive changes have been made to it. Since it was the main entrance to the city, it appears more frequently than other gates in drawings and photographs from the beginning of the 19th century on. For these reasons it has been investigated intensively.

### Previous Excavations

Already in the early 1930s, the Department of Antiquities of the British Mandatory Government under the direction of R.W. Hamilton[1] excavated at the Damascus Gate. During these excavations, part of the Roman gate was exposed, including the outer face of the eastern archway and the base of the western tower. Remains of later periods were also revealed.

In the early 1960s, J.B. Hennessy resumed excavation at the Damascus Gate. This was an extensive project in which many remains of the Crusader period were uncovered, including part of a church and the entrance of a fortified outer gate building. The facade of the eastern archway was also completely exposed. Hennessy's excavations were brought to a halt by the Six-Day War; results were published in 1970.[2]

Damascus Gate: the eastern Roman gateway and the Ottoman gateway above it

### The Stairwell

In 1979, the decision of the Jerusalem Municipality to renovate the plaza in front of the Damascus Gate presented an opportunity for carrying out new excavations in that area.[3]

report: G.J. Wightman *The Damascus Gate, Jerusalem* Biblical Archaeological Reports (BAR) International Series 519 (Oxford, 1989).

[3] The excavations in the area of the Damascus Gate were part of a project to improve the area initiated by the Jerusalem Municipality and carried out by the East Jerusalem Development Corporation. Also participating were the Jerusalem Foundation, the Ministry of Tourism and the Ministerial Committee for Jerusalem. I thank all of them for their help, especially I. Yaacoby, the coordinator of the project.

[1] R.W. Hamilton, "Excavations Against the North Wall of Jerusalem, 1937–38," *QDAP* 10 (1940): 1–57.

[2] J.B. Hennessy, "Preliminary Report on Excavations at the Damascus Gate, 1964–6," *Levant* 2 (1970): 22; and see the final

Damascus Gate: the eastern Roman gateway and entrance plaza

the Old City wall above the Ottoman gate, provided further impetus for excavating.

When the stairwell was cleared of the rubble and debris that had filled it, it was found to be built entirely of huge stones measuring as much as $2 \times 1.5$ m. Some of these ashlars have dressed margins typical of the Herodian period. At a later date, the steps at the bottom of the stairwell had been removed and the walls plastered over to convert it into a cistern. The lower exit of the stairwell was blocked and also covered with plaster. It became clear to us that the steps originally led to the roof of the eastern tower of the gate, whose outer side had been completely exposed during the 1960s.

In the course of our work we penetrated the eastern archway and exposed the interior of the eastern tower. We also examined the remains near the western tower in order to determine their relationship to the present-day gate complex.

The discovery of a stairwell, the upper end of which was incorporated in the upper part of

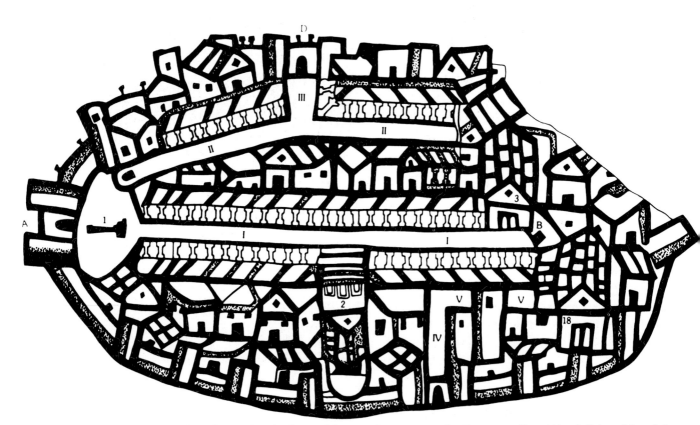

Schematic representation of Jerusalem in the Madaba mosaic map: note the Damascus Gate (A) at left (north) and the pillar in the oval plaza (1) inside the gate

282

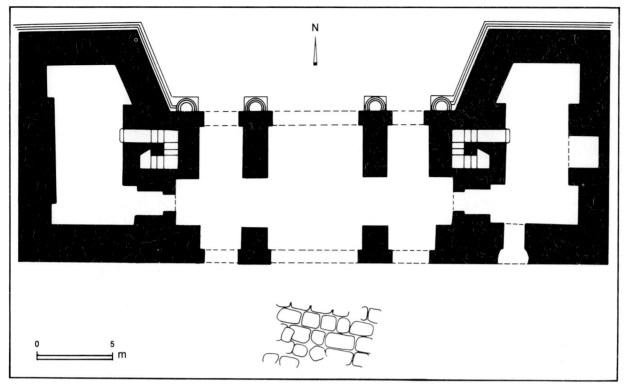

Damascus Gate: plan of Hadrian's Gate complex

## The Towers

The earliest structure to be revealed was a wall of monumental stones discovered by Hamilton beneath the western tower. This wall, 6 m. in length, is preserved to a height of only two courses and describes an angle of 150 degrees. It is the remnant of a large, possibly octagonal structure (tower?). This wall was built directly on the bedrock. The stones have typical Herodian margins.

Above this wall is a tower whose base was constructed in Roman style but which is completely encompassed by a wall of large, rough stones. Adjoining it on the east is the door-jamb of an entrance portal made of smooth, hewn stones. Above it, the remains of an arch were revealed: extremely worn stonework that still bears traces of a beautifully carved, molded profile. The entrance itself was completely blocked by well-laid, smooth stones of medium size. Above all of these is the Ottoman gate structure. Alongside the blocked entrance, Medieval remains include cisterns, a Crusader church, and parts of later walls.

Unlike their western counterparts, the eastern tower and the archway adjoining it are

Damascus Gate: the interior of the eastern tower, looking north

perfectly preserved. Midway between the two towers is located the center archway of the

Roman tripartite gate. It, too, was completely blocked by a later structure. Of the original eastern entrance, the arch, the vault of the ceiling, the doorjambs and the floor have survived. Grooves to allow for the passage of wheeled carriages are cut into the stone sill. In the threshold are holes for the door hinges, and the doorjambs have square recesses for wooden beams once used to bar the door. The pavement is made up of large stones up to 1 m. in length and 60 cm. in width. On its southern side, the entrance room, 9 m. in length and 3 m. wide, was blocked by a stone wall built in Crusader style. The width of the opening is 2.3 m. From the eastern wall of the entrance room, a corridor, 4 m. long and 2 m. wide, leads into the eastern tower. This corridor, too, is built of huge, smooth-faced stones.

The eastern tower has been preserved to a height of 11.8 m.; only its ceiling is a later addition. The tower is built entirely of very large stones, most of which are hewn in typically Herodian style. The tower is rectangular, 11.5 × 6 m., and extends in a north-south direction. At its northwestern extremity, a niche with an angular wall was created, parallel to the tower's outer face. A large part of the original pavement is missing and in many places smaller stones had been used in repairs. The tower has two openings in addition to the main entrance. One of these, with hewn steps leading into the city, is breached in the southern wall. The western wall has an opening, found blocked and plastered over, leading to the above-mentioned stairwell. A small 2 × 2 m.-square compartment is built into the eastern wall. Leaning against this wall was a huge round stone, 2 m. in diameter and 70 cm. thick. When laid on the floor, it turned out to be the lower basin of an olive press. Stone benches were built along the wall on all sides. Thorough investigation revealed that many of the stones used for the benches were also taken from the oil press: the crushing stone, two bases used in pressing and a large stone basin.

Small rectangular slots cut into the northern wall supported the wooden beams of the oil press. Evidently, after the tower no longer served as a guardroom for the soldiers posted at the gate, it was utilized as an oil pressing workshop.

It seems that at a later stage the tower was divided into two stories by arches spanning the walls. Hollowed recesses for the arches are hewn into the eastern and western walls (remnants of arches remain in two of these hollows), while rows of smaller holes were cut into the northern and southern walls, 6 m. above the floor, apparently to anchor wooden

Damascus Gate: the upper (crushing) stone of an oil press at the time of its discovery inside the eastern tower

Damascus Gate: the opening to the stairwell in the western tower

beams which were supported by the stone arches. In the eastern wall, at a height of 10 m., a window blocked with small stones was discovered.

In August 1983, the interior of the western tower was also excavated. This tower was not as well preserved as the eastern one. Although its northern wall and parts of its eastern and western walls rise to a height of 11 m. above the floor, the southern wall is completely missing and only the northern side of the adjoining stairwell remains. This tower is identical in plan and dimensions to its eastern counterpart, but is built as its mirror image. It too was divided into two stories by arches, and apparently was also used as an olive press at some later stage.

## The Roman Plaza

In early 1982, when foundations were dug for a large block of shops on the inner side of the present-day Damascus Gate, very large paving stones were found *in situ* at the level of the entrance of the Roman gateway. We inferred that they were part of the Roman plaza adjoining the inner facade of the gate. This plaza with a pillar at its center is clearly depicted on the Madaba map of the 6th century C.E. It is this pillar that gave rise to the Arabic name for the Damascus Gate, Bab al 'Amud—the gate of the pillar. We decided to extend the excavation area along the inner side of the gate as far as possible in order to reveal the plaza. At the same time, we intended to break through the Crusader wall that blocked the eastern entrance in order to determine its connection with the plaza. It soon became apparent that the wall was 3.5 m. thick and that it was built directly on the plaza pavement.

In addition to the excavation, the breach had to be secured with steel supports to keep the gate structure above from collapsing. As a result work proceeded very slowly, but when the breach was completed a link was created between the eastern entrance and the newly-excavated plaza. We succeeded in exposing a 6–10 m.-wide section of the plaza, extending 30 m. south of the entrance. The pavement is

Damascus Gate: section of pavement in the Roman plaza

Damascus Gate: pavement of the Roman plaza

Damascus Gate: pavement of the Roman plaza with Crusader construction built over it

well preserved; its stones are particularly large —up to 2 m. in length and an average width of 1.2 m. All the stones, with the exception of two, were found *in situ* and most of them were whole. Above the pavement, structures with vaulted ceilings were revealed. Two stages of building may be discerned in these structures. The vast majority of coins from the lower level are of the Ayyubid period, whereas the ceramics found in the buildings date to the Mamluk period. The present-day street leading from the Damascus Gate into the Old City runs directly above the ceilings of these structures.

## Summary

As a result of these excavations the history of the Damascus Gate could be reconstructed. There may have been a gate here already in the Second Temple period, the wall below the western tower representing its remains. The building of the towers and the elaborate tripartite entranceway between them can apparently be dated to the 2nd century C.E., the time of the construction of Aelia Capitolina by Hadrian. The style of the tower bases and of the eastern entrance archway is identical to that of the triumphal arches built during the reigns of Trajan and Hadrian. An inscription discovered by Hamilton above the eastern archway apparently refers to Aelia Capitolina. Whereas the ashlars date to the Herodian period, many such stones were put to secondary use, and we may assume that they were taken from the ruins of the Second Temple period city walls, the walls of the Temple Mount, and the previous city-gate. All these indicate that the Roman gate complex was constructed after the destruction of the Second Temple, in the 2nd century C.E.

The form and function of the gate remained unchanged during the Byzantine period, although some alterations may already have been made in the towers, i.e., their division into two stories, the narrowing or blocking of the side archways, and the conversion of the guardrooms into oil pressing workshops. Possibly, only the central archway continued to be used as an entrance to the city.

During the Early Arab period, the openings were blocked and large cisterns were built in front of them and in the stairwells.

The Crusaders blocked part of the gate completely, and next to the northeastern corner of the gate and at a higher level, they built an outer gate structure at a right angle to the line of the city wall. These structures remained in use under the Ayyubids and were renovated in the Mamluk period. The present gate building was constructed in 1538 C.E., the remnants of the Roman towers forming the bases for the new ones. Above the central Roman archway, the present-day entrance was erected. The street leading from it was built directly above the Mamluk structures.

Damascus Gate: Mamluk building below the Turkish gate

## Bibliography

Magen, M., "Recovering Roman Jerusalem—The Entryway Beneath Damascus Gate," *BAR* 15/3 (1988): 48–56.

# Excavations at the Third Wall, North of the Jerusalem Old City

Vassilios Tzaferis, Nurit Feig, Alexander Onn, Eli Shukron

Several years ago an opportunity arose for conducting intensive archaeological excavations over a relatively large area of about 15 dunams (4 acres) north of the Damascus Gate. It was occasioned by the construction of a major traffic artery (Highway 1) which necessitated an archaeological emergency salvage operation. Because of technical considerations the excavation area was divided among four teams of excavators who worked there during three consecutive seasons, in 1990–1992.*

Each one of these excavations brought to light remarkable structures which filled separate purposes, but together were parts of a complex residential pattern. It turned out that this large area of Jerusalem north of the Damascus Gate evolved in the long history of the city from being an open, uninhabited area until the turn of the 1st century B.C.E., to a sparsely occupied area within the fortified city encompassed by the Third Wall in the mid–1st century C.E., and until the end of the Second Temple period. Finally, in the Byzantine period, this area became a crowded, extramural residential district north of the city walls, that filled highly important religious functions.

* The Third Wall Excavation Project was conducted on behalf of the Antiquities Authority under the general direction of V. Tzaferis. Funding was provided by the Company for the Development of Jerusalem. Excavations in the different areas were carried out by A. Onn (Area A); N. Feig (Area B); E. Shukron and A. Sabrayago (Area C). They were assisted by a team of archaeologists: R. Avner, N. May, R. Abu-Riya, J. Seligman, Y. Rapuano, N. Sanduka, S. Wexler, E. Assaf, and A. Gorzalczany; field surveying was by S. Mandreia. Area D was excavated by D. Amit and S.R. Wolff (see in this volume, pp. 293–298).

## The End of the Second Temple Period

The results of our excavations show that this part of the city, about 300 m. north of the Damascus Gate, was uninhabited throughout most of the Second Temple period. It served for a long time as a source of building stone: Almost in every place where the excavations reached the underlying base rock, clear traces of quarrying were discerned, and in some cases ready-cut stone blocks were found on the spot. A particularly interesting find in this connection was the discovery of an assemblage of about twenty iron quarrying tools in a rock crevice, including worn chisels as well as seemingly new ones that had never been used. These tools were obviously hidden there by workmen for some reason and forgotten, or perhaps the owners were prevented from returning.

Construction work in this area began in the middle of the 1st century C.E. with the erection of the Third Wall that encompassed the northern part of Jerusalem at the end of the Second Temple period. According to Josephus Flavius (*War* V, 135–161) the foundations of this wall were laid by Agrippa I (41–44 C.E.) and its construction was ended only during the First Jewish Revolt against Rome in 66–70 C.E. Expectations of finding additional parts of the Third Wall in our excavation area derived from earlier discoveries nearby of sections of this wall, mainly by E.L. Sukenik and L.A. Mayer in 1925–1927 and in 1940, and in 1972–1974 by S. Ben-Arieh and E. Netzer. The identification, dating, and the course followed by the Third Wall have been the subject of lengthy discussions by many scholars. The discoveries made in the course of our excavations contribute to some extent

287

Bird's-eye view of the excavation Area A at the Third Wall; looking east

to the clarification of certain questions connected with the Third Wall.

Remains of the Third Wall were uncovered in two of our excavation areas. In Area A, a 20 m.-long stretch of the foundations of the wall was revealed, built directly on bedrock. The foundations of the wall, about 4 m. wide, were constructed of small stones and concrete. The excavations in Area B uncovered a small section of the superstructure of the wall itself, built of large ashlars with margins dressed in the Herodian manner. In Area A the excavations exposed the foundations of a tower that protruded northward from the line of the wall. Further east, another tower in the Third Wall was discovered some years previously in the excavations conducted by Ben-Arieh and Netzer. Until now, all the excavations in this area during the past century revealed sections totaling about 500 m. out of the entire line of the Third Wall.

The impressive construction of the Herodian Third Wall attests to architectural, engineering and planning capabilities on a royal scale. It certainly was not built hurriedly under the pressure of current need. Therefore it may safely be assumed that this is indeed the Third Wall mentioned by Josephus.

## The Roman Period
In 70 C.E., with the destruction of the Second Temple, the Third Wall was dismantled and its stones removed for secondary use. The area north of the city reverted to being uninhabited until the Byzantine period (5th century C.E.). The archaeological finds show that during this interval the area served mainly as a burial ground. Of the six tombs discovered in Areas A and B that can be dated to this period, four were of cremation burials commonly practiced by the Romans.

## The Byzantine and Early Arab Periods
Intensive settlement of the area began in the mid–5th century C.E. and continued without interruption until the 9th century C.E. The

archaeological evidence indicates that during this period there was an ongoing Christian presence in a suburb outside and north of the city walls of that time.

We learn from literary sources that important historical and religious events in this area were connected with the Christian settlement in Jerusalem. In the excavations to the north of the Damascus Gate, four monasteries, two hostelries and a large cemetery were discovered. Apparently, these not only served the religious establishment, but also the other inhabitants of Jerusalem over a long period. All these must be added to the main Christian center in this area, the Basilica of St. Stephen and the adjacent monastery and pilgrims' hospice built there by the empress Eudoxia in the mid–5th century C.E. the remains of which were cleared by the Dominican fathers at the end of the 19th century.

Remains of Byzantine period buildings were uncovered directly beneath the surface in this area. The walls—mainly foundation courses —are preserved only to 1 m. above bedrock because of later construction and other damage. The walls are about 70 cm. wide and are built of fieldstones and cement and plastered over. Openings and corners of the buildings are constructed of worked stones.

AREA A. In Area A we uncovered an extensive complex of buildings, over 115 m. long, which comprises a large monastery and a hostelry. In the center of the complex is a large courtyard encompassed by rooms on its eastern side, and apparently also on the western side—most of them for the accommodation of pilgrims— and various service rooms with a kitchen, bakery, and a scriptorium. The residential rooms of the monks are situated to the south of the courtyard where a chapel was discovered, decorated with a colorful mosaic floor. This chapel apparently served the devotional needs of the monks attached to the monastery. Another chapel excavated in the 1930s by D.C. Baramki next to the hostel most probably was used by the pilgrims staying there.

The complex also included a variety of burial caves for more than one body, and rock-cut

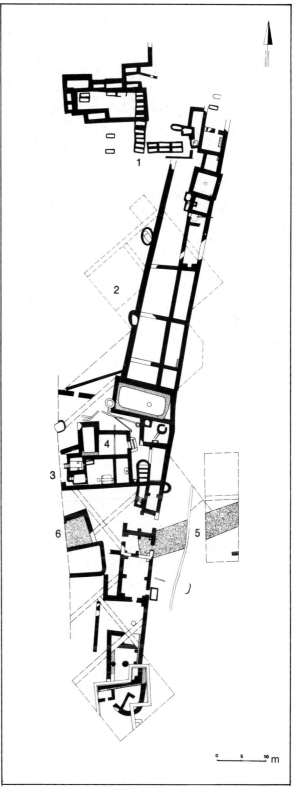

Third Wall, Area A: general plan of the excavations— 1. graveyard; 2. hospice; 3. monastery; 4. chapel; 5. the Third Wall; 6. tower of the Third Wall

Third Wall: view of the chapel with remains of the mosaic floor and the entrance to the crypt; looking east

graves for individual burials. Beneath the chapel we found three burial crypts of identical plan. Each crypt could be entered from the chapel by a separate entrance and had two rock-hewn or built up burial places. A small bowl for sanctified oil, given to the pilgrims as a blessing of the saint, found in one of the crypts probably indicates that local saints were buried there. This corresponds with literary sources that tell us of bones of Christian

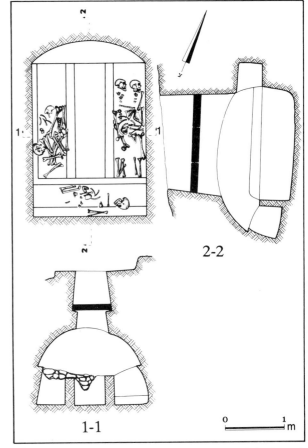

Third Wall: plan and sections of Roman tomb in Area A

saints, including martyrs executed by the Muslim authorities in the Early Arab period, buried in this area. North of the central courtyard is a cemetery for individual burials. The graves are laid out in orderly fashion, side by side.

Several different stages of construction could be distinguished in the complex of buildings in Area A. The earliest of these, from the time of the foundation of the complex in the Byzantine period, dates to the end of the 5th century C.E. and continued in use, with minor alterations, well into the Early Arab period. Apparently, the hostel of the monastery fell into disuse already at the beginning of the 8th century C.E., although the monastery proper and the cemetery continued in use for some time afterward, until the 9th century C.E. In the monastery there is evidence of changes from the 8th century C.E.

Third Wall: the eastern crypt beneath the chapel in Area A; looking west

Third Wall: small stone reliquary decorated with incised, framed crosses that was discovered within a plastered basin inside the chapel

on, which resulted in a reduction of its area and concentration on the area of the chapel with its crypts below, and the cemetery.

**AREA B.** In Area B, east of Area A, part of another especially large hostel was discovered. Its rooms clustered around two inner courtyards, each measuring 40 × 40 m. The floors of these rooms were decorated with mosaics of geometric pattern, except for one of the rooms which seems to have been used as a small chapel and has a more delicate, colorful mosaic floor. In this hostel there is evidence of

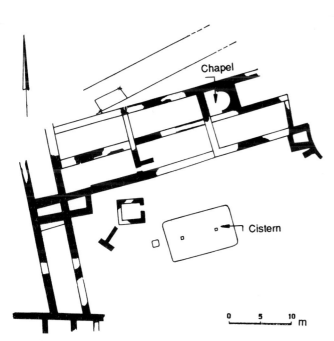

Third Wall, Area B: general plan of the excavations

several stages of construction and building additions. The foundation stage dates to the Byzantine period, most probably the 6th century C.E., and the last stage to the 7th century C.E. The hostelry was abandoned and destroyed in the Early Arab period at the beginning of the 8th century C.E., most probably with the cessation of Christian pilgrimages to Jerusalem at that time.

A sophisticated planning effort went into the provision of water to the buildings discovered in Areas A and B. Below the buildings we found large, plastered cisterns which collected water running off the roofs and paved courtyards by means of an intricate system of drain pipes.

Third Wall: complex of water systems in Area B belonging to the Byzantine hostelry

**AREA C.** Remains of another monastery were discovered in Area C south of Area A. This monastery differs by its better construction from the other monasteries found in this area. The foundation courses are built of dressed ashlars laid on bedrock, and in some places also integrated with it. In the center of this monastery, too, is a courtyard, with rooms arranged on three of its sides. The building was severely damaged in the past, and only the remains of ten rooms are partly preserved. A

291

corridor between the rooms and the court-yard leads to a rock-cut crypt beneath it. A cross is carved on a stone slab that had obviously served as the cover of one of the graves in the crypt. Additional graves belonging to this monastery complex were uncovered beneath the floor in one of the rooms in its southern part. The evidence of the pottery and coins points to the monastery having been founded in the Byzantine period and continuing in use into the Early Arab period.

## Summary

The finds in the areas excavated by us, in addition to the excavation results from Area D (see in this volume, pp. 00–00), show that in this part of the city, north of the Byzantine city walls, there existed at the time four monasteries with adjoining or separate pilgrims' hospices and cemeteries occupying about 3 dunams. All of these served as one functional unit despite the absence of a clear structural connection among them and each being built on a different plan, and differing in dimensions and style. This part of Jerusalem outside the walled city of that period provided services to monks, pilgrims, and the deceased throughout more than four hundred years.

The multiplicity of monastic establishments is undoubtedly due to historic causes of the end of the Byzantine period in the country, including the Persian invasion in the year 614 C.E. and the Muslim conquest in 638 C.E. These events resulted in the destruction of many monasteries and churches in the Judean Desert region, and jeopardized the safe existence of Christian religious establishments outside the towns. Apparently many of the monks who abandoned their monasteries in the desert came to Jerusalem and lived also in the monasteries north of the city walls.

Although the monasteries continued to exist after the Arab conquest, the pilgrims' hostels ceased functioning, attesting to a halt of pilgrim traffic to Jerusalem in that period. The finds here confirm this view.

# An Armenian Monastery in the Morasha Neighborhood, Jerusalem

David Amit and Samuel R. Wolff

In anticipation of impending road construction, a rescue excavation was conducted north of the Old City, on the eastern edge of the Morasha (Musrara) neighborhood.[1] The excavation was one in a series of Third Wall projects carried out in 1990–1992 in the vicinity (see in this volume, pp. 287–292). The site was divided into two areas, North and South. The most significant result was the discovery in the Southern Area of the earliest Armenian monastery to have been identified in Jerusalem.

## Southern Area

The Southern Area is a north-south strip measuring 65 × 20 m. The earliest human activity at the site is represented by signs of stone quarrying. No pottery was found that could date the quarrying with precision, but it is probably related to the construction of the nearby Third Wall at the end of the Second Temple period (1st century C.E.).

The monastic complex of the 6th–8th centuries C.E. consists of the monastery church (A) and residences (B) south of the church unit, a paved courtyard (C), a southern unit of rooms (D), and a water collecting system featuring a huge reservoir (E). All the buildings are oriented northeast-southwest and were constructed on levelled earth-fill deposits that covered the quarries. Some of the walls are founded directly on the bedrock and are pre-

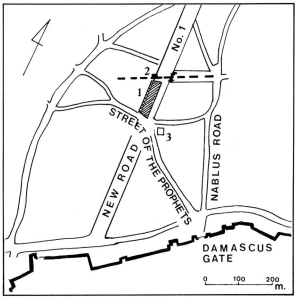

Morasha: general plan of the area north of the Jerusalem Old City—1. excavation sites; 2. line of the Third Wall; 3. The Armenian "Bird" mosaic

served to an average height of 50–80 cm. The walls are built of medium-size fieldstones with small stones filling the interstices. Two large late 19th or early 20th-century buildings were erected over the remains of this complex, causing it much damage.

## The Church Unit (A)

The church unit is located at the northern end of the Southern Area. Prior to its construction this area served as a burial ground in the late Byzantine period (5th–6th centuries C.E.). Several underground crypts and individual tombs (e.g., A3–A7), both rock-hewn and built, were discovered in this area. Stepped corridors lead down to the burial chambers. Some burials were sealed by the construction of the church while others remained

[1] The site is located south of the Street of the Prophets (Reḥov Hanevi'im) and west of Derekh Ḥeil Ha-Handassah. The excavations, conducted from October 1991 through February 1992, were directed by D. Amit, assisted by S.R. Wolff and A. Gorzalczany (field supervisors), D. Gamill (assistant field supervisor), A. Hajian (surveyor) and S. Manderiah (photographer). The Armenian inscriptions were translated by M. Stone; the Greek inscription by V. Tzaferis.

Morasha: general view of Southern Area, looking south

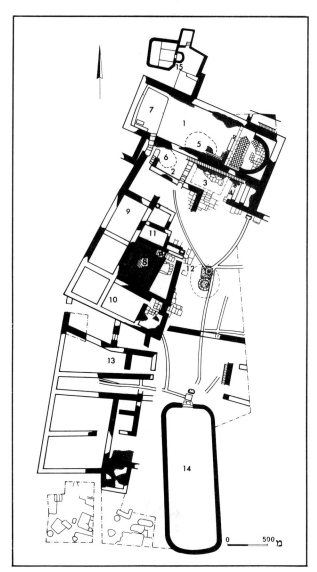

Morasha: plan of Southern Area

accessible after it was completed. A fragment of the marble lid of a reliquary box was discovered in one of the tombs.

The church (A1), measuring 18 × 5.6 m., built on the standard chapel plan, determined the general east-southeast to west-northwest orientation of the monastic complex. In the prayer hall, 13 × 5.6 m., a few sections of a mosaic floor with a floral net pattern framed in a volute border remain. The bema, raised about 20 cm. above the floor of the prayer hall, is paved with white, red and black stone tiles laid diagonally in checkerboard fashion. In front of the bema, a Greek dedicatory inscription in three lines within a *tabula ansata* was discovered. The inscription, which is damaged on its left side, was originally 2 m. long and reads:

> [in the days of Si]lvanus, the god-beloved diacon and head of the monastery, the present
> [mosaic inlay] was done and the apse and annex of the church, of...
> [cubits length] and of six cubits height. Remember me, O Lord, in Thy Kingdom

Paleographic analysis dates the inscription to the 6th–7th centuries C.E.

An entry hall or narthex (A2), measuring 15 × 3.1 m., is at the southern side of the church. Of its mosaic pavement only patches of a geometric pattern remain.

Morasha: Greek inscription from the eastern end of the prayer hall in at the church

The general plan and orientation of the church with a single long prayer hall and apse, and an adjacent long room to the south, are closely paralleled in two nearby chapels.[2]

Under the eastern section of the narthex, a rectangular crypt (A3), measuring 4.3 × 2.5 m., is hewn out of bedrock; its barrel-vaulted ceiling is built of ashlar blocks. The skeletal remains of several individuals were found inside the crypt chamber, with at least one of them in an articulated position. Dispersed among the skeletal remains were two bowls, an exceptional assemblage of glass vessels, and a fragment of a wooden plank (identified as

Morasha: bema and apse of church, looking south

Morasha: glass vessels of the end of the Byzantine period uncovered in the crypt (A3) under the church

cypress) with iron nails hammered into it—apparently part of a coffin. A neighboring tomb (A4) yielded an intact tombstone with an Armenian inscription reading: "Of Petros of Sodk'." Sodk' is a town in the vicinity of Lake Sevan in Armenia. Two additional crypts were found under the western half of the narthex floor. One of them (A5) was filled with stone boulders, and the second (A6), which served as a repository, was filled with heaps of disarticulated human skeletal remains.

Yet another underground crypt with a stepped entrance (A7) was discovered at the western end of the prayer hall. The vaulted

[2] See in this volume, pp. 287–292; and D. Baramki, "Byzantine Remains in Palestine II. A small Monastery and Chapel Outside the 'Third Wall'." *QDAP* 6 (1938): 56–58.

ceiling of the crypt collapsed at some time along with the mosaic floor of the prayer hall above. Cut into the bedrock floor of this crypt are two burial troughs intended for primary burials. The only noteworthy finds from the fill of the crypt and its entrance way are two chancel screen posts with a cross carved into their domed caps, and a stone slab—presumably a tombstone fragment—with three letters in Armenian script preserved, reading: "Abel."

A few isolated tombs (A8) were excavated north of the church. While it is impossible to date these with certainty, the few finds suggest that they were last used in the Byzantine period. One tomb was possibly hewn already in the Iron Age.

### Residential Unit (B)

The focal point of the main residential unit of the monastery is a reception hall (B1) measuring 4 × 5–5.5 m. Its well-preserved mosaic floor features a central medallion, 1.19 m. in diameter, with a seven-line inscription in Armenian script:

> I
> Ewstat' the priest l-
> aid this mosaic.
> (You) who enter this house,
> remember me and my brother L
> uke to
> Christ

Morasha: Armenian inscription from the reception hall in the residential unit

A coin of Arab-Byzantine type found in the foundation of the mosaic floor confirms that it was laid soon after the Arab conquest of Jerusalem in 638 C.E.

A series of rooms (B3, B4) surround the reception hall; several of them were used for storage, others for cooking and other household functions. A rich, varied assemblage of glass vessels and cooking pots was discovered in one of these side rooms. A bath (B2), connected to what appears to be a water-heating installation, and an adjoining entrance or dressing room, served the residents of this unit. A complete bowl with an Armenian abecedary inscription was found on the floor of this room. The rooms in the southern and western wings of the residential unit, which were only partly excavated, may represent the original construction phase of the monastic complex. The reception hall and the other rooms were added later.

A stone-paved courtyard (C) is located east of the residential unit (B) and an additional unit of rooms (D) is adjacent to its southern side. Only the northern and the eastern wings of the southern unit were uncovered. Its orientation differs slightly from that of the main residential unit.

### The Water System

An elaborate system for collecting and storing water was discovered in the monastic complex. A multi-branched network of water channels collected rainwater from the roofs, porches and courtyards of the buildings and led it to reservoirs and cisterns by way of settling basins. The most impressive element in the system is a huge reservoir (E) the capacity of which is estimated at more than 700 cubic meters.

### Summary

Two architectural phases may be distinguished in the building remains of the southern excavation area. In the earliest phase, when the monastery was erected, its church unit (A) was built over an earlier burial ground. This phase probably dates to the 6th century C.E. The complex was expanded in the 7th century C.E., following the Arab conquest, by the addition of the reception hall (B1) and the southern residential unit (D). Additions were also made to the church. The entire complex fell into disuse sometime during the Abbasid period (8th–9th centuries C.E.). These finds constitute a rare example of

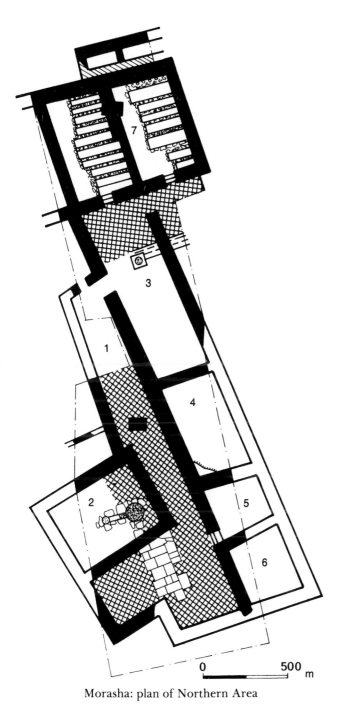

Morasha: plan of Northern Area

Morasha: general view of Northern Area, looking south

a monastic complex of the Umayyad period which surpasses its Byzantine predecessor in relative size and grandeur.

The Armenian monastery adds a previously unknown dimension to our knowledge of Jerusalem in the 7th century C.E. While the Bird Mosaic with its Armenian inscription has been known for over a century, little could be said about it except discussing the mosaic and the text. With the discovery of the Armenian monastery in the southern excavation area nearby, we can now speak of an Armenian neighborhood north of Jerusalem, outside the walls of the city of that time. In addition, the dating of the new Armenian mosaic to the mid-7th century C.E. provides scholars with a

297

benchmark for dating the early Armenian script, which heretofore had been dated only generally and without a solid basis.

## Northern Area

The Northern Area, measuring about 35 × 8 m., is situated a few meters south of the presumed line of the Third Wall. The earliest construction remains revealed in this area, interpreted as yet another monastic complex, consists of a long corridor (1), two large cisterns (2, 3), a row of residential rooms (4–6), and two vaulted tombs (7).

The corridor (1), preserved to a length of 19 m., is paved with a coarse, white mosaic and was apparently open-air, collecting rainwater that ran off the roofs of the adjoining rooms. The residential rooms (4–6) have plain white mosaic floors, or a combination of mosaic and paving stones. Coins from the make-up of the plaster floors yielded dates of the late Byzantine through the Umayyad periods. Most of the coins recovered from probes dug in the earth-fills beneath the floors are of the 4th–5th centuries C.E., the latest of them dating to the reign of Anastasius I (498–518 C.E.). Of special interest is the discovery of a rare coin from the Ethiopian kingdom of Axum, dating to the mid–4th century C.E. (a second Axumite coin was discovered in the Southern Area). Fifteen coins were found in the earth-fill that accumulated above the vaulted roof of the eastern cistern (3), including eight Umayyad and four Abbasid coins. The latter apparently relate to the last-use phase of the monastic complex in the 9th century C.E.

The burial complex (7) consists of two vaulted tombs of similar size and shape whose barrel-vaulted roofs collapsed into the chambers. Both tombs share a common facade wall built of well-cut ashlars. Twenty rectangular box-like burial troughs are cut into the floors of the tomb chambers. Most of the stone slabs which covered them were broken as a result of the roof collapse.

Although the building complex in the Northern Area seems to be more or less contemporaneous with the later construction phase of the monastery in the Southern Area (middle to second half of the 7th century C.E.), there are no grounds for designating it as Armenian. Unequivocal evidence, such as inscriptions, is lacking, and the architectural character of the remains uncovered in the Northern Area differs in orientation and in the construction of the walls and floors from that in the Southern Area. The Northern Area may have a closer affinity to the funerary chapel discovered nearby to the north,[3] and to the monastic complex uncovered more recently to the east (see in this volume, pp. 287–292), than it does with the Southern Area.

---

[3] E.L. Sukenik and L.A. Mayer, *The Third Wall* (Jerusalem, 1930), p. 38.

# The Excavations at Mamilla, Jerusalem, Phase I (1989)

## Aren M. Maeir

With the beginning of the urban redevelopment of the Mamilla neighborhood of Jerusalem, the first phase of a large-scale archaeological rescue excavation project was conducted under the auspices of the Israel Antiquities Authority.[1] The excavated area is situated west of the Jaffa Gate, outside the fortified city walls of all periods, on the northeastern slope of the Hinnom Valley. This area was to be covered over by the realignment and repaving of Jaffa Road.

The excavations added to our knowledge of the extramural areas of Jerusalem. The substantial structural remains that came to light date to: the Second Temple (late Hellenistic-early Roman) period; the late Byzantine-Early Arab period; and the Middle Ages to modern times. Various finds of other periods, mostly in non-stratigraphic contexts, included Iron Age II pottery and various objects dating to the Middle Ages and later.

### The Second Temple (Late Hellenistic-Early Roman Period–1st century B.C.E.)

The earliest architectural phase was found in Area B2, in the northern part of the excavation site. Beneath the remains of later finds, mainly of the late Byzantine-Early Arab period, we discovered the corner of a large structure, its 1.5 m.-wide walls built on the bedrock. The earth-fill inside the corner of the walls contained pottery dating to the first half of the 1st century B.C.E., while the pottery in the fill covering it was of the beginning of the second half of the 1st century B.C.E. The massive proportions of the construction suggest that it may have been part of the fortifications of Jerusalem during the late Hellenistic-early Roman period (1st century B.C.E.)—perhaps the remains of a tower positioned in front of the wall. Elaborate forward defense works (*proteichisma*) are common in Hellenistic fortification systems, and this wall or tower may have been part of such a system. At a later stage, possibly in connection with changes in the fortifications of Jerusalem—particularly the construction of the Second Wall further east—under Herod the Great, this structure was dismantled and covered over by earth-fill.

### The Late Byzantine-Early Arab period (6th–8th centuries C.E.)

This was one of its most intensive periods of development in the history of Jerusalem. Evidence of this period turned up in almost all the areas of excavation and constituted the greater part the finds. The walls we uncovered are constructed both of fieldstones and dressed masonry and are preserved to a height of up to 2 m. The remains of this period were found in three areas.

On the southern side of the excavation, in Area A2, a building complex of rooms and alleys, and possibly a courtyard, was discov-

[1] The excavations were conducted for the Israel Antiquities Authority under the direction of the author. The following assisted during the various stages of work: area supervisors R. Abu-Riya (Area B3), Y. Billig (Area C, assistance in Areas B1, A2), J. Seligman (Area B1), E. Shukrun (Areas A1, A2), D. Stacey (Area B2); archaeologists S. Hananel and O. Raviv; surveying and drafting—B. Arubas; research assistant—Y. Strauss; registration—H. Herzl and D. Shmuel; photography—D. Adar; pottery restoration—M. Ben-Gal and F. Raskin. The excavation was funded by the Karta Jerusalem Development Company, under whose aegis the whole development project is conducted. Phase I of the excavations was conducted in August-October 1989. Phase II, directed by R. Reich in 1990–1992, will be reported separately.

Aerial view of the excavation area at Mamilla along the western side of the Old City, looking north

ered. This complex appears to be a row of three shops opening on a street that led toward the city gate of that period in the vicinity of the present-day Jaffa Gate. Each of the shops consisted of two rooms—an inner and outer room aligned perpendicular to the street—with simple white mosaic floors and various basin-like installations in them. The shops are built on small, stepped terraces, one shop to each step, ascending in the direction of the Jaffa Gate. In one of these shops we

found a particularly rich assemblage of finds, among them a selection of both local and imported pottery, including some rare imported painted ware (Coptic or Transjordanian); a collection of contemporary coins; a small, finely-made ampulla decorated with Christian iconographic figures (Joseph, Mary and the baby Jesus on the flight to Egypt); a beautiful little cross made of red Jerusalem limestone; various glass vessels, and many other items. All these finds were sealed under

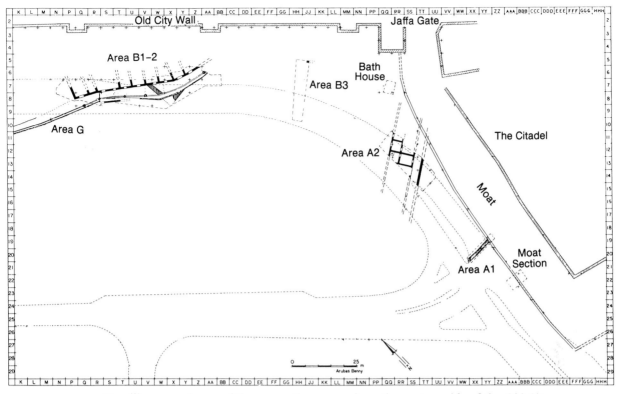

Mamilla: general map of the excavation areas along the western side of the Old City

Mamilla, Area A2: various rooms of the Byzantine shops with plain white mosaic floors; looking south

Mamilla: an ampulla of the Byzantine period from Area A2 adorned on both sides with figures from Christian iconography

Mamilla: small, red limestone cross from Area A2

later layers of the Early Arab period. They represent a rich sample of the late Byzantine-Early Arab material culture of Jerusalem.

North of these shops we discovered what appeared to be either a courtyard or another lane or narrow street. Here too we found a rich assemblage of pottery, coins and glass, including what appears to be industrial glass waste, possibly hinting at the presence of a glazier's shop in the vicinity.

This building complex seems to have been in use for only a limited time. There is evidence of some minimal structural changes and additions to the buildings. What appears to be an extension and continuation of these structures was found during Phase II of the

Mamilla excavations, south and west of this area.[2]

The pottery and coin finds date these buildings to the very end of the Byzantine and the beginning of the Early Arab period. These structures seem to have been part of the extra-mural market and industrial area of Jerusalem. The buildings were all found beneath a well defined layer of earth which sealed the deposits within. Above this were accumulations of debris of later periods, down to modern times.

In the vicinity of this building complex and east of it, the remains of what appears to be a Roman-Byzantine bath-house were discovered. Unfortunately, this building was exposed only in a small pit and was not excavated. It was covered over to preserve it for future investigation.

Additional evidence for construction in the late Byzantine-Early Arab period was found to the north, in Areas B1, B2 and B3. In Area B3, a wide trench excavated down to the bedrock revealed a layer of packed, whitish earth dating to this period—apparently the remains of a road or open area near the city-gate. Protruding from the balk (the unexcavated partition of the excavation grid) at the southeastern corner of the trench, was the corner of a wall that appeared to be contemporary with this area. These finds in Area B3 are related also to the discoveries in Areas B1–B2 of the same period where impressive late Byzantine-Early Arab remains were unearthed.

The earliest construction of this period in the excavation area is an aqueduct supported by a 3–4-m.-high terrace wall. The aqueduct was found to be intact along about 70 m. of its length, running approximately from north to south. Additional sections of this aqueduct were discovered to the northwest in past archaeological work, and in Phase II of the Mamilla excavations to the northeast. We believe that the aqueduct brought water from an external source through the city gate of

[2] The excavations were conducted by R. Reich (see Note 1).

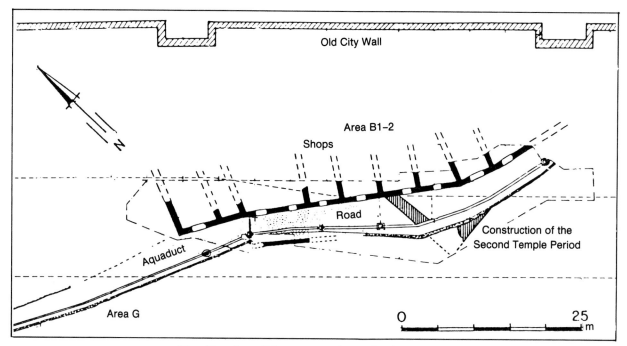

Mamilla: plan of the structural remains in Area B1-2

this period, which was then in the general area of present-day Jaffa Gate. The water could have come from either the Mamilla Pool to the northwest, or from the final stretch of the Roman-Byzantine Upper Aqueduct of which other sections are known from the southern environs of Jerusalem.

The evidence from the excavation appears to indicate that this section of the aqueduct was constructed in the Byzantine period (4th–5th centuries C.E.). The aqueduct apparently continued in use well into the Middle Ages. Concurrently with the construction of the aqueduct, a dirt road was made along its northern side and apparently followed the line of the aqueduct toward the city gate. This roadway continued in use until the end of the Byzantine period and its level was periodically raised.

Toward the end of the Byzantine period a long building was constructed along this road. The part uncovered by us along 50 m. comprised rooms opening on the road. However, neither the interiors of these rooms, nor anything west of the building, could be cleared due to a large Medieval trench that had destroyed much of the earlier material (see below), and because we had reached the limit of our excavation area. The various finds

(processing installations for liquids, storage jars, etc.) in the rooms seem to indicate that these served as shops for mercantile or manufacturing purposes. The building was probably constructed during the latter part of the

Mamilla, Area B2: on the left—the line of Byzantine shops and the street; the aqueduct can be seen in the center; the man at the right stands on the remains of the tower of the Second Temple period; looking southeast

303

found under the building. Most of the channels led rainwater into the aqueduct; others carried off sewage and included sections of piping acting as siphons where they crossed under the aqueduct.

The building and the road appear to have gone through several stages of slight structural renovations, including raising the level of the floor and the road. This attests to a continuous use of the building, at least over several decades.

Among the interesting finds in this building complex are a group of iron weapons found in one of the rooms—perhaps an armorer's shop —including six swords, two spearheads and four or five iron shield-bosses (*umbo*); various metal fixtures of the door of one of these rooms—the lock, key?, and various flanges, nails and other hardware; remains of a plaster wall decoration appear to have Christian religious and architectural motifs.

All of this underlines the extensive extramural activity during the late Byzantine-Early Arab period—which is corroborated by other excavations north of the Old City. Shops, small industry, several access routes, and a water supply system for this part of the city—all these were situated in the immediate vicinity of the western gate of Jerusalem. The archaeological testimony indicates a seemingly uninterrupted continuum between the Byzantine and the Early Arab periods.

## The Medieval to Modern Periods

After the Early Arab period, the area which we excavated was no longer an extensively

Mamilla, Areas B1–2: looking southeast toward Jaffa Gate; note the outer wall with openings to the street of the Byzantine period

Byzantine period, and continued to be in use into the beginning of the Early Arab period, as with the buildings in Area A2.

In some of the rooms were the well-preserved remains of the second story of the building that collapsed on the lower floor. These included overturned mosaic floors, fragments of roofing material and contents of the upper story. A well-planned and executed network of water and sewage channels was

Mamilla, Area B1: hoard of iron swords of the Byzantine period

304

built-up extramural part of the city—until the end of the 19th century C.E. Nevertheless, we did discover various remains from these periods.

The aqueduct continued in use at least to the 11th–12th centuries C.E. and possibly later. This is attested by evidence of the repeated cleaning of the channel over a long period, as well as by the manholes that gave access to the channel from progressively higher ground levels.

At the eastern side of the excavation we came upon a large trench dug approximately parallel to the present city wall. The trench dates to the latter part of the Early Arab period or the Crusader period (11th–13th centuries C.E.), and was apparently part of the city fortifications—probably a dry moat in front of the city wall. This trench was dug into the earlier occupational layers, destroying large parts of the Byzantine construction in the vicinity of the aqueduct. The trench was filled in at some later period.

In the trench were what appeared to be the collapsed remains of a large, well-built wall—perhaps of the city wall of Jerusalem that was intentionally dismantled by the Ayyubid caliph el-Malik el-Muazzam at the beginning of the 13th century C.E. to deny the use of these fortifications to the enemy. Similar remains were uncovered by M. Broshi along the southern part of the city walls (see in this volume, pp. 00–00).

In the excavation area northwest of the Citadel we discovered the remains of the moat built by the Turks in the 16th century C.E. Immediately northwest of the counterscarp (the outer wall of the Citadel moat) is a well-built vaulted conduit that had been cut through and put out of use by the moat wall. This conduit may have served as a drainage channel at an earlier stage of the Medieval citadel. Extensive debris of everyday life of the Medieval and Modern periods covered the earlier remains.

Only in the last decades of the 19th and the beginning of the 20th century did Jerusalem expand significantly beyond the confines of the Old City walls, and this area was again

built-up. Written descriptions and early photographs of Jerusalem show that the area was a busy center and marketplace. In 1898 the moat of the Citadel was filled in and the wall breached to open a new entrance to the city for the state visit of the German emperor Wilhelm II. This is the present road into the Old City next to the Jaffa Gate.

Mamilla, Area A1: the Medieval drainage channel in the background is cut by the wall of the Citadel moat seen in the foreground

## Summary

This excavation exposed a cross-section of the extramural neighborhood outside the Jaffa Gate during several of the major periods of the city's history. In particular, the late Byzantine-Early Arab remains complemented finds from other excavations of these periods in and around the city.

# The Cave of the Birds—A Painted Tomb on the Mount of Olives

## Amos Kloner

A burial cave with birds and trailing vines painted on its walls (Pl. VIIIa, b) was discovered at the end of June 1974 on the western slope of the Mount of Olives, east of the "Church of God." The cave was discovered during the installation of a sewage line on a side road off Samuel ben 'Adayah Street, which leads up to the Mount of Olives from the Rockefeller Museum.[1]

The cave consists of an almost square burial chamber, its walls are 1.73–1.85 m. long; and the 1.65 m.-high ceiling measures approximately 1.7 × 1.7 m. The cave is entered from the west through a narrow, 1.3 m.-long corridor, 50 cm. wide and 50 cm. high. The outside opening was blocked by stone slabs and the inner entrance to the burial chamber was originally sealed by a stone door that was found lying on the floor nearby. Two steep steps lead down to the chamber from the

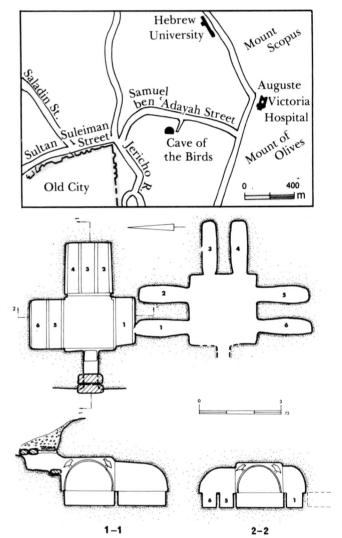

Plan and sections of the Cave of the Birds on the Mount of Olives

inner entrance. An arcosolium is hewn in each of the other three walls. In the benchlike floors of the three arcosolia, burial troughs are carved: one in the southern arcosolium, three in the eastern one, and two in the north-

---

[1] I was informed of the discovery of the cave by a neighbor, S. Marcus. The excavation was conducted on 3–11 July 1974, on behalf of the Department of Antiquities and Museums (today, the Antiquities Authority), under the direction of the present author with the assistance of J. Zias. The photographs are the work of Z. Radovan and Z. Saguiv; the drawings are by M. Krupkin.

In mid-July 1974, after our limited excavation and the registration of the cave, including a 1:1 drawing of the ceiling and walls, the site was visited by Father B. Bagatti, who learned of the existence of the cave from G. Kuhnel. The cave was then still accessible, its entrance sealed by a single stone. At the time, negotiations were held with the Jerusalem Municipality and efforts made to obtain funds for opening an entrance to the cave from the side nearer the "Church of God." Father Bagatti surveyed the cave—recording our pit in the middle of the burial chamber as a burial site—and published his findings in LA XXIV (1974). He failed to report the cave to the Department of Antiquities and Museums and therefore did not realize that it had been excavated by the District Archaeologist.

ern one. The bottom of each burial trough is level with the floor of the chamber. The stone slabs which once covered the burial troughs were not found. The walls of the entire chamber, including the arcosolia and the burial troughs, were coated with a 1.5–2.5 cm.-thick layer of plaster to form a surface suitable for painting on the soft, friable chalky rock. The rock-cut arches of the arcosolia were given their finished form by means of plaster containing an admixture of gravel and sherds.

The plaster and paintings on either side of the entrance door in the western wall have been damaged—most probably by tomb robbers who detached the door sometime in antiquity. The thieves penetrated the cave through a 50 × 40 cm. hole breached in the thin wall of a loculus of an adjacent burial cave. The cave, now known as the Cave of the Birds, was apparently not used for any other purpose in later periods, and the paintings remained untouched. Unfortunately, some of them were badly damaged immediately after the discovery of the cave when workers, and particularly local children, entered the cave and chipped plaster off the walls; only a few days later did the Department of Antiquities and Museums station a guard at the site.

After the discovery of the cave, the excavators concentrated on a partial examination of the accumulated earth. The bottom surfaces of Burial Troughs 2, 3 and 4 in the eastern arcosolium were exposed, the earth being shifted around within the cave but not removed outside. In addition, a small, rectangular area was excavated down to bedrock in the accumulated material in front of the southern arcosolium. This probe led to the decision not to excavate the northern and southern arcosolia or the rest of the burial floor: it was clear that the cave had been thoroughly plundered, for only a few potsherds and fragments of bones were found.

## The Decoration

In the arcosolia the decoration was painted directly on the white plaster; the plaster in the corners of the chamber and on the ceiling had first been painted a deep yellow. A reddish-

Cave of the Birds: flowers painted in the southern arcosolium

brown band, approximately 15 cm. wide, outlines the arches of the arcosolia. A similar but thinner band, about 10 cm. wide, is painted along Burial Troughs 1 and 6 and around the head and foot of each trough.

The flowers painted on the arcosolia walls have green stems, pinnate leaves and pink blossoms. The maximum height of each flower is about 25 cm. The floral decoration in the eastern arcosolium has faded owing to humidity and is no longer visible.

## Corner Decorations

The basic pattern of the decorations in the cave consists of four grapevines, which emerge from the four corners of the chamber and interlace all over the ceiling. Each vine has a single stem, bearing large leaves. On either side of the stem is a bird facing away from it, pecking at large clusters of grapes. Each corner features the same pair of birds: a dove to the right of the stem and a partridge to the left.[2] The coloration of the dove in the southwest corner has faded, but the partridge is intact. The space between the birds and the stem is taken up with vine leaves. Except for some slight damage—mainly to the partridge —perpetrated immediately after the discovery of the cave, the birds in the southeast corner have been preserved almost intact. The coloration in the northeast corner is in good condition but the birds themselves have been badly damaged. In the northwest corner, the dove has been almost completely effaced but for its head and neck, and no trace remains of the partridge.

All the zoological details and the coloration, stripes, shape of tail and even the color of the beak seem to indicate that the right-hand bird in each pair is a rock dove or a feral pigeon. The spur on the dove's leg—if it is indeed a spur rather than a raised claw—presents somewhat of a problem, as does the beak, which is curved too much for a dove. Perhaps it was drawn in this way to match the curved beaks of the other birds in the cave. The details of the chukar partridge are accurately depicted, as are its characteristic coloration, the black stripes on its flanks, the red beak and the spur.

## Ceiling Decoration

Eight birds are painted among the vine tendrils trailing across the ceiling from the corners of the cave. Six of these face toward the adjacent walls; the feet of the other two, in the center of the ceiling, point to the eastern wall. The paintings in the middle of the ceiling have been badly damaged: part of the plaster collapsed due to moisture seeping through a crack in the rock, and more recently, after the cave was discovered, through the vandalism of children in the neighborhood.

Three birds are painted on the ceiling near the western wall. The bird facing left above

the entrance has a curved beak. On its left is another dove whose beak is missing, facing right. To the right of the middle dove is a pheasant that faces left. Although the lower part of its body and tail is damaged, it was apparently longer than 60 cm.; one of the characteristics of pheasants, apart from the red head, is a long, slender tail. Pheasants in the wild are extinct in Israel, and this was probably already so in the late Roman period.

Near the northern wall stands a third dove, 44 cm. long, also with a curved beak, and near the eastern wall, a peacock, 96 cm. long, prances proudly to the left toward a cluster of grapes. Its raised head, body, tail and circular markings are drawn with considerable precision and brilliantly colored in gray, azure and green. The peacock was a common motif in pagan, Jewish and Christian ,art, but it does not seem to have had religious significance here. To the right of the peacock a long-legged bird is drawn, also striding to the left. Its beak and part of its head are missing. Above this bird, too, is a cluster of grapes. Portrayed in the middle of the ceiling are two birds facing one another; however, only their hind parts remain.

As mentioned above, the space between the birds is filled with vine tendrils bearing leaves similar to those painted on the walls. The leaves average about 16 cm. in length; the artist first outlined them in reddish-brown paint and then colored the interior green— dark green in the middle of the leaf and a lighter shade of green around the edges. The same technique was employed for the other figures: first the outline was traced and then the interior was filled in by means of brush strokes. The clusters of grapes are full and heavy, 18–25 cm. in diameter, and give the impression that they are suspended from the middle of the ceiling. The artist achieved three-dimensionality by painting the grapes in black and blue in a sophisticated light-and-shade technique.

The birds in the center of the ceiling are black, gray, blue, green, brown and red—the same hues used for the corner birds. There is no doubt that the ceiling and walls were

---

[2] We are indebted to U. Safriel of the Department of Zoology, Hebrew University, Jerusalem, who helped us to identify the birds.

painted at the same time. The birds, vine leaves and grape clusters in the corners are slightly smaller than those depicted on the ceiling. The artist skillfully planned the distribution of the birds within the available space, subsequently filling in the background with vine tendrils, leaves and grape clusters. The red bands around the burial troughs were probably the last stage in the execution of the decoration.

## Style of Paintings and Date of Cave

Each bird is drawn separately, independently of the other figures in the frescoes. It is not clear whether the lack of perspective is due to

Cave of the Birds: sketch and photograph of the decorated ceiling

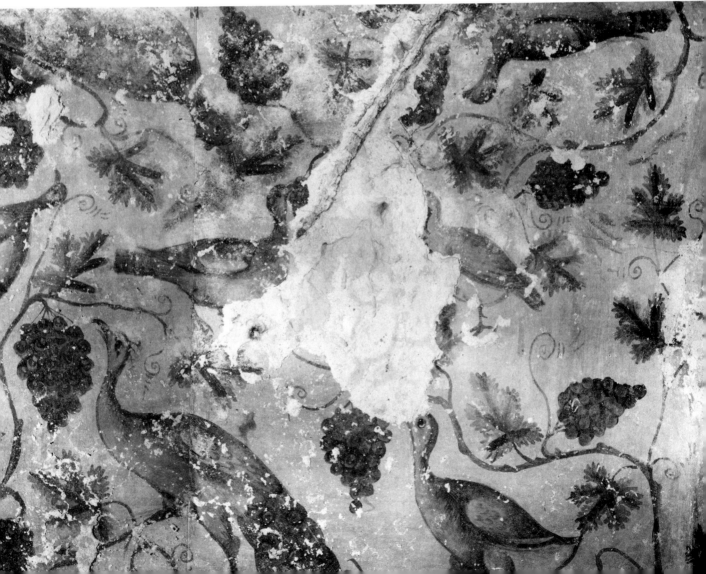

the artist's limited abilities or to restrictions imposed by whoever commissioned the paintings. On the other hand, the artist was obviously quite adept at representing light and shade. Each of the figures is fairly well drawn, recalling the naturalistic art of the classical world.

Comparison of the painting in this cave with other painted tombs of the Roman and Byzantine periods in Israel and the surrounding region, underlines the high quality of the frescoes. It is true that Christian tombs of the Byzantine period, such as those at 'Ein Kerem and Gethsemane in Jerusalem, Kibbutz Loḥamei HaGeta'ot and Bet Guvrin, feature similar elements such as the arcosolia with painted bands as well as representations of birds. But the artistic level in the Cave of the Birds is superior. Moreover, the crosses so typical of Christian Byzantine burial caves, with their schematically and symmetrically arranged decorations, are absent here.

Decorated tombs of the Roman period, such as those at Gerasa, Marwa, Or Ha-Ner, Ashqelon, Ḥanita and the burial discovered by F.J. Bliss and A.C. Dickie near the Tomb of the Kings in Jerusalem, show some minor parallels although there is no real similarity. In its architectural plan and a few details of the decoration the Cave of the Birds recalls a cave at Bet Guvrin published by F.J. Bliss and R.A.S. Macalister, and the cave at Moẓa near the bridge over Naḥal Soreq; however, their dating is still a matter of scholarly controversy. In light of the possible parallels, particularly regarding the artistic conception and execution, the Cave of the Birds seems closer to the caves of the late Roman period. Trailing vines, birds in medallions, peacocks, etc. are indeed very common in mosaic floors of synagogues and churches in our region. These, however, are usually dated to the 5th–6th centuries C.E. while our tomb seems to be earlier.

The details of the design may well have been based on a handbook of patterns which was also used by mosaic artisans. The attention to fine detail indicates that the artist used a good model—apart from his unquestionable talent. His naturalistic approach and care for details, the vigorous composition and arrangement of the birds—albeit unrelated to one another—in a single framework, all attest to a familiarity with the world of Roman painting. This conjecture is corroborated by the artist's skilful use of light and shade to emphasize the grape clusters and the birds.

The technique of burial in arcosolia and the use of an entrance shaft is common in tombs of the 3rd–6th centuries C.E. Neither the scant material finds in the tomb—a few sherds and isolated bone fragments—nor the remains of an inscription in the southern arcosolium are of any help in dating the tomb. Similarly-shaped letters may be found in inscriptions dating to the 2nd–4th centuries C.E., but the available data are too meager to permit a definite conclusion. Given the above considerations, the most probable date for the cave is the end of the 3rd or the 4th century C.E.

The cruciform designs added to the borders of the eastern arcosolium do not resemble Christian crosses typical of the Byzantine period. This, and the absence of other obvious Christian and pagan mythological symbols, raises the possibility that the tomb may have been Jewish. Both vines and birds are motifs found in some Jewish tombs and synagogues of the Roman and Byzantine periods.

# Excavations and Architectural Survey of the Archaeological Remains Along the Southern Wall of the Jerusalem Old City

## Meir Ben-Dov

Following the reunification of Jerusalem in the Six-Day War, the Government of Israel undertook the construction of a new road from Mount Zion down to the Dung Gate. At the same time, outside the Dung Gate, the Jewish Quarter Reconstruction and Development Company began work on a shaft providing access to a service tunnel for the installation of new infrastructure (telephone, electricity, sewage, and water lines). In the course of these public works projects ancient remains came to light, necessitating an archaeological excavation. This was carried out in 1975–1977. The area of excavations extended along the southern side of the Old City wall, from the Dung Gate in the east to beyond the Sulfur Tower (Burj Kibrit) in the west.[1]

### Finds of the First Temple Period

Since the area of the eastern slope of the Western Hill of ancient Jerusalem was already enclosed within the city walls in the late First Temple period, we were not surprised that the excavations uncovered finds of that time. Apart from fragmentary sections of walls in a poor state of preservation due to massive later construction in this area, we found also a large quantity of potsherds of the 8th–6th centuries

[1] The excavations were directed by the present writer under the auspices of the Israel Exploration Society. They were funded by the Jerusalem Foundation as part of the conversion of the area into an archaeological park. In 1981 we conducted a limited excavation on behalf of the Jewish Quarter Reconstruction and Development Company, inside the walls, west of the Dung Gate. Measurements were by the author, P. Adamsky and C. Seiler. The final drawings are by M. Ritmeyer. The drawing of the Tanners' Postern is by C. Seiler. The photographs are the author's.

Aerial view at the excavations area outside the southern wall of the Old City, looking west

311

B.C.E., including several intact oil-lamps, storage jar handles with the royal *lamelekh* seal impressions (two of Mamshat and one of Hebron), and an impression of a private seal belonging to "Tamar daughter of Azariahu."

## Finds of the Second Temple Period

In the Second Temple period this area was densely built up with structures of which only fragmentary remains of their basements survived. Particularly noteworthy among these are several ritual baths (*miqva'ot*) for ritual purification purposes, some hewn in the rock and some built up, and occasionally connected with a small *ozar* (store pool). Near each *miqve* we discovered rock-hewn water cisterns of 20–50 cu. m. capacity. The cisterns and *miqva ot* are lined with a gray plaster of high ash content. The *mikva'ot* share walls with adjoining dwelling rooms. Here were found objects of daily use, among them pottery vessels including some intact ones, and coins comprising also a hoard of 42 silver sheqels of the time of the First Jewish Revolt (41 sheqels of Year Two, and one of Year Five). In addition, there were lathe-turned stone vessels and items of glass and bone. In the southeastern part of the

Southern Old City wall: remains of the Crusader Tanners' Postern built over the remains of the Byzantine lower Cardo

excavation, about 50 m. southwest of the Dung Gate, a large water cistern estimated to have a capacity of several hundred cubic meters was discovered (but not cleared).

In the western part of the excavation area, near the Sulfur Tower, impressive remains of the Lower Aqueduct to Jerusalem were uncovered. This conduit, dating originally to the Second Temple period, brought water from Solomon's Pools south of Bethlehem to the Temple Mount. The section of the aqueduct which was uncovered here to a length of about 20 m. had been partially blocked in later periods. It is cut into the rock to its entire height, sometimes to 1.8 m., and is about 60–70 cm. wide. It is roofed with stone slabs, although along a short stretch it is tunneled entirely through the rock.

## Finds of the Byzantine Period

Two important discoveries in this area belong to the Byzantine period: the lower Cardo street of Jerusalem and a corner of the Nea Church.

Outside the Dung Gate and about 15 m. west of it, a paved section of the lower Cardo street of Jerusalem was uncovered. Part of the street is outside the wall of the Old City and part was uncovered inside the Old City next to the wall. This Byzantine street replaced the main street of the Second Temple period that stretched along the western retaining wall of the Temple Mount. The Byzantine street was constructed about 80 m. west of the previous —Herodian—street which had probably been buried under the heaps of stones fallen from the Temple Mount.

The lower Cardo is paved with very large stones and is partly built over the large water cistern of the Second Temple period. Under the western part of the street a drainage channel was constructed for carrying off surplus rain water and sewage. This channel was still in use during the Ottoman period and was fitted for the same function also during the time of the British Mandate; it was in operation until 1978 when the new service tunnel was completed. On the western side of the street, three column bases were found *in situ* which delimited the street on this side and bore the roofing that shaded the 3.5 m.-wide sidewalk. Fronting the sidewalk was a row of built shops, some of which had contiguous store rooms hewn in the rock behind them. The roadway of the street was 15–20 cm. lower than the level of the sidewalk. Since we could not excavate the eastern side of the street, we were unable to ascertain its overall width. Those parts of the roadway pavement that were uncovered are about 5 m. wide, but the street was undoubtedly wider. The remains of the street came to an end about 45 m. south of the city wall. Judging from the alignment of the drainage channel beneath it, the street apparently veered somewhat to the east and continued downhill and along the Tyropoeon Valley as a stepped street. It seems that the depiction in the upper right-hand corner of the Madaba Map, of what M. Avi-Yona

Southern Old City wall: remains of the outer side of the southeastern corner of the Nea church

interpreted as a representation of the Western Wall of the Temple Mount, is in effect the stepped continuation of our street.

The other important discovery of the Byzantine period came to light in the western part of our excavation, northeast of the Sulfur Tower. There, beneath the foundations of the Old City wall, the massive corner of a very large building was uncovered. Its location identified it as the southeastern corner of the Byzantine Nea Church. In N. Avigad's excavations in the Jewish Quarter the two side apses of this huge church were discovered inside the city wall. The corner section that we found protrudes approximately 11 m. southward and 5 m. eastward from the outer line of the city wall, which at this point makes a wide angle along its course. At the northern end of the eastern side of this corner, beneath the foundations of the present Old City wall, there seems to be the beginning of a curvature in the wall—perhaps part of the large rounded apse that protruded from the exterior line of the eastern wall of the Nea Church. Churches of the period having a similar feature were uncovered in the villages of Judeida and Makr in Western Galilee.

Southern Old City wall: remains of walls adjoining the southern side of the Nea church (after reconstruction)

Adjoining the southern side of the corner of the Nea Church we uncovered remains of walls up to 3.5 m. high. These belonged to ancillary structures of the church complex. Under the extension of these structures inside the city wall is the immense water cistern of the Nea complex with the inscription of the emperor Justinian.

In the excavation area we found remains of residential buildings which include rooms having mosaic floors with different colored patterns. Similar structural remains of the Byzantine period came to light in the excavations conducted by I. Margovsky in the late 1960s west of the Sulfur Tower. His excavation also revealed several rooms with ornamental mosaic floors, and walls preserved to their full height. In some cases even the arches that supported the roofing remain *in situ*. Also south of our excavation, remains of a Byzantine dwelling room with a mosaic floor of floral motif were discovered by G. Edelstein in the early 1970s.

In some of the basements of the houses were workshops with small industrial processing installations such as for tanning of skins. In one of the buildings we found an oven or kiln built of burnt bricks, and in another one, a stone-built installation for conveying water, connected to a built channel with an extension through a lead pipe about 2.5 m. long and 7 cm. in diameter. Pottery, including a few complete oil-lamps bearing crosses, and coins of the Byzantine period were found at the site.

Several water cisterns were discovered beneath and next to the houses. The Byzantine plaster used in these cisterns is of a red coloration due to the large quantity of crushed potsherds that were mixed in as binding material. The large cistern uncovered next to the Dung Gate, probably dating originally to the Second Temple period, was adapted in the Byzantine period to serve as a dwelling or for underground storage by cutting a side opening into its southern wall. A doorway with an arched lintel is built into the opening and on one of the doorjambs the word Akra, in Greek, is incised.[2] The great quantity of potsherds in the rubble filling the entire space inside the cistern dates to the Middle Ages.

The discoveries of the Byzantine period in this location, as well as those in the excavations next to the Temple Mount, show that the eastern slope of Mount Zion and the Jewish Quarter, as also the area of the Ophel, were all densely built up at that time. In some of the structures of the Byzantine period were found Early Arab potsherds, and among them, handles of large storage jars with typical Early Arab seal impressions apparently dating up to the 11th century C.E. This is perhaps an indication that during the Early Arab period Jerusalem maintained its Byzantine dimensions.

## Construction of the Medieval Period

Significant changes were made in the southern city wall of Jerusalem in the 11th century C.E. The architects and builders of the city walls now left a considerable part of the city outside the new fortification line in the south. This new line of fortifications is earlier than the Crusader city walls, for we know that the Crusaders besieged the southern part of the city in 1099 C.E. from the camp they established on Mount Zion. In 1046 C.E. the Persian traveller Nasir i-Khusrau visited Jerusalem and described the southern gates of the Temple Mount (the gates built by the Muslims in place of the original Hulda Gates of the Second Temple period) as open gateways. This would only have been possible if the southern wall of the Temple Mount was included within the fortified walls of Jerusalem. The new southern fortified line of the city could therefore only have been constructed after Nasir i-Khusrau's visit.

Thus, by the end of the 11th century C.E., the southern part of the earlier city was already outside the city walls of Jerusalem. It seems that the new wall was erected in a hurry when the Fatimids were preparing for the expected attack by the Crusaders. The wall of the second half of the 11th century C.E. followed the line it had under the Byzantine emperors and their successors the Arab caliphs; in the south, however, a fundamental change occurred. The area of the city was almost reduced to half, with the new line extending from the Temple Mount to Mount Zion, and leaving the City of David and the present Mount Zion outside the walled area.

---

[2] The inscription was discovered by B. Pixner of the Dormition Abbey on Mount Zion.

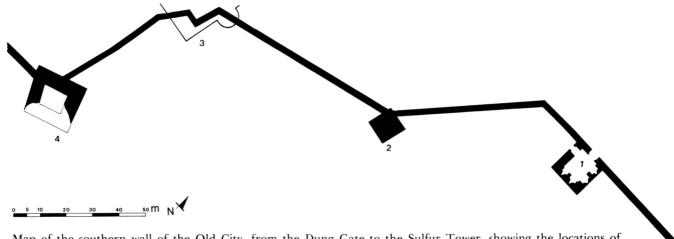

Map of the southern wall of the Old City, from the Dung Gate to the Sulfur Tower, showing the locations of ancient structural remains: 1. Tanners' Postern; 2. tower; 3. Nea Church; 4. Sulfur Tower

After founding the Kingdom of Jerusalem in 1099 C.E., the Crusaders presumably reinforced the fortifications which they had besieged but a few years earlier. We do not know whether the city's defenses were completely destroyed after falling to Saladin in 1187 C.E., or were left standing and, perhaps, only slightly damaged. At the beginning of the 13th century, 'Al-Malik al-Mu'azzam 'Isa, the Ayyubid sultan of Damascus, strengthened Jerusalem's fortifications and even added to them. However, some years later, in 1219 C.E., the same ruler, alarmed by reports of a new Crusader invasion, decided to dismantle the walls of Jerusalem and other fortifications throughout the country. A few years after this deliberate destruction, the Christians returned to Jerusalem: Frederick II concluded an agreement with the Ayyubid sultan of Egypt placing Jerusalem under Christian rule—with the sole exception of the Temple Mount, which remained in Muslim hands.

Since 1968, a number of excavations have been conducted along both sides of the southern line of the Old City walls—mainly by N. Avigad and M. Broshi (see in this volume, pp. 147–155). These excavations revealed impressive remains of the southern fortifications of Medieval Jerusalem, from the end of the Fatimid period to the Ottoman period. In our excavations along the outer side of the Old City wall other well-preserved remains of a Medieval complex of fortifications with towers, a gate, and sections of walls came to

Southern Old City wall: eastern side of the Sulfur Tower of the Crusader and Ayyubid periods beneath the Ottoman tower

315

light—though we could not determine exactly when the component parts were constructed.

In the eastern part of our excavations, next to the present Dung Gate, the remains of a fortified gatehouse (the Tanners' Postern) were uncovered (see below). About 30 m. to the west, a tower built of small stones was discovered in the southern city wall. And 70 m. further west, along the line of the city wall, was another tower built on the foundations of the southeastern corner of the Nea Church. From here the wall turned south, and after a short distance reached yet another very large tower that was uncovered beneath the Sulfur Tower of the Ottoman period. These are the remains of the Medieval Sulfur Tower, built on the foundations of the Fatimid-period tower of the second half of the 11th century C.E.

## The Medieval Tanners' Postern

A few meters west of the Dung Gate, our excavations revealed a massive fortified gatehouse. Medieval literary accounts and maps refer to it as the Tanners' Postern. This name derives from the thriving tanning industry concentrated in the neighborhood near the Temple Mount, where Jerusalem's cattle market was then located.

As was customary in contemporary military architecture, the gatehouse projected outward from the line of the wall. The outer entrance was in the western wall of the gatehouse tower, and the inner one in its northern wall. In both doorjambs of the outer entrance are vertical grooves, probably connected in some way with the operation of the gate. The entrance threshold of the gate is higher than the level of the ground outside the tower, suggesting that access to it from the exterior may have been by way of an earthen rampart. The gatehouse has five loopholes typical of medieval military architecture—two in the southern wall, two in the eastern wall, and one in the western wall next to the entrance. The other opening, the one in the northern interior wall, afforded entry into the city proper. The doorposts of this opening are still visible, although the opening was blocked with well-cemented stones by the Ottoman Turks who

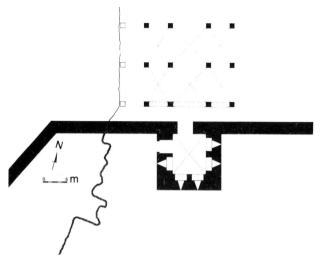

Southern Old City wall: plan of the first story of the Tanners' Postern and structure of vaults built inside the Old City

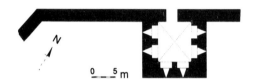

Southern Old City wall: reconstructed plan of the second story of the Tanners' Postern

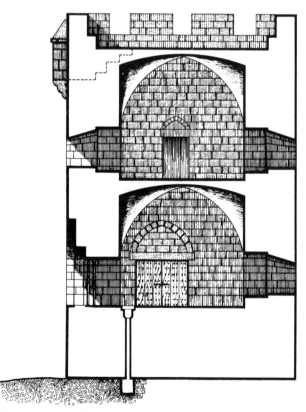

Southern Old City wall: section of the two stories of the Tanner's Postern (reconstruction); note the drainage pipe beneath it

built their city wall on the remains of the gatehouse and moved the entrance to the city here slightly eastward (see below).

The floor of the gatehouse is of beaten earth. At about 20 cm. beneath the floor is a stone-lined sewer channel covered with stone slabs, leading into the sewage system under the Byzantine Cardo. The gatehouse was built

Southern Old City wall: view of western wall with the outer entrance to the Tanners' Postern (reconstruction)

on a solid foundation—the original pavement of the Byzantine Cardo. As usual during the Middle Ages, the gatehouse was probably two stories high, with the upper story identical in plan to the ground floor—except that there may have been an additional loophole in place of the western outer entrance. A door above the inner entrance gave access from the city to

the upper floor of the gatehouse, probably by means of a staircase.

Inside the city, near the entrance to the gate, part of a building with a large number of square piers was exposed during the excavation. Apparently, the crowded conditions within Jerusalem at the time, and the need for roofed public buildings, prompted the city authorities to permit construction directly in front of the city gates—as is the case even today inside the Damascus Gate complex. At this point, we can neither conjecture as to the function of this building nor indicate its full plan, for only a small portion of it was revealed. This structure may have had some relation to the tanners' workshops which gave the postern its name. Completion of the excavations here might provide a more definitive interpretation.

**Construction of the Ottoman Period**

In 1535 C.E. Sultan Suleiman the Magnificent renovated the walls of Jerusalem. The southern wall, parts of which had remained virtually in ruins since the demolition in the early 13th century C.E., required considerable work. The new wall followed the line of the later Medieval wall and was built upon its remains. Although the Ottoman towers were constructed on the ruins of Fatimid, Crusader and Ayyubid period towers, the new gates in the southern wall were positioned differently, perhaps because the north-south arteries of Jerusalem now followed different courses. The western gate on Mount Zion was moved some 100 m. to the west, and has since been known as the Zion Gate, or Gate of David's Tomb, while the new eastern gate—the Dung Gate—was built approximately 20 m. east of the Medieval Tanners' Postern.

**The Dung Gate**

The new Ottoman gate was called Dung Gate by the Jews, after one of the city gates in the south of Jerusalem mentioned in connection with Nehemiah's reconstruction of the city walls in the mid–5th century B.C.E. (Nehemiah 2:13; 3:14; 12:31)—though the gate of Nehemiah's days was situated some 600 m.

south of Suleiman's wall. The Arabs call it the Moors' Gate, Bāb al-Magharibah in Arabic, after the nearby residential quarter which was then inhabited by North African (Maghrebin) Muslims, and from the gate in the western wall of the Temple Mount of the same name.

A basic change in the Ottoman Dung Gate was made in the early days of the British Mandate, probably in the late 1920s, when most of its construction was removed leaving only an opening in the city wall. In 1953, the Jordanian authorities again altered the form

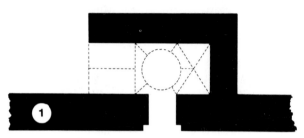

Dung Gate: plan of the original stage with the gatehouse built inside the city wall

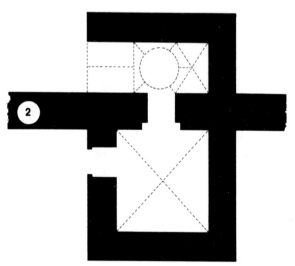

Dung Gate: plan of the second stage, after the additional gatehouse was built outside the city wall to strengthen the defenses

Dung Gate: plan of the third stage, during the British Mandate, when both parts of the gatehouse were removed and only the original opening was left in the city wall

of the Dung Gate by broadening it to permit the passage of motor vehicles. A reinforced concrete lintel was built above the new opening; this was replaced in 1985 by an arched, stone-lined lintel giving the gate its present form. As no formal records of the British modification seem to have been preserved, reconstruction of the original Ottoman plan of this gate has been a difficult task. A few veteran Jerusalemites still recollected the main features of the Turkish Dung Gate, the remains of which were still standing at the beginning of the British Mandate. With their help, I was able to trace its remains and understand its plan and architecture.

When Suleiman the Magnificent's masons renovated the walls during the mid–16th century they built a gatehouse inside the city, leaving a small opening in the city wall about 1.2 m. wide and 2.5 m. high. This narrow aperture, intended for pedestrian use, was barely wide enough to allow the passage of a loaded donkey. The facade of the postern was decorated by relief carving in the stone. The lintel consisted of a single large stone, with a carved six-pointed star design above it. Over the lintel was a gadroon arch with a multiple-taled floral relief above it. These decorative motifs were commonly used by the craftsmen who carved the decorative reliefs in the Ottoman Old City wall. In the outer side of the city wall, above the roof level of the gatehouse, was also a corbeled machicolation that overhung the entrance of the gatehouse on the outside. This feature of military architecture is typical of all the Ottoman gates in Jerusalem.

Still visible on the inner face of the Ottoman wall are the imposts of the vaults that once formed the inner gatehouse roof. The roof of the narrow gatehouse consisted of three consecutive sections: a small cross-vault; a domed vault; and a barrel vault. The gatehouse, entailing a ninety-degree turn, is typical of the gates built by Suleiman in the Old City wall of Jerusalem. The same feature can be seen in the gatehouses of the Ottoman fortresses at Ras al-'Ein and at Solomon's Pools. It differs from the typical medieval

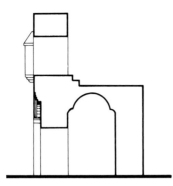

Dung Gate: section of the original gate (reconstruction)

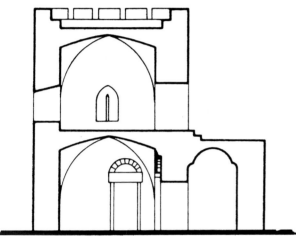

Dung Gate: section of the second stage, one story high inside, and two stories high outside the city wall (reconstruction)

The Dung Gate during the time of the British Mandate, after removal of the outer gatehouse

Facade of the Dung Gate in its original stage (reconstruction) after removal of the outer gatehouse

gatehouse plan which has the gatehouse projecting outside the line of the defensive wall.

At a later stage an additional gatehouse was built outside the entrance. The date of this addition cannot be determined, though drawings and photographs from the second half of the 19th century clearly show this outer gatehouse. This strengthening of the defenses of Jerusalem was probably one of the measures taken to offset the decline of Ottoman power in the late 18th century. The construction of this gatehouse follows the traditional design of medieval gatehouses. It stood outside the city wall, two stories high, obstructing the ornamentation of the original gate facade. The entrance to the gatehouse was in its western side, perpendicular to the city wall, with loopholes in its walls. In order to permit access to the second story above the roof of the outer gatehouse, the machicolation over the original gateway was dismantled, thus creating an opening. This opening remained after the British removed the outer gate tower, and can be seen in photographs taken before the Jordanian alterations of 1953.

319

Dung Gate: reconstruction proposal conserving the original gate and leaving passage for modern traffic

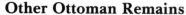

The Dung Gate after the construction in 1985

## Other Ottoman Remains

Remains of the Ottoman period revealed in our excavations comprise also sections of the aqueduct to Jerusalem. As mentioned above, this conduit from Solomon's Pools to the Temple Mount, originally built at the time of the Second Temple period and used in later periods, was restored by Suleiman the Magnificent and was subsequently repaired several times during the four centuries of Ottoman rule. Now, however, the water was conveyed in pottery pipes made in sections about 45 cm. long and 22 cm. in diameter. Other parts of this pipeline can still be seen on the southern slope of Mount Zion. This pipe passes over the ruins of the Sulfur Tower of the Medieval period and enters the city northeast of the tower. Apart from the aqueduct, no other distinct remains of the Ottoman period were found—except for remains of a few enclosures for livestock that were built at the end of the 19th century and at the beginning of the 20th century by the owners of the land at the foot of the southern city wall.

## Bibliography

Ben-Dov, M., *The Fortifications of Jerusalem—Walls, Gates and the Temple Mount* (Tel-Aviv, 1983) (Hebrew).
Prawer, J. *The Latin Kingdom of Jerusalem. European Colonialism in the Middle Ages* (London, 1972).
Wilson, C., *Ordnance Survey of Jerusalem* (London, 1865).

# A Mamluk Basin Rediscovered

## Myriam Rosen-Ayalon

The many Mamluk madrasas of Jerusalem have recently been subjected to comprehensive study. Of these, the Tankiziyya, dated to A.H. 729/1328–9 C.E., is undoubtedly one of the most beautiful. The building is located at the southeastern end of the Street of the Chain, next to gate to the Temple Mount. The madrasa is named after the emir Tankiz, who ruled Syria and Palestine under the sultanate of ā-Naṣir Muhammad ibn-Qalā'un. Despite the ravages of time, the sumptuous aspect of the building is still in evidence. The impressive facade and the architectural details inside the building—particularly the colored marble revetments and veneers, and the glass mosaics in the miḥrab niche—attest to the rich decoration characteristic of the Mamluk style. Now we can add another dimension to the art history of this madrasa.

The cruciform (court-iwan) plan of the madrasa is typical of other contemporary madrasas, although in the Tankiziyya these features

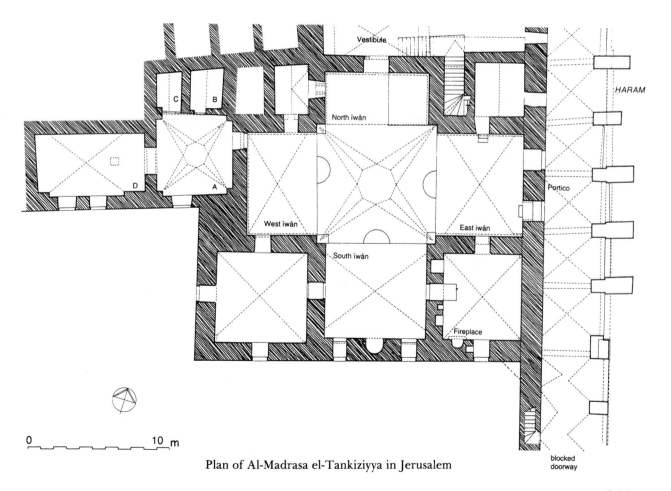

Plan of Al-Madrasa el-Tankiziyya in Jerusalem

are not necessarily repeated. The central part of the building which was intended as an open courtyard is roofed except for a small opening in the center of the ceiling. As in every madrasa, there is a water basin in the center of the court of the Tankiziyya. Here, the basin is fed by the ancient aqueduct from Solomon's Pools near Bethlehem. The repair of this conduit was one of the public works projects undertaken by Tankiz to assure the supply of water to the Temple Mount in Jerusalem.

The pool is built of stone in an octagonal form, although the northern side of the parapet has the form of a broad, concave niche. This niche, in line with the miḥrab in the southern wall of the building, emphasizes the direction of the qibla—the direction of prayer. That was the appearance of the basin for a long time, and it was described as such in various publications. Recently, however, what seemed to be the bottom of the basin was discovered to be artificial fill. After being cleaned out, the entire basin was revealed in its full splendor.

The Tankiziyya basin

Al-Tankiziyya: view of interior; looking south

Inside the low stone parapet framing the basin above the level of the floor, another, inner, frame was discovered one step down. Seven of the horizontal facets of the lower, stepped frame structure are composed of seven triangular blocks alternating with six semicircular niches. Apparently because of the curved form of the eighth, northern, side of the exterior parapet, the craftsmen had to interrupt the decorative structural pattern on that side of the lower, inner frame, and so, an inward-facing, shallow concave niche at that level connects the two triangular blocks at either end of it.

On the horizontal surface of the inner, lower-level stepped frame was revealed polychrome marble marquetry in the best tradition of Mamluk architectural decorative art. The decoration of the basin is executed in a combination of two techniques. One entails parallel, colored marble strips lining the flat surface above each of six small semicircular niches. The other technique is in evidence in the small triangular forms between the apex of each large triangle and the rounded tops of the two adjacent niches: these little triangles are inlaid with marble tesserae measuring about 1 cm. on the average. The colors are mainly black and white, arranged in a star-like pattern. The large triangular areas are revetted with gray-white marble contrasting with the rich coloration over the semicircular niches. This polychrome effect is achieved by the use of black, white and orange marble strips. The sequence on each of the niches is: black; white; orange; white; black; white; black; white; orange; white; black. An interesting decorative detail is the small semi-circular protrusion on the black strips at the ends of each color sequence, that is inserted in the white marble surface of the adjoining pale-hued triangles.

The architectural decoration of the basin conforms with the other decorative elements of the Tankiziyya building, particularly with that of the miḥrab. The interior of the miḥrab is inlaid with alternating strips of marble in black and white. This technique is known from several other miḥrab niches of the Mamluk period, and perhaps already from the Ayyubid period.

The fountain in the Victoria and Albert Museum, London

In Mamluk architecture, alternating multicolored marble revetment, or masonry, is known as *ablaq*. This is reflected in the decor of the basin in the way the black, white and orange strips are applied. Usually, *ablaq* motifs are in two colors, the most common combinations being black and white, or red and white. Every addition to these two colors creates a rich polychrome effect. The architectural decor of another building in Jerusalem, also attributed to Tankiz, features a similar combination of colors—white, black and orange. This is the ornate gate structure leading from the Temple Mount to the Cotton Market (Sūq a-Qattānīn).

As in the case of the marble strips, there are also other examples of Mamluk structures where marble mosaics cover areas of small triangles—in the rich decorative style of this period. One close parallel can be seen in a water fountain now in the Victoria and Albert Museum in London. This example, which is a fountain rather than a basin, has not been dated but is similar in many of its details to the decoration of the Tankiziyya basin. This tradition persisted in the art of Syria and Egypt until the 17th and 18th centuries C.E.

There is no problem in dating the Tankiziyya basin. The building bears an inscription of Tankiz and the historical background for its construction is known. A similar basin—also of indeterminate date—in the Cairo Museum of Islamic Art, exhibits several features that

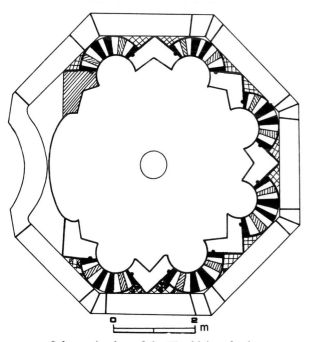
Schematic plan of the Tankiziyya basin

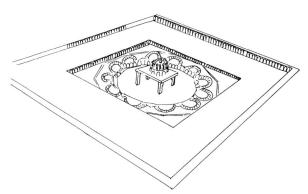

The basin in the Cairo Museum of Islamic Art

fit in with the basin in the Tankiziyya. Unlike the fountain in London, the item in the Cairo museum is closer in its decorative conception to the Tankiziyya basin and helps complement the picture. Although the form of the basin in Cairo is square and not octagonal, it also has an outer parapet constituting an upper level, and a lower-level, stepped frame with small niches. This creates a different effect from the alternating play of triangles and semicircles in the Tankiziyya basin. Both basins however share a common decorative technique: each basin is revetted with multicolored marble mosaics—both levels in the Cairo basin, and only the lower, inner level in the Jerusalem basin. Since the Cairo basin is not dated, it has been suggested, on the strength of compari-

son, that it is contemporneous with the basin in the mausoleum of Qalā'un in Cairo, i.e., the second half of the 13th century C.E. (A.H. 684/1285 C.E.)—fairly close to the time of the Tankiziyya. Another interesting detail in the Cairo Museum basin is the form of the opening in its center through which the water issued. It seems that in the course of time the basin in the Tankiziyya lost its spout, and, at an unknown later date, a section of a column surmounted by a fragmentary carved stone capital was affixed to it to give it the form of a vase. In contrast, in the center of the basin in the Cairo museum is a small, pretty fountain on four little pillars that form a sort of platform for the decorative spout. Perhaps a similar fountainhead originally graced the Tankiziyya basin as well.

The beautiful, colorful basin in the Tankiziyya adds to the overall impression of magnificence of the madrasa. Beyond complementing the architectural ornamentation of the building of which it is part, the basin exhibits characteristic features that enhance our understanding of the Mamluk architectural style in general, which is here expressed mainly in the various kinds of colored marble revetment. It is the only example known so far of a splendid, decorated Mamluk basin in Jerusalem, and very likely in the entire country.

## Bibliography

Briggs, M.S., *Muhammedan Architecture in Egypt and Palestine* (New York, 1974).
Burgoyne, M.H., *Mamluk Jerusalem* (London, 1987).
Rosen-Ayalon, M., "A Neglected Group of Miḥrabs in Palestine," in: Sharon, M. (ed.), *Studies in Islamic History and Civilisation in Honour of Professor David Ayalon* (Jerusalem, 1986), pp. 559–561.
van Berchem, M. *Matériaux pour un Corpus InscriptionumArabicarum. Jérusalem-Ville* (Cairo, 1923).
Wiet, W., *Album du Musée Arabe du Caire* No. 14 (Cairo, 1930).

# Major Archaeological Activities in Jerusalem, 1967–1992[*]

Hillel Geva

**1. N. Avigad, 1967, MOUNT SCOPUS, NORTHEAST OF JERUSALEM**
Burial cave of Nazirite family of the Second Temple period (1st century C.E.).

**2. V. Tzaferis, 1968, GIVʿAT HA-MIVTAR, NORTH JERUSALEM**
Burial caves of the Second Temple period (1st century B.C.E.–1st century C.E.) with ossuary bearing inscription "Simon the Temple builder," and another ossuary containing skeletal evidence of death by crucifixion.

**3. Amiran and A. Eitan, 1968–1969, TOWER OF DAVID CITADEL, OLD CITY**
Exposure of the inner face of the northwestern corner of the First Wall of the Second Temple period with an inner tower of the Hasmonean period and inner reinforcement to the city wall of the days of Herod; buildings of the Hasmonean period and foundations of Herod's palace (1st century B.C.E.–1st century C.E.); reinforcement of the city wall and buildings of the Byzantine period (and see also Nos. 23, 27).

**4. D. Ussishkin, 1968–1970, SILWAN VILLAGE, SOUTHEAST OF THE OLD CITY**
Survey and publication of tens of burial caves of the First Temple period (9th–7th centuries B.C.E.).

**5. B. Mazar, 1968–1978, THE OPHEL AND THE SOUTHWESTERN CORNER OF THE TEMPLE MOUNT**
**First Temple period:** royal building—Beit Millo (9th–6th centuries B.C.E., and see also No. 28); tombs (9th–8th centuries B.C.E.).
**Second Temple period:** structures and water installations of the Hellenistic and Hasmonean periods (2nd–1st centuries B.C.E.); exposure of the southern wall and the southwestern corner of the Temple Mount with contiguous streets, plazas, stairways to the Ḥuldah Gates, walls supporting the stairway to Robinson's Arch and various buildings of the Herodian period (end of 1st century B.C.E. and 1st century C.E.).
**Roman Period:** structures.
**Byzantine Period:** the Ophel wall and its towers, various structures, public building—hostelry;
**Early Arab period:** four palaces of the Umayyad period (7th–8th centuries C.E.); buildings of the Fatimid period (10th–11th centuries C.E.).

**6. M. Ben-Dov, 1968–1978; D. Bahat, 1985–1990, WEST OF THE TEMPLE MOUNT, OLD CITY**
Excavation of tunnel along the Western Wall of the Temple Mount; exposure of entrance to Warren's Gate; rediscovery of Hasmonean aqueduct northwest of the Temple Mount; exposure of Herodian construction at the northern end of the Western Wall of the Temple Mount and the tower at its northwestern corner, with adjacent quarry and

---

[*] This list covers the major archaeological activities of the last twenty-five years (1967–1992) in the area of ancient Jerusalem. The excavation results are summarized in the articles presented in the two volumes of *Jerusalem Revealed*. Dating of the finds, identifications, and conclusions are those of the excavators. It supplements and updates the "Table of Major Archaeological Activities in Jerusalem," by Y. Shiloh, in the first volume of this series: Yadin, Y. (ed.), *Jerusalem Revealed* (Jerusalem, 1976), pp. 131–136.

paved street; cleaning and exploration of the complex of underground vaulted structures of the Medieval period.

## 7. A. Mazar, 1969, SOUTH OF JERUSALEM
Survey of aqueducts from Solomon's Pools to Jerusalem of the Second Temple and Roman periods to the Ottoman period.

## 8. N. Avigad, 1969–1982, JEWISH QUARTER, OLD CITY
Excavations in many areas:

**First Temple period:** section of fortifications along the northern line of the First Wall: the Broad Wall (Area A), tower—gate? (Area W), city wall and tower (Area X–2) and buildings in various areas of the late First Temple period (8th–6th centuries B.C.E.).

**Second Temple period:** sections of fortifications along the northern line of First Wall: tower (Area W), fortified (Ginat) gate complex (Area X–2); buildings of the Hasmonean period (1st century B.C.E., Areas E, J); street and buildings: Palatial Mansion and Burnt House of the Herodian period (end of 1st century B.C.E.–1st century C.E.) with evidence of destruction by the Romans in 70 C.E. (Areas B, F, M, P).

**Roman period:** rooftiles of the Roman Tenth Legion.

**Byzantine period:** Cardo (Area X), church structures and cistern of the Nea Church complex (Areas D, T; and see also No. 20), bath house (Area C), and buildings in most of the excavation areas.

**Early Arab period:** southern city wall and gateway (10th–11th centuries C.E., Area T).

**Crusader period:** public building (Area T), roofed market building (Area X).

**Ayyubid period:** tower—gate? along the southern city wall (Area T, and see also No. 17).

## 9. V. Tzaferis, 1970, GIV'AT HA-MIVTAR, NORTH JERUSALEM
Burial cave with inscription "I, Abba, son of the priest..." of the Second Temple period (1st century B.C.E.–1st century C.E.).

## 10. D. Bahat and M. Broshi, 1970–1971, THE ARMENIAN GARDEN, OLD CITY
Section of fortification along the western line of First Wall and foundations of Herod's palace of Second Temple period (1st century B.C.E.–1st century C.E.); complex of Crusader palace (12th century C.E.).

## 11. A. Kloner, 1971, GIV'AT HA-MIVTAR, NORTH JERUSALEM
Burial cave with ossuary bearing inscription "of the House of David" of the Second Temple period (1st century B.C.E.–1st century C.E.).

## 12. D. Bahat and M. Ben-Ari, 1971–1972, NORTHWESTERN CORNER OF OLD CITY WALL
City wall, Tower of Goliath and moat of Crusader and Ayyubid periods (12th–13th centuries C.E.).

## 13. G. Barkay, A. Kloner and A. Mazar 1971–1972, NORTH OF THE OLD CITY
Survey and publication of burial caves of the late First Temple period (8th–6th centuries B.C.E.).

## 14. M. Broshi, 1971–1972, ARMENIAN HOUSE OF CAIAPHAS MONASTERY, MOUNT ZION
Buildings of late First Temple period (8th–6th centuries B.C.E.); Hasmonean and Herodian buildings of the Second Temple period (1st century B.C.E.–1st century C.E.); remains of construction of Holy Sion Church complex and street of Byzantine period; buildings of Early Arab period; outer wall of church and Monastery of Holy Mary of Mount Sion complex of the Crusader period.

## 15. R. Reich and H. Geva, 1972, MOUNT SCOPUS, NORTHEAST OF JERUSALEM
Complex of five burial caves of the Second Temple period (1st century B.C.E.).

## 16. S. Ben-Arieh and E. Netzer, 1972–1974, NORTH OF THE OLD CITY
Section of city wall and towers along the line of the Third Wall of the end of the Second Temple period (1st century C.E.); monastery

complex of the Byzantine period (and see also Nos. 34, 35).

### 17. M. Broshi, 1973–1978, WEST AND SOUTH OF THE OLD CITY

Structure and burial caves of the late First Temple period (8th–6th centuries B.C.E.); sections of fortifications along the western line of the First Wall of the Second Temple period: tower of the 2nd century B.C.E., city wall and four towers of the Hasmonean period (2nd and 1st centuries B.C.E.), reinforcements of the city wall and these towers, and stepped entrance structure to a conjectured gate of the time of Herod the Great (end of 1st century B.C.E.); section of Byzantine city wall; city wall, towers and gatehouse? (and see also No. 8) of the Ayyubid period (beginning of the 13th century C.E.).

### 18. A. Kloner, 1974, MOUNT OF OLIVES, EAST OF THE OLD CITY

Tomb decorated with paintings of the Byzantine period.

### 19. M. Broshi, 1975–1976, CHURCH OF THE HOLY SEPULCHER, OLD CITY

Remains of construction activity of the late First Temple period (8th–6th centuries B.C.E.); foundation walls of raised podium (*temenos*) supporting the temple and basilica erected by Hadrian in the Roman period (2nd century C.E.); foundations of the Constantinian church complex of the Holy Sepulcher of the Byzantine period (4th century C.E.).

### 20. M. Ben-Dov, 1975–1977, 1981, SOUTH OF THE OLD CITY

Buildings and water installations of the Second Temple period (1st century B.C.E.–1st century C.E.); secondary (eastern) Cardo street, corner of the Nea Church and adjacent buildings (and see also No. 8) of the Byzantine period; city wall towers and gateway of the Medieval period (12th–13th centuries C.E.) along the line of the southern wall of the Old City.

### 21. A. Kloner and D. Davis, 1975–1978, WEST OF THE OLD CITY

Burial caves of the late First Temple period (8th–6th centuries B.C.E.); section of the Lower Aqueduct of the Second Temple to Ottoman periods.

### 22. G. Barkay, 1975, 1979–1980, 1988–1989, KETEF HINNOM, SOUTHWEST OF THE OLD CITY

Burial caves of the late First Temple period (8th–6th centuries B.C.E.); continuation of burials during Second Temple period; cremation burials of the Roman period (2nd–3d centuries C.E.); Monastery of St. George Outside the Walls with church and graves of the Byzantine period.

### 23. H. Geva, 1976–1980, TOWER OF DAVID CITADEL, OLD CITY

Southern Tower at the northwest corner of the First Wall with Hasmonean and Herodian stages of construction of the Second Temple period (1st century B.C.E.–1st century C.E.); structural remains of the camp of the Roman Tenth Legion (2nd–3rd centuries C.E.); sections of the city wall, tower and buildings of the Byzantine period; round corner tower and buildings of the Early Arab period (7th–8th centuries C.E.); sections of fortifications and structures of the Medieval to Ottoman periods (and see also Nos. 3, 27).

### 24. D. Chen, S. Margalit and B. Pixner, 1977–1988 (intermittently), MOUNT ZION

Remains of fortification and buildings of the late First Temple period; reexamination of the gate in the southwestern corner of the city wall including an early stage of the Gate of the Essenes in the line of the First Wall of the Second Temple period, and two later stages of use of the Roman and Byzantine periods.

### 25. Y. Shiloh, 1978–1985, CITY OF DAVID

Excavations in many areas:

**Bronze Age:** Early Bronze Age structures; city wall of the Middle Bronze Age (18th century B.C.E.) and structures in successive occupation levels of the Middle and Late Bronze

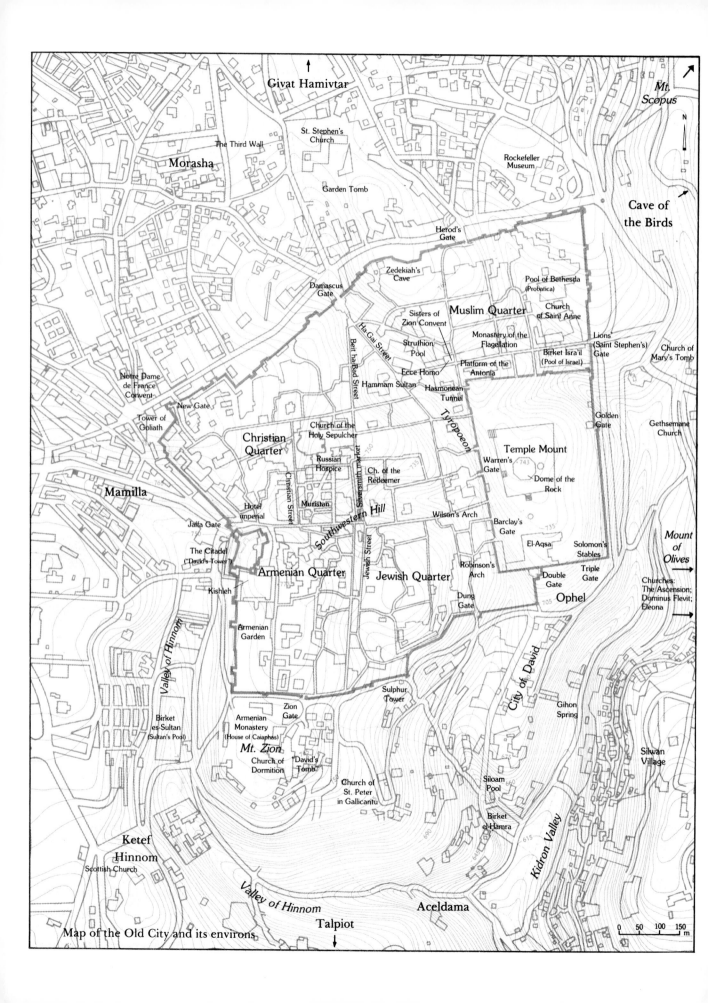

Givat Hamivtar

*Mt. Scopus*

N

Morasha

The Third Wall

St. Stephen's Church

Rockefeller Museum

*Cave of the Birds*

Garden Tomb

Herod's Gate

Zedekiah's Cave

Pool of Bethesda (Probatica)

Damascus Gate

Sisters of Zion Convent

Muslim Quarter

Church of Saint Anne

Ha-Gai Street

Struthion Pool

Monastery of the Flagellation

Birket Isra'il (Pool of Israel)

Lions' (Saint Stephen's) Gate

Church of Mary's Tomb

Beit haBad Street

Ecce Homo

Platform of the Antonia

Notre Dame de France Convent

Hammam Sultan

Hasmonean Tunnel

New Gate

Church of the Holy Sepulcher

Tyropoeon

Golden Gate

Gethsemane Church

Tower of Goliath

Christian Quarter

Russian Hospice

Temple Mount

Warren's Gate

743

Christian Street

Ch. of the Redeemer

Silversmith market

Dome of the Rock

Mamilla

Muristan

Southwestern Hill

735

Hotel Imperial

Wilson's Arch

*Mount of Olives*

Jaffa Gate

Barclay's Gate

735

The Citadel ("David's Tower")

Jewish Street

Armenian Quarter

Jewish Quarter

El-Aqsa

Solomon's Stables

Kishleh

Robinson's Arch

Double Gate

Triple Gate

Churches: The Ascension; Dominus Flevit; Eleona

Armenian Garden

Dung Gate

Ophel

705

City of David

Birket es-Sultan (Sultan's Pool)

Sulphur Tower

Gihon Spring

Zion Gate

Armenian Monastery (House of Caiaphas)

*Mt. Zion*

Church of Dormition

"David's Tomb"

Silwan Village

Church of St. Peter in Gallicantu

Siloam Pool

Birket el-Hamra

Ketef Hinnom

Scottish Church

Valley of Hinnom

690

615

Kidron Valley

Valley of Hinnom

Aceldama

Talpiot

Map of the Old City and its environs

0  50  100  150 m

Ages on the eastern slope of the City of David (Area E).

**First Temple Period:** city wall (Area E), dam and city wall at the southern issue of the Tyropoeon Valley of the late First Temple period (Area A, 8th–6th centuries B.C.E.); stepped stone structure of the Davidic period (10th century B.C.E.); residential houses: House of Aḥi'el, Bullae House and Burnt Room (Area G) of the end of the First Temple period (7th–6th centuries B.C.E.).

**Water Systems:** clearing of Warren's Shaft; investigation of the Siloam tunnel (Area B) of the First Temple period.

**Second Temple Period:** sections along the eastern line of the First Wall: city wall and tower of the Persian and Hasmonean periods (5th–2nd centuries B.C.E.) and Hasmonean earth glacis (Area G); city wall and blocked opening of the Hasmonean period (Area D); additional construction at the Tyropoeon dam and the city wall (Area A); terraces of the Hellenistic and Hasmonean periods on the eastern slope of the City of David outside the line of the city wall (Areas D, E); remains of Hasmonean (1st century B.C.E.) construction in the Tyropoeon Valley (Area H).

**Byzantine Period:** structures (Area H) and partially rock-cut structure (Area K).

### 26. M. Magen, 1979–1984, DAMASCUS GATE, NORTHERN WALL OF THE OLD CITY

Structural complex of the Roman Damascus Gate and pavement of its inner courtyard erected by Hadrian (2nd century B.C.E.).

### 27. R. Sivan and G. Solar, 1980–1988, TOWER OF DAVID CITADEL, OLD CITY

Fortification and building remains of the late First Temple period (8th–6th centuries B.C.E.); clearing of the exterior face of the northwest corner of the First Wall of the second Temple period including the early Middle Tower, the early stage of the Southern Tower of the Hasmonean period (1st century B.C.E.) and several stages of the city wall between them of the Second Temple period (Hasmonean and Herodian periods); stepped installation of the Hasmonean period (1st

century B.C.E.); Byzantine city wall (and see also Nos. 3, 23).

### 28. E. Mazar and B. Mazar, 1986–1987, OPHEL

Complex of massive royal buildings (Beit Millo) including sections of fortification and gatehouse—Water Gate of the First Temple period (9th–6th centuries B.C.E., and see also No. 5).

### 29. G. Avni and Z. Greenhut, 1989, KIDRON VALLEY, SOUTH OF THE CITY OF DAVID

Sumptuous burial caves of the Second Temple period (1st century B.C.E.–1st century C.E.).

### 30. A.M. Maeir, 1989, MAMILLA, WEST OF THE OLD CITY

Corner of a structure (tower?) of the Second Temple period (1st century B.C.E.); complex of buildings, street and aqueduct of the Byzantine and Early Arab periods (6th–8th centuries C.E., and see also No. 33).

### 31. V. Sussman, 1989, MOUNT SCOPUS, NORTHEAST JERUSALEM

Burial cave of the Second Temple period (1st century B.C.E.–1st century C.E.).

### 32. Z. Greenhut, 1990, NORTH TALPIYOT, SOUTH JERUSALEM

Burial cave with ossuary bearing inscription: "Joseph son of Caiaphas" of the Second Temple period (1st century B.C.E.–1st century C.E.).

### 33. R. Reich, 1990–1992, MAMILLA, WEST OF THE OLD CITY

Burial caves of the late First Temple period (8th–6th centuries B.C.E.) and Second Temple period (5th–1st centuries B.C.E.); burial cave and chapel of the Byzantine period; complex of buildings of the Byzantine-Early Arab periods (6th–8th centuries C.E., and see also No. 30).

### 34. V. Tzaferis, N. Feig, A. Onn, and E. Sukron, 1990, NORTH OF THE OLD CITY

Section of city wall and towers along the line of the Third Wall of the end of the Second

Temple period (1st century C.E.); cremation burials of the Roman period (2nd–3rd centuries C.E.); monasteries with rooms, chapels and tombs of the Byzantine and Early Arab periods (5th–8th centuries C.E., and see also Nos. 16, 35).

## 35. D. Amit and S. Wolff, 1991–1992,
MORASHA, NORTH OF THE OLD CITY

Armenian monastery including rooms, chapel and burial caves of the Byzantine and Early Arab periods (5th–8th centuries C.E., and see also Nos. 16, 34).

# Glossary

ABBASID—Early Islamic dynasty ruling from Baghdad (749–969 C.E., in Palestine).

ACROTERION (pl. ACROTERIA)—ornamental element at the apex or outer angles of a pediment.

A.H.—Latin: Anno Hegirae; year of the Hegira of the Muslim calendar.

ANTA (pl. ANTAE)—Pier or square column formed by enlarging the end of a wall on either side of a door or in a corner.

APSE—Arched or dome-roofed semicircular or polygonal recess.

ARCHITRAVE—Horizontal beam of stone or timber spanning the interval between two columns or piers; the lowest component of an entablature.

ARCOSOLIUM (pl. ARCOSOLIA)—Arched niche over sarcophagus-like trough in which corpse was inhumed, hewn in wall of burial cave.

ASHLAR—Rectangular block of hewn stone.

ASTRAGAL—Simple molding around the neck of a capital masking the break between the column and the capital.

AYYUBID—Muslim dynasty ruling from Cairo (1169–1250 C.E.).

BALLISTA—Military engine for hurling projectiles.

BARAITA—Traditional Jewish interpretation or statement of biblical law not included in the Mishnah.

BASILICA—Long-halled public building divided into a nave and aisles by rows of columns, often with an apse at one narrow end.

BEZEL—Groove and flange holding a gem in place.

BOSS—Protruding central part in the face of a worked building stone or ashlar having dressed margins.

BROADHOUSE—Building whose focal point is situated in the long wall.

BULLA(E)—Seal of written scroll, usually of clay, often stamped with seal impression.

CARDO—Main north-to-south street of the Roman-Byzantine city.

CHAPEL—Small, or subordinate place of worship.

CRYPT—Room or vault under the floor of a church used for burial or to inter relics.

CUBIT—Ancient unit of measure based on length of forearm from elbow to tip of middle finger, about 50 cm. in length depending on the period.

DEFECTIVE ORTHOGRAPHY—Hebrew spelling without use of vowels.

ENGAGED—As an architectural element, such as a pilaster or column, built into a wall and partially protruding from it.

ENTABLATURE—Horizontal superstructure carried by columns comprising an architrave, frieze, and cornice.

FATIMID—Muslim dynasty ruling from Cairo (968–1171 C.E.).

FERRULE—Metal band or cap enclosing end of a tool or weapon handle, or staff, to strengthen it and prevent splitting and wear.

FIBULA—Buckle or clasp for fastening garment, usually at the shoulder.

FIELDSTONE—Unworked stone used in building.

FRESCO—Watercolor painting on wet plaster.

FRIEZE—Middle decorative component of entablature, often with relief carving.

GABLE—Triangular wall enclosed by sloping ends of ridged roof; triangular decorative feature over door or window.

GADROON ARCH—Accordion-like decorative molding of small cushions around upper part of arched doorway or window.

GENIZA—Repository for sacred objects, books, manuscripts and documents.

GLACIS—Embankment sloping up to outer fortification wall to expose attackers.

GRAFFITO (pl. GRAFFITI)—Drawing or writing scratched on wall or other surface.

HALAKHA (pl. HALAKHOT)—The body of oral law based on authoritative rabbinical interpretations of the Bible but not actually specified in it.

HEADER-AND-STRETCHER—Method of masonry construction of rectangular stone blocks laid alternately parallel and perpendicular to the face of the wall.

HORROR VACUI—Aversion to empty space.

331

IN SITU—Latin: in the original place.

IWAN—Vaulted, sometimes raised hall open on one narrow side to central court in Islamic buildings.

KAKULA—Arabic name for local soft, friable, porous chalk or limestone, used as building material in roofs because of its light weight.

KOKH (pl. KOKHIM)—Rectangular burial niche hewn horizontally, perpendicular to wall of cave tomb; loculus.

LINTEL—Horizontal crosspiece over door or window carrying weight of structure above it.

LOCULUS (pl. LOCULI)—Rectangular burial niche hewn horizontally in wall of cave tomb (KOKH) in Hebrew.

MACHICOLATION—Projecting gallery or parapet over outer side of fortified gateway, with opening at the bottom from which boiling oil, stones or projectiles could be dropped on attackers below.

MADRASA—Muslim theological school.

MAMLUK—Military dynastic caste ruling from Cairo (1250–1517 C.E.).

MASORETIC—Accumulated Jewish tradition regarding the correct Hebrew text of the Bible.

MELEKE—Arabic name for a local semi-hard limestone used for building.

MENORAH—The seven-branched candelabrum that stood in the Holy of Holies in the Temple in Jerusalem.

METOPE—The square space between triglyphs on a classical frieze.

MIḤRAB—Niche, usually of apsidal form, in mosques or other Muslim religious buildings to indicate the direction of Mecca.

MIQVEH (pl. MIQVA'OT)—Jewish ritual bath.

MISHNAH—Earliest codification of Jewish oral law compiled around 200 C.E.; the main component of the Talmud.

MIZZI ḤILU—Arabic name for a hard local limestone used for building.

NARI—Arabic name for soft layer overlying limestone and chalk, not used for building.

ONOMASTICS—The study of names.

OPUS SECTILE—Inlaid paving or wall decoration made of cut flat pieces of stone and colored marble.

OSSUARY—Container for bones of the dead in secondary burials.

PEDIMENT—Triangular gabled end of a ridged roof in classical architecture.

PIER—Mass of masonry or massive column supporting a ceiling or the spring of an arch.

PILASTER—Rectangular column; see ENGAGED pilaster, above.

PLENE ORTHOGRAPHY—Hebrew spelling with added vowels.

PORTICO—Colonnaded entrance to a building.

REPOSITORY—Storage pit in burial cave for discarded bone material and funerary offerings.

REVETMENT—Retaining wall; embankment or added construction of stone and/or earth to thicken and reinforce defensive wall; facing of stone or other material.

ROTUNDA—Round building, hall, or room, usually roofed with a dome.

SALTIRE—X-shaped cross motif.

SARCOPHAGUS—Stone coffin.

SHEPHELAH—Foothills between the Judean Mountains and the coastal plain along the Mediterranean Sea.

STOA—Portico having a wall on one side and pillars on the other.

STRIGIL—Knife-like metal or bone instrument for scraping skin during a bath.

STUCCO—Plaster or cement used for coating wall surfaces, or for molding architectural relief ornamentation, cornices, etc.

TABULA ANSATA—Frame of Roman and post-Roman inscription with a triangular "ear" at either side.

TALMUD—The main corpus of Jewish civil and ceremonial law which includes the Mishnah and the Gemara. Two compilations exist: Jerusalem, or Palestinian, Talmud (ca. 400 C.E.) and Babylonian Talmud (ca. 650 C.E.).

TEMENOS—Sacred precinct enclosure of a temple.

TESSERA (pl. TESSERAE)—Small cube of limestone, marble or glass used in mosaics.

TETRASTYLE—Building or portico having four columns in front.

TOSEFTA—Collection of teachings and traditions closely related to the Mishnah.

TRIGLYPH—Decorative element of a slightly projecting tablet with two vertical grooves between two half-grooves, usually alternating with metopes on a classical frieze.

TYMPANUM—Recessed space, usually triangular, enclosed by slanting cornices of a pediment and often ornamented with carving.

UMAYYAD—Early Islamic dynasty ruling from Damascus (661–749 C.E.).

VOUSSOIR—Outer, wedge-shaped or curved stone forming a vault or arch.

# Index